C0-AUG-968

EDMUND KEAN

KEAN AS SIR GILES OVERREACH

EDMUND KEAN

BY

Harold Newcomb Hillebrand

AMS PRESS, INC.
NEW YORK
1966

Reprinted with the permission of the
Original Publisher, 1966

AMS PRESS, INC.
New York, N.Y. 10003
1966

Manufactured in the United States of America

CONTENTS

ILLUSTRATIONS

ACKNOWLEDGMENTS

In gathering the materials for this biography I have been very greatly aided by several persons to whom I wish to express my gratitude. First, to Mr. W. J. Lawrence, who, as soon as he learned of my purpose, placed at my disposal a number of items, including his transcripts of the Mary Kean letters, and was in other ways most considerate and helpful. Next, to Mrs. Hall of the Harvard Library and Mrs. Enthoven of the Victoria and Albert Museum, who did everything they could to facilitate my researches in their collections. To Mr. Henry E. Marquand and Miss Edith Carey of St. Peter Port, without whose aid I could not have written my chapter on Guernsey. To Mr. Messmore Kendall and Mr. Frederick King of New York and Mr. J. S. Dodd of Brooklyn for allowing me to examine their collections and cite therefrom, as hereinafter noted. To Mr. Allardyce Nicoll for kindly reading proof; and to Mr. G. C. D. Odell, for his sympathetic interest and advice. Biographical clue-hunting is a game which has its own fascinations; but it is made doubly pleasant when it brings the player into contact with such very agreeable people.

I wish also to acknowledge the courtesy of the officers of the Harvard Library, the Victoria and Albert Museum, and the British Museum for allowing me to reproduce pictures, bills, and letters in their possession.

HAROLD N. HILLEBRAND

URBANA, ILLINOIS
March 13, 1933

CHAPTER I

CHILDHOOD

"THE birth and parentage of Edmund Kean are, apparently, equally unknown." Thus wrote Procter in 1835, adding that "no such information exists as his biographers can use with *entire* confidence." Reluctantly the present biographer is compelled to admit that in spite of three sizable biographies[1] and a great many articles, reminiscences and notes, the ninety years and more which have passed since Procter's book appeared have cast not the smallest ray of light on the vexing problem. The evidence is all in the form of testimonials long after the fact. Much of it is so clearly market-place gossip that it can be instantly dismissed; a little of it has a sufficient look of authority so that at least a strong presumption may be said to exist as to the actor's parentage. But the date of his birth remains a mystery which only a baptismal registry or some such practical document will clear up, and the present biographer has thus far failed to discover anything of the kind. The best he can do is to display the evidence such as it is, hoping that the reader, in default of enlightenment, may derive at least some amusement from its contradictions.

Of the several persons who at one time held the key to the mystery, the one who today most attracts and baffles conjecture is Miss Charlotte Tidswell. This lady was for about forty years a member of the Drury Lane company, from which she retired in 1822. Her earliest participation, so far as I have been able to trace her, was in March of 1783, when she played Eleanora in Congreve's *Mourning Bride*. Report has it that she was the daughter of an army officer and took to the stage when her father's death left her destitute; has it also that she was at one time "protected" by the Duke of Norfolk, and by him introduced to Garrick. Certain it is that she filled during her long stage career the humbler rôles of comedy and tragedy, plodding conscientiously through her round of confidantes and waiting women, never ill or temperamental, the steadiest of walking gentlewomen.

[1] Procter, Bryan Waller (Barry Cornwall), *Life of Edmund Kean.* 2 vols., London, 1835. Hawkins, F. W., *Life of Edmund Kean.* 2 vols., London, 1869. Molloy, J. Fitzgerald, *Life and Adventures of Edmund Kean.* 2 vols., London, 1888.

Even the most voluminous of stage biographies of the day give her but a scant and vague paragraph.

Her one connection with fame is her connection with Edmund Kean, on whom, in his childhood, she kept a casual but protective eye and to whom all his life she stood in close personal relations. She undoubtedly knew the circumstances of his birth. Had she chosen she could have cleared all ambiguity. She did indeed say something on the subject and is the authority from which important later accounts derive, but what she really said is either so contradictory in itself, or has been so garbled in repetition, as to be more confusing than helpful. Here is her testimony as reported by Procter:

> The introduction of our hero to this world of actors, is derived from Miss Tidswell. "On the 17th of March, 1789 . . . at half past three in the morning, Edmund Kean, the father, came to me, and said—'Nance Carey is with child, and begs you to go to her, at her lodgings in Chancery Lane.' Accordingly I and my aunt went with him, and found Nancy Carey near her time. We asked her if she had proper necessaries? She replied, 'No, nothing'; whereupon Mrs. Byrne begged the loan of some baby clothes, and Nancy Carey was removed to the Chambers, in Gray's Inn, which her father then occupied; and it was here that the boy was born."

Turning to Hawkins we find, preceded by a declaration that "the parentage and birthplace of Edmund Kean are not involved in the slightest uncertainty," the date given as November 4, 1787, and the words of Miss Tidswell thus recorded:

> "About half-past three in the morning," writes Miss Tidswell, the actress, "Aaron Kean, the father, came to me and said 'Nance Carey is with child, and begs you to go to her at her lodgings in Chancery-lane.' "

The rest of her brief story agrees with that in Procter. Hawkins does not say that he took his date from Miss Tidswell, but that is, I think, the implication of his paragraph, and if he did not take it from her then there is no telling where he got it. And what are we to make of a witness who in two places gives a different birth and parentage? This confusion is beyond solution, for neither Procter nor Hawkins tells us where they found the testimony they quote. The former reports what Miss Tidswell *said*, the latter what she *wrote*. If she wrote (that is, published) anything on this subject or any other, I do not know where. That both biographers could quote, with such discrepancies, from the same source, or that Hawkins would quote from Procter and silently alter him to fit his own theories, seems scarcely credible. Furthermore, Procter did not place much credence in Miss Tidswell's statement, since he was of the opinion that all the evidence he had was unreliable. And we, at our distance, can only guess where the truth may lie, wondering, for example, whether old age had played havoc with Miss Tidswell's once accurate memory, or whether, perhaps, the whole story of Nancy, Aaron, and Edmund might not be a herring drawn across the true track. So much, for the time being, for Miss Tidswell.

The dates assigned for Kean's birth in all the accounts are either March 17, 1789, or November 4, 1787. There is no reason to suppose that either is correct, but of the two the second is the more likely. The earlier notice-writers incline to it, and the date 1789 has been doubted by more than one either because Kean looked too old for it, or because they questioned whether, precocious though he certainly was, he was quite as precocious as he wished to seem. Probably he did not himself know just when he was born, and it is frequently reported that he used to pull his birth date after him as he moved through life, from 1788 to 1789 and even to 1790, in his eagerness to cut a youthful figure. All in all, he seems to have inclined towards March of 1789. Thus he dates a letter written to Douglas Kinnaird in 1821 "19th of March My Birthday," and writing to Mrs. Clarke on April 4, 1810, he remarks that he was twenty-one three weeks ago. But the most that can be said for the evidence of these letters is that Kean really believed that he was born at such a time. They prove nothing. So far as there seems to be any weight of opinion in this none-too-important matter, that weight is for 1787.[2]

[2] In 1839 Charles Kean placed in the parish church at Richmond a tablet to the memory of his father. This tablet now informs the curious (and in my own case an astonished) visitor that Kean died in 1833 "Aged 48." But from several drawings of the monument at Harvard, I find that the lettering has been twice recut. In one case it reads "Aged 45," in others "Aged 46," there being other changes also in the rest of the inscription. These alterations are doubtless the result of renovations. One such renovation was carried out by Mr. F. B. Chatterton, of Drury Lane, on or about 1870. Correspondence relative to it may be found in the *Era* for January-February, 1871.

As to Kean's parentage the case is not much clearer. Nance Carey, paired indifferently with Edmund or Aaron Kean, is the favored mother. But Miss Tidswell also has been suspected, indeed by the actor himself, who was more than once heard to speculate, "Why did Miss Tidswell take such care of me, if she were not my mother?" Why indeed. And knowing the old story of Miss Tidswell's intimacy with the Duke or Norfolk, he liked to fancy himself that nobleman's offspring. Others did too; at least the story was common property and got itself printed in the London papers as soon as Kean was famous. An old story goes that the Earl of Essex openly twigged the Duke with his paternity one evening in the lobby of Drury Lane Theatre, only to draw forth a graceful denial: "I assure you that I should be very proud to acknowledge him; but this is the first intimation that I have received on the subject." And it has also been said that the Duke, having enough of the story, demanded from the actor a disavowal, and got it. No one, except perhaps Kean, has ever really believed in his connection with the nobility. That Kean may have thought more seriously of it than he did of his numerous other biographical fibs is suggested by the fact that he called his sons Howard and Charles, names that are familiar to the line of Norfolk but strange both to the Keans and the Careys.

Finally Kean has been thought to be the product of the loves of Moses Kean and Miss Tidswell. This seems to be a modern theory, for I find the suggestion nowhere among the older speculations, and arises, I presume, from suspicion that Miss Tidswell was the real mother and from some rather uncertain evidence that she was on intimate terms with Moses. One J. Addison, writing to the *Sunday Times* on June 2, 1833, states that "Miss Tidswell was spoken of as the wife of Moses though not publickly announced as such nor did she reside with him about the year 1787 or 8." If this is true, it would sufficiently account for the fact that Kean habitually referred to Miss Tidswell as his aunt, a relationship otherwise puzzling to explain.

But the weight of testimony seems to be for Nancy Carey and Edmund Kean. I refer not to the repeated iteration of these names, most of which can be dismissed as mere parroting, but to a few declarations having a grave and circumstantial air of authority which may not lightly be disregarded. One of these is the statement of J. Addison in the *Sunday Times*, referred to above.[3] After stating that the youngest of the three brothers was Edmund, "with whom I was particularly intimate," the writer goes on as follows:

> Edmund was an extremely smart young fellow—was Clerk to Welmot [Wilmot] the Surveyor at the time he built the Royalty Theatre[4]—he had great abilities as an orator and was at an early age a distinguished speaker at debating clubs from those at the Lyceum & Coachmakers Hall to the free and easy clubs at Public Houses—The three Brothers lived together at 9 Little St. Martins Lane their sister Mrs. Price (a widow) kept their House . . . my intimacy with Edmund was interrupted by his attention to Miss Carey daughter of Geo Sav Carey & our evening walks generally terminated at the door of Careys Chambers in Gray's Inn—he died about the age of 22 or 23, previous to which he had been disordered in his intellect—Moses died before him.

Pasted below the Harvard transcript, in the same writing, is this memorandum:

> Mr. T. Hill told me he knew Keans Father well—he was a Speaker at the Mitre Fleet Street—Coach Makers Hall & Spring Gardens—had long dark hair & was with Wilmot the Surveyor *20 May 1833*.

The next testimony comes from one Mr. Lush, of Charles Square, in the form of a note to the *Gentleman's Magazine* of August, 1833,[5] correcting the obituary in the June number. He says that the actor's father was Edmund, who nearly fifty years ago was apprenticed to a surveyor, a relative of Lush's; that he debated at Coachmaker's Hall; was afterwards for a short time an architect in Long Acre; was ruined by dissipation and brought to be a copying clerk in Lush's office; and died by walking off a parapet of the roof of his lodgings. Mr. Lush

3 In the Theatre Collection at Harvard in an extra-illustrated set of Hawkins' *Life of Edmund Kean* is a manuscript copy of the letter printed in the *Times*, headed "J. Addison | Camden Cottage | Camden T | May 28." The date being a few days in advance of the publication, one may infer that the paper is a transcript, not from the newspaper, but from the original letter, and that J. Addison, whoever he may have been, was the author thereof. I have taken my copy from this transcript.

4 Erected in June, 1787, by John Palmer, the actor. The story of its prosecution by the patent theatres and Palmer's devices for evading the law is told in Percy Fitzgerald's *New History of the English Stage*. II, 323 ff.

5 See CIII, Part II, 98.

adds that the chief instrument in Kean's education was an aunt, Miss Price, of Green Street, Leicester Square, "a very amiable woman."

Both these accounts, inasmuch as they lay claim to a personal acquaintance with the elder Edmund, must be taken seriously. Indeed Addison, unless his story of Edmund's courtship is pure fancy, pretty well clinches the matter. To their evidence should be added the significant facts of the actor's name, his acknowledgment of Nancy Carey as his mother by settling an allowance on her and by calling her to him before his death, the lifelong silence of Miss Tidswell who would have been constrained by no ethics or practice of her profession from claiming the great tragedian as her son if such he was, and his complexion. On the last matter a few words should be said. Kean was dark, with black hair and piercing black eyes. The reminiscent critic of the *Athenæum* of May 18, 1833, described him as having "an Italian face," but most often it is called Jewish. The writer of an important memorandum in the *New Monthly Magazine* for 1834[6] remembered seeing Kean as a child in 1796, accompanied by his mother Mrs. Carey and a boy Darnley, a reputed son of Mrs. Carey by another father; he was "a pretty boy, but unquestionably more like a *Jew* than a Christian *child*." More than one writer has wondered if Kean had Jewish ancestry,[7] but no proof has been forthcoming, the query seeming to arise from such inconclusive circumstances as Kean's dark coloring and the names of his uncles, Aaron and Moses.

We shall proceed, then, on the accepted likelihood that Edmund Kean and Nancy Carey were the parents of the actor. Of the father very little is known. We have seen that he was in 1787 clerk to Wilmot the surveyor, that at some time afterwards he set up as an architect, and that he was a famous spouter among the debating clubs. He also, like his brother Moses, had the gift of imitation. In the Harvard Theatre Collection is a playbill of the Royalty Theatre, Well Street, for September 9, 1788, announcing: "For this night only, Sound without Sense, Or, The Portrait of a Debating-Club," consisting of imitations of public men, "By the Author, Mr. Edmund Keen, being his

[6] See New Series, XL, Part I, 434 ff.

[7] See, for instance, *Notes and Queries*, 10th Series, I, 449, where the suggestion is made that the name may originally have been Cohen.

first appearance on the Stage." He also was a principal dancer in a ballet pantomime *The Algerian Pirates* and took part in a program of catches. This is beyond doubt the tragedian's father. Yet he was not the only man on the stage in those days bearing the name Keen or Kean. Among the Harvard playbills is one of the theatre in New Street, for June 23, 1790, announcing *Othello,* with "A Messenger" played by "Mr. Keen." This was almost certainly not our Edmund, who seems to have stuck by his imitations. Tom Dibdin, in his *Reminiscences,* tells us that at Manchester in 1791 he played with a Mr. and Mrs. Keene. It is possible that this was the man of the New Street theatre. The only other notice I have of Edmund on the stage comes from a Brighton playbill in the Burney Collection at the British Museum.[8] The occasion was a benefit performance for Moses Kean at the New Theatre in Duke Street, September 1, 1790. After the play of the evening, it is announced, "Mr. Kean will give his Evening Lounge, In which he will be assisted by his Brother, Mr. Edmund Kean, who will present the audience with Sound Without Sense; or, The Portrait of a Debating Society. Consisting of Imitations of Public Speakers, on the Discussion of the Question, '*Which is more proper to oil a Man's Wig with, Honey or Mustard.*' "

The close of Edmund's brief life was melancholy. Madness seized him, brought on, Mr. Lush implies, by dissipation. He had sunk into a mental lethargy when his brother Moses died, the sight of whose body, so the story goes, aroused him, but only for a moment. He relapsed into stupor, then, one day, about his twenty-third year, walked off the roof of his house. All in all, Edmund was fitted to be the father of the great Kean. For he could leave him, besides the black hair and eyes and the taste for imitations, the fatal streak of dissipation and madness which played havoc with his life.

As to the two brothers of Edmund senior much need not be said. Nothing, in fact, can be told of Aaron, except that he was a tailor and possibly a drunkard. Of Moses much more is known, for he was a man of some eminence in the theatre by reason of his imitations of public persons. He was the Foote of his day, even to the wooden leg. As to his age, or the beginnings of his stage career, I have no knowledge.

[8] Burney playbills, Miscellaneous, press mark 937 f. 2.

He made his first appearance at the Haymarket in August of 1784, his second on August 26, as the Gentleman in the Balcony in *The Manager in Distress* by the elder Colman.[9] At Covent Garden he first came out on May 6, 1785, playing the title rôle in Foote's *Devil upon Two Sticks;* and he made his début at Drury Lane on June 4, 1789, as Mrs. Cole in *The Minor* by Foote. Although he played now and then at both the patent houses, he was never a regular member of either company. Usually he was traveling about the country with a program of imitations which he called his *Evening Lounge.* He entertained, for instance, at Bristol, Theatre Royal, on January 5, 1789 (first appearance), and again on January 12 and 19, alternating with Bath, where he performed on January 8, 13, and 17.[10] On October 31 of the same year we find him at the Town Hall, Cambridge, this time, interestingly enough, joining forces with George Saville Carey, the father of Nancy, who did the same kind of thing. With Carey he played again at Cambridge on February 23 and 25, 1790, and we find him alone at Oxford, at the Mitre Inn, on November 19, 1790, and again alone at Cambridge on December 11.[11]

This association of Moses Kean and Carey is of some importance to the genealogical problem of Edmund Kean, because it establishes a connection between the two families. George Saville was the son of Henry Carey, who wrote the ballad operas, *Chrononhotonthologos* and *The Dragon of Wantley,* and lives through *Sally in Our Alley.* Henry went mad at the end and committed suicide, adding perhaps his mite of dry rot to the stock which was to produce Kean. Of his son, George, little is known. He was, according to Oxberry in his *Anecdotes of the Stage,* a posthumous child, began work as a printer, then tried the stage and failed, and finally discovering his bent as a public lecturer, he remained a lecturer for forty years. He died in 1807 at the age of sixty-four. "He possessed," says Oxberry, "musical taste and knowledge to an eminent degree; but with all he was never enabled to do more than support the appearance and conduct of a decent honest man." He has left behind him a dozen or more come-

9 Harvard playbills.

10 Harvard playbills.

11 Burney playbills, British Museum, Miscellaneous, 937 f. 2.

dies and dramatic skits, all of which are well forgotten. As to his lecturing, it seems to have consisted of a program of mimicry, in the style popular at that day, in which a considerable number of imitations of popular actors and singers were strung along a thread of discourse. His staple offering was, I suppose, his *Lecture on Mimicry*, which he published in 1776 with a portrait of himself holding a comic mask and a mirror, and which describes itself as being "delivered with great applause, at the Theatres in Covent-Garden and the Hay-Market, and the great Room in Panton-Street. In the Course of which were introduced A great Variety of Theatrical Imitations. To which is added Jerry Sneak's Return From the Regatta; and A Lecture on Lectures." As to the quality of his art I have met with no expressed opinion, but inasmuch as Moses Kean, who was excellent, deemed him worthy of association, we may safely infer that he was at least respectable.

Had he other children than the wayward Nancy? I do not know. Our knowledge of her is very meagre. She was an actress all her life, probably a very bad one, for she never rose above the humblest parts in provincial companies, and much of her time was spent in Bartholomew Fair. In comparison with her Miss Tidswell may be said to have had a brilliant career. The only biographer of her son to furnish any data as to the mother is Hawkins. He says that she ran away at the age of fifteen to join a company of strolling players, and that when the strolling business was bad she peddled wares on the London streets. How far Hawkins is justified in calling her "worthless" and "inhuman" we scarcely have the means of knowing. All her connections, or disconnections, with her son in his childhood are but unsubstantial rumor. In one place you will read that she kept the child two years before abandoning it, in another that she kept it only three months. One knows not whether to imagine her as hard and coarse, or shallow and flighty. Poor as she was, abandonment may have been a necessity. But there is really no need to hunt excuses for the behavior of Nance Carey. Whatever she did or did not do for Edmund, she seems to have resigned his upbringing easily to others, and she left no tender recollections in her son's mind. When they went a-strolling together, so he used to tell later, she beat him and took his money from him. And no doubt the £50 annuity which he later settled on her was ample remuneration for whatever small troubles she had taken in his behalf.

That there were other members of the Carey family than George Saville and Nancy is implied in various casual and uncorroborated statements. The author of an important manuscript account of Kean's boyhood[12] gives Nancy's authority for it that she had a brother "who played on the guitarre and sang," and with whom she was wont to give soirées in the villages adjoining London. The *New Monthly* memoir[13] credits her with another son, Darnley, by a different father, and asserts that Darnley played for many years at Astley's Amphitheatre and was still alive in 1833; he is in fact mentioned in Nancy's letter to Edmund, shortly before his death, as a married man with a family. There may also have been a daughter. One finds, for example, among the company of the Royal Circus and Surrey Theatre from 1816 to 1819, a Mrs. Carey and a Miss Carey. But here, as in almost every case where a Mrs. Carey is mentioned in the playbills, one cannot feel perfectly sure that the Mrs. Carey is our Nancy, though one may fairly allow the probability. Like uncertainty rests on a playbill of Richardson's traveling theatre announcing *The Africans, or, The Deserted Island,* with Mrs. Carey and Mr. H. Carey in the cast. There is no date, but the bill must be subsequent to July 29, 1808, when *The Africans* was first produced. This H. Carey may well have been the brother whom Nancy is said to have had, and who may have been called Henry after his maternal great-grandfather. But one cannot be sure of any of these bills except in one instance. At the Theatre, Peckham, on September 22, 1814, a Mrs. Kean played in *The School of Reform* and *Plot Counter Plot*. The *Theatrical Inquisitor*, commenting on the Peckham season, declares Mrs. Kean to be the mother of the Drury Lane actor, and remarks further that "the likeness is astonishingly great." The same commentary also notices a "Mr. Kean" as among the Peckham company, but his name does not appear on this particular bill. The adopting of the name Kean, in view of Edmund's recent great success in London, is easy to understand, but

12 See Appendix I.

13 See above, page 6.

ANN CAREY

apparently she did not keep to it, for she is spoken of to the end of her life as Mrs. Carey.

The childhood of Edmund is well-nigh mythical. Though many stories became current after 1814, none of them seems to rest on sounder authority than Kean himself, which should raise an instant presumption that they were untrue. The rest were gathered after his death, by Procter and Hawkins, and have an air of fabulous uncertainty. Who cared for him in his earliest infancy? Procter says the mother did, and that she relinquished him to Miss Tidswell at the age of two, who then offered him to Aunt Price, but that on her rejecting him the father put him to nurse with some woman unknown. Hawkins would have it that Nancy abandoned him in a doorway at the age of three months, whence he was taken by a poor couple and cared for until, at the age of two, his mother claimed him again. Mr. Lush, whose communication to the *Gentleman's Magazine* has been cited before, says that the chief instrument of his education was Mrs. Price, of Green Street, Leicester Square, "a very amiable woman," and an aunt.

There is no composition in these news
That gives them credit.

But we may, I think, once and for all dismiss Hawkins as having any weight in a doubtful matter. Where he got the many details of fact with which he supplemented and "corrected" Procter, unless he made them up in his own head, I have no notion. But because in so many cases his corrections are demonstrably wrong, and because it is scarcely probable that, writing so long after the event, he should have access to reliable information whose source is alike unknown to those who wrote before and after him, he may be safely passed over except where he may be securely checked by corroboration. He undertook, for example, to make Mrs. Price the sister of Nancy Carey, although Procter had stated and stated correctly, that she was a sister to the brothers Kean. Addison says that "their sister Mrs. Price (a widow) kept their House." We may therefore conclude, striking a kind of average of the testimony of Procter and Lush, that the infant Kean was more or less looked after by Mrs. Price and Miss Tidswell, with perhaps a few occasional shillings from the father.

It is probable that he had some trouble with his legs. Procter lays the blame on the woman with whom the father put him to nurse, who so neglected her charge that he "grew bowlegged, knock-kneed, walked on his ankles, and exhibited other symptoms of his nurse's care," as a result of which he had to wear irons on both legs until he was seven or eight. But Procter does not explain how such neglect, which might well produce these results in an infant learning to walk, could affect a child of two. Hawkins has another version which need not detain us. Still another, which may well be nearer the truth, tells that he fell from a horse while riding in a circus at the age of six or seven, and broke both legs. At the time when he presented himself to Mrs. Clarke, when he must have been about eleven, he was wearing one leg-iron. But whatever accident he may have suffered in childhood, his legs were straight and strong enough throughout his later manhood.

He seems to have had a little desultory schooling. Both his biographers (and others) speak of short sojourns at day schools in or near Leicester Square. One was kept by a Mr. King in Chapel Street, Soho. Quite possibly he attended these long enough to pick up the rudiments, but it is not likely that he ever spent much time in any of them. He seems to have been a restless, migratory, incorrigible sort of boy who was always running away from his Aunt Tidswell or his Aunt Price or his Uncle Moses. But he was quick enough in his mind, eager when his curiosity was aroused, so that a little schooling may have gone farther with him than with most boys. During the traveling years of his adolescence and early manhood he was zealous in study and self-instruction, as his commonplace books show. It is probable that he taught himself, in these years, most of what he knew. W. Donaldson, the actor, recollected that when he played Hoddesdon, in Hertfordshire, in 1817, a Miss Sams, of the town library, told him "she well recollected Edmund Kean, at the age of sixteen, acting in the town-hall with Humphrey's company; and many a time she obliged him with the loan of a Greek lexicon."

But another kind of schooling than the three R's is of more immediate concern to us. It is generally affirmed by all the biographers, albeit with a sad confusion of dates which shows how much these reports depend on mere hearsay and which could easily have been corrected by a reference to Genest, that Kean was nursed in his childhood by Drury Lane, which became his playground and even gave him such employment, from time to time, as might lie within his powers. Hawkins indeed has it that he was instructed by the various masters there—in dancing by D'Egville, the ballet master, in fencing by Angelo, and in singing by the great Incledon. No doubt Kean in later years said so, even as he said that he attended Eton, and no doubt with as much truth. On the face of it, the story has plausibility, for what could be more natural than that Aunt Tidswell should take him with her on her daily visits, or that she should attempt to win for her stage-smitten charge a few of those childish parts which frequently came along with the repertory? Nor indeed can one reasonably refuse to entertain the idea that he knew well the interior of Drury Lane, or that, so far as crotchety door keepers and pestered managers would allow, it was his playground. Tradition has it that he played there on sundry occasions, but there are reasons for thinking that these occasions were sporadic, and that he was not regularly employed.

His earliest appearance is supposed to have been as Cupid in an operatic version of *Cymon* based on earlier ballet. This opera was produced on December 31, 1791, when, having lost their theatre by fire, the Drury Lane company were active in the King's Theatre in the Haymarket. The sponsor of this story is Michael Kelly, the genial and popular possessor of a fine Irish-Italian tenor voice, who composed the music and sang the leading rôle. In his *Reminiscences* he tells of looking over a number of children for the part of Cupid, and of being struck by one with a fine pair of black eyes. "I chose him, and little did I then imagine that my little Cupid would eventually become a great actor: the then little urchin was neither more nor less than—Edmund Kean. He has often told me that he ever after this period felt a regard for me." It is a pretty story, but alas! the playbills cut the ground from under Maestro Kelly's bland recollections. Cupid was played by Master Gregson. Who this lad was or what became of him I do not know; he was playing children's parts in 1797, but disappeared thereafter.

The popular goblin story belongs to 1794. In that year the newly built theatre in Drury Lane was ready for occupancy. On Monday, April 21, the opening was celebrated by a splendid production of *Macbeth,* with Kemble and Siddons in their famous rôles. As had come to be the custom, a great deal was made of the supernatural machinery, with choruses and ballets of witches and, as a novelty, a ballet of sprites or infant goblins. During the incantation scene of Act IV, at the song *Black Spirits and White,* this crowd of little boys came scurrying onto the stage like winged beetles. The effect was more comical than impressive, and they were discontinued after a few performances. Kean was later fond of telling a yarn to the effect that during the execution of their steps he tripped up his brother sprites so that they tumbled "like a pack of cards," greatly to the wrath of Black Jack Kemble. This escapade can hardly have improved his standing at Drury Lane, where Kemble was stage manager as well as leading tragic actor.

On June 8, 1796, he played Robin in *The Merry Wives of Windsor,* as is proved by bills which have quite recently come to light.[14] The occasion was the benefit of "Mr. Burton, Misses Heard, Tidswell, & Mrs. Bramwell." He is listed as "Master Kean." This seems to be the first known instance of the appearance of his name on a playbill.

He has been credited with the part of the page in Cibber's *Love Makes a Man,* a comedy frequently in revival at Drury Lane. I have found performances scattered from October 4 to November 8, 1792, and others on June 12, 1797, December 19, 1798, and November 23, 1799; there were doubtless more. None of the bills makes mention of a page, with one curious exception, which concerns the production of June 12, 1797.

The regular bills for this night, of which there are two in the Burney Collection at the British Museum and two at Harvard, bear at the top: "For the Benefit of Messers. Phillimore, Denman, Cooke, Stokes, Miss Tidswell, Miss Heard, Mrs. Benson," showing that the occasion was an omnibus benefit for the walking ladies and gentlemen. The program began with *Love Makes a Man,* followed with Mrs. Jordan in *The Spoiled Child,* went on to imitations by Mr.

[14] Through the acquisition of the playbill in question by Mrs. Enthoven at the Victoria and Albert Museum and by the Harvard Theatre Collection.

For the Benefit of Mr. Burton, Misses Heard, Tidswell & Mrs. Bramwell.

Theatre Royal, Drury-Lane.

This present WEDNESDAY, JUNE 8, 1796.

Their Majesties Servants will act a Musical Prelude in One Act, called

The PURSE; Or, Benevolent Tar.

The Baron, Mr. PACKER, Edmund, Mr. DIGNUM,
Theodore, Mr. TRUEMAN, Will Steady, Mr. WATHEN,
Page, Miss MENAGE. Sally, (First Time) Miss LEAK.

After which Their Majesties Servants will Revive (by particular desire)
Shakespeare's Comedy of The

MERRY WIVES of WINDSOR.

Sir John Falstaff, Mr. PALMER,
Fenton, Mr. TRUEMAN, Shallow, Mr. WALDRON,
Slender, (1st. Time) Mr. RUSSELL, Mr. Page, Mr. PACKER,
Mr. Ford, Mr. WROUGHTON,
Sir Hugh Evans, (First Time) Mr. DODD,
Dr. Caius, Mr. WEWITZER, Host of the Garter, Mr. MOODY,
Bardolph, Mr. HOLLINGSWORTH, Pistol, Mr. R. PALMER,
Nym, Mr. Webb, Robin, Master Kean, Simple, Mr. Burton.
Mrs. Page, Miss POPE,
Mrs. Ford, (First Time) Mrs. GOODALL,
Mrs. Ann Page, (First Time) Miss HEARD,
Mrs. Quickly, Mrs. HOPKINS.

Edmund Kean aged 9 years.

To which will be added, not acted these Six Years, a Pastoral Opera
in two acts, called The

GENTLE SHEPHERD.

Sir William Worthy, Mr. AICKIN,
Patie, (First Time) Miss DECAMP,
Roger, Mr. DIGNUM, Symon, Mr. MOODY,
Glaud, Mr. SUETT, Bauldy, Mr. DODD.
Peggy, (1st Time) Miss Leak, Jenny, (1st Time) Miss Mellon.
Mause, Mrs. BOOTH, Madge, Miss TIDSWELL.

Printed by C. Lowndes, Next the Stage Door. Vivant Rex et Regina!

To-morrow, The BELLE'S STRATAGEM and The SULTAN,
Doricourt, (For that night only) Mr. LEWIS.
Of the Theatre Royal, Covent-Garden.
Letitia Hardy, & Roxalana, Mrs. JORDAN.
Being positively the last time of her Appearance this Season.
End of Act the First and Second of the Play FAVOURITE SONGS by
Mr. BRAHAM, Signora STORACE, and Madame MARA.
For the Benefit of the Widow, and three Orphan Children of the Late Mr. Benson.
The 13th. 14th. and 15th. nights of MAHMOUD, will be on Friday, Saturday,
and Wednesday, next.

THE EARLIEST KEAN PLAYBILL

Caulfield, and ended with Grimaldi in the ballet of *The Scotch Ghost*. At the foot of the bills, above the announcements of coming attractions, is the cachet: "Printed by C. Lowndes next the Stage-Door," showing that they were issued by the official printer to the theatre. Nowhere is any word of Kean or of page. Yet the Harvard Theatre Collection possesses a unique bill of quite different composition, which begins, "For the Benefit of Miss Tidswell," without mentioning the other sharers. It is not a bill for the performance itself but a preliminary announcement, for instead of the formula "This present Monday" etc. one finds "On Monday next." It is short, or else mutilated, because it comprises only *Love Makes a Man* and *The Spoiled Child.* The listing of characters varies in a few points from the official bills, the capital difference being that at the end of the male *personæ* appear the words: "Page, Master Kean." The whole set up of the bill is sufficiently curious, so that I wrote to Mrs. Lillian A. Hall, in charge of the Theatre Collection, and received a reply which reads in part as follows:

> The paper and its condition are the first noticeable discrepancies. Unfortunately the bill has been mounted and I cannot determine the texture, but it is not at all like the paper of that period, or similar to that used in bills of that year. It is also evident that somebody has tried to make the paper resemble an old foxed bill, but the process leaves me in no doubt this was also a very poor imitation not in the least convincing.

Forged playbills are of course not uncommon. To condemn this bill, however, on the testimony of only one expert would doubtless be over hasty. Yet the bill is suspect, and not only on the grounds offered by Mrs. Hall but from the peculiar form of the announcement. Artists for whom benefits were given usually had tickets printed which they went about to sell, but did they issue handbills of this kind? I have never heard of a similar instance.

Two other parts have been credited to the boy Kean, neither of which I have been able to check. One is Prince Arthur in *King John.* I have found performances of this play on March 14, 1795, with Master Welch as Arthur, and on January 1, 1802, with Miss Kelly, but none with Kean. Procter and Kelly both say that in 1798 he played Blue Beard in pantomime, not the full grown butcher of course, "but the diminutive *boy*-Blue Beard, who, before the commencement of the tragedy, appears in perspective, riding over the hills." This most successful opera was produced January 16, 1798, the book by Colman the Younger and the music by Michael Kelly.

Before reviewing the evidence for Kean's connection with Drury Lane in his childhood, one other rather important piece of testimony remains to be considered. It consists of a report of a conversation held, presumably about 1800, between Mrs. Clarke, who had befriended Edmund, and Miss DeCamp, a well-known actress of Drury Lane.[15] It runs as follows:

> She [Miss DeCamp] said he would never, she was assured, be anything but an actor, and that she was sure the moment he was let out of my friend's hands his mother and uncle would seize upon him. He had all his father's talent, who was a wonderful mimic. They were on both sides, Careys and Keans, too full of talent, but the Carey family formed an objection to his being engaged at Drury Lane, otherwise he was the cleverest child they had ever seen. He had also done himself an ill office in provoking the anger of Mr. Kemble, who had caught him at one of the rehearsals behind the scenes mimicking his tones and actions to the great amusement of the underlings gathered round. Mr. Kemble had shoved him aside so roughly that he fell through a trap door and lamed himself for some time.

If any weight at all may be allowed this statement, written down many years after the conversation took place and by a third person, it helps to strengthen the general impression, derived from what little we know of his career there, that he was not regularly employed among the children at Drury Lane. Many boys appear on the bills between 1792 and 1800—Masters Gregson, DeCamp, Harlowe, Welsh, Chatterley, Menage, Elliott, Tokeley, Heather, Walter, Ellis, Wells, Johnson, Weal, Smith, Beton. It would seem strange that "the cleverest child they had ever seen," if he were really open to engagement, did not appear more frequently. Furthermore, the list of parts which begins in 1794 with a dancing goblin and closes in 1798 with a supernumerary Blue Beard shows no progression. One is driven to the conclusion that his appearances were sporadic, that he was picked up on occasion, probably through the influence of Aunt Tidswell, and

[15] See below, page 18, and Appendix I, page 357.

that he was more familiar with the wings of Drury than with the stage.

What then was young Edmund doing all this time, when he was not at the theatre? If we only knew! Yet, although certainty is beyond our reach, we may at least make a shrewd guess, that he was for the most part with his mother. The biographers are full of stories allocating him to London in the combined cares of Uncle Moses, Aunt Tidswell, and Aunt Price. They draw attractively-decorated pictures of lessons in elocution and stage behavior from Uncle Moses and Aunt Tidswell, of long hours of drill in the great Shakespearean rôles—Richard, Hamlet, Lear, Othello; of his restlessness and unruly flights from home with subsequent capture; of attempts to cage the wild young hawk by locks, cords, and even a brass dog collar, about the inscription on which the biographers cannot agree. There is no way of knowing how much fact and how much fiction there is in all this. On the face of it, there seems to be every likelihood that the boy's theatrical relatives should take an interest in his education for the stage, provided they concerned themselves about him at all. But such feeble checks as we are able to apply to the biographers cast a doubt upon their whole story. One of these is the important reminiscences published in the *New Monthly Magazine* of May, 1834. This takes the form of notes gathered from various unnamed witnesses who professed to have had personal knowledge of Kean at different periods. Witness number one testifies that he saw Edmund first in April of 1796. "I am certain of the day, because I met Mrs. Carey, Edmund, and Darnley . . . the day when *Vortigern* was performed" (i.e., April 2, 1796). The following September he played Tom Thumb at Bartholomew Fair at a public house, his mother being Queen Dollabella. Old Richardson (the owner of a well-known traveling tent theatre, which was carried from fair to fair) engaged him then and subsequently. He broke his leg when a boy riding an act of horsemanship at Bartholomew Fair.

Even the biographers, with characteristic inconsistency, add corroboratory hints that the boy was usually away from London. "When the boy grew old enough," says Procter, "she [his mother] took him with her." And again, "These truant habits existed all his life, with the exception only of the time when he lived with Mrs. Clarke . . .

He was, in effect, migratory." Procter, whose constant willingness to confess insecurity proves at the same time his good faith and the frailty of existing knowledge, admits that he does not know where the boy lived, although he thinks Miss Tidswell had most of his time. But if that were so, it would seem to have been prior to 1796.

The time has come to speak of Kean's relations with Mrs. Clarke. The authority for this long anecdote, told with embroideries and omissions by Procter and Hawkins, is a manuscript once in the possession of John Forster and now among the papers left by him to the Victoria and Albert Museum. It is unsigned, undated, written on letter paper in a feminine hand. The lady who figures as benefactress is never called by name, but referred to only as "my friend." Hence there is no absolute certainty that she was Mrs. Clarke, yet Procter identifies her by that name and the probability is strengthened by letters from Kean a dozen or more years later to a Mrs. Clarke of 5 Caroline Place, Guilford Street, in which he calls himself "your once favored protégé." Inasmuch as the document is printed at the end of this book, there is no need, at this point, to rehearse in full its narrative.

Suffice it to say, that at some indeterminate time Mrs. Clarke, through Dr. Young, the father of the tragedian Charles Young, was introduced to Nancy Carey, then a peddler of perfumes, who spoke to her at various times of her son Edmund as "a wonderful little boy with an astounding genius for acting." She said he was at present with a lady, a Roman Catholic, who had taken him and was bringing him up "quite genteely." Presently Mrs. Clarke met the boy himself, was taken with his beauty, his charming manners, and his histrionic swagger, let him act scenes from *Richard III* before a group of friends, was still more taken with him, and ended by annexing him almost as a member of the family. So he lived on under her affectionate eye for an indefinite period which might be months or even a couple of years, attending school and acting his rôles occasionally at the houses of her acquaintance, until a slight put upon him by an inconsiderate guest so wounded his feelings that he ran away and was gone seven days, at the end of which he was found half starved by the ostler of a neighboring mews and brought home. His story was that he had made his way to Portsmouth and offered himself as a sailor, "but nobody would take him." Whereupon Mrs. Clarke, feeling the responsibility of guarding the wild young hawk to be more than she could manage, and feeling that he needed a man's control, cast about to find some accommodating gentleman who would take over her charge, at length coming to terms with Captain Miller of the Staffordshire Militia, stationed at Windsor Castle. He carried the boy to Windsor with him. But first she allowed Edmund to give a public recital at an exhibition room in Chancery Lane, which was so well attended that he gathered in between forty and fifty pounds. At Windsor he performed for the officers, became acquainted with Eton boys who smuggled him into their rooms, and recited twice before the King and Queen at the Castle. Leaving Windsor he went to Oxford, armed with a letter from an Eton boy to his elder brother, and there his success with the students was equally great. He was received into the apartments of some of the most distinguished students, including those of "the late reverend worthy and accomplished Mr. Conybeare, who had, he told me himself, the honor and pleasure to present to the future Kean the first copy of Shakespeare's plays he had ever possessed."

Here ends the story, all of which is most interesting and very likely in the main outlines true, inasmuch as we know that Kean was protected at one time by a Mrs. Clarke, a woman of means and social position. The whole force of this important document, one is bound to admit, suffers from the obscurity which veils the authorship. Who wrote it? Some woman friend of Mrs. Clarke, clearly enough. When was it written? Not until after Kean's death. Perhaps it was set down for Procter in 1834, when he was gathering materials for his book; in fact, that seems altogether likely. But 1834 is a long time after the events narrated, and the information is at second hand. We are dependent on the memories of two persons, and in matters relative to Kean, the biographer quickly learns to distrust everyone's memory. Yet some assurance may be drawn from the fact that the incidents dealt with, until near the end, fall within the personal observation of Mrs. Clarke. Therefore one is unwilling to reject the pretty story, which, if perhaps adorned in certain details, may very well be true in the essential outline.

Who was Mrs. Clarke? No one has ventured to identify her, nor do I know that it would be possible on the slender clues we hold. When Kean wrote to her on May 4, 1810, he addressed her at her London house in Caroline Place, Guilford Street. In his next letter of May 17, he wrote to her at Lady Wooton's Green, Canterbury. I have wondered whether she may not have been the wife of Clarke the banker, of Clarke, Coutts and Company, with whom in his days of prosperity Kean banked his money and to whom we have several of his letters.

How old was Kean when he went to Mrs. Clarke? The story says eleven—"a slender, pale, diminutive boy, really eleven years of age but not taller than nine." That would make the year to be 1798, if we choose 1787 as the birth date. The close of his association with the Clarkes may be tentatively set in or about 1800. Witness number two of the *New Monthly* reminiscences before alluded to, says that "about 1800" Kean, described as "the infant prodigy, Master Carey," gave readings at the Rolls Rooms in Chancery Lane, among other things reciting the whole (!) of *The Merchant of Venice*. This occasion might plausibly be identified with that performance in Chancery Lane whereby Mrs. Clarke benevolently found the money with which to launch her protégé on the wide world.

If we are right in supposing that the protection of Mrs. Clarke ended about 1800, we must believe that her account of his subsequent movements needs emendation. For she sends him to Windsor and then vaguely to Oxford, whereas there is reason to believe that he was in London between 1800 and 1802. These years must compose, or be embraced in, those during which he was known about town as a distinguished spouter and amateur actor. The same witness who recalled the Rolls Room performance, had it from one Cobham, an actor and "a playmate of Kean's," that about 1802 Carey was acknowledged by the "private" actors of London to be "the best amateur then extant." And on the word of the same authority, he was given leading parts at a private theatre in Lamb's Conduit Street, despite the fact that he could not bear his part of the expenses. If the memories of various anonymous gentlemen are to be trusted, we must picture Kean at this time as flitting about the outskirts of the legitimate

For the BENEFIT of

Mifs TIDSWELL.

Theatre Royal, Drury Lane.

On MONDAY next, JUNE 12, 1797,

Their Majefties Servants will act a Comedy called

Love Makes a Man

Or, The Fop's Fortune.

Antonio, Mr. DOWTON,
Charino, Mr HOLLINGSWORTH,
Don Lewis, Mr. KING,
Carlos, Mr. BARRYMORE,
Clodio, Mr. PALMER,
Sancho, Mr. SUETT,
Monfieur, Mr. WEWITZER,
Governor, Mr. PHILLIMORE,
Don Duart, Mr. CAULFIELD,
Don Manuel, Mr. HOLLAND,
Pedro. Mr. BANKS, Jaques, Mr. TRUEMAN,
Prieft, Mr. DENMAN, Lawyer, Mr. WATHEN,
Page, Mafter KEAN,

Angelina, Mifs HEARD,
Louifa, Mrs. POWELL,
Elvira, Mifs TIDSWELL,

End of Act I. "*CHELSEA QUARTERS*" Compofed by Mr. SCHROEDER.
By Mr. COOKE.
End of Act IV. "*When on board our Trim Veffel*" Compofed by Mr. CARTER
By Mr. COOKE.
To which will be a Farce called The

SPOIL'D CHILD.

Little Pickle, Mrs. JORDAN.
Old Pickle, Mr. SUETT, Tag, Mr. R. PALMER,

Mifs Pickle, Mifs TIDSWELL,
Maria, Mifs HEARD,
Margery, Mifs BOOTH, Sufan, Mrs. [illegible]

PLAYBILL (FORGED?) OF "LOVE MAKES A MAN"

theatre, acting with societies of amateurs, reading at exhibition rooms, ready for a turn at anything from acrobatics to singing prettily to the harpsichord, now and then given a chance to do something at one or another of the minor theatres, but never fixed at one kind of work or with one group of workers. Stories which one does not know whether to believe or disbelieve, float vaguely to us out of the distance. Roach, a bookseller of the neighborhood of Brydges Street and Drury Lane, recollected that Kean acted Richard in his garret with a Scotch lass for Lady Ann. One Edwards, an amateur, was attracted to him from the time of the Rolls Room spouting, and in later years was wont to boast that he taught the boy all he knew. This we may pardonably doubt, and yet when all such memories are liberally discounted there remains as an undiscountable residuum a recollection, shared by several persons, of Kean as a gifted boy in the first years of the new century active among the entertainment halls and minor theatres of London. And this recollection is further supported by the one indisputable fact which we possess in this connection, namely that in the spring of 1802 Kean did recite at Covent Garden. Here, at least, the biographers and the playbills are at one. The occasion was a benefit on May 18 for Knight, when, between the comedy and the farce, were offered "(By particular desire, and for this Night only) Recitations by the celebrated Master Carey (His First appearance on this Stage)." Procter says that the piece recited was Rolla's address to the sun, and that Kean was too hoarse from a recent performance at the Sans Souci exhibition hall to make much of an impression. It is not important to know whether these details are true. What is important is that about the age of fifteen Kean was presented to a Covent Garden audience as "the celebrated Master Carey." Behind this phrase lie indeterminate years of preparation, which, vaguely as we can see them, must have been somewhat as they are described in the biographies—years of tramping and starving with his mother, of knocking about from Aunt Tidswell to Uncle Moses to Aunt Price, of running away to Richardson's migratory theatre and coming home again, of fragmentary training from one or another person with whom he happened to be, years of tumbling, singing, dancing, horseback riding, mimicking, reciting, learning Richard, learning Hamlet, learning Othello, learning *The*

Merchant of Venice complete, with an interlude of sobriety and decorum under Mrs. Clarke's wing, culminating in a miniature fame among the spouting houses of London. To this career, which occupies what I have generously called the childhood of Kean, the recital at Covent Garden in May, 1802, must have seemed to fit the climax. Who knows with what high hopes and swelling heart he went to assist his friend Knight, trusting perhaps to arouse the formidable patrons of Covent Garden as he had aroused the patrons of Sans Souci and the Rolls Room, or his indulgent friends in Guilford Street? It might be important after all to know if he was hoarse and "received no applause." But stop! Let Molloy and Hawkins imagine the boy's disappointment, his humiliation, the collapse of his far-flinging hopes of being received as a petted hero into the bosom of Covent Garden, the despair with which he set his foot on the twelve long years of wandering that elapsed before his way led him to delirious prosperity at Drury Lane. This is austere history, with a free reign to imagination but a stout curb to fancy. And all that history has to report is that "the celebrated Master Carey" did, by particular desire and for this night only, speak some sort of piece in Covent Garden on a spring evening in 1802.[16]

Approximately here closed the pillar-to-post childhood of Kean and began the more earnest post-to-pillar career of his young manhood. But before closing, one more semi-mythical escapade remains to be spoken of—the voyage to Madeira. Procter mentions it in a brief chapter as an adventure of uncertain date but certain authenticity, since "the fact rests upon more than one statement, and is confirmed by his [Kean's] own assertions." The last-mentioned authority may raise a smile; the others, adumbrated in the phrase "more than one statement," are unfortunately vague. Hawkins, and before him Phippen, tells the story at greater length, to the effect that in his eighth year Kean shipped as cabin boy on a vessel bound for Madeira, dis-

[16] It is curious that Kean should have been billed at Drury Lane in 1796 as "Master Kean" and at Covent Garden in 1802 as "Master Carey." Did he use the one name on the professional stage and the other among amateur circles? Or was the boy at Covent Garden not our Edmund at all? Mrs. Enthoven is skeptical on this point. Yet who else could be implied as "the celebrated Master Carey?" Neither Darnley nor any other of Ann Carey's possible children is known to have had the least reputation.

liked the life on shipboard, pretended to have gone deaf from a cold, and got himself sent home on the sick list. It is a good yarn to spin in after years over the port and cigars, about one's shrewd and venturesome infancy, but is it true? For my own part, I believe not, though I cannot disprove it. But in the Clarke narrative is an incident which sounds suspiciously like the germ of this story. When Kean ran away from Mrs. Clarke, he made his way to Portsmouth (as he afterwards told her), where "he offered himself for a sailor but nobody would take him. He had been repulsed—rudely treated, beaten, half starved . . . ;" and so he begged his way home again. Here is all the basis that would be needed for one of those fictions with which the later Kean was fond of adorning the early Kean. A voyage to Madeira was nothing to a man who, out of a passing sojourn at Eton, could embroider a three year's residence in that school.

CHAPTER II

WANDERING YEARS

THE old story that Kean spent the years between 1803 and 1806 at Eton has long been exploded.[1] A thorough examination of the school registers has revealed no one by either name he might have used. The story was got up, doubtless, to add a lustre of gentility and letters to his record, just as he gave the press to understand, at the time of his Drury Lane triumph, that he had been a subaltern in the army. But no doubt he had visited Eton in his travels, and the time was probably 1803. Whether he came there with Richardson's troupe or with some other, there is no knowing. The Clarke narrative represents him as going to the Windsor garrison in company with Captain Miller and thence establishing acquaintance at the school, but it is very hard to reconcile that account with so late a date. For if Kean went to live with Mrs. Clarke at the age of eleven, he can scarcely have stayed with her until he was sixteen. All other accounts represent him as going to Windsor with a company of strollers, and as being honored with a command to recite before the king and queen. This much-repeated story, although concerned with that part of his life which we must regard as prehistoric and of the kind to draw suspicion on itself, may still be true. At any rate Procter gives a kind of authorization for it, as being told long after to Mrs. Kean by Mrs. Heath, wife to a former Eton master. Said Mrs. Heath: "We had your husband for two or three days when he was a boy. The Eton boys were so fond of hearing him, that they asked Dr. Heath to permit him to recite, which he assented to. It was thus that the king heard of him, and had him recite before him." There is nothing inherently improbable in this, for it was a day of infant spouters and the star of Master Betty, the greatest of the tribe, was soon to rise over Ireland. And George III was a devoted, if somewhat whimsical, amateur of the stage. Unluckily no eyewitness has reported the momentous meeting, which is said to have netted Master Carey two guineas.

Between May of 1802, when we know Kean to have been in Lon-

[1] See, for example, *Fraser's Magazine*, VIII (1833), 753.

don, and Easter of 1804, when we know he joined the company of Samuel Jerrold at Sheerness, Kean was in all probability on the road. Procter sketches at this point a tour into Scotland under a manager who, he thinks, was Moss, supporting his account with tales of hardship and of a love affair with some dim Scotch lass. It may be. Or it may be that he was in the west of England or in the east midlands, or anywhere else at all, for until we can pick up a trace of him in some town we never feel sure that we know. And the first trace does not turn up until the spring of 1804.

Blanchard Jerrold is the sponsor of what meager news we have about Kean's association with the Jerrolds. Samuel Jerrold, the manager, had for many years headed a company which served the southeastern towns in the neighborhood of Sheerness. By a second wife he had had Douglas Jerrold, born in 1803, who in time won fame as a man of letters and whose biography[2] was written by his son, Blanchard. The brief memoranda on Kean which it contains were obtained at second hand and set down long after the event, Douglas himself being much too young to remember the actor at the time when he was a member of his father's company. Nevertheless, the Jerrolds, who were an industrious and intelligent family, may be taken as competent witnesses.

Kean, then, joined the company at Sheerness on Easter Monday, 1804, but whence he came we are not told. He still dressed as a boy and called himself Carey, though he must have been seventeen. His salary was fifteen shillings a week. He opened in *George Barnwell* and harlequinade, stayed with the company the rest of the season, played all kinds of parts, and was very successful in comedy. He is said to have made hits in *Wattey Cockney* and *Risk* and with the popular song about the *Unfortunate Miss Bailey*. The only serious rôle besides Barnwell that is mentioned is Rolla, presumably in Sheridan's *Pizarro*.

The one thing of note in this account is that a boy of seventeen should have been engaged to play leading rôles. But in fact there is nothing surprising in that. The lesser provincial companies were usually so short in people and so long in repertory that everyone, unless

[2] *The Life and Remains of Douglas Jerrold*. London, 1859.

he was reduced by age to playing old men or unless the manager arrogated all the leads to himself, was qualified to shine as a star. And competent young fellows thoroughly routined who could turn a neat double somersault as harlequin and carry off the grand manner of Alexander or Rolla were none too common. A talented actor, of whatever age, might languish in the provinces for his salary, but never for rôles. In a company of greater magnitude Kean would have played second parts, as he did the following year in Belfast. His position with Jerrold, then, merely shows that the company was among the lower orders of its own class.

Here let me pause to voice a lament, which might be repeated at intervals throughout this chapter, that no history of the provincial companies of the 18th and 19th centuries has ever been written. In some cases we have town chronicles of a sort, as for example those of Bath, Exeter, Liverpool and Norwich. But even for the major circuits, such as York, Norwich, Canterbury, and Swansea, information is rare and scattered, and of the minor circuits we know practically nothing at all. This is one reason why it is so hard to trace the provincial careers of famous actors who nourished their seedling art in country barns until it blossomed at Covent Garden or Drury Lane. I have found nothing about the Jerrold Company of 1804, despite a search through the available Kentish newspapers. In 1806, besides Sheerness, they were playing at Lydd, in Kent, a town which may well have been on their circuit in 1804, but beyond that I do not know their territory. Samuel Jerrold did not lease the Sheerness Theatre until January of 1807, but he seems to have made that his headquarters for some time previously.

Nor do I know what constituted his season, whether he played all the year round, or only into the autumn. From the fact that on January 6, 1806, he was announcing in the *Kentish Gazette* the opening of his Sheerness Theatre, I presume that he may regularly have played during the winter. In that case Kean may have stayed with him through the Christmas season of 1804-5.

By February, however, he was back in London. A communication to *Notes and Queries*[3] first called attention to the existence of a Kean

[3] Eighth Series, IV, 538, submitted by W. F. Waller.

At the Theatre, Wivell's Billiard Room,

CAMDEN-TOWN.

This present Evening, Friday, Feb. 15, 1805,

Will be presented the Romantic Opera of

The Mountaineers,

OR

Love and Madness:

Octavian, Mr. KEAN
Bulcazen Muley, Mr. NEWMAN
Roque, Mr. SMITH
Count Virolet, Mr. COLLINS Killmalock, Mr. THOMAS
And Sadi, Mr. GROSETT.
Zoradia, Mrs. GROSETT
And Agnes, Miss BARNES.

End of the Play

A Comic Song, by Mr. Grosett

To which will be added the Farce of

The Spoiled Child,

Little Pickle, Mrs. GROSETT
Old Pickle, Mr. NEWMAN John, Mr. KEAN.
And Telamachus Tag, (the Author and Actor) Mr. GROSETT.
Miss Barbara Pickle, Miss BARNES.

PIT 2s. GALLERY 1s. Doors to be opened at 6, and begin at 7.

Jones, Printer, Chapel Street, Soho.

PLAYBILL OF "THE MOUNTAINEERS"
CAMDEN TOWN, 1805

playbill for February of 1805. It has been reproduced by Mr. W. J. Lawrence in an article of which I shall speak frequently.[4] The place is "the Theatre, Wivell's Billiard Room, Camden-Town," a quite unchronicled amusement hall, the date is February 15, and the bill is composed of the younger Colman's popular melodrama, *The Mountaineers*, and Bickerstaffe's farce *The Spoiled Child*. In the first, "Mr. Kean" played the lead, Octavian, a favorite part with him; in the second, John. One other bill of this theatre is preserved, at Harvard, dated March 2. This time Kean is playing the secondary part of Wilford (Sir Edward Mortimer was probably at this time rather too mature for him) in Colman's *Iron Chest* and Jerry Sneak in Foote's *Mayor of Garrat*. "Preceding the Play, Mr. Kean will recite the favorite Tale of Alonzo and Imogine. End of the Play The Favorite Song of the Post Captain, by Mr. Kean." Thus, in the manner of the theatre of that day, he was rewarded for condescending to Wilford.

He left Camden Town very shortly after this performance, and his consequent movements have been established by Mr. W. J. Lawrence in a valuable essay (the only scholarly essay, in fact, which has ever been devoted to Kean), contributed to the *English Illustrated Magazine*.[5] It seems that manager Michael Atkins of the Belfast Theatre had come to London for recruits and carried back with him, among others, Kean and Miss Macauley, of the Haymarket Theatre. They arrived at Belfast on March 21, and the season opened on the 27th. Not much is to be got from local papers or extant bills about Kean in Belfast, but that little has interest. In May the company was "strengthened" by the addition of Miss Mudie, a prodigy of six who was hailed as a female Betty and was destined to be hissed from Covent Garden the following November. Her benefit performance, on May 31, was announced as *The Country Girl*, but this was replaced by *Douglas*, "owing," as the Belfast *Newsletter* explained, "to the indisposition of Mr. Keane, who was to have played the part of Belville." Mr. Lawrence, reading between the lines, believes that the illness was merely

[4] A copy of this bill exists in the collection made by Mr. Houdini and now the property of Mr. Messmore Kendall of New York. Whether or not it is the same bill noted by Mr. Lawrence I cannot say.

[5] *A New Chapter in the Life of Edmund Kean*. August, 1901.

an excuse to avoid playing with an infant phenomenon, toward whom, as is well known, Kean had a rooted objection. On a later and more celebrated occasion he refused to act with Master Betty himself. Because Belleville was the leading male rôle of *The Country Girl,* it does not follow that Kean was habitually given leads at Belfast. The evidence is indeed quite to the contrary, the case of Belleville being explicable on the grounds of his short stature, which would match him well with the diminutive heroine.

On June 3 he played David in *The Rivals,* on June 28, Henry Moreland in Colman's *Heir at Law* and Dermot in O'Keefe's *Poor Soldier,* none of these being first-line parts. On August 2 the company was genuinely strengthened by the arrival of Jack Bannister, of Drury Lane, one of the most popular actors of the day. In his opening comedy, Mrs. Centlivre's *A Bold Stroke for a Wife,* Kean played Sir Philip Modelove. Early in August, also, came Chalmers from Bath and Mansell from Dublin, both playing leads. Evidently the company was being equipped for the august approach of Mrs. Siddons.

The great queen of tragedy was now paying what was to be her farewell visit to Belfast. This occasion has been utilized for another Kean legend, successfully exploded by Mr. Lawrence's investigation. Procter gives two versions of Kean's association with Siddons, one of which, as he remarks with shrewd humor, "is derived from Kean, and the other rests on very respectable authority." According to Kean, Mrs. Siddons was to open as Zara in Congreve's *Mourning Bride,* with Kean opposite her as Osmyn. Elated by such an honor, he drank too deeply, with the result that the part vanished from his memory, reducing him to frantic stuttering which enraged the lioness. But in the next play, Home's *Douglas,* in which he played Norval to Siddons' Lady Randolph, he did so excellently that the lioness was surprised into admiration, and after the play commended him as follows: "You have played very well, sir, *very* well. It's a pity—*but there's too little of you to do anything.*" The story has been much repeated, with variations. Yet it is certainly a fiction. Manager Atkins had not brought Chalmers and Mansell to Belfast for the purpose of letting young Kean play Kemble to Mrs. Siddons. His position in the company all along was a minor one. Furthermore, the Siddons repertory disagrees conclusively with the story. She played for five consecutive nights, beginning August 19, in this order: *Venice Preserved, George Barnwell, Macbeth, Mourning Bride, The Stranger. Douglas,* it is to be noticed, was not given.

Procter's second story, the one "of very respectable authority," may well be true. It goes to the effect that Mrs. Siddons, feeling unwell at rehearsal time, requested the company to run through the play at her lodgings. They all repeated their lines as is frequently done at rehearsal, that is, with indifference, except for one "little man who was to play one of the secondary characters," and who "although he had not a great deal to do . . . endeavoured to do his best." This caught the great actress's attention, who remarked when he had finished: "Very well, sir—very well. I have never heard that part given in the same way before." The difference in versions is striking.

Of Kean's movements for nearly a year after leaving Belfast there is no trace. Hawkins places him, in March of 1806, with Moss's company in Dumfries and later with Butler in Northallerton. This is evidently the same northern tour that Procter dated some three years earlier, but which dating is right would be hard to tell. Procter fills in the winter of 1805-6 with an engagement in Mrs. Baker's Kentish circuit, but this is certainly incorrect; also with a story of his swimming the Thames in order to reach Braintree in Essex and catching therefrom an ague. But we are not on certain ground until June of 1806, when we find him at the Haymarket, London. It may be worth while to mention a story from Hawkins, that he owed his engagement to one of the Haymarket staff, who saw him play Octavian in Northallerton, but according to Procter, he owed it to Miss Tidswell.

A good deal has been made of the Haymarket engagement as one of the major crosses in Kean's wandering years. He came to London, we are told, in the expectation of playing leads, and was bitterly mortified to be palmed off with serving men. But the chances are strongly against this romantic hypothesis. The Haymarket was the third most important theatre of London, a kind of summer supplement to the patent theatres, which were usually closed during July and August, and it recruited its forces from the favorites of both institutions. With such veterans as Fawcett, Mathews, Liston, Winston, and Wewitzer engaged for the season of 1806, there was small chance that a young and unknown stroller should even dream of playing leads. Arrogance, with respect to London at least, did not come to Kean until fame brought it. At this period of his career he was a diffident enough young man, and he who, in 1812, would be writing to manager Arnold that third- or fourth-line characters at Drury Lane were the summit of his ambition, would scarcely, in 1806, aim at the first line in the Haymarket. Furthermore, Procter tells us that he was engaged for "small parts."

The season opened on June 9 with *The Mountaineers,* in which Octavian was played by Rae and Kean was a goatherd; in the afterpiece, *Fortune's Frolic,* he was a clown. Rae was the tragedian of the troupe, of which the main line, as befitted the summer weather, was the lighter phases of comedy. He was a young man, a little older than Kean, with whom it is reported he had played and spouted as a boy—a handsome fellow who had risen quickly in his profession and of whom a good deal was expected. He never fulfilled these expectations, for he had no more than ordinary talent, but eventually settled down to playing second-line parts at Drury Lane. When Kean opened there in 1814 as Shylock, Rae was the Bassanio, and he supported the great star in many another play after that. He was what is called a respectable actor, and has left but the faintest echo in the dramatic hall of fame. But now he was cock of the walk in his own line. The story is told of his patiently rehearsing a scene of *The Iron Chest* for an effect which Kean could not get, finally giving it up with, "Never mind, sir, we'll try it tonight." Kean was hurt, said nothing, and never forgot. But in 1817, when Rae had taken the East London Theatre and was playing *The Iron Chest,* Kean sat in a front box, elaborately attentive. This is one of those stories which, though they may not be true to the life of Kean, are true to his nature, for it seems that he had a tenacious memory for all slights and most kindnesses, and loved to pay in kind.

The season of 1806 proceeded at the Haymarket quite without any event of the slightest importance. Besides a few plays which are still remembered, such as *Hamlet, The Mountaineers, The Iron Chest, The Clandestine Marriage, The Heir at Law,* the repertory was composed of forgotten trifles: *Five Miles Off, Follies of a Day, The Water-*

man, Catch Him Who Can, Blue Devils, The Weathercock, Paul and Virginia, The Gay Deceivers, We Fly by Night. The spirit of the younger Colman lay authoritatively on the Haymarket. On most of the bills I have been able to see the name of Kean does not appear, either because he took no part or because his part was too insignificant to notice. He had some kind of small work to do in Tom Dibdin's *Five Miles Off* (produced July 9 and frequently repeated), he was Rosencrantz in *Hamlet* (August 12),[6] a servant in *The Iron Chest* (June 23), a goatherd in *The Mountaineers* (June 9), Carney in *Ways and Means* (June 12), John in *The Heir at Law* (June 10), Dubbs in *The Review* (June 10—this part was taken at times by Johnston, when Kean may have been ill), a servant in *John Bull* (June 19), landlord in *The Prisoner at Large* (June 26), an alguazil in *She Would and She Would Not* (July 1), a servant in *Speed the Plough* (June 14), and a fifer in *The Battle of Hexham* (June 16). Truly a humble list. An analysis of the complete Haymarket season shows that until July 18, with one exception, Kean played in every performance, but that thereafter his name is frequently missing from the bills. I have no notion of what the trouble was, if there was trouble.

Another favorite story of Kean at the Haymarket illustrates a trait which certainly belonged to the struggling apprentice but which the master in later years frequently lost, that of putting himself into every part with all his energy. It is said that he tried to make of Carney, a very minor person in *Ways and Means*, a real character, contrary to the invariable rule of walking gentlemen that their parts were to be played in a manner equivalent to their own positions in the company, which is to say, as badly as possible. One of his fellow actors, probably one of the same tribe, observing his efforts with surprised contempt, exclaimed: "Look at the little man—he's trying to act; he's trying to make a part of Carney!"

One does not, of course, know what Kean thought or what he felt during his one season at the Haymarket, but one can imagine it with a good deal of certainty. Even granting that he went there with full

[6] These are dates of first performances. All the plays were, of course, repeated several times.

knowledge of what would be given him, a man who has played Octavian and Rolla, though in barns, does not stoop gracefully to waiters and alguazils. We know that Kean was through the later years of his provincial exile like a hound straining at his leash, that he was immensely conscious of his powers and ate his heart in despair at those powers wasted on the desert. Even in these youthful days he must have been conscious of something within him which his smug metropolitan associates had never known and would never know, in spite of their maddening air of having arrived at the center. He may have knocked at other doors. He may have, as Hawkins says, gone to John Philip Kemble, now at Covent Garden, and been coldly rejected. But whether or no, he must have seen that in the closed circle of the London theatres there was as yet no place for him. His way led out again toward the circumference, the provinces which were the bitter training school and battleground of every great actor, where if he had to starve he could at least starve as Octavian and not as a goatherd. And so into the provinces again he went.

According to the fourth witness of the *New Monthly* memoirs, he went directly to Mrs. Baker's in Kent, and this appears to be correct. Substantiation comes from a newspaper clipping among the Kean miscellanea at Harvard,[7] which lists fifty-five of his performances at Tunbridge Wells, derived, the anonymous correspondent tells us, from bills "in the possession of Mr. Clifford, printer." The list has every appearance of veracity, agreeing with the partial list given in the *New Monthly* and furthermore with the one bill of this Tunbridge Wells season that I have been able to find. Kean opened on September 22, 1806 (probably his first performance with Mrs. Baker, inasmuch as the Haymarket season closed on the 15th) as Lord Hastings, the hero of Rowe's popular tragedy *Jane Shore*, and Peeping Tom, in the musical farce of that name by O'Keefe. The times, it would seem, had changed, in that the young fellow who was fit only to play Carney at London was deemed fit to play Hastings at Tunbridge. But the elevation, though considerable, was not so great as Mrs. Baker's opening night makes it seem. Doubtless she was trying out her new man, doubtless playing up his Haymarket connection

[7] Unnamed and undated. If only the busy tribe of clippers would identify their cuttings!

for its advertising value. At any rate, as the subsequent course of the season shows, Kean filled a secondary place in her company, which was, if not one of the best in the provinces, certainly one of the most substantial.

If the annals of provincial theatres at this period are often wretched in almost every aspect of life and art, they are at least rich in odd persons. No character of Dickens is more whimsical than Tate Wilkinson of York, or Elliston, the prince of hocus-pocus, or Mrs. Baker of the Canterbury circuit. About this last person far too little is known; it is a pity that some one of the literary wags among her contemporaries, who knew and relished her, did not write her history. It would make excellent reading, besides constituting an important chapter of that unwritten book whose lack I have before lamented, the chronicle of the provincial stage. She looks out from an occasional page, as in the *Reminiscences* of Tom Dibdin, or Dickens' *Memoirs of Grimaldi*, or Mrs. Mathews' *Anecdotes of Actors*, but we get no more than passing glimpses of her.

Tom Dibdin, who knew her well, tells us most. She had, apparently, in her early years been mistress of a puppet show; then, left a widow without any resources but her native energy, she had acquired a company of living actors and by prudent management had grown from little to more, until, toward the end of the 18th century, she was the owner of half a dozen theatres in various towns. Most of these she built herself, with dwelling houses attached, for she loved to be comfortable. The Rochester Theatre was built in 1791, the Maidstone in 1796, the Tunbridge Wells in 1802 (this last at a cost of £3,000). In addition to these she had theatres in Canterbury (built about 1790 and a source of unbounded pride), Feversham, Deal, and perhaps elsewhere.

She was illiterate and vulgar, yet shrewd, active, domineering, capable, and kind-hearted. Quite untutored in the nicer ways of business, she nevertheless dealt effectively with her affairs by the simple expedient of keeping her hand and eye on everything. She always took in the gate moneys herself, having arranged the approaches to her theatres so that patrons of box, pit, and gallery passed equally before her window, and when her five hours' vigil was over she betook her-

self promptly to bed, carrying her evening's cash in a large front pocket. Having no faith in banks and being ignorant of any other form of investment than new theatres, she kept her money in various boxes, jars, and canisters. Dibdin tells that when, after years of persuasion, she at last consented to invest in stock, she dug out of various hiding places seven hundred gold guineas, a gold Jacobus, several foreign coins, and a Bank of England note for £200, which last document she had guarded for seven years as a curiosity. It is doubtful if she had ever played a part in her own company (beyond occasional back-stage duties as prompting, beating the drum at coronations, and such like); at least, by the time Dibdin first met her (in 1789) she confined her attentions to business management, leaving rehearsals and all conduct of stage affairs to her subordinates. Her prosperity seems to have rested primarily on her native sagacity, secondly, on her parsimony in dressing plays (which drew more than one protest from the local press), and thirdly, on the practice of nepotism. In Dibdin's day her forces included two daughters, one of whom later married Dowton, the popular comedian of Drury Lane, and thus formed an alliance by which her mother profited, a sister, Miss Wakelin, who danced, acted, kept the wardrobe and cooked, and two relatives by the name of Ireland, father and son. In addition to these she had two or three lieutenants of such long standing as almost to become members of her family—Gardner, her stage manager in 1789, who was still with her in 1802, if not later, and Long, whom Dibdin knew as prompter but who by Kean's day had risen to be manager. These persons formed a stable nucleus of her company, which she ruled with regal absolutism, a despot whose sudden turns of temper must have been trying to the uninitiated, but a benevolent one, from the largeness of an honest and kindly heart.

The routine of her days went something as follows. In the morning she went to market, posted her accounts, manufactured the next day's playbill with scissors and paste from old bills, thus avoiding the mystery of penmanship, and in the time that remained before dinner held a levee for all who had business with her. Then came the family dinner with the addition of one or two privileged members of the company, and after dinner she went to her place at the box office.

Promptly on the fall of the last curtain she retired to her room, having provided a substantial cold supper for the rest of her family. Both Dibdin and Dickens have recorded samples of her demeanor at the box office, which united authority, maternalism, and an excited volubility. The following from Dickens:

"Now, then, pit or box, pit or gallery, box or pit?" was her constant and uninterrupted cry.

"Pit, pit!" from half-a-dozen voices, the owners clinging to the little desk to prevent themselves from being carried away by the crowd before they had paid.

"Then pay two shillings,—pass on, Tom-fool!" such was the old lady's invariable address to everybody on busy nights, without the slightest reference to their quality or condition.

Dibdin selects a busy evening at Tunbridge Wells:

"Little girl! get your money all ready while the gentleman pays.—My Lord! I'm sure your lordship has silver; and let that little boy go in while I give his lordship his change.—Shan't count after your lordship.—Here comes the duke! make haste! His Royal Highness will please to get his ticket ready while my lady—now, sir! now, your Royal Highness!"—"O dear, Mrs. Baker! I've left my ticket in another coat pocket."—"To be sure you have! take your Royal Highness's word: let his Royal Highness pass: his Royal Highness has left his ticket in his *other* coat pocket."

According to Mrs. Mathews, children would frequently come towards the end of an evening's performance and offer threepence or fourpence for a glimpse at the show, which she would take if she were in sufficiently good humor. In fact, she sometimes took pledges—a knife, a pair of scissors, even on one occasion a dove—which were to be redeemed the next day for the price of admission. Mrs. Baker was more than the mistress of a chain of theatres; she was an institution of a kind to be regarded, throughout her sphere of influence, with laughter, affection, and respect. One more anecdote before we finish with her. A woman with a squalling baby had left the theatre, by public consent, in the midst of a performance. Mrs. Baker obligingly returned her entrance money, saying as she did so in her hurried, urgent way: "Foolish woman! foolish woman! don't come another night till half-price, and then give the poor baby some Dalby's Carminative!"

Under such motherly and autocratic supervision did Kean remain from September of 1806 until September of 1807, playing all kinds of parts. The only tragic leads assigned to him were Hastings and, no doubt because of his youth, Norval in *Douglas*; otherwise he played second or third parts, like Gratiano in *The Merchant of Venice*, the Lieutenant of the Tower in *Richard III*, Major Fitzharding in *The Iron Chest*, Hephestion in *Alexander the Great*, Lenox in *Macbeth*. In comedy his best parts were Bob Acres in *The Rivals*, Caleb Quotem in *The Review*, Frederick in *Lover's Vows*, Dr. Lenitive in *The Prize*, and Peeping Tom. Besides these he filled a miscellaneous assortment of parts in forgotten melodramas, comedies, and afterpieces, and on almost every night he sang a comic song. The Tunbridge season ran into November of 1806, reopened in July of 1807, and closed again in September. During the winter he went with the company to other towns on the circuit, but as to this part of the season there is almost no information. That he was in Maidstone in February, 1807, is proved by a Harvard bill of February 14. It was his own benefit performance, yet on an occasion when, of all others, he might be expected to shine in stellar light, we find him occupying a most humble place. In *School for Friends* he played Double Jug, and in the farce of *Catherine and Petruchio*, the Tailor. And what is still more surprising, the various songs which filled the intermissions were all done by others. The company, so far as this bill covers it, consisted of Messrs. Dobbs, Long, Giles, Kebby, Girton, Cantelo, Younger, Waldegrave, Mesdames Dobbs, Long, and the Misses Walcot and Drake.

The only other bill of the Baker engagement which I have found comes from Tunbridge Wells and dates September 5, 1807. *Adelgitha*, the new tragedy by Monk Lewis, was chosen, in which Kean played the unimportant rôle of Tancred. Between acts of the afterpiece he sang "The Four and Twenty Puppet Shews." Members of the company not appearing on the Maidstone bill are Messrs. Rackham and Sloman, Mesdames Dowton (Mrs. Baker's daughter), and Keys, and Misses Stratton and Wakelin.

The subordinate place which, on the whole, Kean filled in this engagement might be laid to the superior quality of the company, were it not known that Mrs. Baker, except when she employed London stars for special and short occasions, went in for economy rather than quality. Although her circuit was more prosperous and respected than that of Jerrold, there is no reason to think that anyone in her regular company was more talented than Kean even in this early stage of his career. The reason probably lies in the fact that her company was pretty much a closed organization, being mainly composed of relatives and old retainers who would naturally be unreceptive towards a newcomer. And this is all the more likely because she left the business of casting and direction almost entirely to her lieutenants. The commentary which Kean made a few years later not only bears this out but shows that, however content in some respects he was with Mrs. Baker's management, he felt that he was unjustly dealt with in the rôles for which he was cast.

These feelings are expressed in a letter[8] written to Mrs. Clarke in 1810 and therefore prior to the time when he began to adorn his early life with imaginative arabesques. There is no reason, in this case, to disbelieve his testimony. The letter is dated May 17, 1810, from Waterford in Ireland, and is addressed to Mrs. Clarke at Lady Wooton's Green, Canterbury. Here is the part which concerns his sojourn with Mrs. Baker:

Above all things I shou'd like to be in Mrs. Bakers company again but Mr. Long who officiates for her in the business of the Theatre, has an unaccountable objection to *small* men which aversion he carries to so great an excess that I firmly believe had Mr. Garrick offered himself as Candidate to Mr. Longs Management, He even *He* wou'd have been rejected this is somewhat hard to think, that an ignorant Man, of no kind of consequence in our profession, shou'd start an objection which has been overlooked in the first Theatres in the three Kingdoms viz. Edinburgh, Birmingham, Cheltenham, Margate, Dover, &c &c in all which I have sustained the principal characters of the Drama, with universal approbation the Audiences of these Theatres have overlooked my *figure* & have thought only of my Acting.

When I was last in Mrs. Bakers company I was extremely ill treated he Mr. Long kept me in the back ground as much as possible & frequently gave those characters, which undoubtedly were mine, to fellows, who cer-

[8] At Harvard—hitherto unpublished, I believe.

tainly wou'd have adorned the handles of a plough, but were never intended for the Stage, but these met Mr. Longs approbation because they were *taller* than me.

I think if these matters were intimated to Mrs. Baker herself, it might be of essential service to me. My writing to her is useless, as this *Manager* arrests her Letters & answers them as he pleases.

Of the serpent in Mrs. Baker's paradise Dibdin gives the following thumb sketch:

Her prompter, from being very tall and corpulent, was distinguished as "Bonny Long"[9] . . . he was remarkable for being never out of temper,—a miracle for a prompter—and for having ten fingers, and no thumbs.

Mr. Long's objection to Kean probably came from the distaste which men of tall stature not uncommonly have for short fellows. He was no doubt a hard cross to the aspiring youngster. Yet it is interesting to note that in spite of him Kean yearned to be again with Mrs. Baker, "above all things," although at the time of writing he was with Cherry's company, one of the better sort, where he was comfortable and well treated.

Blanchard Jerrold says, rightly, that Kean returned to Samuel Jerrold's company in 1807. The only playbill of this engagement which I have seen is one at Harvard. It is headed "Theatre, Sheerness. By their Majesties' Servants" and is dated December 5, 1807. The plays were *Jane Shore* and *The Young Hussar* (by W. Dimond, Jr., new the previous March), in which Kean acted Hastings and Florian, both male leads. Other participants were Messrs. Lewis, Fitzbury, Russell, Phillips, Jerrold, Briggs, Mesdames Jerrold, Inchbald, Lewis, and Miss Wallack. More information about the Jerrold season is provided, not by Blanchard, but by Douglas, who seems to have written out all that he knew of Kean's association with his father for Procter. This account was also used by Blanchard, but his recension is not so full as Procter's. From the latter, then, we learn that Kean returned to Sheerness at the increased salary of a guinea a week, opening in *Alexander the Great*.

[9] Dickens says he was called "Bony" Long from being thin, but Dibdin was in a better position to know.

An officer in one of the stage boxes annoyed him by frequently exclaiming—"Alexander *the little*." At length . . . Mr. Kean folded his arms and approached the intruder . . . and with a vehemence of manner and a glaring look, that apalled the offender, retorted "Yes,—with a GREAT SOUL!"

The story is worth repeating, partly because the authority of Jerrold gives it some validity,[10] and also because, whether strictly true or not, it is true to the character of Kean. Jerrold adds that in the "farce" of *The Young Hussar* which followed, Kean's powerful acting caused one of the actresses to faint, an absurdity of statement which would not have resulted if Jerrold had remembered that *The Young Hussar* is not a farce, but a serious play of strong emotions.

Kean remained in Sheerness with increasing favor, says Jerrold, until early in 1808, when it seems he had some quarrel with one of the townspeople. This enemy, to be revenged, set a press-gang after him, so that he had to go into hiding and at length escaped aboard the Chatham boat. He is also reported to have made himself useful to the company by his ingenuity in devising machinery for the pantomimes, particularly in adapting them to the manager's meager purse.

For the events of 1808 we are almost wholly dependent on the biographers. Following dubiously in the lead of Procter, we find Kean about March in Gloucester, where he took service under manager Beverley. But either the company was very bad or the citizens of Gloucester were among those who do not go much to the theatre, for the season was disastrous. We are told that, in the hope of putting a little money in their pockets by that precarious expedient, a benefit, Kean banded with Jack Hughes, destined to win comic success in London, and posted the bills for *A Cure for a Heartache*. But benefits in an indifferent or hostile town are worse than precarious, they are hopeless, as it turned out in this case. When the time came to begin, the house contained one shilling and sixpence. And as it would be less expensive to stop than to go on, the disheartened promoters sent their audience of three home.

In the company at Gloucester were two Irish girls, sisters, from Waterford, by name Mary and Susan Chambers. How they came there

[10] It is only fair to the principle of skepticism, however, to state that the story has also been laid in Croydon.

is uncertain, but certain it is that they had but recently set foot on the stage. A correspondent to *Fraser's Magazine*[11] says that Mary had come to England as governess in the family of a Mr. and Mrs. Congreve, of Mount Congreve, near Waterford, and had then gone stage-struck, but he does not account for Susan.[12] The latter seems to have made but a short go at acting, for in a few years we find her settled again at home. Doubtless she discovered that she had no talent and wisely withdrew. And so might her sister Mary have done, who was likewise without talent, had she not fallen in love with Kean and been loved by him. No doubt it is one of the great gifts of providence that our futures are closed to us. If Mary Chambers had been able to see through the coming years, with all the privation and misery of the beginning and all the loneliness and bitterness of the end, she might well have recoiled in horror from the step she was soon to take. But she could not see, and so she entered into matrimony as blithely and as ignorantly as she had entered upon the stage.

The *Fraser's Magazine* correspondent says that at Gloucester Mary Chambers played important rôles, and since he speaks of playbills in his possession to prove it, doubtless it is so. In *The Mountaineers* she played Floranthe to Kean's Octavian, in *Tekeli* (a melodrama by Theodore Hook) she was Alexina, in *The School of Reform* (a serious comedy by Thomas Morton) she was Julia. But we must suppose that some reason other than her talents accounted for her prominence in the Gloucester company; perhaps, as not infrequently happened, she was featured merely because she was new—"Floranthe, by a Young Lady, being her first Appearance on Any Stage"—or perhaps the company was too poor to afford a better choice. At all events, she had no talent, as her subsequent career proved, and eventually found her place among those listed at the bottom of the *dramatis personæ*.

After about three months at Gloucester the company moved to Stroud, in the same county. Here Kean played Archer in *The Beaux' Stratagem* badly and Hastings in *Jane Shore* well. Stroud was a small

[11] *Fraser's Magazine*, VIII (1833), 500.

[12] A bill for the Theatre Royal, Cheltenham, of September 3, 1807, shows that a Miss Chambers played Jacqueline in *The English Fleet*. Her sister, who may have come over later, does not appear.

town, the theatre was small, and the receipts were smaller still. And so Beverley, hoping that an attraction of magnitude would put money in his purse, engaged Master Betty, the Infant Roscius, who, after extraordinary triumphs at Drury Lane and Covent Garden in 1804-5, had been touring the provinces with dwindling success. He came and was billed in two of his famous parts, Norval in *Douglas,* and Hamlet. Kean was to play Glenalvon and Laertes. At least, so said the bills, but Kean was of a different mind. When the time came for performance Glenalvon was missing, and missing he remained for two days. On the third he came home, footsore and hungry, but still furious. "I am starved," said he. "I have eaten nothing but turnips and cabbages; but I'll go again, as often as I see myself put in such characters. I'll not play second," he ended, "to any man—except to John Kemble."[13] This revolt has usually been credited to a prejudice on Kean's part against infant phenomena. But Betty was scarcely an infant at this time, being seventeen and therefore only four years younger than Kean. The explanation is rather to be found in Kean's growing pride, his feeling that first-line parts in Beverley's company were his prerogative, and his objection to being ousted from his rights by any man, short of the great Kemble himself.

Beverley having dissolved his company at Stroud, Kean and the Misses Chambers went to Cheltenham, where they took service under Watson. Procter says he acted there without pay until he had proved his excellence, but this is an unlikely story, and the more unlikely because Watson was the owner of the Gloucester theatre and must have known Kean there. And at Cheltenham, in July, the rapidly growing affection between him and Mary Chambers came to a head. The ceremony was performed, not at Cheltenham, but at Stroud, a circumstance which suggests that the publication of the banns, a matter of three weeks' time, had begun before they left Stroud. They were married July 17, 1808.[14] It is reported that a Miss Thornton, daughter

[13] This story is usually placed at Stroud. But a memoir in the *Literary Gazette,* June 1, 1833, page 346, assigns it to Weymouth, and to a later date. Betty entered Oxford in July, 1808, returning to the stage in 1812. If Weymouth is really the place of the passage at arms with Kean, the year must then be 1812, or possibly 1813.

[14] A certified copy of the marriage certificate is printed in *Fraser's Magazine, loc. cit.*—"No. 2227. Edmund Kean of this parish, bachelor, and Mary Chambers of this parish,

of the boxkeeper of the Cheltenham theatre, lent the bridegroom half a guinea to defray his expenses, and that the mistress of "The Dog" tavern provided a wedding breakfast.

And so began a union which brought to the bride much happiness but still more misery. Malicious gossip has charged Kean with marrying under the misapprehension that Mary Chambers was heir to considerable money. There is not the slightest reason for thinking so. What is far more likely, beyond the force of mutual attraction which needs no explaining, is that he contemplated such an arrangement as was constantly being made in his profession, by which two players joined hands for their mutual advantage. Chiefly, it made for economy, in that the family income would be nearly doubled whereas their expenses would not. No one can know whether, in the flush of passion, Kean believed his bride to be the talented actress she was not, and conceived the hope that they would walk on to glory together, united in fame as they were in wedlock. If so, his disappointment may have partly accounted for his subsequent dissipations and neglect. Probably he thought little beyond the present, that he needed to marry and was in love. We have not much to go on in picturing Mary Kean. The few letters we possess, written five years later in the height of wretchedness, suggest a simple, sentimental, pure, and unaffected creature, one who was fitted by nature to cleave to her husband in spite of the infinite grief he brought her and to whom motherhood came as an absorbing passion. The brief picture that Grattan draws of her[15] in the early days after success had come in London enables us to form some notion of her in her bloom.

She was, in her own home, and surrounded by everything that might dazzle the mind's eye, and dizzy the brain of almost everyone, a fair speci-

---

spinster, were married in this church by banns, this seventeenth day of July, in the year one thousand eight hundred and eight, By me, H. C. Adams, Clerk.

This marriage was solemnized between us, { Edmund Kean
Mary Chambers

In the presence of { Wm. Hy. White,
Steph. Howell,
Susan Chambers."

[15] Grattan, Thomas Colley, *Beaten Paths: and Those Who Trod Them*. 2 vols., London, 1862. II, 184.

men of natural character. Her head was evidently turned by her husband's fame, and the combined consequences were bodied forth with exquisite naïveté. But there was withal a shrewdness, an offhandedness and tact quite Irish: and, what was still more so, a warm-hearted and overflowing recognizance of ever so trivial a kindness, or tribute of admiration offered to "Edmund" before he became a "great man."

The years of wandering which succeeded the marriage, cruel as they frequently were, must have fulfilled in some measure the hopes which she had as a bride. It is true that in December of 1813 she wrote with emphatic underlinings to her old friend Miss Roberts of Waterford, *"Happiness I have never known,"* but she wrote this when life was utterly black before her and the immediate past did not bear thinking on, so that much may be discounted. Certain it is that she loved her husband and trusted completely in his genius, and when a woman loves her husband and believes in him, her life must have its moments of great joy. Moreover, she was one of those women for whom the only legitimate business of life is marriage. No, her real unhappiness was not in these early years of struggle, but later, when in her middle age, discarded, pensioned, ill, and forgotten, she had nothing left her but bitter memories and her son Charles. But let no one minimize her nearer afflictions. She herself has left one vivid sketch of the downward course of her hero. She is again writing to Miss Roberts:[16]

My first step to Misery was going on the stage. My character I preserved pure and unsullied, I then married, my Husband possessed of every Talent requisite for his profession, educated to give grace to that talent; and could he have endured patiently a little longer, Fortune might have rewarded his very great abilities. To forget sorrow he first took to Drinking—every dissipation follow'd of course. His Nights were spent with a Set of wretches a Disgrace to Human nature. One step lead on to another, till ruin, inevitable ruin was the end.

Nor did her woes come entirely from the difficulties of life immediately around her, for she tells in another letter that "Mr. Kean's aunt has been trying to prevent his living with me—oh! you know not half of what I am suffering." This aunt was of course the ambiguous Miss

16 Written in September, 1813. See below, page 88.

Tidswell. Her antipathy to Mary was doubtless the effect of jealousy, of possessive instinct offended in respect to the only person in whom she had a deep interest, who, she felt, belonged to her more than to anyone else. Whatever the cause, she nourished so strong a resentment that when the Keans were destitute in London she would not come near them or offer them assistance, and in Edmund's affair with Mrs. Cox she sided with the mistress against the wife.

Procter says that as a result of a quarrel with Beverley, who for some reason was displeased with the marriage, Kean left his company and went to Warwick, where he obtained an engagement at one guinea a week; but that he was not happy there because all the best parts were preempted by established members of the company, to wit Chatterley, Waring, and Mason; and that because of his displeasure he left them and went to Walsall (in Staffordshire), taking service with Watson. But this is all very unsatisfactory, because when we find him in December playing in Birmingham he is again with the Cheltenham company and with him are Messrs. Chatterley, Waring, and Mason, nor is he at that time playing second rôles to them. Furthermore, Procter involves himself in contradiction by taking Kean to Cheltenham under Watson and then making him quarrel with Beverley. The facts of the matter are probably, that Kean did not leave Watson's company, but went on with it. Walsall seems to have been customarily in the Cheltenham circuit; whether Warwick was also I cannot say.

In October, says Procter, the company moved from Walsall to Birmingham. But no positive trace of them there occurs before December. And in Birmingham they remained, with the exception of a seven weeks' pause, until the following summer. The Harvard collection is fortunate in having a goodly number of their bills, which give us a very fair idea of the season and of Kean's business. The company called itself "Their Majesties' Servants, from the Theatre Royal, Cheltenham." It gave the following performances:

Monday, December 5, 1808: Thomas Morton's *Speed the Plough* and Charles Kemble's *Plot and Counterplot.* Kean was respectively Henry and Don Leon; no part for Mrs. Kean. The company was composed of Messrs. M'Gibbon, Chatterley, Waring, Mason, Robinson, Shuter, Moore, Villars, Hilliard, Melvin, Slaney, Mesdames Waring, Watson, Jun., Chatterley, Hilliard, Farmer, Moore, Misses Hudson, Walcot, Manessier, and the Misses Fleming. Also a Mr. Richer performed on the tight rope. Days of performance were Mondays, Wednesdays, and Fridays.

Monday, December 12: *The School for Scandal* and *The Bridal Spectre, or, Alonzo and Imogine.* Kean was Joseph Surface and Alonzo; his wife a "lady of the court" in the afterpiece. This afterpiece is described as "Dibdin's much admired Ballet D'Action, founded on the popular Ballad of Monk Lewis, and originally got up by Mr. Richer at Sadler's Wells."

Friday, December 16: *The Busy Body* (by Mrs. Centlivre) and *The Bridal Spectre.* Kean played only in the ballet.

Monday, December 19: Morton's *School of Reform* and *Don Juan* (a *ballet d'action*). Kean was Frederick and Scaramouche.

Wednesday, December 28: *The Point of Honour,* translated by Charles Kemble from Mercier (Kean as Durimel), *The Black Forest, or, Parental Cruelty,* a pantomime (Kean as Monsieur l'Abbé), and *The Devil to Pay, or, The Wives Metamorphosed,* an old ballad farce by Charles Coffey (Kean as Sir John Loverule). Mrs. Kean appeared only in the third piece, playing Lettice.

January 12, 1809: *The Siege of St. Quintin,* by Theodore Hook (Kean as Count Egmont, Mrs. Kean as Margaret), *The School for Authors,* by John Tobin (Kean as Cleveland), and *Peeping Tom of Coventry,* a comic opera by John O'Keefe (Kean as Harold).

January 20: *Man and Wife, or, More Secrets than One,* a new comedy by S. J. Arnold (Kean as Lord Austencourt, Mrs. Kean as Fanny), and Fielding's *Tom Thumb* (Kean as Noodle). A note at the foot of this bill announces that after next Thursday, January 26, the theatre "will be suspended for seven weeks."

During the intermission the company traveled, but the only report of their itinerary I have to make is that on February 9 they played at Lichfield. In *Perouse, or, The Desolate Island* (of which more later)[17] Kean played Powantowski, while Chimpanzee, which was later to be

[17] See below, page 52.

one of Kean's "big" rôles on the provincial stage, fell to Chatterley. In Colman's farce *Blue Devils,* Kean played Megrim. The company is announced as "Mr. Richer's Cheltenham Company."

After their return to Birmingham:

April 3: Bickerstaffe's ballad opera, *Love in a Village,* with the great Incledon and no rôle for Kean, also *The School for Authors,* with Kean again as Cleveland. New persons, or persons who had not appeared on previous bills, are Miss Wood, of the Theatre Royal, York, Mr. Mortimer, Mrs. Fleming and Mrs. Creswell.

May 11: *Speed the Pough,* as before, and Colman's farce, *Ways and Means,* with Kean as Scruple.

May 15: *Man and Wife,* as before.

May 17: Chatterley's benefit. Monk Lewis' *Castle Spectre* (Kean as Earl Osmond), and *The False Friend,* probably the musical piece by J. C. Cross recently produced (Kean as Mandiville, the false friend).

June 5, the first night of the summer season. The personnel of the company was almost entirely changed by the acquisition of various persons from London and the provinces. These were Messrs. Blanchard (Covent Garden), Kent (Drury Lane), Townshend (Theatre Royal, Richmond), Hamerton (T. R., Dublin), Norman (T. R. York), Entwisle (T. R., Manchester), Rayner (T. R., York), and Fawcett, Mesdames Thomas Dibdin (Covent Garden), Emery (Covent Garden), Townshend (T. R., Richmond), Beynon, and the Four Misses Adams, dancers (T. R., Haymarket). Old members retained were Messrs. Mason and Slaney, Mrs. Fleming, and the Miss Flemings. Kean had no part in the first piece, Cherry's comedy, *The Soldier's Daughter* (Mrs. Kean as Mrs. Malfort), but played Don Carlos in *Lover's Quarrels,* presumably the adaptation of Vanbrugh's *Mistake* by Thomas King.

June 7: *The Beaux' Stratagem* and *The Sultan.* Kean had no part in either, but his wife played Dorinda and Sultana Elmira.

June 8: Tobin's *Honeymoon* (Kean as Duke Aranza) and *The Irishman in London,* by William Macready[18] (Kean as Captain Seymour and Mrs. Kean as Caroline).

[18] The father of the famous actor, William Charles.

A consideration of the above schedule shows that, whereas Kean was not by any means the star or leader of the company, he was certainly not an underling, but had a fair share of good parts. Unfortunately for him, if the bills we possess are a true indication of the general repertory, the management inclined to comedy, farce, and melodrama, so that he was obliged to take parts in which his special abilities could not shine. Comedy was not his forte, although, as a result of his early acrobatic training, he was a brilliant harlequin. Therefore he might have just grounds to feel dissatisfied with the opportunities which were afforded him in the Cheltenham company. Yet on the score of general quality it was the best assortment of actors he had yet played with, and this may have been the principal reason why he spent so much as eight months in Birmingham.[19]

According to Procter, Stephen Kemble, a brother of John Philip and a very fat one, came to Birmingham for a few performances in the spring, but if so he left no impression on any of the bills we have. Kean is supposed to have played Hotspur so well as to surprise the huge Falstaff into an admission that brother John could not have done better. But I have no faith in this.

The Keans left Birmingham in June, shortly after the summer season had started, so that their remotion was not due to the breaking up of the company. What the reason may have been one can only guess. Perhaps the influx of so many important personages from various Theatres Royal discouraged him. Perhaps it was a forced move.

19 But none too good at that, if we may trust the recollection of William Charles Macready. As a boy of fifteen he visited the Birmingham theatre during his Christmas holidays (evidently on December 16) and he later recorded the event in his reminiscences: " 'Richer, the Funambulist!' was the large-letter attraction of the playbills. The play was 'The Busybody,' very badly acted, and the after-piece was a serious pantomime on the ballad of 'Alonzo and Imogene.' Richer represented the Baron 'all covered with jewells and gold,' and a female porpoise, rejoicing in the name of Watson, being the manager's wife, ungainly and tawdry, was the caricature of the 'fair Imogene.' As if in studied contrast to this enormous 'hill of flesh,' a little mean-looking man, in a shabby green satin dress (I remember him well), appeared as the hero, Alonzo the Brave. It was so ridiculous that the only impression I carried away was that the hero and heroine were the worst in the piece. How little did I know, or could guess, that under that shabby green satin dress was hidden one of the most extraordinary theatrical geniuses that have ever illustrated the dramatic poetry of England!"—Macready, *Reminiscences*, ed. by Sir Frederick Pollock. London, 1875. I, 23.

Procter says that he was oppressed by debts, although his salary had been raised from a guinea to thirty shillings, which, with his wife's stipend, would bring their combined resources well above two pounds. Now, two pounds ten shillings, or whatever it may have been, was not a comfortable competence, even in those days, yet two people could live on it, and were doing so all over provincial theatredom. So if Kean had managed to roll up a debt of £15 there was something wrong in his domestic economy. The source of trouble doubtless lay, even then, in his dissipation. No man can have got drunk as often and as deeply as he is reported to have done without spending far more than he was earning. With nine out of every ten player folk the margin between paying all bills and paying only the most urgent was so small as to require the maximum of economy and sobriety. So long as they had steady occupation they could subsist, but let them stumble against even the smallest obstacle and they were face to face with starvation. The annals of these fascinating vagabonds are full of privation and suffering. Had not John Philip Kemble himself lived on turnips stolen from the fields he passed by? Probably a considerable portion of their trials they brought on themselves, through their pride and restlessness, being always on the go, taking offense at one manager and passing on to another, not infrequently falling between the two stools, with lamentable results. The six years which elapsed between the marriage of Kean and his arrival at Drury Lane are known to have been filled with wretchedness—"Happiness I have never known," was Mary Chambers' summary of them. Yet one may occasionally wonder why. Kean was young, hard working, gifted, and for most of that time he was a member of three stable companies. Debt and privation were the common lot of strolling players, but they were not quite a primal curse. One cannot avoid the conclusion that Kean's imprudent and dissolute courses were the chief cause of all his ills in this his early life, as they were the whole cause in his latter end.

Yet one ought at the same time to regard him with charity. Between the tippling of these cruel early days, which found the only available nepenthe in strong liquor, and the sodden debauchery of prosperous after years lies a world of difference. When he was his ordinary self Kean was quiet, modest, winning. But he was possessed of a demon. "He used to mope for hours," someone, probably his wife, has said, "walking miles and miles alone, with his hands in his pockets, thinking intensely on his characters. No one could get a word from him. He studied and slaved beyond any actor I ever knew." A demonic energy inhabited him and wrecked the economy of its mansion. He was inordinately ambitious. True to the tribe into which he was born he was the constant prey to vanity, restlessness, jealousy, and envy. Most of the men who were his fellows he regarded with contempt. He was like a runner straining to reach a goal which forever retreated. Chafing against fortune which tied him to an ignoble slavery for petty tyrants, he looked toward London as Christian looked toward the Delectable Mountains. Had he possessed the true vagabond's temper, that happy-go-lucky carelessness which tempered the winds of destiny to most of his fellows, he would have been happier, and so would the poor woman, his wife. But in that case he probably would never have reached Drury Lane and glory. Or had he been given the phlegmatic equanimity of John Philip Kemble he could have borne his disappointments. But instead he ate his heart, and fell into spells of moodiness from which he escaped into violent intoxication. And thus he consumed his vital forces, leading the way to that melancholy dissolution with which his life prematurely ended.

If one would see the prosperous and smiling side of provincial theatre life, let him turn to the *Reminiscences* of Tom Dibdin. And why, might he then impatiently demand, should that nonentity, that handy man to the patent theatres, who ground out trash as a hand organ grinds a stale tune—why should he have ridden so easily before a fair wind while Kean, a genius, tacked as furiously and almost as vainly as the Flying Dutchman? The answer is easy. Dibdin was a cheerful, likable soul, never for a moment above the needs of his immediate occupation, who could play a light part decently, sing a comic song more than decently, write, as easily as a hen lays eggs, anything from a topical song to a pantomime, or paint a back drop, or do a competent turn as stage manager. To the country theatre of that day such a man was a whole company in himself. Audiences loved him, managers caressed him, even his fellow players liked him. But Kean had nothing with which to win that kind of allegiance except his dexterity as harlequin. He was primarily a tragic actor, and the lot of the tragedian in the countryside has always been a hard one.

The Keans did not leave Birmingham until he had found a place elsewhere, to wit, in the company of Andrew Cherry, who owned a very respectable circuit embracing Swansea and Carmarthen in southern Wales and Waterford in Ireland. No doubt the wishes of Mary, who might thus revisit her home, had weight in the decision. Cherry was a Limerick man, born in 1762, son of a bookseller, who had begun his career as printer's devil and had run away to the stage at the age of seventeen. Since then his life had been passed in numberless provincial theatres until his merits as a comedian brought him in 1802 to Drury Lane. But in spite of very good success there, he broke away[20] in order to enter the provincial field as manager, and doubtless preferred to be king in a small realm rather than a mere subject in a great one. Besides his accomplishments as an actor he was the author of several comedies and small pieces, of which *The Soldier's Daughter* attained some measure of popularity. Report makes of him a man of kindly heart, and he certainly must have been a capable manager, for he built up in his small circuit of small cities a good will which established him on a firm position with his patrons and gave him a sound reputation among the profession.

Tradition has it that the journey from Birmingham to Swansea, a matter of a hundred and eighty miles, was performed on foot, the family purse having but twenty shillings in it, and these only because Cherry had advanced a loan of two pounds. And Mary Kean was six months heavy with child. Procter gives a picturesque account of their Odyssey—the little tragedian carrying a bundle of clothes and four swords and the weary woman dragging her double burden after him. The twenty shillings carried them with the utmost parsimony to Bristol, where they arrived penniless, scarcely more than half way to their destination. But an appeal to Cherry brought another two pounds

[20] In 1807, I think, at the time when he leased the new theatre at Swansea. See *Monthly Mirror* for July, 1807.

and the five days required for this transaction gave them a needed rest. So they trudged painfully on, with fifteen shillings in pocket for the eighty miles that remained, stinting themselves of food and gratefully accepting such occasional kindnesses as were offered them. In this manner they completed a journey which was without notable adventures, without romance, even without any danger except, in the case of Mary Kean, that of dying in some ditch by the way. In later years the man used to recall this experience with that glamor which prosperity throws over past hardships, but I doubt if the woman ever thought of it without a shudder.

The first bill to record for Swansea[21] is dated June 23, 1809. *Speed the Plough* was given (with Kean as Henry) and *Catherine and Petruchio,* Garrick's popular rearrangement of Shakespeare, with Kean as Petruchio. The company included Messrs. Cherry, Ford, Woulds, Bickerton, Whitlock, Thompson, Cumberland, Niblett, Horton, Mesdames Cherry, Gunning, Thompson, Bickerton, and Miss Cherry. This performance must have been the first, or very nearly the first, after Kean's arrival.

Cherry was favorably impressed by the new recruit, for he kept him some two years and gave him leading business, except when any personage of importance paid the company a fleeting visit. Soon after his arrival he put him on as Rolla in *Pizarro,* casting Mary in the important role of Cora.[22] The latter action was probably a gesture of courtesy toward the new lady and was not often repeated, for Mary Kean's status at Swansea quickly became what it had been at Birmingham.

The Keans remained in Swansea all summer, with Edmund given plenty of work to do and fearing no rivals among his regular associates. But later in the summer, after the close of the Bath season, arrived Bengough, a second-rate actor though in Cherry's company a notability, with the result that Kean's sun was in considerable measure eclipsed. Yet he had now and then a rôle which was not pre-

[21] All the bills cited for Cherry's company are, with one exception, from the Harvard collection.

[22] Thus Procter, corroborated by the memory of Mrs. Cherry. See *Fraser's Magazine,* VIII (1833), 501.

empted by the visitor. Thus on September 4 we find him playing one of his favorite parts, that of Octavian in *The Mountaineers.* The occasion was his own benefit, for which, of course, he had the choice of bill. Therefore it is interesting to see that he added one of those pieces which more than any others give the early nineteenth-century stage an air of theatricals in a nursery and which need the pen of a Dickens to describe them. This was the pantomime of *Perouse, or, The Desolate Island,* confected in 1801 by John Fawcett, after Kotzebue, with music by Moorehead and Davy and at this time still popular. The bill of this performance informs the public that the piece was "Never Acted in this Theatre," and that it is got up "with the Original Overture, Music, Scenery, Dresses, and Decorations . . . under the direction of Mr. Kean. Mr. Kean assures the Public that neither pains nor expence have been spared to render this most interesting Spectacle worthy the attention of an enlightened Public." Being master of the occasion, he could now elect for himself the choicest morsel of the *dramatis personæ,* that which at Lichfield nine months before had fallen to Chatterley, to wit, Chimpanzee.

The editors of the invaluable *Biographia Dramatica* have supplied us a sketch of the contents of this classic. Perouse, the great navigator, is represented to be wrecked on a desert island, where he is variously endangered by native tribes. "He builds a hut, and is greatly assisted in preserving his life by a little savage called Champanzee [*sic*], an animal approaching something nearer to the human form and rational faculties than the Ourang-outang." When later on Kean repeated the rôle in Waterford he was seen by Grattan, who recorded his impressions thus: "He then finished with Chimpanzee the Monkey in the melodramatic pantomime of *La Perouse* and in this character he showed agility scarcely since surpassed by Mazurier or Gouffe and touches of deep tragedy in the monkey's death-scene which made the audience shed tears." Shades of Burbage, Betterton, and Garrick! If some descendant of the Shandy family would but erect a theatrical Hall of Fame, in which the rôles of the great tragedians were pictured or carved, what a curious promenade one might make from the early giants—Tamburlaine, Richard, Lear, Hamlet—down through the stuffed but dwindling heroes of the seventeenth and eighteenth centuries, until, in the old curiosity shop of the nineteenth, he arrived with stupefaction at Chimpanzee, the Monkey!

On September 13, 1809, a boy was born to the Keans, who christened him Howard Anthony, and destined him for the navy. He was blessed with health and a beauty which increased as he grew; he developed quick parts and a bent for the stage. On his mother's testimony he was the essence of all that is captivating in childhood. He became the idol of his parents. But he lived only four short years.

On September 13, Mrs. Whalley took a benefit, choosing as her *pièce de résistance* Colman's *Iron Chest.* Kean had no part, but in *The Miller of Lochmaben* he played Sandy.

On September 22 came Bengough's benefit, with *King Lear* and *Robinson Crusoe.* Kean played respectively Edgar and Friday. And on September 27 he played Faulkland in *The Rivals.* The bills for that evening also carried the notice: "Between the Play and Farce, the celebrated Dying Scene of Harlequin. Harlequin—Mr. Kean, (In which Character he will leap through a Balloon of real Fire.")[23]

While at Swansea, we are told, Kean made the acquaintance and won the interest of Mrs. Ann Curtis, or Hatton as she was called at this time, the eccentric sister of Mrs. Siddons, who after a sensational and disreputable career had settled in the Welsh seaport, had taken to writing poetry and novels under the mellifluous name of Ann of Swansea, and had established a kind of literary salon there. By 1809 she must have been at least forty and upwards; "she squints—a large woman," wrote someone of her ten years later. It is said that she fell in love with Kean and wrote a play for him, but that is scarcely more than rumor, and what the play was or whether it was ever acted no one knows. Yet a friendship seems to have existed between the actor and the novelist, which is corroborated by the circumstance that Kean used her name in his letters of application to the London managers.[24]

The numerous benefit performances which appear in September

23 British Museum, Add. MSS, 18,590.

24 For a sketch of Mrs. Curtis' life see Percy Fitzgerald, *The Kembles,* II, 98 ff. And for Kean's connection with her, the *New Monthly Magazine for* 1834 (Part I, page 443, and Part II, page 52).

are a sign that the Swansea season was drawing to its close. From there the company moved to Carmarthen and then to Haverfordwest, but when these moves were made is uncertain, and nothing of importance is known as to what was done there, unless a long story of a pantomime goose may be counted among the Kean memorabilia. No Carmarthen bills have come to my attention, but Harvard has two for Haverfordwest. The first, of February 5, 1810, announces *The Young Quaker,* a comedy by O'Keefe, followed by Hook's popular melodrama, *Tekeli.* In the first, Kean played Young Sadboy, in the second, the title rôle, featuring a broadsword combat in Act III. The company was practically the same that acted at Swansea, with the addition of Messrs. Hale and Wheeler. On February 16, in *The Castle Spectre,* Kean repeated the rôle of Earl Osmond, and in *False and True,* a comedy by the Rev. Mr. Moultru, he played Lealto and his wife Lauretta.

In mid-April the company passed over to Waterford, where it remained several months. Of this first Waterford visit practically nothing is known beyond the reminiscences of Thomas Colley Grattan. From Mrs. Cherry, *via* the before-mentioned contributor to *Fraser's Magazine,*[25] we learn that Mrs. Kean acted only once there, for her husband's benefit, the reason being that her engagement had been temporarily suspended at his request, in order that she might not be prejudiced in the eyes of family and friends by the inferior rôles she was accustomed to play. The benefit comprised Mrs. Hannah More's tragedy, *Percy,* with Kean as Douglas and Mary as Elwina, followed by the performance of *Perouse* which drew the applause of Grattan. As to Grattan's meeting with Kean there is some uncertainty because the informant himself is exceedingly vague as to dates, but the probabilities are that it took place in 1810. Although his account[26] is always quoted at this point in Kean biography and therefore must grow tedious to those who have looked into the matter, it cannot be passed by, because it is the only first-hand portrait we have of the actor in these early days.

[25] Volume VIII (1833), pages 501-2.

[26] First published in the *New Monthly Magazine.* Afterwards incorporated in *Beaten Paths; and Those Who Trod Them,* II, 175 ff.

Grattan was then a subaltern in the town garrison; this was long before he turned to literature and writing, and his life was that of any gay young military buck. Passing the town theatre one evening with a friend, he observed that *Hamlet* was posted and proposed that they go in. But as *Hamlet* meant to them nothing much but the fencing scene, they adjourned to a billiard hall after arranging with the boxkeeper to call them for the fifth act. They entered the theatre as the duelling began.

> The young man who played Laertes was extremely handsome, and very tall: and a pair of high-heeled boots added so much to his natural stature, that the little pale, thin man, who represented Hamlet, appeared a mere pigmy beside him. Laertes commenced (after slurring . . . through the usual salute) to push cart and tierce, which might, as far as the scientific use of the small-sword was concerned, have been as correctly termed cart and horse.

Grattan's companion was for leaving the theatre at once;

> and I might have agreed, had I not thought I perceived in the Hamlet a quiet gracefulness of manner, while he parried the cut-and-thrust attacks of his adversary, as well as a quick glance of haughty resentment at the uncivil laugh by which they were noticed. When he began to return the lounges *secundum artem*, we were quite taken by surprise to see the carriage and action of a practised swordsman . . .

Upon their inquiring of the boxkeeper who the little man was,

> she told us that his name was Kean; that he was an actor of first-rate talent; chief tragic hero (for they were all honourable men) of the company; and also the principal singer, stage-manager, and getter-up of pantomimes, and one of the best harlequins in Wales or the West of England.

Having been told also that he gave instruction in fencing and boxing, they engaged to take lessons from him in the first of these sciences and thus began an association which in Grattan's case ripened into a friendship of many years' duration. He was pleased with his new acquaintance.

> Nothing could exceed Kean's good conduct and unpresuming manners during some weeks that I knew him in this way. Several of the officers of the garrison met him with us on these occasions, and a strong interest was excited for him. He owed to this cause, I believe, rather than to

any just appreciation of his merits, a good benefit, and some private kindnesses.

The only bill for this first Waterford season that I have seen (again at Harvard) is dated Thursday, May 10, 1810, and offers the popular melodrama of *The Exile*, with Kean in the leading rôle of Daran. It is of more than ordinary interest in that Count Calmar was played by Sheridan Knowles, thus proving that the Knowleses were in the company at this time. The friendship of the leading tragic actor and the leading tragic dramatist of their day thus began at Waterford in 1810.

To the spring of 1810 belong two interesting letters to Mrs. Clarke, the patron of his childhood, which, because they relate so closely to one another, I place here together, although the first was written from Haverfordwest and the second from Waterford.

(To Mrs. A. Clarke, 5 Caroline Place, Guilford Street, London; forwarded to Lady Wooton's Green, Canterbury.)

April 4th 1810

Dr Madam|

I beleive when I last had the pleasure of seeing you, You expressed a hint that hearing of your once favor'd Protegee wou'd not be wholly disagreable to you, upon which I take the liberty of writing you. My Situation & circumstances are much altered since I was last in London, it is but three weeks back since I arrived at that age, which is stiled Manhood 1 & 20 & I am both a *husband* & a *Father*, a charge indeed for the pocket of a Country Actor, but a burthen I am proud of, as I have a good heart to divide my sorrows with, which in return takes no *pleasure*, but what I participate in, it has taught me likewise to know, that heaven has always some blessing in store to reward the Unfortunate. My boy is now 6 months old, & I have taken the liberty of calling him Anthony, a name, most entitled to My respect in this world, it is my intention if I can command *Interest* sufficient, to get him as early as possible in the Navy—"& let him carve his fortune with his sword" he cannot spend his lîfe better than in the Service of his King & Country, & tis a profession which at once entitles him to the respect of high & low. that which I have the Misfortune to be in, is full of difficulty & uncertainty—chance—may give one Actor a Chariot while a Superior one—in Abilities—has scarce the means to purchase a dinner—& the examples set before us are so bad & the Members so unworthy, that he must have fortitude indeed, that can abstain from all the *vices* of a *Theatre*—the Circuit I am in at present, is very respectable both from the conduct of the Manager (Mr *Cherry* late of the Theatre Royal Drury Lane) & the size of the Towns, of which the principles are—*Swansey* —*Carmarthen*—*Haverfordwest*—(from which *place* I write & which gave birth to the greatest Genius's of the Drama—the Kemble family) in Wales! —& Waterford in Ireland—I have the vanity to suppose that in my profession—I am as great a favourite in the aforesaid Towns—as any that have yet appeared, if I may Judge from My Benefits which in every one have been extremely good, & the very great applause I nightly receive, I need not tell you Madam, that in this & all professions depending on the Public there is nothing lends so much to the promotion of our success, as being noticed by our Superiors, in which I have been hitherto most fortunate & which has given Me in private Life—as well as public, an ascendancy over My Brother professionals, Mr Cherry intends to open the Waterford Theatre on a very great scale on Easter Monday. & I assure you I have very great expectation of being very much taken notice of there, if I cou'd procure a Letter or two—of recommendation, it wou'd greatly increase those expectations "In te spes est" if Madam you were not too much wearied with the kindnesses you have already shewn (& which the more Matured I grow—the less I cease to admire) wou'd assist Me once again—You cou'd most materially serve Me on this occasion as doubtless among the numerous Circlle of Yr friends some one or two may have Connexions at Waterford, & I am bold to say, that my present Character & Actions [will no]t disgrace any recommendation, whatever [At all] events I shall be most happy to hear that you & Mr Clarke are well, & that you may continue in health & prosperity will be the constant prayer of him, who never can forget the numerous obligations he lays under to you, & which are stampt Indellibly in the heart of

Your Grateful St
Edmund Kean

Theatre
Haverfordwest
Wales

PS be kind enough to indulge Me with an immediate answer—My best respects to Mr Clarke—Mr Good & Family if you will take that trouble—we sail for Ireland—Monday week

An immediate reply from Mrs. Clarke, probably inclosing the desired introductions and certainly inquiring with interest about his marriage, drew the following letter.

Theatre Waterford. May 17th 1810

Dear Madam|

tis impossible to describe the heartfelt pleasure I felt, at the receipt of your very kind Letter. I truly rejoice to hear Mr Clarke & yourself are in health. long long may you enjoy that health. & in the possession of your paternal home continue to enjoy every blessing & uninterrupted happiness tho' I must say I am selfish enough not to rejoice at your removal from London. chance may bring *Me* there again, & I assure you one of the chief inducements that could lead Me thither wou'd be once again to see My best friends Mr & Mrs Clarke but as you have so highly honoured Me with your correspondence I must content Myself with that, to give you a description of Mrs Kean as she ever has & still continues to appear in My eyes is impossible. but if a brief recital of the circumstances which brought us together will suffice, I shall endeavour to comply with your request, Miss Chambers—that was, is of a respectable Family in Waterford, the town from which I write (& to which let Me add in My profession I am no small favourite) but feeling an early inclination & very great talent for the Stage, herself & Sister totally unacquainted with the World or its artifices left their friends without any previous knowledge & went to England to embark in the most dangerous of all professions to unprotected females. Fortune however was more kind to them than they were to themselves by Mrs Keans very great Theatrical merit & their Ladylike conduct in general they acquired friends & were universally respected, after performing at the Theatres Royal Cheltenham, Plymouth &c I had the honour of meeting her at Gloucester. I was instantly struck with the similarity between her & Miss Owenson's [?] *wild Irish Girl,* & certainly if She resembled that character in her manners, She is not at all deficient in copying her heart our courtship was not tedious, we read each other's Sentiments in our eyes. I soon led her to the Altar by which She made Me the happiest of Men. the plays in which we had to act were placed uniformly in our favour. I had to sustain a principle character in *"Gallantry & Courtship"* I shortly after witnessed her admirable Acting in *"Love for Love"* our services were mutually required in the "Wedding day" & the differences of "3 weeks after Marriage" were laid aside for that delightful Comedy the "Honey Moon" You will think me vain in again mentioning how great a favourite I am in Waterford, the great applause I nightly receive, & the flattering encomiums (entirely unsolicited) I receive in the papers daily—prove that they think somewhat highly of Me. I have taken the liberty of enclosing one that appeared in this days paper. knowing that you will not dislike to hear of the popularity of your former little favourite. I shall go to Swansey next Summer, & then My engagement with *Mr Cherry* closes, unless I choose to renew it. Above all things I shou'd like to be in Mrs Bakers company again but Mr Long who officiates for her in the business of the Theatre, has an unaccountable objection to *small* Men which aversion he carries to so great an excess, that I firmly believe had Mr Garrick offered himself a Candidate to Mr Longs Management, He even *He* wou'd have been rejected this is somewhat hard to think, that an ignorant Man, of no kind of consequence in our profession, shou'd start an objection which has been overlooked in the first Theatres in the three Kingdoms viz. Edinburgh, Birmingham, Cheltenham, Margate, Dover &c &c in all which I have sustained the principle characters of the Drama, with universal approbation the Audiences of these Theatres have overlooked My *figure* & have thought only of My Acting

when I was last in Mrs Bakers company I was extremely ill treated he Mr Long kept Me in the back ground as much as possible & frequently gave those characters, which undoubtedly were mine, to fellows, who certainly wou'd have adorned the handles of a plough, but were never intended for the Stage, but these met Mr Longs approbation because they were *taller* than Me I think if these matters were intimated to Mrs Baker herself, it might be of essential service to Me. My writing to her is useless, as this *Manager*, arrests her Le[tters] & answers them as he pleases, I certainly must [be a] great acquisition to such a company as hers, as indepe[ndently] of Abilities (of which with Her, there is a very small [?][27] I have a most magnificent Stage wardrobe, which they have not, & every part I play, I dress with equal Splendour, if not sometimes more, than they are dressed in London, if Madam, Mrs Baker shou'd fall in your way & you wou'd take the trouble of mentioning this subject to her you wou'd oblige Me exceedingly, & dear Madam with every prayer for Yours & Mr Clarkes prosperity & Happiness, I remain for ever

With Unabated Gratitude & Affection
Yours truly
E. Kean

To the year 1810, or thereabouts, belong four notebooks now a part of the Forster collection in the Victoria and Albert Museum, which give an interesting glimpse into Kean's methods of self-culture. Only the first, in the order in which they are arranged, is dated (1810);

[27] Some words are torn away with the seal.

it is merely a guess as to whether the others preceded or followed it. One may regret that so much private memoranda should yield nothing but exercises in language, but at least one can see how the ambitious young actor was going about to fill the gaps in his education, and some of these notations show an unexpected curiosity. Book I, for example, besides a few pages of Latin and Italian phrases, contains "Ethelreds Promise in the Saxon language," with the Anglo-Saxon and the English in parallel columns, a "Translation of Taliesin in the Ancient British or Welch Language," and the Greek alphabet. Books II and III are filled with Latin phrases. Book IV, besides a collection of foreign phrases mostly in Latin, contains some pages of botanical exposition, some historical notes, and a few commentaries on Shakespeare by eighteenth-century editors. The deduction which may be made from the materials, and their proportions, suggests that he was doing some desultory though serious reading, but especially that he was concerned with picking up a knowledge of Latin, the language which before all other school accomplishments marked the educated gentleman. His Greek, Italian, Anglo-Saxon and Welch were signs merely of temporary interest; his Latin he pursued with more permanency, but it is to be doubted if he could ever read a passage of Latin, or cared much to learn. What he wanted was phrases to adorn his written and oral conversations, to give a turn to his style and to himself the air of a school-bred man. The products of this harmless affectation are scattered through his letters and speeches, which are rarely without their tag of Latin. Kean was not an intellectual man; one may smile at these schoolboy notebooks, but after all how many strolling players in their early twenties, burdened with the responsibilities of a family, were doing even so much to widen the horizon of their minds? In this respect, as in others, the apprentice Kean was a better man than the master he became.

Procter says that Kean remained in Cherry's company for two years, following again the round of Swansea, Carmarthen, and Haverfordwest. We must take his word for it, because all trace of Kean is lost during the summer, autumn, and early winter of 1810-11. Yet since we find him again with Cherry in Waterford early in 1811, the chances are that Procter is right.

[illegible] of [illegible]

ne quid simile [illegible]	Do so no more
[illegible]	I have done my part
Ah che bella Cosa	Oh how charming
Vecchio Ladro. —	— an old Rascal
Per devozione —	— from Piety
Vicaria —	Town Hall
Mercato —	Market Place
Munificenza —	by the Munificence
Date me qualche cosa	give me something
Marito —	— Husband.
La mia disgrazia	how unfortunate I am
[illegible]	Know
[illegible]	— Yellow
Pons Sublicius	so called from Sublices signifying Piles, in the Volscian language
[illegible] — I drink this Cup to You	
Pons Paolo	Budge [illegible] a Cup

[illegible] in this Cup

Latinus

Vox populi vox Dei	That must be the [illegible]
[illegible]	which [illegible] then [illegible]
Dilatae [illegible]	[illegible] upon thy mouth [illegible] fill it
[illegible]	Butter from the kine & milk from the flock
In te domine speravi	in thee oh Lord, I have put my trust,
Ne sutor ultra crepidam	a cobler should not go beyond his last
In expugnandis urbibus.	in reducing towns
Aeternitas —	— Eternity
Mai piu representata	has never yet been performed
Le Statue Parlanti	the speaking Statues
Rex sapiens dissipat impios	a wise king disperses the wicked
[illegible] caput [illegible]	This blood [illegible] be upon thy head
Ara Primogeniti Dei	— first born of God.

TWO PAGES FROM KEAN'S COMMONPLACE BOOK, 1810

The first notice I have of this second Waterford season is dated January 9, 1811, when the Waterford *Mail* announced a repetition of *The Exile,* with Kean again as Daran. Other members of the company were Messrs. Cherry, Ford, Knowles, Stuart, Santer, Niblett, Barry, Woulds, Wilkie, Bur, Pennyman, Mesdames Cherry, Whaley, Knowles, Gunning, Misses Charteris, Cherry, and Master H. Cherry.

January 16,[28] Colman's *John Bull,* with Kean as Job Thornberry.

January 30, *The Wanderer* (probably the historical play of that name by Charles Kemble), with (for the fifth time) *Brian Boroihme.* No casts are given.

February 13(?)[29] for the benefit of Mr. and Mrs. Knowles, *Leo, or, The Gipsy* (no cast).

A special interest attaches to these last two plays, because they were both composed by Sheridan Knowles, who was at this time on the first steps of a career that led him after many years to eminence as the author of *Virginius* and *The Hunchback,* and because of the close friendship which subsisted between Knowles and Kean. No greater interest attaches to any episode of Kean's early life than to this association of two incipient stars. Unfortunately their later association is not to the actor's credit. When, after the Waterford days, the two next met, in Glasgow, Kean was a spoiled hero and Knowles a starved pedagogue in a country school. And when the poet offered his latest tragedy, of *Caius Gracchus,* the actor was cool and lofty: he had, he said, a dozen manuscripts of tragedies in his desk, but if his friend insisted, he would read it. So the pedagogue took himself and his manuscript off, in a dudgeon. Then later the actor, in a more friendly mood, suggested to the poet that a good subject might be got out of Virginius, which so worked upon the poet that, in a fine frenzy, he completed the play in three months;[30] but when he offered it to Drury Lane another play on the same theme had already been

[28] This and the next two notices are from the Waterford *Mail.* I am also indebted for information concerning Kean at Waterford to two articles by W. J. Lawrence: (1) "Edmund Kean at Waterford," *Irish Weekly Freeman,* March 17, 1911; (2) "The Old Waterford Stage," Dublin *Evening Telegraph,* April 27, 1912.

[29] So announced. But an extant playbill for February 13 gives a quite different selection of plays—See below, page 63. Probably the bill was changed.

[30] Writing it on a school slate!

accepted. And thus, by Kean's own neglect of his present advantages and forgetfulness of past enthusiasms, the best play of his time slipped through his fingers and into those of his surly rival, Macready. There is a pretty irony in the fall of these events.

But at Waterford, when as yet no disquieting successes had broken in upon their equal poverty, the two men were firm friends and abettors. Knowles was busily wooing two muses. In August of 1810 he had printed at Waterford a volume of *Poems on Various Subjects*, but the results of this and his other poetic efforts had been anything but encouraging. In Richard Brinsley Knowles's story of his father's life[31] we read that at the time he joined Cherry's company (in 1810) he had become so despondent over the chances of literary composition that "he had thrown down his pen in despair of lifting it again," and might never have done so, had not Kean, "that noble, enthusiastic, fine little fellow," encouraged him to go on. Such is the testimony of Sheridan Knowles himself. If this was actually the case, we may conclude that *Brian Boroihme*, as well as *Leo*, owed its existence to Kean. On the authority of R. B. Knowles the former play was a rewriting of a play of the same name by D. O'Meara, and was intended more for horses than for men, thus showing that its reviser was abreast of the latest developments in the drama. Kean acted Brian and Knowles, Voltimer. It was very successful, drawing crowded houses for many nights. On the same authority it was revived in 1837 at Covent Garden, when Knowles played Brian himself.

For our knowledge of *Leo, or, The Gipsy*, which was never published, we are indebted to Procter, who came into possession of the greater part of the manuscript[32] and printed selections of it in his *Life of Kean*. We need not enter into details. The play is in bad blank verse and concerns the love life of two gipsy youths; Leo loves Helen, the daughter of a landed gentleman, and Hugo sighs for Chloe, who prefers the landed gentleman's supposed son, Ferdinand; Hugo is for a little murdering, but Leo, all valor and virtue, at the same time protects him from his evil impulse and Ferdinand from a knife in the

[31] *Life of James Sheridan Knowles*. Privately printed for James McHenry. London, 1872.

[32] That is, the first two acts and part of the third. Procter surmises that the fourth and fifth acts are lost, but a witness of the benefit performance speaks of it as a play in three acts.

back. The tone is heroic. Kean, we know, played Leo; Knowles almost as certainly played Hugo. Procter tells us that Kean was so enthusiastic over the play and his rôle that when he came out at Drury Lane he would have done so in Leo if the text could have been found, but this may scarcely be believed. He knew himself and his public too well to risk anything less than Shakespeare.

Mr. W. J. Lawrence has recorded two Waterford playbills.[33] The first of these is dated February 13, the day for which the Waterford *Mail* announced *Leo* for the Knowles benefit. Evidently a substitution was made for some reason—perhaps *Leo* could not be got ready in time—and Cherry decided to use that day for his own benefit. He chose as the principal piece a concoction of his own, with music by Domenico Corri, which had been brought out at Drury Lane in 1806, while he was a member of that company. It was called "The Grand Operatic Drama of The Travellers, or Music's Fascination," and was built round the idea, suggested by Corri, of using the national airs of various kingdoms and tracing the progress of music from old China to modern England. Each of its five acts was laid in a different country, the whole being linked together by the participation of five travelers: Zaphimiri, Prince of China (Kean), Koyau, his Preceptor (Knowles), O'Gallagher, an Irishman (Cherry), Musidora (Mrs. Gunning), Celinda (Miss Cherry). At Drury Lane Elliston had played Zaphimiri, Braham Koyau, and Johnston O'Gallagher. Knowles, then, was the Braham, or principal singing gentleman, of Cherry's company. After the opera came *The Lying Valet*, with no part for Kean.

The second bill is for Santer's benefit, on March 7. It consisted of Colman's comedy *The Poor Gentleman*, a comedy ballet called *The Rival Lovers*, and Colman's *Review*. Kean played only in the first, taking the part of Frederick Bramble.

On July 18, 1811, Mr. and Mrs. Kean took their "farewell benefit" under the patronage of the mayor.[34] The plays billed were *Douglas* and *The Review*. This is the last notice from Waterford.

[33] Dublin *Evening Telegraph*, April 27, 1912. These were formerly owned by Arthur Hunter of Manchester, but he has disposed of them and I have no idea where they are now.

[34] Advertisement in the Waterford *Mirror*. Communicated to me through the kindness of Mr. Lawrence.

Of far more value, however, than any amount of dry statistics of performance is a review of the Waterford season contained in a letter to the *Hibernian Magazine* signed "Thespian" and printed in the issue of May, 1811.[35] The letter bears date of May 7. After stating that the company is now at Clonmell for a few weeks and after some miscellaneous comments on the company and the repertory, the critic goes on as follows:

> Mr. Kean is entitled to precedence next [i.e., after the Cherrys]: a young man, who to any stage would be an ornament; his fort is tragedy. In Octavian, he really showed a degree of excellence that astonished me; his Hamlet, Osmond, and Jaffeir, were equally good; but his figure is much against him, being low, though well formed and graceful; his acting bears a strong resemblance to Young's, who perhaps, he may some day rival.[36] He also possesses some literary talent, having produced a Melo Drama at his benefit, entitled, *The Cottage Foundling, or, The Robbers of Ancora.*[37] It is not without merit, particularly the part of a dry old fisherman, performed by Cherry; yet the audience gave no great marks of approbation. I am told that he intends offering it at Covent Garden.
>
> Mr. Knowles seems gifted with abilities more for writing than acting, yet he sings a tolerable good song . . . At his benefit he produced a play of three acts that really had a very just claim to the applause it was received with; it was called *Leo, or the Gipsies.* Leo, by Mr. Kean, was well supported; and Miss Cherry, as one of the Gipsies with whom Leo was in love, went through her part with her usual vivacity.

The Cottage Foundling never came out at Covent Garden; indeed it is doubtful if any town but Waterford saw it. Procter says that the author sent it by post to Miss Tidswell in so bulky a package that the actress refused to pay the enormous charges on it, and so it was lost. But in a York bill of October, 1811,[38] it is spoken of as in preparation for the Lyceum Theatre, London, though probably it never came to production. Other compositions by Kean, dating from the Cherry period, have been mentioned. One of the witnesses cited in the *New*

[35] Called to my attention by Mr. Lawrence.

[36] An interesting prognostication in the light of the future rivalry of these men. How Kean would have foamed at being told that his style resembled Young's!

[37] Should be "Ancona."

[38] See below, page 67.

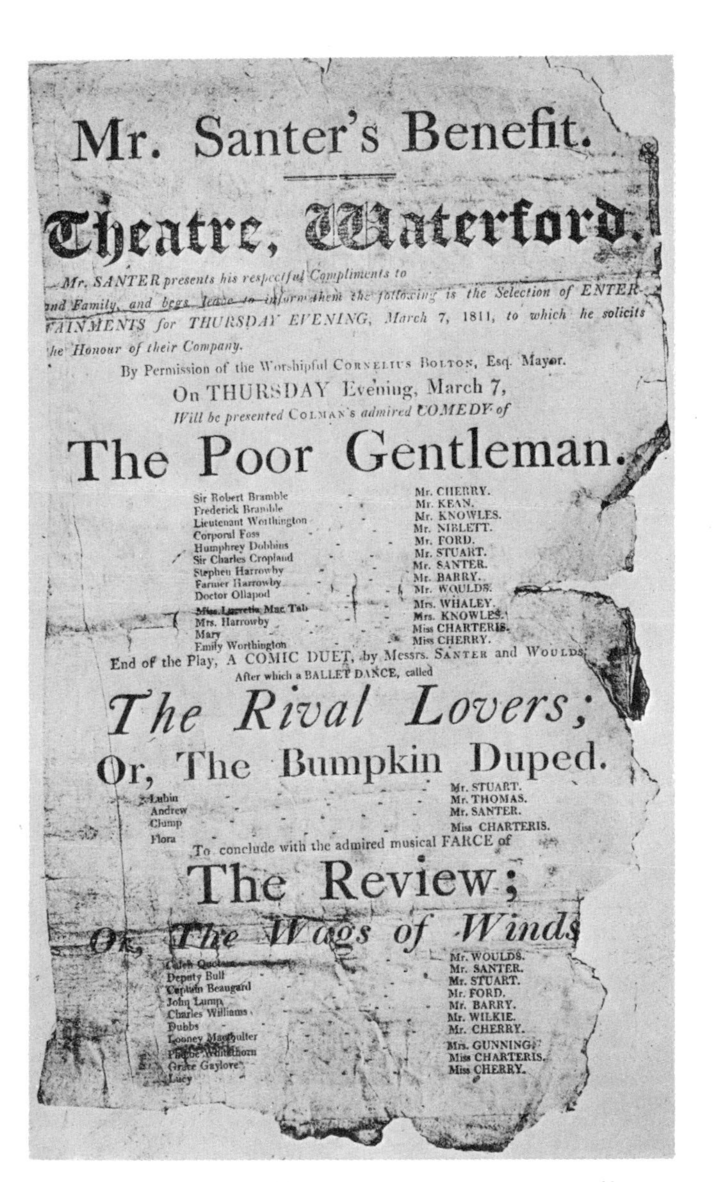

Mr. Santer's Benefit.

Theatre, Waterford.

Mr. SANTER presents his respectful Compliments to
and Family, and begs leave to inform them the following is the Selection of ENTERTAINMENTS for THURSDAY EVENING, March 7, 1811, to which he solicits the Honour of their Company.

By Permission of the Worshipful CORNELIUS BOLTON, Esq. Mayor.

On THURSDAY Evening, March 7,

Will be presented COLMAN'S *admired COMEDY of*

The Poor Gentleman.

Sir Robert Bramble - Mr. CHERRY.
Frederick Bramble - Mr. KEAN.
Lieutenant Worthington - Mr. KNOWLES.
Corporal Foss - Mr. NIBLETT.
Humphrey Dobbins - Mr. FORD.
Sir Charles Cropland - Mr. STUART.
Stephen Harrowby - Mr. SANTER.
Farmer Harrowby - Mr. BARRY.
Doctor Ollapod - Mr. WOULDS.
Miss Lucretia Mac Tab - Mrs. WHALEY.
Mrs. Harrowby - Mrs. KNOWLES.
Mary - Miss CHARTERIS.
Emily Worthington - Miss CHERRY.

End of the Play, A COMIC DUET, by Messrs. SANTER and WOULDS.

After which a BALLET DANCE, called

The Rival Lovers;
Or, The Bumpkin Duped.

Lubin - Mr. STUART.
Andrew - Mr. THOMAS.
Clump - Mr. SANTER.
Flora - Miss CHARTERIS.

To conclude with the admired musical FARCE of

The Review;
Or, The Wags of Windsor

Caleb Quotem - Mr. WOULDS.
Deputy Bull - Mr. SANTER.
Captain Beaugard - Mr. STUART.
John Lump - Mr. FORD.
Charles Williams - Mr. BARRY.
Dubbs - Mr. WILKIE.
Looney Mactwolter - Mr. CHERRY.
Phœbe Whitethorn - Mrs. GUNNING.
Grace Gaylove - Miss CHARTERIS.
Lucy - Miss CHERRY.

PLAYBILL OF "THE POOR GENTLEMAN"
WATERFORD, 1811

Monthly memoir, which I have drawn upon several times before, says that he contrived a "ballet of action," called *Zoa and Koa,* which became popular in the provinces, and a "piece" called *The Fisherman's Hut* of which Cherry averred that Kean wrote nothing but the bad English in it, whatever that may mean. All but the names of these compositions has vanished, for which no doubt their author is to be congratulated.

Only one other event of importance needs to be repeated in connection with Waterford, namely, the birth of a second son, John Charles, on January 18,[39] 1811. This boy in the fulness of time won for himself a considerable reputation on the stage, where, if he did not equal his father in genius, he more than surpassed him in sobriety, chastity, and business prudence.

[39] This date is probably correct, although I have not seen the baptismal entry. Arthur Hunter formerly owned a certified statement by Henry Archdale, Vicar of Kilmeaden, etc., that he baptised the child on January 26, and that it was five or six days old. Mr. Lawrence kindly gave me a copy.

CHAPTER III

WATERFORD TO GUERNSEY

BETWEEN July and December of 1811, that is between Waterford and Exeter, lies a gap which must be filled by the biographers. As to Kean's reasons for leaving Cherry nothing is known, unless there is truth in the story that Cherry refused to advance his salary from twenty-five to thirty shillings. He might better have stayed with Cherry at any price, rather than throw himself on the world as a masterless player. We are told that he applied to various managers—at Bath, Liverpool, Dublin—without success. Then began what, in Procter's account, was a painful pilgrimage, of the kind which is only too common in the annals of wandering actors. His route lay through Whitehaven, Dumfries, Annan, Carlisle, Appleby, Penrith, Richmond (in Yorkshire), to York, a route, so to speak, of tears and curses. It is a story neither good to tell nor to hear, of harassed plans, of desperate hopes, of arguments with surly landlords, of cringing to indifferent officials, and beseeching-the-favor of indifferent patrons, of laboriously copying out beguiling handbills announcing recitations to which nobody came, of the slow conversion of their few not absolutely necessary belongings into bread and meat. Here and there they had better luck, enough to keep their heads above water, and they encountered a few Samaritans. One such adventure is recorded in a scrap of writing preserved in the Forster Collection in the Victoria and Albert Museum. As it is a reminiscence of Mary Kean, written down in her old age, I give it *literatim:*

> In Richmond (Yorkshire) we suffered privations of more than common my Husband took a Room in the principal Inn & gave recitations singing &c. a gentleman who kept a large establishment for the Education of Young gentlemen w[as ver]y kind & the young gentlemen called next day with their pocket money & left it with the Landlady directed to Mr Kean the sum amounting I think to eleven shillings & sixpence there is something in the generosity of youth.

And Procter tells that at York, where the wanderers were in such straits that Kean thought seriously of enlisting as a soldier, they were relieved through the generous assistance of one Mr. Nokes, a dancing master, who opened his school room to Edmund for recitations and whose wife slipped a five-pound note into the hand of Mary.

To York belongs the interesting handbill owned by Dr. Doran and printed in his *Annals of the English Stage.*[1] It is said to be in Kean's own writing.

Under Patronage.

Ball Room, Minster Yard,
Thursday Evening, October 10th, 1811,

Mr. KEAN,
(*Late of the Theatre Royal Haymarket and Edinburgh, and Author of the Cottage Foundling; or, Robbers of Ancona, now preparing for immediate representation at the Theatre Lyceum*),

and

Mrs. KEAN,
(*Late of the Theatres Cheltenham and Birmingham*)

Respectfully inform the Inhabitants of York, and its Vicinity, that they will stop

FOR ONE NIGHT ONLY,

On their way to London; and present such Entertainments that have never failed of giving satisfaction, humbly requesting the support of the Public.

Part I.

A Scene from the Celebrated Comedy of

THE HONEY MOON;

Or,

How To Rule A Wife.

Duke Aranza . . Mr. KEAN. Juliana . . Mrs. KEAN.

Favourite Comic Song of "Beggars and Ballad Singers,"
In which Mr. Kean will display his powers of Mimicry in the well-known characters of London Beggars.

[1] It appears only in the earlier editions, being omitted, curiously enough, in Lowe's edition (1888).

IMITATIONS

Of the London Performers, viz.—

Kemble, Cooke, Braham, Incledon, Munden, Fawcett, and

THE YOUNG ROSCIUS.

Part II.

The African Slaves' Appeal to Liberty!!!

Scenes from the Laughable Farce of

THE WATERMAN;

Or,

The First of August.

Tom Tug (*with the Songs of "Did you not hear of a Jolly Young Waterman" and the pathetic ballad of "Then farewell my trim-built Wherry"*) .... Mr. KEAN.

Miss Whilhelmina .... Mrs. KEAN.

After which, Mr. Kean *will sing in Character,*

George Alexander Stevens's Description

of a

STORM.

Part III.

Scenes from the Popular Drama of

THE CASTLE SPECTRE.

Earl Osmond . . Mr. Kean. Angela . . Mrs. Kean.

Favourite Comic Song of the "Cosmetic Doctor."

To Conclude with the Laughable Farce of

SYLVESTER DAGGERWOOD,

Or,

The Dunstable Actor.

Female Author . . . Mrs. Kean.

Sylvester Daggerwood.......Mr. Kean (*in which character he will read the celebrated play-bill written by* G. Colman, Esq., *and sing the "Four-and-Twenty Puppet Shows," originally sung by him at the Theatre Royal, Haymarket.*)

Each character to be personated in their appropriate Dresses, made by the principal Theatrical Dress Makers of London; viz., Brooks & Heath, Martin, &c.

First Seats . . 2*s.* 6*d.* Back Seats . . 1*s.*

Doors to be open at SIX, and begin at SEVEN precisely.
Tickets to be had at the PRINTER'S.

From York the wanderers journeyed to London, where they counted, mistakenly, on the friendly offices of Aunt Price and Aunt Tidswell. Aunt Price grudgingly kept them for a few days (she cannot be blamed for feeling inadequate to the sudden addition of four mouths), but Aunt Tidswell would have nothing to do with them. Meanwhile they were looking about. And fortunately there came at this time a call from Exeter.

As to the time of his joining the Exeter company there is some uncertainty. William Cotton[2] says that he opened there on December 2, 1811, as Octavian, and that on December 3 he played Shylock with such effect as to move Hughes, his manager, to offer him a contract for three years at two guineas a week. But Molloy prints a letter from Kean to Hughes written before leaving London with the date 1812. Therefore, unless Molloy has made an error in reading, Cotton must be wrong. At all events, I have come across no Exeter playbills before January 15, of 1812. The letter, since it was unknown to Procter and Hawkins, and since letters of this date are rare, is worth repeating.

Tavistock Row, Covent Garden, 1812.

To —— Hughes Esq., *Sadlers Wells Theatre.*

Dear Sir,

Having travelled lately some hundred Miles with a large family and most expensive baggage, I am left in London in a situation (which many of our brother professionals are acquainted with) *Non est mihi argentum.* It is My wish therefore to depart by to-morrow's coach for Weymouth, but I frankly confess I at present have not the means; if, sir, you would oblige me with the sum of ten pounds, Mr. Finch or Miss Tidswell will become Answerable for my immediate appearance at Weymouth, and Mr. Hughes might proceed to the reduction of ten shillings per week till the debt is

2 *The Story of the Drama in Exeter; with Reminiscences of Edmund Kean.* London and Exeter, 1887.

discharged. As I am fully sensible this is a great obligation from a stranger, it is my wish to pay any interest on the money you may please to demand, and as Mr. Hughes, Junr. will have the means in his own hands, there can be no *doubt* of the payment, and I shall bear the recollection of your kindness Παρ' ὅλον τὸν Βίον. I should not ask so great a favour, but My Aunt, whose purse was ever open to my necessities, is at this moment as bare in pocket as myself, and another Relation from whom I have been in the habit of receiving Supplies is not in London. I can only say, sir, however exorbitant the request may appear to a stranger, there is no Manager who *knows me* would refuse it; it is My intention, should fortune favour my designs, to make the Situation you have offered me a permanency, and as I have ever shown unremitting attention to my professional duties, I despair not of joining your approbation to the public's, and of making it pleasant to all parties. The money I write for is for immediate service, and if you would commit it to the charge of the bearer—My Servant—it would be brought very safe to Me, and to-morrow we would depart for Weymouth.

I am, Sir,

With the greatest Respect, yours,

E. Kean.

This Hughes was one John Hughes,[3] manager of the theatres at Exeter, Plymouth, and Weymouth, who by discipline and careful attention to business had brought his country affairs to a sound condition and had for several years kept a foot in London as proprietor of Sadler's Wells, to which no doubt he gave most of his personal attention. The Hughes at the other, or Exeter, end was his son Richard.[4]

Kean's letter shows that he joined the company, or meant to join the company, at Weymouth. By January the company was in Exeter.

[3] Procter jumped to the unwarrantable conclusion that the Hughes of Exeter and Sadler's Wells was the Jack Hughes with whom Kean played at Gloucester and Cheltenham in 1808. But the sketches of Richard Hughes in *The Thespian Dictionary* (1805) and of Hughes in *The Biography of the British Stage* (1824) dispel the confusion. Jack Hughes went to Richmond, where he was manager for a time, and in 1813 to Drury Lane. He may, however, have been of the same family as John and Richard.

[4] My authority for this paragraph is chiefly a communication from "Old Actress" to the *Era* of June 13, 1869. John, she says, was in 1812 an old man of 70. Richard, his eldest son, married Miss Bish, the lottery office keeper's daughter. His second son, Henry, married Miss Wentworth of Covent Garden, who then became a great favorite in Exeter and appears on many bills as "Mrs. H. Hughes."

There are few Kean bills[5] before December of 1812, but enough to show that he stayed with the company. On January 15 Kean played Duke Aranza in *The Honeymoon* and Rosenberg in the popular melodrama *Ella Rosenberg*. On April 13, Incledon being engaged, was given *The School for Fathers* (an alteration of Bickerstaffe's *Lionel and Clarissa*), with an epilogue by Goldsmith spoken by Kean as Harlequin, "in the course of which he will take A Leap through a Balloon of Fire!" After it he played the Prince in *Cinderella*, the dances of which were "got up under the direction of Mr. Kean." Among the company were Messrs. Middleton, Tokeley, T. Short, Warsdale, Loveday, Horton, Quantrell, Pitt, Master Pitt, Mesdames Loveday, Quantrell, Middleton, H. Hughes, Johnston, Warsdale, and Miss Warsdale. Harvard possesses an interesting bill of April 14 announcing Kean as Alexander in *Alexander the Great* and Romaldi in *A Tale of Mystery*. But apparently he played neither part, for nearly all the names of both printed casts are crossed out in ink and other names written in. Such corrections on old bills are quite common and represent last minute changes. But rarely was a casting so thoroughly remade as in this case. For Romaldi, H. Johnson was substituted, and for Alexander, Betty. This was, of course, the former Infant Roscius, Master Betty, now, after four years at Oxford, returning to the stage.[6] One would be glad to know more of the circumstances of this performance, for remembering Kean's jealousy of Betty, one can be sure that he would not yield Alexander with any good grace. According to Procter he took a benefit on April 20, playing Luke in *Riches*, William in *The Sailor's Return*, and Frederick in *Of Age To-morrow*.

In August the company was in Totnes. On the sixth Kean had a benefit, for which he arranged a feast of varieties. The play was *The Merchant of Venice*, with himself as Shylock: after which, "Mr. Kean will dance a new Pas de Deux." Next came

[5] A number of bills are in the Dyce Collection at the Victoria and Albert Museum: the rest of those cited here are at Harvard.

[6] The return was a failure, for the electrifying child-actor had developed into a stodgy, unromantic young man. For a time his past fame lent him a certain interest; then he dropped from the stage altogether.

a new grand Serious Pantomime . . . called *The Savages, Or, Love and Hatred*. Performed upwards of 50 Nights, at Astley's Royal Amphitheatre Westminsterbridge London. Got up under the direction of Mr. Kean!! With distinguished approbation, in the Theatres Royal Dublin, Edinburgh, York, Birmingham, Cheltenham, Richmond, Weymouth, Canterbury, Exeter, &c. In the course of the Pantomime the following peculiar performances. A Savage 'Pas de Trois' Mr. Kean, Miss Warsdale, and Master Pitt. Otaheitan method of using the Bow and Arrow. Several Extraordinary Combats, by Messers Kean, and Tokeley, with Bamboos, Battle Axe, Shield, and Sword. Savage Distraction Delineated by Mr. Kean. A most affecting scene of an Infant preserved from the hands of an Assassin, by the Magnanimity of the elder brother Hugo. This truly Interesting Piece concludes with the death of Yassedo, destroyed in a surprising Combat by Kojah, the restoration of Illa, and her Children to the Arms of their Father and Husband. Savage Dance of Peace. Being an exact representation of the Otaheitan method, as described by that wonderful Navigator, Captain Cook.

Kean, of course, took the part of Kojah, the noble savage.

New persons in the company, as shown by this bill, were Mr. and Mrs. Edwards, Mr. Gregory, but chiefly, in the light of his future reputation, John Vandenhoff.

By October 24 the company had moved to Weymouth, their composition being the same as at Totnes with the addition of Mr. and Mrs. Bennett and Mr. Miller. Weymouth was in those days a fashionable watering place and a Hughes stronghold, although it may be supposed that with the cessation of the yearly visits from George III the resort had lost some of its *ton* and the theatre some of its patronage. Nevertheless, that great favorite, Mrs. Jordan, had been engaged. Her last performance fell on the twenty-fourth, as Lady Teazle in *The School for Scandal*, with Kean as Charles Surface. The famous romp, who also played with Kean in Exeter, is said not to have been pleased with her leading man, and to have declared, after doing Mrs. Centlivre's *The Wonder*, that "she had never played to so bad a Don Felix in her life."

If Cotton is right in saying that Mrs. Jordan played in Exeter in October of 1812, the company must have gone there directly after her closing performance of the twenty-fourth. Beginning in December and extending through the following March the extant bills are numerous, as the following list will show. Kean played:

December 9, Don Felix in *The Wonder.*

December 11, Sir Edward Mortimer in *The Iron Chest.*

December 14, Othello (Mrs. Kean as Emilia), additions to the company having been Messrs. Perkins, Congdon, Mason (Iago), and Miss Rivers (Desdemona).

December 16, Macbeth.

December 18, Frederick Bramble in *The Poor Gentleman.*

December 21, Hamlet.

December 26, Hastings in *Jane Shore.*

December 28, Beverley in *The Gamester,* and Harlequin in *The Corsican Fairy.*

December 30, Henry in *Speed the Plough.*

January 5, 1813, Harry Dornton in *The Road to Ruin,* with *The Corsican Fairy.*

January 8, Malvogli in *The Doubtful Son* (by W. Dimond).

January 12, Sir Edward Mortimer, with *The Corsican Fairy.*

January 13, Reuben Glenroy in *Town and Country.*

January 15, Captain Thalwick in *How to Die for Love,* with *The Corsican Fairy.*

January 18, Richard III. In *The Wood Demon* Mrs. Kean played the Spirit of Alexina.

January 19, *The Birth-Day* (no part for Kean), with *The Corsican Fairy.*

January 20, Octavian in *The Mountaineers,* with *The Corsican Fairy.*

January 22, Harry Dornton.

January 25, Frederick Bramble, to the Sir Robert Bramble of Munden.

January 26, Faulkland in *The Rivals,* to the Sir Anthony of Munden.

January 29, Gossamer in *Laugh While You Can* (by Reynolds) to the Bonus of Munden.

February 2, Doricourt in *The Belle's Stratagem,* with *The Corsican Fairy.*

February 3, Young Marlowe in *She Stoops to Conquer,* with *The Corsican Fairy.*

February 5, Daran in *The Exile,* and Captain Thalwick.

February 9, Count Belino in *The Devil's Bridge,* and Tristram Fickle in *The Weathercock* (probably the farce by J. T. Allingham).

February 10, Count Belino.

February 16, Malvogli, with *The Corsican Fairy.* (The "popular New Tragedy of Remorse" is announced for rehearsal.)

February 22, Don Christoval in *The Student of Salamanca,* with *The Corsican Fairy.* (In the latter Mrs. Kean replaces Mrs. H. Hughes as the Protecting Spirit, but without the song which had been advertised heretofore with the part.)

February 26, Count Belino.

March 1, Shylock: also a "Serious New Pantomime" got up by Kean, called *Nautical Heroism, or, The Indian Ambuscade,* with Kean as First Savage. This, we are told, was based on an incident which happened to Commodore Byron on his passage through the Straits of Magellan. Among the things promised are: "The Method of Ambuscade employed by the South Americans against their Enemies: Military Exercise of the South Americans. Capt. Byron in personal contention with the Indian Chief, with that disinterested liberality that ever characterizes the British Tar, teaches him the use of the weapon that is employed against himself."

March 2, Earl Osmond in *The Castle Spectre.* (*Remorse* is announced for Friday, March 5.)

March 8, Mr. Ferment in Morton's *School of Reform* (Mrs. Kean as Shelah); also Rugantino in Monk Lewis' melodrama of that name.

March 9, Othello and Rugantino. Mrs. Kean played Emilia.

March 11, Young Rapid in Morton's *Cure for the Heartache*; also Damon in a "new comic dance" called *Hurry Scurry.*

March 15, Bronzely in *Wives as they Were,* and Florian in *The Young Hussar.*

March 17, Don Alvar in Coleridge's *Remorse* (produced March 5).

March 19, Charles Surface in *The School for Scandal,* "by Desire of Richard Hippisley Tuckfield, Esq. High Sheriff of the County of Devon;" also *The Corsican Fairy.*

March 24, Count Belino and *The Corsican Fairy.*

March 25, Shylock. (Mrs. Kean was a dancing lady in *Don Juan,* a pantomime.)

March 26, Cato in Addison's tragedy, with *The Savages,* under the "Patronage of Mrs. Buller, of Downes." The occasion wins solemnity from the patron, who, as her title almost necessarily implies, was an august personage and wins interest from the first appearance on the stage of Howard Kean, who played Hugo, one of the children of Kojah—that one who Magnanimously rescued his Infant brother from the hands of an Assassin.[7]

As this list shows, Kean was indisputably the leading man of the Hughes company, both in tragedy and comedy. Procter reports that he was also greatly in demand for Harlequin, to such an extent that on his recovery from an illness the manager placarded his return, not as Shylock or Count Belino, but with the promise that "Mr. Kean will Resume the character of Harlequin this Evening." He may well have been the determining factor in the remarkable popularity of *The Corsican Fairy*. Another conclusion, to which the Exeter list leads, is that by the close of his engagement he had formed practically the whole of the repertory on which he based his reputation in London. One cannot, of course, in view of our fragmentary knowledge of his previous career, say what new rôles he essayed at Exeter, but considering that he had not had anything like metropolitan practice since Birmingham, and that none of the places in which he played between Exeter and London were qualified to bring out his powers, it is not unreasonable to suppose that the year and more he spent there ripened his art to a full maturity. He had the authority of position, he had constant practice in the most exacting rôles of tragedy, and, Mr. Cotton insists, he was greatly admired by the connoisseurs of the town.[8] Molloy, with what security I know not, states that his interpretations of Shakespeare aroused a lively interest which resulted not only in verbal debate but in the production of essays and pamphlets. Exeter was scarcely a London, but it contained men of discrimination in matters of the theatre, in short a critical public such as he could

[7] The bill of this performance is printed, with some errors, by Molloy.

[8] Cotton quotes from a local paper: "We have scarcely ever known a performer, in this or any other theatre, who possessed so great a versatility of talent as Mr. Kean . . . Whether he pourtrays the Jew, or trips it on the light fantastic toe, as *Harlequin* or the *Prince* in *Cinderella,* in either character he interests, he delights his audience—he is indeed a universal favourite."

not have found in Waterford or even in Swansea. An unsigned memoir in the *Literary Gazette* for 1833,[9] written in the form of personal recollections, says that a certain Mr. Nation of Exeter was the first person to perceive that Kean was a genius, that he talked Shakespeare with him by the hour and taught him much, and that he brought Dr. Drury to Exeter to see Kean. If this last statement is correct, then to Mr. Nation belongs the honor of setting Kean's foot on the road to Drury Lane. The same writer, who knew Kean at the time, testifies that "he was unaffected and pleasant in his manners, and most unassuming."[10]

All in all, one might be justified in assuming that Exeter, after the bitter months of northern wandering, came as a haven of peace, success, and respectability. So indeed it might have been had the man willed to make it so. But he still lived the double life; habit had rooted itself in him; when he was with sober men like Nation he took on their sober coloring, but his nights were spent at the tavern, where he drank his little money away. And there was illness in the family. A glimpse into the darker corners of the picture is given by a letter of Mary Kean to her girlhood friend, Margaret Roberts.[11] It is dated Exeter, July 4, 1812.

I must own, my Dear Marg^{t}, your letter was written very hastily. I shall not however comment on it, except on the word *passion*—which I did not at the time merit; nothing was farther from my Bosom than passion of any kind. I was so ill no one expected I should ever get better—the two boys dying in measles and hooping cough, Edmund entirely ruining his health with Drink. I saw nothing but misery before me, and the repulse I met with from Mrs. Hunt, when I expected her interest did rouse what little feeling I had. As I expected we had but 6 pound in the House for our Benefit—we were out of pocket[12] . . . We leave this day three weeks

[9] June 1, page 346.

[10] He is also the authority for the story of Kean's second (?) encounter with Master Betty, during the Weymouth engagement. The writer met him one night wandering disconsolately in the rain. "I must feel deeply," he said; "*he* commands overflowing houses, *I* play to empty benches, and I know my powers are superior to his."

[11] Sent to me by W. J. Lawrence. It has not, I think, been printed before.

[12] This must refer to the Exeter benefit of April 20. Kean had not belonged to a company since leaving Cherry.

for Weymouth . . . If you have any bits of silk Muslin you can send it or any old thing. Little Howard is very delicate, the Measles has weakened him much. Mr. Kean's aunt has been trying to prevent his living with me—oh! you know not half what I am suffering.

Kean knew well that there was no future for an actor who remained in the provinces, no matter what the local critics might say of him. True fame, and the fame that pays, could only be won in London. Therefore he bombarded the patent houses with letters which were predestined to be thrown in the waste basket or to be answered with vague and meaningless promises. Probably, too, the pressure of domestic worry made him think at times of Covent Garden and Drury Lane not as fields of glory but as entrances to the modest comfort of a living wage. Such is the mood of a letter[13] to Arnold, the Drury Lane manager, written from Weymouth on September 23, 1812.

Theatre Royal Weymouth
Septr 23^{d} 1812

Sir | When I was last honor'd with your Correspondence you closed your very polite letter, with the assurance, "that at a future opportunity, you wou'd be enabled to pay more attention to my application." this flattering assertion emboldens me to again address you, nor cou'd I in my humble opinion time it better than the approaching renovation[14] of Drury Lane Theatre, if the Services of so humble a Candidate for public favor, wou'd be accepted, I shou'd feel myself most happy in becoming a Member of the new Community. from my earliest days I have been accustom'd to take a leading line of business. & consequently must have a Theoretical knowledge of everything concerned with it. & I find the fame gained by acting Richard & Hamlet in the Country is not so *estimable* or *profitable*, as the Richmond or Tressel, Laertes or Horatio, in London! to be settled in the Metropolis in a *third* or *fourth* rate Situation, & on a salary sufficient to support my family with respectability wou'd be the summit of my ambition. You will Sir I hope pardon me for this frankness, your reported liberality encourages me to be more explicit than the nature of such applications admit of, & tho I have been fortunate in gaining the public approbation wherever I have acted, I need not tell you Sir, so well acquainted

13 In the Harvard Theatre Collection.

14 He refers to the new theatre, opened on October 10. The previous theatre had burnt to the ground in 1809.

with (Dramatic Concerns) that the best situation in Provincial Theatres, is not a livelihood. M[r] Dowton is very well acquainted with me, & I am convinced will give an impartial account of my Talent.

I am Sir &c &c
Yours
E Kean

But even such humility had no effect on the hard-headed Arnold.

The story has been current from early days that Kean was dismissed from Hughes's company for drunkenness and insubordination. He is supposed on one occasion to have been too intoxicated to play his part, which was taken over by one of the Hugheses, and by way of revenge to have sat in a box and jeered at the unhappy performer all evening. There is no truth in it. The company left Exeter for Guernsey in April of 1813, and with it went the Keans.

No part of the life of Kean has been so grossly misrepresented as the few months which he spent in Guernsey. Procter's account, although wrong by a year in date and otherwise unsubstantial, is not altogether away from the truth, but what may be called the standard account is not only untrue in every particular but is a libel upon the people of a very charming island. Briefly it is this:

Shortly after the company opened at St. Peterport Kean played Hamlet. Thereupon one of the newspapers published a scathing review, from which a long passage is cited by Hawkins and others[15] but which will be sufficiently illustrated by the following excerpt.

> Even his performance of the inferior characters of the drama would be objectionable, if there was nothing to render him ridiculous by one of the vilest figures that has been seen on or off the stage, and if his mind was half so qualified for the representation of Richard III, which he is shortly to appear in, as his person is suited to the deformities with which the tyrant is supposed to have been distinguished from his fellows, his success would be most unequivocal. As to his Hamlet, it is one of the most terrible misrepresentations to which Shakespeare has ever been subjected . . .

A little while after, upon his appearance as Richard, Kean was greeted with such a storm of hisses that the play was overwhelmed. For a time he struggled on, then losing his prudence in righteous anger he ad-

[15] It seems to have been given currency first by Francis Phippen in his *Authentic Memoirs of Edmund Kean*, 1814.

EDMUND KEAN

vanced to the edge of the apron, glared upon the mob, and uttered his famous and apocryphal—

Unmannered dogs, stand ye when I command.

From now on he was the object of general persecution.

Strolling companies in the island [I quote from Hawkins, who might have reflected that not more than one company could stroll in Guernsey at a time] were warned that the slightest disposition to shield "the fellow Kean" from the consequences of his "audacious insult" to the intelligent audience would certainly bring upon them a large share of public disfavour; private people were solemnly enjoined, for the sake of their own credit, not to assist in any way "the ignorant, incompetent blackguard."

At length the governor, Sir John Doyle, took pity on the castaway, protected him, and so insured to him a measure of patronage and quiet.

And so Guernsey has endured for over a hundred years the stigma of having been blind and deaf to the merits of the greatest actor of the day, of having hissed him off the stage only a few months before the audiences at Drury Lane would be shouting him to the skies. I dare say Guernsey has not felt the stigma keenly; it has continued to be a prosperous and respected isle. Yet, since there is not a word of truth in the story, no reason exists why even so light a shadow of blame should be suffered any longer to persist. It is true that an occasional voice of protest has been raised.[16] But a popular myth is hard to scotch, and I suspect that in this instance Guernsey has been ruthlessly sacrificed to enhance the element of dramatic contrast in Kean's life, as if the gloom which preceded his apotheosis were not dark enough in reality, but must be made still more horrid. The hisses of Guernsey make a picturesque background to the plaudits of London.

On April 17, 1813, *Le Miroir politique*[17] carried an advertisement of manager Hughes that the theatre[18] would be opened on Easter Monday, the 19th, for a short season. The play would be *The Mountaineers*, with the following persons: Octavian, Mr. Kean (from the

16 For example in *Fraser's Magazine*, VII (1833), 745.

17 I was enabled to examine a file of this rare newspaper for 1813 through the courtesy of Miss Edith Carey, of St. Peter Port.

18 The Theatre Royal was built in 1791. It was destroyed about 1900 in extending the buildings of the Royal Court.

Theatre Royal, Dublin); Bulcazin Muley, Mr. Hamilton (from the Salisbury Theatre); Ganem, Mr. Congdon (from the Theatre Royal, Windsor). After the play, *Blue Devils* and *The Savages.*

The company played three times a week.[19] Unfortunately the Guernsey papers, after the custom of the provincial press at large, carried only such occasional reviews as might be offered by some interested amateur, and manager Hughes inserted paid notices only when the mood struck him. But from one source or the other we can patch out a pretty fair schedule, especially for the latter part of the season.

On Wednesday, May 19, was given a "new comedy," *The Sons of Erin,* reviewed in the *Miroir politique* for May 22. The critic was friendly. He found that Mr. Wright's face and figure were finely adapted to the coxcombry of Sir Frederick, and that "Mr. Kean was equally happy in *Fitz-Edward.*" Other members of the company who took part on this evening were Messrs. Loveday, Perkins, Tokeley, Congdon, Gregory, Cox, Hughes, Cooke, Master Rivers, Mesdames Hughes, and Loveday, Misses Rivers and Quantrell. From other sources are to be added Messrs. Hamilton, H. Hughes, and Bennett. It would seem, from a remark dropped apropos of Cooke, that he had played in *The Man of the World* at some time since the theatre opened.

Saturday, May 22, *The Royal Oak, or, The Preservation of King Charles the Second,* and *The Review.*

Wednesday, May 26, repetition of *The Sons of Erin.*

May 29 the *Miroir* carried the following remarks:

We observe with satisfaction, that the Theatre has been rather less thinly attended of late than at the beginning of the Season. The talents of the Company are altogether such, as deserve encouragement, and cannot fail of producing much entertainment, when the parts are properly cast. We cannot but approve of the manner in which Mr. Kean fills most of his tragic characters. His attitudes are easy, his action judicious, and his tones as good as the badness of his voice will allow. He would however do well

[19] The following notices are drawn from *Le Miroir politique, Le Mercure de Guernsey et Publiciste de Saint-Pierre-Port,* and *The Star, or Guernsey Weekly Advertiser*; the last two, through the courtesy of Henry E. Marquand, of the Guernsey Star and Gazette Company.

to confine himself as much as possible, to characters of a serious cast. There is a certain combrous solemnity about him which incessantly keeps his *vis comica* in the background. His efforts to be lively are entirely unavailing; and his mirth, like Macbeth's Amen, sticks in his throat. But take him all in all, and he is a Performer of no inconsiderable merit. Let him not therefore (however thin the audience or scanty the applause) lessen that merit by occasional fits of languor and negligence.

Monday, June 7, *George Barnwell* and *Cinderella.* The reviewer complained that the play was sadly mishandled, being curtailed to an hour's time and very badly performed. But of Kean he said that what he lost as Barnwell he made up in the pantomime.

Wednesday, June 16, *The Gazette Extraordinary* (without Kean) and, for the tenth time, *Harlequin's Choice,* with Kean as Harlequin.

Mr. Kean was in one of his fits of idleness; they come now so often that a stranger would really fancy that he *did not play for his own amusement.*

Monday, June 28(?),[20] *Othello.*

Mr. Kean was this evening in full possession of all that fire of which we have too often to lament the absence. He gave to Othello all that energy which the part demands, and displayed with great discrimination, the varying and tormenting passions that alternately preyed upon the noble but unhappy moor [*sic*]. Dignified, feeling, and impressive, throughout, he drew forth our admiration—our sympathy—our tears.

Wednesday, June 30, *The Battle of Hexham* and *Modern Antiques.* In the play "Mr. Kean and Miss Rivers were, as usual, conspicuous."

Monday, July 5, Mary Kean took her benefit, with *The School for Scandal* and *Cinderella.* Between the two pieces Messrs. Congdon and Kean sang "the celebrated Duet of *All's Well,* from the opera of the English Fleet." Kean also played Charles Surface in the comedy.

About the middle of the third act [reported the *Miroir*] Mr. Kean came forward and made a suitable apology for his non-attendance at

20 This date is not certain, the source being a review in the *Star* on Tuesday, July 6, which does not mention the night of performance. Since it could not have been Saturday the third, when Kean failed to appear at all, or Monday the fifth, when *The School for Scandal* was given, the most likely date is Monday, June 28.

the Theatre, on the preceding Saturday, we do not wish to be too severe, but sincerely hope he will bear in mind that it was the second time of his apologizing for the like offence, and that he has pledged himself, *the Audience shall not be again disappointed.* [Then the reviewer salved his reprimand by remarking that the Charles Surface was very good.]

Wednesday, July 7, "For the Benefit of Brother Perkins. Past Master of Lodges 738 and 838, R. A. E. S. E. M. on the Registry of Ireland," *Wives as They Were and Maids as They Are,* with *The Honest Thieves.*

Friday, July 9, *Douglas* and *Right and Wrong.*

Wednesday, July 14, for the benefit of Congdon, *The Young Hussar, The Old Maid,* and a concert of songs in which Kean took part.

Friday, July 16, *Man and Wife* and *A Tale of Mystery.*

Monday, July 19, for Miss Rivers' benefit, *Venice Preserved* (with Kean as Jaffeir) and *Catherine and Petruchio.*

Wednesday, July 21, *The Way to Get Married* (with Kean).

Saturday, July 24, for Mrs. Hughes's benefit, *The Turn Out, Personation,* and *The Budget for Blunders.*

Wednesday, July 28, for Kean's benefit, *Hamlet,* followed by the ballet *Chiron and Achilles* and the farce *Lock and Key.*

A photographic copy of a bill for this event hangs in the Guille-Allés Library at St. Peterport. As it is of the greatest rarity, for Guernsey bills seem to be nonexistent, I reproduce it hereunder.

REAL HORSES.

The Pupil of Nature!

Master Howard Kean

His first and only Appearance this Season

Shakespeare's most celebrated Play!!!

For the benefit of

MR. KEAN.

On Wednesday Evening July 28th, 1813
will be presented Shakespeare's most admired Play of

HAMLET;
Prince of Denmark.

Hamlet . . .	Mr. Kean	Guildenstern . .	Mr. Gregory
King	Mr. Warsdale	Grave Digger . .	Mr. Tokeley
Horatio . . .	Mr. Bennett	The Ghost . . .	Mr. Wright
Laertes . . .	Mr. Hamilton		
Osrick . . .	Mr. Perkins	Queen	Miss Rivers
Polonius . . .	Mr. Loveday	Player Queen . .	Miss Quantrell
Rosencrantz .	Mr. Congdon	Ophelia	Mrs. H. Hughes

To which will be added a Grand Ballet, (in one Act), called

CHIRON & ACHILLES

Never acted but at the Theatre of Paris, and the King's Theatre, London, in the course of which Achilles enters in a Car, drawn by

REAL HORSES

Chirons instructions to the Infant Achilles, in the ancient mode of war, the celebrated

SHAWL DANCE

(As performed by Madame Parisot, at the Opera House, London,)
By Miss Warsdale

Chiron (the instructor of Achilles) . . Mr. Kean
Achilles . . . . Master Kean
Thetis . . . . Mrs. Warsdale
Dancing Nymphs, the Misses Warsdales

The whole to conclude with the much admired
Laughable Musical Farce, called the

LOCK & KEY

Captain Cheerly . . . . Mr. Congdon
Brummagem . . . . Mr. Loveday
Ralph . . . . Mr. Tokeley
Captain Vale . . . . Mr. Perkins

Fanny . . . . Miss Quantrell
Laura . . . . Mrs. H. Hughes

Tickets to be had of Mr Kean, at Mrs. Rotell's, New-Town, and at Mr. Greenslade's, where places for the boxes may be taken.

Greenslade Printer Guernsey

Saturday, July 31, Miss Rivers, having failed in her first benefit, took a second, with *The Soldier's Daughter* and *The Forty Thieves.*

Monday, August 2, for Miss Quantrell's benefit, *The West Indian* and *Paul and Virginia.*

Saturday, August 7, for Bennett's benefit, *Education* and *The Hunter of the Alps.*

Monday, August 9, being the last performance of the season, for H. Hughes's benefit, *The Africans* and *Blue Beard.*

An analysis of the Guernsey season proves conclusively, I believe, that the stories which have been given currency are quite without foundation. Those newspapers which I have been able to find—the *Miroir politique*, the *Mercure et Publiciste*, the *Star and Advertiser*, and the *Gazette de Guernsey*—either say nothing at all (like the *Gazette*) or speak of Kean with friendly interest rising to admiration. It is scarcely conceivable, had such a riotous and untoward scene taken place as is told of in connection with *Richard III*, that it would not have got into the press. The so-called Guernsey review of *Hamlet* must be false. It is tied to the theory that *Hamlet* was given soon after the arrival of the company,[21] yet it is far more likely that *Hamlet* was given for the first time at Kean's benefit, late in the season, and in any case Kean's identity and talents had been established on the opening night in *The Mountaineers.* There seem to be only two ways of explaining this review: either it is a fabrication for some unknown motive, or else it comes from a provincial newspaper of some other town which, perhaps because the first sponsor had it only as a clipping, was assigned by guess to the wrong place.

Kean's sojourn in Guernsey, then, seems to have been not unlike his sojourns in other towns. Yet, although it contained none of the startling disagreements with which it has been decorated, still there are grounds for believing common report to be right in saying that all did not go well. On two occasions at least Kean had to make public apology for failure to appear on nights when he was billed. Also he is reproved more than once for listless acting. As to the causes of such lapses the press says nothing, but tradition lays them to drink. Proc-

[21] The opening sentence points in that direction. "Last night a young man whose name the bills said was Kean made his first appearance as Hamlet," etc. And the whole tenor of the review clearly relates to a first appearance.

ter's story may not be true, that Kean greeted his wife on her arrival with the jubilant announcement, "I can get brandy here for eighteen-pence a bottle—I can drink it instead of beer!" But the fact stated was true, and one may be sure, without adventuring too far in the direction of pure fancy, that a hard drinker in England would be a harder drinker in Guernsey.[22] It is not at all unlikely that Procter is right in stating that Kean's habitual drunkenness and his consequent irregularities at the theatre so displeased the citizens of St. Peterport that he fell into their bad graces, with disastrous effect on his benefit. Nor is it improbable that, as Procter says, he quarreled with Hughes and refused to go with the company when it quit the island. The two men are said to have fallen out over *The Royal Oak*, in which Kean was cast as Charles I so much against his will that on the night of performance he lay perdu in a tavern, sending Hughes a message that "King Charles had been beheaded on his way to the theatre;" then in his exalted state entered a box and roared sarcastic applause at Hughes, who was sweating through the part. The story is the same at which I have glanced in connection with Exeter. I hazard no opinion on it.

There was one bit of off-stage comedy, however, played in Guernsey of which we are given an imperfect glimpse in the press. Among the company was a temperamental Irishman, William Henry Halpin Hamilton, to give him his full titles, who must have cut quite a dash among the local belles, judging by the number of poems he sent to the newspapers addressed "To ———." On one occasion he turned his talents at verse in another direction. The *Star* of June 29 carried an *Epistle, addressed to N. I. H.-Esq.*, which is a satire in heroic couplets aimed at some critic (not N. I. H.) who had dispraised the comedian.

> Damn'd as an actor, by a school boy's frown!
> Who tears the budding laurels from my crown!!

And so on. There is no need to repeat the whole of it.

[22] Mr. Marquand had it from his father that on one occasion, when Hughes came forward to announce the "unavoidable" absence of Kean, someone called out, "Search the public houses." On this hint the fugitive was found, but he was so drunk that he had to be supported through his part. The incident may be apocryphal, but that such a tradition lingers in Guernsey is not without interest.

This charge seems to have called forth a counter attack, which in turn drew from the aggrieved Hamilton a long letter in the *Mercure et Publiciste* of July 3. Inasmuch as the opening paragraph of the copy I examined has been clipped away, it is impossible to say exactly what the counter attack was, or from whom it came, but various hints given in the body of the letter make it clear that it was in the form of a searing letter or article, and that it was made in reply to the *Epistle.* "My poetic insertion of Tuesday," so runs the closing paragraph, "was aimed against critics in general, and I began with the only one that ever assailed me." But the most interesting part of the letter touches on Kean, who seems in some way to have got embroiled.

My *"ill conduct"* towards Mr. Kean, has, I am aware, been very industriously whispered about. I am glad you mentioned it, for it gives me an opportunity of refuting the charge. Those busy fly-flaps, those ephemeral gnats styling themselves "Anonymous," must ever be considered a public evil by rational men—they render even our friends the object of suspicion, and that suspicion I had as much right to attach to Mr. Kean as to any other person. Our correspondence *was* perfectly "civil," and a challenge *was* the result—but I had previously communicated to Mr. Kean my notion of that courage which distinguishes a *man* from a *brute,* and my reply was this—"Mr. Kean knows my opinion of courage, consistently with that opinion I cannot *meet* him—he is at liberty to attack me and I pledge my honor that no legal advantage shall be taken—I will resent his blows to the last, but I will not *meet* him." I am extremely sorry that I never received your thundering message, but I assure you that I never heard you named but by accident, and that by another gentleman of the Company; so that I am free from the uncandid, illiberal and dishonorable crime of betraying your trust.

From this it appears that some hostility, probably founded in jealousy, existed between Hamilton and Kean, which would have passed from words to blows if Hamilton, with a true Pistolian flourish, had not played the man's part against the brute's, and that the unnamed adversary, who would seem to have been friendly to Kean, had made allusion to it. Thus the irritated feelings of all parties escaped into vocal and harmless wind. But before the quarrel died Hamilton, in the *Star* of July 6, addressed a letter "To the Public," in which he charges his *"good friend* 'Anonymous,'" with having circulated a false report "that in consequence of my letter of Saturday last, he had met me in the streets, collared me, and shook his cane in my face." The wits of Guernsey must have made oblation to their gods for the presence of William Henry Halpin Hamilton.

The circumstances under which Kean left Guernsey have been variously and vaguely reported. Certain it is that he did not accompany Hughes at the close of the season, but whether the cause was a quarrel or unpaid debts it is impossible to tell. The chances in either case are that he would be left penniless, so that there is reason for believing the common story that he raised the necessary money by giving one of his family recitals at the Assembly Rooms.[23] It is said that Sir John Doyle, governor of the island, and other notables were patrons on this occasion.[24]

23 Now part of the Guille-Allés Library.

24 The account of Kean's wanderings up to this point is, of course, incomplete from lack of information. Particularly interesting is it to note that at Guernsey he was announced as "from the Theatre Royal, Dublin," and more than once, in letters and bills, he spoke of having played in Edinburgh. But I have found no verification for either place and am unable even to guess when he may have been there. An old tradition has it that he played Hamlet in Edinburgh with great success in his very early days.

CHAPTER IV

OPPORTUNITY

ONE would like to be able to follow every step of Kean's movements from his leaving Guernsey, for we are now approaching that change of fortune which has scarcely its equal in the annals of the theatre and the intervening months are filled with torments beyond anything which the unlucky pair has experienced thus far. But although the way is made a little clearer by Mary Kean's letters, too much still remains dark.

Early in September we find them again in Exeter; at least Mary and the children are there, for Kean has gone to London—with what end in view we can only guess, possibly to launch another vain assault on the entrenched managers. That his situation was desperate may be guessed from the fact that he deserted his family, left them without a penny, to pick up a living as best they could. From her refuge with Miss Hake, feather maker, with whom they had lodged during their former stay in Exeter, Mary Kean directed a forlorn letter to her friend Miss Roberts.[1]

My Dear Margaret — Exeter Septr 5th 1813

after two years of severe trouble I once more address you. When last I wrote to you my letter I know displeased you. I wrote hasty, but Heaven is my witness, my Heart was pure—that has never err'd. Misery gave a quickness to my words that should not be. You knew not *all my sufferings.* Poverty I bore & could have borne with patient resignation to the will of the Almighty. I know not whether Susan has read you, or sent you, any of my letters. My first step to Misery was going on the stage. My character I preserved pure and unsullied, I then married, my Husband possessed of every Talent requisite for his profession, educated to give grace to that talent; and could he have endured patiently a little longer, Fortune might have rewarded his very great abilities. To forget sorrow he first took to Drinking—every dissipation follow'd of course. His Nights were spent with a Set of wretches a Disgrace to Human nature. One step lead on to another, till ruin, inevitable ruin was the end. I am now with two Lovely Boys pennyless, friendless. He is gone to London.

[1] Printed by W. J. Lawrence in the Dublin *Evening Mail,* Sept. 30, 1912.

Disease on Disease has ruin'd my Health—I cannot act, none will engage one incapable of supporting a line of business. What can I do. I have written to my Dear Sister—and my Dear Margaret will you advise me. Heartbroken I write to you. You have been my *Sister*, my FRIEND, I never had a thought concealed from you. Wild in ideas—my imagination warm in my favorite project—now pining in Misery—I can boast of nothing but a Heart & character unsullied—nothing to blush for, but my Misery. I write to you, Dear Margaret, for advice, shall I say for assistance. Could you send me the smallest trifle. Do not I beg of you be offended. If I could get to Ireland could I, think you, get my Bread in any way whatever. I wish to preserve my children off the Stage. Howard is wonderfully clever, but could I make them good clerks, they might, if they grow up with the Dispositions they have at present help me in my old age. Could I, think you, keep a little School? I want nothing but a bare subsistence—my tears blind me—you cannot read this. Will you write by return, tell me of my Sister, my Mother. Oh my Dear Margaret, could I be near you & my Sister, could I end my Days in peace, see my children able to assert their own [talents],[2] then if it pleased the Almighty [I care not] how soon I slept in quiet. Do not de[lay] my Dr. Margaret, write I pray by return. If you can send me a trifle I know your Heart—but write at all events—make me happy by hearing from you, & tell me what you would advise. I know your Distresses—I know all you have had to encounter, at least I think I may guess it. My best Love to all y[r] Sisters, & believe me, Dr Marg[t], your sincere & affect[e] Mary Kean

Direct for me, Miss Hake, Feather Maker, No 211 Fore Street Exeter.

From her next letter (to her sister[3]) we learn that in her distress she used the only asset she had, the talents of her boy Howard, that meanwhile she left Exeter for some unmentioned town, and that in response to her frantic letters Edmund returned from London. He found himself a place, probably with Henry Lee, the manager of a small circuit centered upon Taunton in Somerset.[4] This Lee was a man who, for his oddities of character, stood out among his fellow managers, themselves a group of odd characters. His chief claim to

2 A few words have been torn away with the seal.

3 See page 101.

4 Procter has him playing an engagement of four nights at Teignmouth for a Mr. Fisher, some confirmation for which occurs in Kean's letter to Drury. See Appendix II, page 358.

glory and the constant theme of his lamentations was that Colman the Younger had stolen Caleb Quotem, in *The Review*, from one of his own comedies. He was fat but without the phlegm which usually goes with fatness, mercurial, taken with odd fancies, like all his fellow managers a master of chicane but a clever actor in certain rôles and expert in the trick of making sixpences do the work of pounds. Furthermore, and this is more to the point in the present case, he carried beneath his vast waistcoat a kindly heart.

The month of October was spent in Barnstaple in Devonshire. Of this engagement I have found one bill,[5] a *de luxe* edition, so to speak, printed on silk, so interesting in relation to the Kean family and so characteristic of provincial pomp and circumstance, that I reproduce it in full. The reader will notice that Master Howard is again headlined, and in the same *ballet d'action* in which he had performed in Guernsey.

Under the Patronage of
MAJOR ELRINGTON
and
OFFICERS OF THE DEPOT,

The Pupil of Nature
MASTER HOWARD KEAN!!!
Will make his First and only Appearance, in the Barnstaple Theatre,
For the Benefit of
MRS. KEAN.

On Thursday, October 28, 1813
Will be presented the admired Tragedy of
VENICE PRESERVED;
Or, A Plot Discovered.
JAFFIER, MR. KEAN.

Bedamar, Mr. Hewitt	Elliot, Mr. Whitlock	
Priuli, Mr. Hallam	Renault, Mr. Lloyd	Belvidera, Mrs. Kean
Spinosa, Mr. Hearn	And Pierre, Mr. LEE	

[5] In the collection of Messmore Kendall, of New York (formerly the Houdini collection).

End of the Play, a serious Ballet in one Act, performed only in the
Theatres of Paris, Lisbon,
and the King's Theatre London, called
CHIRON and ACHILLES.
(Got up by *Mr. Kean*, with particular attention.)
Aided by appropriate Dresses, Music, &c.
The Part of Achilles by Master Kean,
(a Child of Three Years old)
Chiron, *Mr. Kean.*
Centaurs, Messrs. Hallam, Hewitt, Willis, Hearn, Lloyd, and Whitlock,
Thetis, Mrs. Brown.
Dancing Nymphs, Miss S. Bence, and Mrs. Hearn. Nereids
attendant on Thetis, by young Ladies and
Gentlemen of the Town.

In the Course of the Pantomime the following peculiar Performances.
An exact representation of the
Group of Centaurs, from the Paintings of Buonoretti.
Celebrated Shawl Dance, (as performed by Madam Parisot, at the King's
Theatre, Haymarket) by Miss S. Bence.
Achilles instructed in the Ancïent Mode of War by Chiron, in which
Master Kean will introduce a Classic Delineation of the
GLADIATOR DE MORI.
Dance by the Nereids.
The Grecian Method of Ambuscade,
Forming in an Instant, from an almost imperceptible motion, Concealment for an Army however considerable.

Mr. Kean will recite Goldsmith's celebrated Epilogue in the Character of
HARLEQUIN.
And will Leap through a Balloon of Real Fire.
[To conclude with the farce of *The Road to Glory.*]

Meanwhile Kean's efforts to get a foothold in London were producing results, though far from what he had most at heart. Robert William Elliston, successful actor and prince of theatrical mountebanks, had about this time acquired possession of the Olympic Theatre in Wych Street and was making preparations to open it for the approaching season. It is quite possible that Kean, on hearing of the new venture, had dashed off to London to see if he could not find a place in it. Indeed Mary Kean leads one to think so.[6] However that may be and whatever may have been the *pourparlers* in London, it was October before Kean received a definite offer from Elliston. The following letter[7] of acceptance was written from Barnstaple on October 2:

Barnstable Oct. 2nd 1813

Sir | I have this moment rec'd your proposals for the Wych Street Theatre, id est, Little Drury,[8] & much lament your letter not finding me, as a neglect of answering, must have appeared negligent or abrupt which failing I do not rank in the Catalogue of my follies.
the terms Miss Tidswell, by your authority mentions to me is the Superintendence of the Stage business, the whole of the principle *Line of business*!!! & an equal division of the House, on the night of the benefit, with three guineas per week allotted as salary.
these terms I own do not bring my expectations to a level with the respectability of the establishment, but I place so firm a confidence in your reported liberality, that on the proof of my humble abilities & assiduity towards the general promotion of the business you will be inclined to increase it, *that I accept your present proposals,* simply requesting you to name the extent of the Services expected from me & what time you expect me in London (be kind enough to allow me as much as possible, as I am making out the time very profitably) I stay here three weeks shall be glad to hear from you immediately

Yours Obediently
E Kean.

What such a decision meant, none knew better than Kean. It meant the surrender of all his dearest hopes. Under the conditions of monopoly which existed in London the legitimate drama, from Shakespeare to Monk Lewis, was the jealously guarded prerogative of the two great patent houses for the winter season and of the Haymarket for the summer. Repeated efforts on the part of the minor theatres had

[6] See her letter, page 102.

[7] First printed by George Raymond in *Life and Enterprises of R. W. Elliston,* London, 1857, but condensed and garbled. The original is at Harvard.

[8] The new name which Elliston gave to his theatre. It reverted before long to the Olympic.

not been able to break that tenacious hold. The repertory of the Olympic must be restricted to burlettas, musical farces, operettas, pantomimes, ballets, and melodramas. At the Olympic, Kean could play Chimpanzee and Count Belino but not Shylock or Richard. Moreover, to close with Elliston meant the death blow to his chances at Drury Lane or Covent Garden, whose managers looked to Bath, Dublin, and Liverpool for their recruits, or to almost any provincial house rather than to the minor theatres at their doors. Only the despair of fruitless struggle and the pressing need of the moment could have moved him to such an action.

According to a statement made later by Kean, Elliston on October 8 returned to the Barnstaple letter an evasive reply, saying that he was uncertain when he would be able to open his theatre and inviting Kean to write him again within a month.

Meanwhile an important correspondence in quite different quarters was under way. Dr. Joseph Drury, headmaster at Harrow, amateur of the theatre, and a close friend of several of the managing committee at Drury Lane, had become aware of the excellences of Kean during his summer residence near Exeter. Indeed so forcibly was he impressed that sometime in September he urged Pascoe Grenfell, a member of the committee, to bring the provincial player to the attention of Drury Lane. Three items of the ensuing correspondence are preserved at Harvard. On October 3, the day after Kean's letter to Elliston, Grenfell wrote to some unnamed person who may have been a fellow committeeman or perhaps Arnold, the Drury Lane manager, to the effect that he had recently been in company where a young actor was extravagantly praised; that he was especially impressed by the words of Dr. Drury and thought, therefore, that he might be worth trying; and that, as he had forgotten the man's name, he had written to Mrs. Drury to find out. With his letter he enclosed a note from Mrs. Drury, dated September 30, saying that "The name of the actor recommended so strongly by Dr. D—— to Mr Grenfell is Kean." The "tip" was duly communicated to the powers of Drury Lane.

Now it so happened that the affairs of that great institution had been going none too well, as we shall see more fully in the next chapter. Patronage, always a fickle quantity, had fallen from bad to worse; the previous year had ended in a deficit; the new year had opened wretchedly; the company finances were in bad shape, nor was there anything in the prospects of the new season that promised a happier outcome. Something must be done to lure back the indifferent public, but what? Something could be done with a new pantomime, much could be done with a new dramatist, but a new actor, if he were lucky enough to hit the popular taste, could do still more. And of all three expedients a new actor was the cheapest. It cost only a few pounds to bring him out, and if he failed, as most likely he would, he could be quickly sent off again. Therefore, when the Honorable Pascoe Grenfell, backed by the respectable word of Dr. Drury, proposed that a young fellow in Dorset be looked over, the committee paid attention. Indeed, their plight being what it was, they could not afford to do otherwise. And so the proper machinery was set into motion.

Meanwhile Drury wrote to Kean, apprising him of the step which he had taken. The effect we can easily imagine. Here at last was opportunity knocking at the door; the chilly guardians of old Drury were taking counsel; forgotten were Wych Street and the tempestuous Elliston, or remembered only with distaste; hope sprung awake again, in a fever of impatience. But the machinery of large concerns moves slowly, especially when it is driven by a committee of gentlemen amateurs. October dragged on without anything being done. Finally, at the end of the month, Kean's fraying nerves drove him to write to his patron, who was then at Cockwood, in Devonshire.

October 29th 1813
Theatre Barnstable

Sir | the state of suspence I have been in on account of my poor little boy, who has just recovered from a most alarming illness prevented me from the pleasure of addressing you before with a heart fill'd with anxiety, I now request the Issue of your kind application to the Proprietors of the Drury Lane Theatre, if Sir, soliciting your advice wou'd not be deemed intrusive I wou'd learn whether a personal application to Mr Whitbread aided by the powerful influence of Dr Drury's recommendation wou'd not be more serviceable than distant correspondence, I have offers from Mr

Elliston, for a new theatre in Wich Street, his proposals are by no means advantageous, & the nature of the entertainments I am afraid, detrimental to the reputation of a Dramatic actor, it is however a reserve in case of the failure, of the more desirable point. I leave Barnstable for Dorchester on Wednesday or Thursday next (where I play six nights) I need not say how proud I shall feel by the favor of a line from you—in the meantime Sir allow me to thank you for all the flattering marks of attention I have rec'd from you which must be ever foremost in my remembrance & with sincere respect I sign myself

Yours Obediently

E Kean

Revd Dr Drury

This appeal seems to have spurred Drury to a renewal of effort. On November 7 he writes to someone in authority at Drury Lane (probably Mr. Whitbread) that he has that same day sent word to Kean, now at Dorchester, desiring him to notify the present correspondent when he can be in London for an interview. Mr. Grenfell has offered to introduce him to Mr. Arnold. "Mr. Kean is a stranger to me,"[9] the Doctor continues, but having followed him in several rôles he is convinced of his ability. But for some reason Kean was not sent for to London; instead manager Arnold was dispatched, on a reconnoitering party, to Dorchester, where he arrived on the fifteenth of November.

In view of the fact that Kean was from the beginning aware of these important councils, it may seem strange that just at the time when everything was moving as favorably as possible at Drury Lane he should have again closed with Elliston. But from an ironic whim of chance Drury's letter to Kean, written also on November 7, did not reach its destination until the thirteenth. Meanwhile poor Kean had fallen into a state of discouragement far more acute than his letter of October 29 gave expression to. One gathers that Drury, with the best intentions, had prudently refrained in his correspondence from raising too lively an expectation of success in the Drury Lane negotiations; had in fact leaned so far backward that the unhappy actor, fretted by the weeks of delay and his pressing necessities, began to look on the whole business as just another pricked bubble. And he

[9] A significant declaration. It disposes of all the stories of Drury's friendly interest in the boy Carey—if indeed they need further disposing.

felt desperately the need of doing something, for his darling Howard was gravely ill, his wife was mad with fear and wretchedness, and his engagement with Lee at Dorchester was drawing near a close. So in November 11 he wrote again to Elliston declaring his readiness to join the Wych Street company as soon as he should have finished with Lee. Two days later came the delayed letter from Dr. Drury bringing the unbelievable news that he was as good as engaged at Drury Lane, and on the following day came manager Arnold, doubtless to learn why no answer had been returned to his friendly overtures.

The memorable proceedings of November 15 at the Dorchester Theatre were a favorite subject of reminiscence with Kean. Granting that the story lost nothing in the telling, the assured facts render the occasion one of the great moments in the lives of the players. Kean was depressed; his favorite boy, Howard, lay seriously ill, he had closed with Elliston and thereby had shut the gate on his dreams of glory, circumstance had beaten him. Therefore, he entered without enthusiasm upon the part of Octavian. But soon he noticed, easily distinguishable among the sparse provincial audience, an unprovincial gentleman in a stage box, who, without applauding, lent an attentive and understanding ear to the doings on the stage. The artist, perceiving the connoisseur, braced himself to his best. At the close of the play, while dressing for Kojah in *The Savages* under the stage, he heard the stranger questioning Lee as to the identity of the little man and Lee bragging right loyally—"a wonderful clever fellow; a great little man."—"But he is very small."—"His mind is large."—When Kean returned above ground the stranger introduced himself as Arnold of Drury Lane. "I staggered as if I had been shot," Kean used to say. "My acting in *The Savages* was done for. However, I stumbled through the part," and then he rushed home to tell Mary.[10]

[10] In the Houdini-Kendall collection is a Dorchester playbill for this night, Monday, November 15, 1813. Although the company is the same as at Barnstaple, announcement is made that Mr. Kean has been engaged at "a considerable expense," an advertisement which, though probably mendacious, shows that Kean had something of a reputation in those parts. The bill consisted of *The Mountaineers* and *The Savages*. A note written in ink declares it to be the self-same bill used by Arnold, inherited by his son and purchased by T. A. Lacy in 1868.

THEATRE, DORCHESTER.

Mr. LEE presents his respects to his Friends and the Public in general, and begs leave to inform them that his best exertions will be used to render the amusements of the Theatre worthy their attention and patronage. In addition to his regular Company, he has engaged for SIX NIGHTS (at a considerable expence) Mr. KEAN, whose abilities have been honored with applause in most of the Theatres Royal in the Kingdom.

On MONDAY EVENING, 15th of NOVEMBER, 1813,

Will be presented the admired TRAGEDY, of the

Mountaineers,

Count Virolet, ... Mr. HEWITT,
Sadi, ... Mr. WILLIS,
Kilmallock, ... Mr. HALLAM,
Bulcazin Muley, ... Mr. LLOYD,
Roque, ... Mr. CLIFFORD,—Ganem, ... Mr. HEARN,

The Part of Octavian by Mr. KEAN,

Zorayda, ... Mrs. CLIFFORD,—Floranthe, ... Mrs. HEARN,
And Agnes, ... Miss BENCE.

The celebrated Song of the 'BRITANNIA' by Mr. CLIFFORD.

A Favorite SONG by Miss BENCE.

A COMIC SONG by Mr. WILLIS.

After which a New PANTOMIMICAL BALLET (got up under the Direction of Mr. KEAN) called the

SAVAGES,

Or, LOVE and HATRED.

Kojah (Husband to Illa) Mr. KEAN.—Yaspedo (a Rival Savage) Mr. HERBERT LEE,
Pomatowski .... Mr. WILLIS.
Koah (his confederate) .... Mr. LLOYD.
Scampowtoo, ... Mr. HEWITT.
Dominapaw, ... Mr. CLIFFORD.—Wamptum, ... Mr. HEARN.
And Nigero, ... Mr. HALLAM.
Illa, (Wife to Koja) .... Miss S. BENCE.—Oro, ... Mrs. BROWN.
Umbo, ... Miss THOMAS.—And Coba, ... Mrs. HEARN.

In the course of the PANTOMIME the following performances,

A SAVAGE PAS DE TROIS,

By Mr. KEAN, Miss BENCE & Miss S. BENCE,

Desperate Combats, &c. &c.

With Bamboo, Battle-Axe, Shield, and Broadsword.

The Savage Dance of Peace,

As described by the celebrated Circumnavigator, CAPTAIN COOK.

☞ Doors open Half past Five, begin Half past Six o'Clock.

BOXES, 3s.—PIT. 2s.—GALLERY. 1s.—Second Account, Half past Eight—BOXES, 2s. PIT, 1s. 6d.

Days of Performing, Mondays, Wednesdays, and Fridays.

G. Frampton, Printer, adjoining the County Hall, Dorchester.

This is the identical bill obtained by Mr. Arnold when he went to the Theatre to see Kean act — prior to his engagement for Drury Lane — sold by his son and purchased by T. H. Lacy — 1860

THE "ARNOLD" PLAYBILL, DORCHESTER
NOVEMBER 15, 1813

Arnold stayed a day or two longer, saw him play *Alexander the Great,* then talked with him graciously and with a nice warmth of praise, representing "in the language almost of a parent" how unwise it was for a new actor to risk the trial of London under the handicap of a large salary, and finally offering an engagement of three years at the advancing rate of eight, nine, and ten pounds a week. The feelings with which Kean listened to the angelic messenger can easily be guessed. Triumph was dominant. At last the citadel of Drury had capitulated, the drawbridge was down, the portcullis raised, and the committee, bearing laurels, advanced smiling to receive him. What mattered the terms of payment? Eight pounds was riches to a man who would have gone for three. The thought of Elliston must have been somewhere in his mind, but without much sense of guilt attending on it. Was he really engaged by Elliston? That gentleman had never said so. And anyway, one could always get out of an engagement.

He closed with Arnold unhesitatingly, one must admit unscrupulously, without mentioning the negotiations with Wych Street. Here no doubt he committed a tactical error; had he spoken of Elliston, explaining the whole confusing situation, Arnold might have helped him get clear of his entanglements. Yet, on the other hand such was the jealousy between London managers, he might have broken off negotiations at once: "I am sorry to hear that you have closed with Mr. Elliston, but such being the case you must expect nothing further from Drury Lane. Sir, I bid you good day." Rather than be blasted with words such as these he chose to keep his own counsel and thereby, when the truth came out, gravely offended Arnold and the rest of the Drury Lane management. One need not waste much sympathy on Elliston. He may indeed have counted Kean among his forces for the coming season, but in his characteristic way he had shilly-shallied so vexingly and kept his intentions so dark that Kean had reason to plead that he did not know whether he had been taken or not. Nevertheless, Kean was technically in his power, for he could display a fairly definite offer and two very definite letters of acceptance. On that evidence he could, and did, accuse Kean of bad faith. And bad faith in fact there was, only it was against Drury Lane rather than

Elliston. The hullabaloo that the Little Napoleon of Wych Street raised has a ring of virtuous insincerity, like a clamor among pots and kettles.

On November 19 Kean wrote to Elliston:

Sir,—Since I last wrote to you, I have received a very liberal offer from the proprietors of Drury Lane Theatre. It gives me unspeakable regret that the proposals did not reach me before I had commenced negotiating with you; but I hope, sir, you will take a high and liberal view of the question when I beg to decline the engagement for Little Drury. Another time I shall be happy to treat with you.

But Elliston was instantly certain that he wanted Kean, that he had engaged him and would keep him. And to that effect he made reply. The tug-of-war had begun.

On the twenty-first Kean wrote a letter to Drury, full of Latin and protestations of gratitude. In Dorchester, on the twenty-second, Howard died. Both parents, in their different ways, were wracked by the loss, for Howard was the apple of their eyes. Mary nursed a grief that ate like cancer, with never-ending pain. Edmund, manlike, eased his pain with cursing, drinking, and frenzied walks into the country. Mary sat at home with the three curls she had cut from her boy's head and wept tears that brought her no relief—wept for the six years of married wretchedness, wept for the blank future years, wept because the golden curls had changed color before death. With the pride of her *petit-bourgeois* class she insisted on burying her son in the best style they could manage. The coffin was "handsome, an angel bearing an infant." Four girls in white carried it, others, also in white, strewed flowers. Into the grave of Howard went something of both the parents which never came out again. Kean, it seems, never transferred to his second son the pride and affection that he bore toward his first, but Mary turned to her remaining boy as the one solace left in the general ruin of her life.

Howard was buried on the twenty-fourth of November. Early in December Kean was in lodgings at 21 Cecil Street, Strand, thanks to a good-natured loan from manager Lee. He had come down, posthaste, to fulfill his engagement with Drury Lane. And at first everything was propitious; Arnold received him with smiles and he was paid his first week's salary of £8. But the complexion of affairs soon changed for the bad when news came from Wych Street of his bargain with Elliston. The high Drury Lane powers were angry. Arnold, who had been so friendly and so fatherly at Dorchester, now looked coldly upon him. "Young man," said he, "you have acted a strange part in engaging with me, when you were already bound to Mr. Elliston." The young man explained as best he could, but how was he to explain away those two unequivocal letters of acceptance which were in Elliston's hands? And after all, he could not say that Elliston had *rejected* him. The managers and owners of Drury Lane felt aggrieved, they felt that they had been put upon by the little scoundrel of a provincial Garrick, they dropped a curtain of offended reserve between them and him, and they ordered the treasurer not to pay him his salary. Poor Kean was desperate. His financial quandary, acute as it was, he no doubt felt less than the mockery of having that prize, of which he had dreamed long years, snatched from him at the moment it was within his grasp. He launched appeal after appeal at the flinty heart of Elliston. Thus on the sixth of December:

Sir,—The fate of my family is in your hands. Are you determined to crush the object that never injured you? . . . Through your means I am deprived of my situation in Drury Lane Theatre, unless I produce a document from you that I am not a member of the New Olympic. How can you reconcile this more than Turkish barbarity? . . . You have become a thorn in the side of my young fortune. I shall conclude by simply requesting you to inform me whether I am to become a member of the Theatre Royal, Drury Lane, or again, penniless, hopeless, and despised, am I to be cast again in the provinces, the rejected of this great city, which should afford a home to industry of every kind. With my family at my back will I return, for the walls of Wych Street I will never enter.

To this demand, for it can scarcely be termed a plea, Elliston replied in a tone of indignant surprise:

To any man with the smallest gift of intellect and the dimmest sense of honour, it must appear that on the 11th of November, and previous to that time, you deemed yourself engaged to me, and that subsequently a more attractive offer having been made, you held it convenient to consider a pledge as idle as words muttered in a dream. All my engagements are made and fulfilled with honour on my part, and I expect an equal punctuality from others.

He was between the devil and the deep sea. On the one hand the Drury Lane managers refused to employ him unless he could show a release from Elliston, on the other they warned him that if he played in any other London theatre they could bring an action at law against him. He wrote to the proprietor, Whitbread, who prudently "knew nothing of the matter;" he wrote to Drury, who urged him to "bear all, bear all, only come out." During his days he loitered about the precincts of Drury Lane, where the actors snubbed him and laughed among themselves at his figure and the huge capes under which he buried himself. Day after day the odd little man hung silently about, pathetic, ridiculous, and grimly tenacious. At other times he pursued Elliston, who, as proprietor of the Wych Street Theatre in London proper and of the Surrey across the river, was continually bustling from place to place and never could be found. Nor when found would he give anything but a torrent of words. At length a meeting was arranged between Arnold, Elliston, and Kean. But it turned into a monody from the Wych Street manager, who scarcely gave space for Arnold to slip in a word and roared the culprit actor into defeated silence. When the storm had subsided, Arnold stated his position in no comforting terms, namely, that Kean was undoubtedly a member of Drury Lane and could be sued for breach of contract if he should play at any other theatre. And with this the conference ended.[11]

The deadlock lasted two weeks. Then, just before Christmas, Elliston suddenly yielded to a compromise, by which an actor was to be supplied him from Drury Lane at a salary of £2, to be paid by Kean. The penalty seemed to the culprit to be a severe one, but it was that or nothing and he consented. Christmas in this year fell on Saturday, and Friday was pay day. The most important thing to him now was his salary. But before the warrant would be issued he must get from Elliston a signed release, and by this time it was Friday morning.

From ten till three [so he wrote to Drury], I was employed in running east, west, north, and south of this great city, after Mr. Elliston. At three,

[11] For the full text of Kean's long letter to Drury concerning his disputes with Elliston and Arnold, see Appendix II.

I fortunately encountered him at the Surrey theatre, and received from his own hands the required document; and hastened immediately, overcome by fatigue and anxiety, to Mr. Arnold . . . For nearly one hour I waited in the passage with the rest of the menials of the theatre—had the mortification of seeing them all conducted to his presence before myself; and when summoned at last to appear, was, with the continued brow of severity, informed that I had no claim upon the treasurers. My engagement had all to begin again.

Evidently the culprit was to be severely disciplined. Nor was he paid the following week, for on January 6 Kean wrote to manager Lee:

My business is not yet settled. Dr Drury is determined to try his interference. & has come to London for that purpose. Saturday next determines my fate—when I assure you, that I have rec^d but one weeks Salary since I have been in London, you may well conceive I have not one pound (or even shilling) in my possession.

What further obstacle postponed a settlement, after the trouble with Elliston had been adjusted, is not explained. Presumably the visit of energetic and kind-hearted Drury bore its expected fruit. What would Kean have done without him?

And how had he lived for four weeks and more in London on the one week's salary and the five pounds that Lee had lent him? Procter says that the family was fed by the Misses Williams with whom they lived, and Kean bears this out when he speaks of "the generosity of strangers, in whose house I had by accident taken apartments." Meanwhile Mary sat at home, weeping for sorrow over her boy Howard and for despair over her present fortunes. Having no friend in London in whose company to ease her stuffed bosom, she overflowed to her distant sister.[12]

[21 Cecil Street, Strand]
Dec^br 26th 1813

My Dearest Sister,

Sad & Melancholy ever is my theme to be at this happy season, while thousands are revelling in Luxury. I with many other forlorn ones, shed the tear of Misery—*no hope now—no, no resource*—cold, cold in the Earth is that jewel that was my only consolation. But to tell my tale. I know not, Dear Susan, whether I mentioned that Mr Elliston had about 3 months ago engaged Edmund to be Stage Manager to a little theatre he meant

[12] Printed by W. J. Lawrence in the Dublin *Evening Mail*, Sept. 30, 1912.

to open in the stile of Sadlers Wells. He was to give him 3 pound a Week —it was not to open till Christmas. Out of a situation & in great Distress—very reluctantly he accepted it, knowing he could never get into either of the great Theatres after muming there; but not seeing any other resource, came up to town, left me, as I before mentioned, without one farthing. I wrote Madly to you—left Exeter—but I had a GEM in my possession that got me a livelihood. Oh, Dear Susan, tell me I have no sin to answer for in exposing his innocence, his angel form, to gain a dinner for his parent —the thought sometimes harrows up my soul. But to go on. I wrote to Edmund, he came. Arnold, Drury Lane Manager, hearing so much of him came down, saw him play and engaged him with every prospect of *Success*—of *greatness*—but transient has been our hopes of happiness—for Elliston, when Edmund went to the treasury to get him his sallary, forbid it, said he was engaged to him. The Drury Lane Managers could not bring him out—Lawyers were consulted—Elliston had the prior claim —so here we have been in this great city in expensive Lodgings these three weeks without one sixpence sallary. He can play in neither Theatre without paying a Hundred pound to get clear of one to go to the other. Whitbread, enraged that Edmund should conceal he was engaged to Elliston, has withdrawn his Countenance, in short, Dear Susan, we are now at the very Climax of Misery—*happiness I have never known,* nor do I now feel that sorrow for the loss of it—I *should, a few weeks ago.* My only regret is I am prevented from relieving that Misery I have so often been a Martyr to myself. My poor mother too—I thought her few remaining days would be comfortable. I feel callous to it all—my only pleasure is when I shed tears, *they* relieve me. Miss Tidswell would not come near me or give us one farthing. I am not well enough to go out—or do I know one human being to get employment. However, do not feel uneasy, my Dearest Susan, I can't long bear all this weight of Woe. I would give worlds, my Dear Sister, to see you *once more.* Would you like a lock of my Boy's Hair? *It changed, his Golden* Locks changed very much a few hours before he died. I have 3 Curls. He died November Monday 22nd, & was buried Wednesday 24th, 4 oclock in the afternoon. Your letter was so feeling when you mentioned him that I keep it to read two or three times a day. I have no one to speak of him, his father can't name him—and as I left Dorchester where he is inter'd, as I gave a last look at his grave, my Heart strings cracked—my soul, my happiness lay entombed there. As it was the last expence I was at for him, I had him carried to his last home as well as I could. The people of the house conducted it. His father gave Directions.

His coffin was handsome, an angel bearing an infant, the plate on it—his name and age. I got up to see him carried out. Four girls dressed in white bore his coffin, others, all white, strewing flowers; while *he*, the Loveliest flower, was insensible to all. But no mourners had he—no tear wet his grave. I could not see the earth laid on the sweetest child ever mother had —and his Father was nearly insane. As we took leave of his corpse, his angelic countenance, with that look of his glory and seraphic smile it ever possessed, seemed to say, "Mama I grieve for you—but do not grieve for me—you know not how happy I am." Dear Susan, I am never happy but in writing, or thinking of him—so excuse this letter of blots and tears. I hope you can read it. That I could but see you! Had I money to pay my passage from Bristol I would walk there.

Tho' I know not where I shall be, or where we go—answer this as soon as possible, as I may get it, or it will be sent where I am. Little John is not well—he too is a beautiful Boy but should I lose him—I wish I knew in what manner to earn my Bread or how I could get support. I have no one to apply to, for none will hear me. Oh that Heaven would please to hear me & lay me by my Boy—with my little John.

Miss Chambers (Unsigned)
Coalnamuck,
Lodge,
Carrick on Suir,
Ireland

But while Mary was thus surrendering herself to despair, Edmund, with right instinct, was hanging on like a battered but obstinate bull-dog. Drury kept urging him to "bear all, bear all—only come out." And in the end they won. The committee, which had been flinging one provincial actor after another into the breach only to see them die as promptly as they came forward, turned at last, wearily and without much hope, to the little man from Exeter. If he failed, they were at least rid of him quickly. So on Saturday, January 22, the Drury Lane advertisement in the *Times* carried, in small print among the notices of bills for the next week, a statement that "on Wednesday, Mr. Kean, from the Theatre Royal, Exeter, will make his first appearance at this Theatre as *Shylock* in the Merchant of Venice."

CHAPTER V

TRIUMPH

On the twenty-fourth of February, 1809, Drury Lane theatre had burned to the ground. The ensuing audit revealed an incredible state of insolvency. Since 1778 the theatre had been controlled, had indeed almost been owned, by Richard Brinsley Sheridan, that popular genius famous over the English world for his wit, his parliamentary debates, his debts, and his comedies. As a manager he had been a wonder, in that during the thirty years of his reign he had not gone bankrupt as many times. The most improvident and irresponsible of mortals, he had through sheer effrontery and by pushing his debts in front of him, succeeded, one can scarcely say how, in keeping his expensive ship afloat. A blandly seductive liar, a master of promises he never meant to keep, skilful at postponements, vanishing neatly at ugly crises, he was the despair of all those who had to work under him. About him was a constant clamor of unpaid creditors—tradesmen for furniture sold a year ago, shareholders for their percentages, landlords for rent, actors and managers demanding overdue salaries. Yet the man had loyal followers, who sweated for him while they complained. Certainly no man had been more useful to him than John Philip Kemble, who for fifteen difficult years served as manager and chief tragic actor. Yet in 1798 we find Kemble recording in his notebook that his salary arrears for the last season alone were £363.16.0, and that for antecedent arrears he held Sheridan's bond of £903.18.0. But John Philip's patience had broken at the end of 1802, when he and his great sister had passed over to Covent Garden.

For upwards of forty years the rival patent theatre had been governed by Thomas Harris, a man without any vestige of literary or personal brilliance, who never thought of his playhouse except as an investment, and who by hard business sense and a keen nose for public favor had made a very nice living for himself. He had every quality for direction that Sheridan lacked, and so well did he have his government in hand that when his theatre burned in September of 1808,

DRURY LANE IN 1814

he was able to build and open a new one by September of 1809. But the affairs of Drury were in such chaos that it took nearly two years to find out how they stood. Then when, in October of 1811, a proposal for financing and rebuilding was made, it was disclosed that the total debts of the theatre amounted to half a million pounds, of which more than £50,000 was owing to authors, actors and tradespeople! In the face of this thundering liability Sheridan, bankrupt and broken, gave way. The general direction was turned over to Samuel Whitbread, a wealthy brewer and member of Parliament who might be expected to give the enterprise the business understanding it stood so direly in need of, all claims were settled at twenty-five per cent, new stock was sold, a committee of nineteen among the major stockholders or proprietors was chosen to assist Whitbread, Samuel Arnold was appointed manager, plans for a building were ordered from Benjamin Wyatt, and promptly thereafter work was begun. The new theatre, which with some important revisions of the interior is the one which stands today, opened on October 10, 1812.

It opened grandly, with *Hamlet,* to a capacity audience which brought in the extraordinary sum of £842.[1] Lord Byron read a poetic address, which was not in his best style, to be sure, but was good enough, inasmuch as it added to the general brilliance the presence of the most-talked-of poet in London. All society was there, admiring the handsome new playhouse, the handsome new costumes, the handsome new stage decorations, and the handsome new committee of management. There was much laughter, among the knowing ones, over the vexation of a score or so of bards whose addresses had been invited and then rejected. There was to be more laughter when those bards appealed to the jury of the public by publishing their slighted offspring. The laughter was to rise mightily at the appearance of Horatio Smith's witty parodies of the *Rejected Addresses.* All in all, His Majesty's New Theatre in Drury Lane began to do business under the most favorable auspices of confidence and good nature. For the first fortnight the intake averaged nearly £600 and by the close of that season the receipts had amounted to £75,584. Looking back upon the

[1] How extraordinary, can be judged from the fact that the average intake in average seasons was around £250.

last full season of 1807-8, when the receipts were just under £50,000, Mr. Whitbread and his committee might justly feel that business was very good indeed.

But no public is more fickle than that which goes to the theatre, or more insistent in its demand for novelty. And this ancient truism was brought sharply home to the committee on the opening of the season of 1813-14. For the past year the new theatre and the change in management had sufficed to hold the public fancy, but one year was enough to exhaust that source of attraction. The new season began with all the buoyancy of a deflated balloon. The initial intake, on September 11, of £410, although less by half than that of a year ago, was not too bad. But on the sixteenth the receipts were only £310, on the eighteenth they had fallen to £133, and at the close of the first fortnight the books showed an average of slightly over £250. It was extremely disquieting. Nor did the progress of the season bring encouragement, for although matters did not go worse, they certainly went no better. At this rate the theatre, loaded with a heavy building debt, would go bankrupt. The managers consulted, argued, asked one another what was to be done, and shook their heads unhappily.

From outside, voices of complaint began to be raised. The *Theatrical Inquisitor*, in December, laid the blame on Whitbread's system of economy. The stage is poorly equipped. "The best actors are rejected on a principle of economy, the number of inferior assistants diminished, and their salaries curtailed." The receipts are perhaps as much as £100 below what they would be with a different management, "so that to save £30 they lose £100, that is £70 complete loss to the concern, besides the public being dissatisfied, and the actors oppressed, adding injustice to imprudence, and disappointing all parties, through a mistaken mode of conducting the business." Disapproval also is expressed for the new system of control. "A committee is at all times ill fitted for interfering with such concerns; but when we consider that Mr. Whitbread is a man of regular habits of business, rather stern and rigorous, than yielding to circumstances, it cannot be expected that a concern which never can admit of strict regularity, will flourish under his management." The *Theatrical Inquisitor* here expressed a skepticism which was no doubt shared by all persons of professional experience in the theatre and which the following years were amply to confirm. Committee management of a theatre was folly. And Whitbread, with all his business acumen, was not the man to choose for leader, divided as he was between Parliament and his brewery and inexperienced in those peculiarly temperamental problems of the stage. A man like Thomas Harris was needed, who would give to Drury Lane his whole attention and his years of practical wisdom, but in all London there was no second Harris and certainly no one wanted a second Sheridan.

However, there was the situation, confronting the committee with a grim clarity. Drury Lane had lost favor with the public. Its prosperity of the year before had cut into the receipts of Covent Garden, but now the rival house was having its revenge. Without either Kemble or Siddons (for the great Sarah had retired in June and Kemble was on leave of absence) it was doing a prosperous business which ran well over £400 per night and in which £500 nights were frequent. Company for company, then, Covent Garden was worth £150 per night more to its shareholders than Drury Lane. What was to be done? The causes must be found and remedied.

One cause at least was apparent, that Drury Lane was pitifully weak on the tragic side. In comedy they had Liston and Munden, artists of the first class, but in tragedy they had no one. And, although they tried it, they could not run on comedy alone. At Covent Garden, besides Kemble, were Young and Conway. Charles Mayne Young, a young man of twenty-six, had already developed abilities and a style, based on the classicism of Kemble, which placed him favorably in the public eye and distinguished him as the only tragic actor worthy or likely to fill the shoes of his great master. Conway, though of a quality inferior to Young, was a competent actor, and what is more important to the box office, a very handsome one. In Mrs. MacGibbon, brought down from York, Harris did not indeed find a successor to Siddons, but she was none the less an actress who added appreciably to the strength of the repertory. These three made a strong trio.

Whether or not this lack in tragic strength was their capital weakness, the Drury Lane committee conceived it to be so and began earnestly to peer about among the provincial Hamlets for a man of talent.

Hence they gave attention to the recommendations of Dr. Drury, hence they dispatched Arnold to Dorchester, and hence they summoned Kean to London, just as they were ready to summon anyone for whom a good word had been spoken. But Kean, as we have seen, ran foul of Whitbread's business principles, which, as the *Theatrical Inquisitor* said, were "rather stern and rigorous, than yielding to circumstances." Meanwhile, as he shuttled despairingly between Arnold and Elliston, the country Hamlets came, strutted their hour, and went away, leaving behind them an indifferent public and a committee whose perplexities grew with each failure. So at last the will of one rather absurd little man won against the harassed uncertainties of some thirty men, who, more to be rid of him than with any hopes of success, instructed Arnold to post his name.

The proceedings of the famous twenty-sixth of January are among the dear memories which historians of the theatre love to dwell on. The one rehearsal which was deemed sufficient was called for twelve o'clock. A listless group of actors gathered—Rae, the old acquaintance of Haymarket days, as Bassanio, Powell as Antonio, Wrench as Gratiano, Philipps as Lorenzo, Oxberry as Launcelot Gobbo, Miss Smith as Portia, Mrs. Bland as Jessica. And listlessly, as befitted a routine rehearsal, they ambled through their lines. Even Kean was restrained, for the sole concern at present was to arrange the details of business and this was not the time to extend himself. Nevertheless, some hints of novelty escaped through the formal monotone of his address, some threats that his Shylock would depart from the model to which the genius of Macklin and Cooke had given a sacred authority. Raymond, the acting manager, became alarmed. "It is an innovation; depend upon it, it will never do." "I wish it to be an innovation," rejoined the little man from Exeter, and Raymond, throwing up his hands, consigned the obstinate provincial to his damnation.

The weather that evening is said to have been bad—the air filled with a smoky drizzle and the ground foul with the slush of melting snow. It should, of course, be bad: the great stage manager of fate could hardly overlook so appropriate a setting. Certainly the audience that gathered that night at Drury filled no more than a quarter of the huge auditorium; the gate receipts showed a few shillings over

£164. Neither before nor behind the curtain was there any stir of anticipation. In an obscure dressing room Kean, savagely aloof from the sneers and the shallow compliments of his associates, fitted a black wig over his head. A black wig on the Jew who from the days of Burbage had worn red hair! Eyebrows went higher, but since the little man from Exeter was certainly damned anyway, what did it matter if he was damned in black or red? A few wished him good luck as he made his way to the wings and took his stand in wait for his cue—Drury out of the depths of his faith, Bannister out of his customary good nature, Oxberry because they had been boys together. The curtain rolled up.

Conventionally, and listlessly, Bassanio exposed his love and his poverty to Antonio; with a hollow gaiety Portia chatted with Nerissa over her lovers. Then, marvellously, the atmosphere changed as genius entered upon the scene. "There came on," wrote many years later one of those who had been present, "there came on a small man, with an Italian face and fatal eyes, which struck all." "Three thousand ducats: well—," said the small man. The fatal eyes rested on Antonio: the Italian face was alive with meaning. "I could scarcely draw my breath," Drury told Kean afterwards, "when you first came upon the stage. But directly you took your position and leaned upon your cane, I saw that all was right." And all was indeed as right as right could be. The Shylock he unfolded was seen to be new, and therefore it was interesting; but what was far more important it was seen to be alive, alive with energy, in every muscle, glance, and intonation. The arms and hands were eloquent, the whole face spoke before the words were uttered, the eyes, the marvellous black eyes which were Kean's most precious instrument, darted intelligence. As the familiar lines fell from his lips they seemed to be rediscovered, as though for the first time was revealed their true meaning. Applause began to clatter, marking those passages in which the new energy seemed most happy. The discriminating among his auditors soon noticed a sardonic quality in this Shylock, a fund of contemptuous scorn which ran as a master theme through the varied phases of delineation. At every opportunity it was released, and whenever it was released it startled applause.

> Hath a *dog* money? is it possible
> A *cur* can lend three thousand ducats?

Line after line bit incisively into the hearers' ears. There was something new, something admirable, at every moment. And the by-play—the constantly varying, almost bewildering play of hands, mouth, eyebrows—never except in the memories of those who knew Garrick, had anything been seen like it.

The end of the scene found an audience galvanized into life. But Kean had not yet shown them what he could do. There remained, of course, the trial scene, but especially the great duo with Tubal in which the floodgates of Shylock's passion are opened their widest. Here Kean counted on nailing his victory to the masthead. And he did. No passage in the range of tragedy lay more securely in the fortress of his powers. The volcanic intensity of feeling, the broken utterances, the sudden passages from grief to exultation as Shylock learns alternately of Jessica squandering ducats in Genoa and Antonio's ships lost at sea, were Kean's histrionic specialty, in which, perhaps, he excelled over any other English actor who has lived. The audience lay in the palm of his hand, whooping for joy. "How the devil so few of them kicked up such a row," said Oxberry, who listened from the green room, "was something marvellous." With the trial scene Kean scored again, this time making as much as he could of the sarcastic humor of Shylock and even giving a turn that way to passages which had been stamped by foregone masters as severe or savage. For instance,

> An oath, an oath, I have an oath in heaven:
> Shall I lay perjury upon my soul?

was spoken with sardonic gaiety, and

> I cannot find it [i.e., a surgeon]: 't is not in the bond,

with what the *Examiner* called "a transported chuckle." Towards the end, in the abject abasement of Shylock he manifested a subdued fury, and as he left the stage he shot one last defiant sneer at Gratiano. His was a bitter Jew, unsentimentalized after our modern fashion, who, like his Richard, fought to the very last.

He left the stage the same little man, to outward appearance, that had entered it some two hours earlier, but in reality all the difference in the world lay between them. Probably no one in the theatre besides himself and Dr. Drury realized quite what had happened. Yet

KEAN AS SHYLOCK

that something respectable had happened was clear to all. The absurd little man from Exeter, who for weeks had encumbered the passageways of Drury with his capes and his tragic eyes, had made a hit. In the manner with which his manager and colleagues congratulated him was nothing of the perfunctory. But he pushed by them to his obscure dressing room that he might get as quickly as possible into his street clothes and as quickly as possible to his lodgings in Cecil Street. There sat Mary trembling for news. He burst through the door. "Mary," he cried—the words are embedded too deeply in the Kean tradition to be questioned,—"Mary, you shall ride in your carriage, and Charley shall go to Eton." And then no doubt, with the blissful content of a captain who has come to port after many storms with rich merchandise, they sat down to a hot supper.

In the morning came the newspapers. Only two had sent representatives, the *Morning Post* and the *Morning Chronicle*. The *Morning Post* exhibited a controlled enthusiasm. It spoke of his "marked and expressive countenance," of his "voice deep and sonorous, clear and articulate," which he managed "with infinite address." His opening scene was excellent, in the scene with Tubal his transitions were admirable, and in the trial scene he showed "much intelligence and mastery of his art." His one fault was a too great activity, a too great juvenility of movement. The *Chronicle* had sent William Hazlitt, than whom no critic in London could have been found more inclined by natural bias to sympathize with Kean's style of acting. A passionate lover of the drama, who loved to see Shakespeare acted passionately rather than "correctly," he had long been a rebel against the acknowledged authority of John Philip Kemble and had long deplored the absence of genius from the stage. Kean was to him like an electric shock. He palpitated with delight at discovering that here at last was the genius, the passionate, natural, and skilled tragedian, the Moses who was to lead Shakespeare out of bondage, and he set about proclaiming the joyful news to London.

For voice, eye, action, and expression, no actor has come out for many years at all equal to him.

There have been, he admitted, actors of Shylock more successful in conveying the idea of rigid will and brooding malignity.

But in giving effect to the conflict of passions arising out of the contrast of situation, in varied vehemence of declamation, in keenness of sarcasm, in the rapidity of his transitions from one tone and feeling to another, in propriety and novelty of action, presenting a series of striking pictures, and giving perpetually fresh shocks of delight and surprise—it would be difficult to single out a competitor.

As to pointing out individual beauties of interpretation, the critic professed himself to be helpless

where almost every passage was received with equal and deserved applause.

On the following day (Friday, January 28) he published a long descriptive paragraph about Kean, closing with the iteration that

his performance was distinguished by characteristics which at once fix him in the first rank of his profession.

So far so good. Kean had not indeed leaped into fame overnight—too many newspapers were silent about him, including that important voice, the *Times*—but he had made a hit, he was known, and he was talked about. His next appearance would clinch the matter. In regard to this next appearance some fabulous matter has crept into history. Tom Dibdin is in part responsible. Inasmuch as he was prompter for Drury Lane at this time his reminiscences might reasonably carry authority, yet on this point, as in the case of Michael Kelly, vanity played tricks with his memory. His story is that Kean's success was so inconsiderable

that little notice was taken of it either in or out of the theatre, and for a few days scarcely anything was said respecting him. A necessary, but unexpected change of play, on some occasion, caused the usual question,—"What shall we act?" from the stage-manager: I immediately advised a second appearance of the "new gentleman."

In Hawkins the story takes on a more romantic embellishment, for now it is Lord Byron who comes to the defense of the actor against a committee so incredibly blind that it was on the point of dropping Kean's name from the bills. We are even told the noble gentleman's speech of remonstrance, which can have been obtained in no other way than by a communication with his ghost. As a matter of fact, neither the second appearance of Kean nor the time of it was ever in question. On January 27 the Drury Lane bills, among the announcements of coming plays, carried the note that "Mr. Kean, who performed the part of *Shylock* last night . . . will repeat the character on *Tuesday*," which was repeated on each subsequent bill. It is absurd to suppose that the managers of Drury Lane could not read the most conspicuous of signs. The one thing which might excite surprise is that they did not proclaim an immediate repetition, and we can only suppose that they did not feel secure enough about the new gentleman's favor to interrupt their schedule.

That Kean's success, except with a few, was moderate rather than spectacular is proved by the subsequent receipts for *The Merchant of Venice*. On February 1 the attendance doubled, the intake being a little over £325. This showed a real curiosity as to the new actor, but still the house was far from being full. On February 3 the receipts fell to £203, on the fifth they were £211, on the eighth they dropped to £193, and on the tenth they recovered to £244. There is nothing wonderful in these figures; the most that can be said, in comparing them with the receipts of performances in between, is that Kean was holding his end up. But what they do not show is that Kean's reputation was gaining ground steadily about London. The *Times* had got round to him at last, and on February 4 allowed him its qualified approval.

> We have seldom seen a much better Shylock. If he be inferior to Kemble in those peculiarities which distinguish that great actor, and to Cooke, in the force which he, above most performers, could give to particular passages, he need have no fear of a successful competition with any other man on the stage who attempts the sordid and malignant Jew.

There was a sting in this, because Kemble's Shylock was one of those parts in which the great classicist was not happy, but the *Times*, to whom Kemble was the faultless artist, could hardly be expected to concede his inferiority in any line. Continuing its appraisal of Kean with condescending patronage, the *Times* found that he was "not deficient" in stage business, that his face, although not so strongly marked as one could wish, was expressive, that his conception was good, his gestures natural to the part, and his voice not unsuitable. But whatever was lacking to it of warmth was supplied in full measure by Leigh Hunt's *Examiner,* whose critic[2] rose, like another Hazlitt, to the enthusiasm of discovery. He dwelt, for the greater glory of Kean's soul, on his bodily defects—his insignificant person and his hoarse voice, "somewhat between an apoplexy and a cold." Against such handicaps the artist could delight only "by the display of sheer excellence exposed to the calculating effect of understanding." And he succeeded triumphantly.

> There was an animating soul distinguishable in all he said and did, which at once gave a high interest to his performance, and excited those emotions which are always felt at the presence of genius—that is, at the union of great powers with a fine sensibility. It was this that gave fire to his eye, energy to his tones, and such a variety and expressiveness to all his gestures, that one might almost say "his body thought."

The playbill of February 1 had carried the announcement that *Richard III* was in preparation. The performance took place on Saturday the twelfth. In disclosing himself to the London public Kean ordered his campaign most shrewdly. Shylock made an excellent opening. The part is short and packed with opportunities. Moreover, the Jewish gaberdine served to conceal his low stature, which might have provoked ridicule in any other rôle. Then when the ear of the town had been won and its curiosity aroused, he meant to bring on his show piece by which to dazzle with the display of the full range of his virtuosity. After that he would be ready for the great tests of *Hamlet* and *Othello,* which, if he endured them successfully, would secure him firmly on his throne.

And the campaign worked to perfection. On the evening of February 12 an audience of very respectable size gathered in Drury Lane. The house held a little over £350, certainly not enough to justify the manager's decree that "no orders would be admitted," but enough to show that the town was interested. Moreover, it was not a chance collection of spectators such as had greeted him on the memorable twenty-sixth of January. All the critics, professional and amateur, were there. In a way it was a more formidable test than the first per-

[2] Perhaps Thomas Barnes, who wrote the Parliamentary articles for the *Examiner,* and seems to have covered the theatre during Leigh Hunt's imprisonment in 1813 and 1814.

formance had been because it was a test before connoisseurs. But at least one great obstacle was removed, that of indifference. The audience which assembled for Richard may have retained some doubt as to whether the new actor was all that his admirers said he was, but at least they were prepared for something uncommon. And they got it. The performance was from the first soliloquy to the death a triumph keyed to the pitch of trumpets and hosannas. The little tragedian was in everything he did prodigious. He was the master virtuoso who swept through the gamut of moods, throwing his hearers, with each change, into new ecstasies. His technical dexterity alone was amazing. There was nothing here of the noble dignity, the statuesque poses, the measured declamation of Kemble; here were the thunder and the lightning, here were storms and bursts of sunlight, here were the colors of the rainbow and the terrible shadows of crime and death, here in a word was nature in all her enchanting variety. So, in their own manner, thought the two thousand or more persons in the spectator's benches, who beat their hands together in a continuous rattle of approval and at the end stood up shouting. The little tragedian bowed again, and again, and again. His heart swelled; in two weeks he had made himself king of Drury Lane, the house of Sheridan and Garrick; it was from now on his plaything; Mr. Whitbread and the honorable committee of management would be his obedient servants; he looked benignly over a shaking panorama of hats and handkerchiefs. And in the wings, clad in the robes of the Duchess of York, stood Miss Tidswell. What thoughts passed through the head of the woman of mystery we do not know, but as she stood there watching the investment of—shall we say her son, or her nephew, or merely the boy she birched in the old days?—surely her heart swelled in her bosom also.

The press on the following Monday, with varying emphasis, sustained the triumph. From the *Times*, of course, unqualified approval was not to be expected, but within the limits of its prejudices it did well by the new actor. "He is evidently a player of no ordinary cast, and as from his youth he will not want time for improvement, he is in all probability destined to shine in his profession." He possesses considerable powers of mind and discriminated many difficult passages with judgment. "He excelled in the cutting and sarcastic; but he was not equally fortunate in the loftier darings of the heroic." Finally he is to be praised for imitating nobody and being himself.

The *Morning Post* was more cordial, showing at the same time a just feeling for the weaker aspects of the performance. In its first review, while it pointed to certain scenes as being very fine, it complained that the aspect of the whole was marred by an excessive levity verging on comedy; for example, in the wooing of Ann at the line "I swear, bright Saint, I am not what I am," he "strutted across the stage, rubbing his hands, and laughing in a manner which we could almost venture to compare with that of Mr. Lovegrove in Gobbo." But on attending the next performance the critic found, or professed to find, that the objectionable levity had been toned down. On further examination of the actor in the part, his enthusiasm rose. Of the many fine points he selected three for special mention. One was the play of Kean's features when he is taunted by the little Duke of York. "A finer picture of stifled rage, and affected composure, can hardly be conceived. This is not marked by a grim aside, nor is it accompanied by any theatrical flourish. It is done without effort, and its delicacy constitutes its strength." His exit into his tent, in the last act, was "one of the finest pieces of acting we have ever beheld, or perhaps that the Stage has ever known." The death scene was greatness itself.

But all other flattering noises were drowned in the pæans sung by the *Examiner* and the *Chronicle*. The former was in an ecstasy. "We cannot recollect any performance,—the very finest exhibitions of Mrs. Siddons not excepted,—which was so calculated to delight an audience, and to impress it with veneration for the talents of an actor . . . To go through all his excellences would be to write a pamphlet." The reviewer then gave some excerpts from the pamphlet that might be written and closed with a burst of emotion over the death scene. "We have felt our eyes gush on reading a passage of exquisite poetry, we have been ready to leap at sight of a noble picture, but we never felt stronger emotions, more overpowering sensations, than were kindled by the novel sublimity of this catastrophe." The ardor of Hazlitt fell short of this exuberance, but that was because he carried within him an ideal delineation of the heroes of Shakespeare which perhaps

KEAN AS RICHARD III

only a god among actors could have realized. The defects of Kean were due to that human fallibility to which even the greatest are subjected.

> It is possible [he said], to form a higher conception of this character (we do not mean from seeing other actors, but from reading Shakespeare) than that given by this very admirable tragedian: but we cannot remember any character represented with greater distinction and precision, more perfectly *articulated* in every part . . . If Mr. Kean does not completely succeed in concentrating all the lines of the character, as drawn by Shakespeare, he gives an animation, vigour, and relief to the part, which we have never seen surpassed . . . He gave to all the busy parts of the play the greatest animation and effect. He filled every part of the stage.

His chief fault lay in the very exuberance of his talent, under which he sometimes overwhelmed the part. But none the less Hazlitt found the performance strewn with beauties, the more notable of which he recreated with all the vehemence of his enthusiasm.[3]

[3] The entry of Henry Crabb Robinson in his diary for March 7 is valuable, partly for its descriptive details and partly as giving the intelligent reflections of a man who was biased neither for nor against the actor. He lets us see, as the partisan critics do not, both sides of the picture.

"At Drury Lane, and saw Kean for the first time. He played Richard, I believe, better than any man I ever saw; yet my expectations were pitched too high, and I had not the pleasure I expected. The expression of malignant joy is the one in which he surpasses all men I have ever seen. And his most flagrant defect is want of dignity. His face is finely expressive, though his mouth is not handsome, and he projects his lower lip ungracefully; yet it is finely suited to Richard. He gratified my eye more than my ear. His action was very often that of Kemble, and this was not the worst of his performance; but it detracts from his boasted originality. His declamation is very unpleasant, but my ear may in time be reconciled to it, as the palate is to new cheese and tea . . . His speech is not fluent, and his words and syllables are too distinctly separated. His finest scene was with Lady Anne, and his mode of lifting up her veil to watch her countenance was exquisite. The concluding scene was unequal to my expectation, though the fencing was elegant, and his sudden death-fall was shockingly real. But he should have lain still. Why does he rise, or awake rather, to repeat the spurious lines? He did not often excite a strong persuasion of the truth of his acting, and the applause he received was not very great. Mrs. Glover had infinitely more in the pathetic scene in which she, as Queen Elizabeth, parts from her children. To recur to Kean, I do not think he will retain all his popularity, but he may learn to deserve it better, though I think he will never be qualified for heroic parts. He wants a commanding figure and a powerful voice. His greatest excellencies are a fine pantomimic face and remarkable agility."

Kean was evidently "new cheese" to Robinson; as his palate grew accustomed he liked the actor more and more.

It may be well here to mark those passages which struck all critics into admiration. In the opening soliloquy, at the words

> So lamely and unfashionable
> That dogs bark at me as I halt by them,

Kean pointed at his deformity and gave such a tone to his words that he drew a loud round of applause; and this remained to his death one of his best points. In the wooing of Ann he was fascinating. To use the words of Hazlitt, "he seemed, like the first tempter, to approach his prey, certain of the event, and as if success had smoothed the way before him." The grace of his postures at the beginning of the scene was striking, as he leaned against the proscenium arch awaiting the approach of Ann. In the tent scene of the last act, as he bade his lords good night, he made a sensation by the suggestive power of his byplay, when he stood for a moment drawing lines in the ground with the point of his sword, as though lost in foreboding thought. But all previous successes were dimmed in the radiance of his death, that "sublime" catastrophe which lifted a shouting audience to its feet.

> He fought [it is Hazlitt again who speaks], like one drunk with wounds; and the attitude in which he stands with his hands stretched out, after his sword is taken from him, had a preternatural and terrific grandeur, as if his will could not be disarmed, and the very phantoms of his despair had power to kill.

With the success of *Richard III* Kean became definitely a personality in London and the subject of much drawing-room conversation—argument rather, for his qualifications were the theme of unending disputes which followed the cleavage of that day, between followers of the traditional or classical taste and enthusiasts for the new naturalism. The drift of such debate is well reflected in the diary of Joseph Farington, the painter, who cared little for the theatre himself but knew many people who did, and who received through them echoes of controversy. Thus on March 2 he recorded that "Thomson & Owen spoke to me of the extraordinary talents of Edmund Kean, a new actor in Tragedy, and of his being perfectly *original* in His manner of representing characters," and that "*Wroughton*, an Old Actor, spoke of Him as having much of what *Garrick* possessed."[4] But on March 7

[4] Farington, Joseph, *The Farington Diary*. Edited by James Greig. N. Y. 1927. Vol. VII (June, 1811-Dec., 1814).

he was being told that the actor was "puffed beyond His claim, probably to fill the Drury Lane Theatre which was reduced almost to Bankruptcy." On March 30 Farington had "company to dinner," whose conversation seems to have turned chiefly on the new tragedian and to have been entirely hostile. John Taylor, the journalist, led the attack, declaring in his absolute way, "He is an *Humbug*: His acting is often false, & without anything like classical taste. He is a *Pot-House* Actor." Farington recalled that Wilson had once said, "I wd. not give Sixpence to see Him again," Someone else told of Morton the playwright's retort to Pascoe Grenfell, as they were coming away from *Hamlet*. "Well," said Mr. Grenfell, "You have seen Hamlet."—"No," replied Morton, "I have not seen Hamlet." Taylor wondered what Sir George Beaumont would say. But it was not until late in April that Beaumont was able to see Kean and deliver his valued opinion. He was all warmth—"no actor since Garrick exhibited so much genuine *feeling of nature*. At times, sd. He, he appears to be Richard himself. He never, sd. He, can have dignity or grace, His person is too diminutive, but He is a true natural actor, and wholly free from the measured and artificial practise of the Kemble school." On May 3 the chief Kembleite of the Farington group, Taylor, and the chief disciple of naturalism, Beaumont, met in open battle, as no doubt they did on many other occasions. "Taylor sd. 'Kean has art in His acting in attempting to give touches of nature, but it is low, vulgar art, without dignity or elevated conception of character.' —Sir George did not yield to this opinion." Later on in the same month, at a time evidently when he was not under the constraint of Taylor's caustic tongue, Sir George expanded on the beauties of the actor, whom he had by now seen also as Othello. There was at times, he said, "a fire in his acting that was electric," his smile was bewitching, and he rejoiced that "such a man had appeared on the stage to bring it back to truth and nature."

After this fashion went the conversations about the new tragedian in Farington's drawing-room, and in a hundred other drawing-rooms other champions of classic Kemble similarly vented their sarcasm on the vulgar upstart, other champions of nature gave thanks to heaven for sending them a redeemer, and every now and again some mild gentleman would mildly observe, braving the sneers of the intransigeants, that it might be possible to enjoy both Mr. Kemble and Mr. Kean.

Within the walls of Drury Lane all was smiles. On March 5 a new contract was signed for five years at £16 per week the first year, £18 the second, and £20 the last three. On March 14, following the success of *Hamlet*, the stipend was raised to £20 flat.[5]

One day Whitbread called upon the Keans and put a draft for £50 into Charles's hand. Presents flowed in: £100 from Lord Jersey, £50 from the Duchess of St. Albans, who in her maiden days as Miss Mellon had been a goddess of the stage, £500 from the Drury Lane committee; Lord Essex and several other gentlemen gave him each a share in the theatre. He was allotted of course the best dressing room. Wherever he looked he saw deference, curiosity, and envy.

Only one small, ominous incident marred the perfect concord of his triumph, but it was so insignificant that it passed unnoticed by himself and everyone else. On the first night of Richard he suffered from a cold which became so much worse that his next appearance had to be postponed to the nineteenth of February. In itself it seemed nothing. Colds were common things among actors, and so were postponements. But a note in the *Post* on the eighteenth stated that the exertions of his performance as Richard had so weakened him that he expectorated blood. That spot of blood, to us who can view the whole course of his life, is a sign full of grave warning. Disease had already laid hold of him. At the moment his foot crossed the threshold of success the internal disintegration had set in which was to blight his powers and waste his body.

On the nineteenth of February Kean resumed the part of Richard. Nothing more clearly illustrates the hold which he had taken on the affections of the town than the solicitude with which the public watched his convalescence. They would not have him play again until he was fully recovered; and suspicion having got abroad that the managers were forcing him to return while he was still ill, so much resentment was expressed that Arnold thought it prudent to contradict the rumor with a letter from Kean himself, which the actor

[5] From the Drury Lane records of plays and receipts in the British Museum, Add. MSS, 29,711.

willingly furnished. On the nineteenth the house held £544, on the twenty-fourth, £592, on the twenty-eighth, £608, and on March 3, £655. The free list was suspended. It was a furor. Many accounts have come down of the crushes at these and subsequent performances of Kean's first season. In those days there were no reserved seats in the pit, which occupied the whole of the main floor, or in the gallery. The consequence was a seething mob blocking the streets about the theatre and when the doors were opened a battle in which hats were crushed, feet bruised, clothing disheveled, and tempers spoiled. On one occasion two provincial players came up to see *Hamlet*. Being hardy men they fought their way into the pit, but found themselves in a corner where they could see nothing of the stage. There was no help for it but to pay the extra fee and go into the boxes, but getting out was almost as hard as getting in. At length, however, bruised and out-of-pocket, they found themselves on the last bench of a top tier box against the proscenium, where, by standing up and craning, they could look almost perpendicularly down upon the stage. Such were the not uncommon experiences of amateurs of the drama while the Kean fury lasted. In those days, when visiting a popular star was a form of mob athletics, there was a zest about theatre going which our times do not know. A man who arrives, torn but triumphant, on his few inches of bench will relish the play for which he has risked his life more than one who walks down just as the curtain rises to a seat which an obliging management has reserved for him. An electric expectancy lies over the auditorium which communicates itself powerfully to the people behind the curtain. Probably this is the ether in which great actors, as great actors were understood in the old days, thrive. Our modern theatres are never taken by storm. Gone are the surging masses, the tramplings of frenzied feet, the pantings, the grunts, the cries of pain or alarm, and the curses. Gone too are the great actors, the noble lads who could make all split and bring three thousand people surging to their feet.

On Saturday, March 12, Kean played Hamlet. This was designed boldly to set the capstone on his success, for Hamlet was above all other rôles the one by which the supereminence of a tragedian was proved. He might indeed win fame in a limited or special repertory, as Macklin and others had done, but if he aspired to take his place with Garrick or even with Kemble he must show that he had not only brilliance in character parts like Shylock and Richard, but also universality and intellectual depth. He well knew that of all the great Shakespearean rôles Hamlet is the most formidable on account of the awe which generations of critics and eminent actors have thrown about it. It is the holy of holies of the tragic stage. Also, it is hedged about with passionate prejudice, for every critic has rooted ideas as to how it should be interpreted and will cry murder at whatever he may consider a violation of its sanctities. It is a catechism of "points" which everyone knows by heart, so that the progress through it of a man on trial, especially of one who like Kean has established a reputation for novelty, is a passing from one ambuscade to another. The mediocre player may trudge about in it as he pleases to the world's complete indifference; but for the challenger to title, all traps are set and guns trained. And by this time London was beginning to realize that in Kean a challenger had appeared worthy of contending with the great Kemble. Now Hamlet was one of those rôles whose title had for years, by general acclamation, been vested in Kemble. That actor had a commanding figure, a fine intellectual face, a studied grace of deportment. His specialty was "noble Romans," so that he shone beyond rivalry as Brutus, Coriolanus, and Cato. To Hamlet he brought the beauty of his presence and the virility of a somewhat narrow but highly intelligent mind. What his Hamlet lacked in fluidity or contrast it made up in nobleness. Now in this contest Kean was under a physical disadvantage from the start. The roughness of his voice he could discount, because Kemble was himself no song bird. But his insignificant, unprincely stature, hitherto condoned by the gaberdine of Shylock and the deformity of Richard, would be revealed to the full in Hamlet's solemn black. The contrast he would make against Kemble's heroic presence would be a handicap which could be offset only by forcing a victory of mind over matter. But again in this respect there were serious problems, for Hamlet did not "lie" within his powers so easily as had his two previous rôles. In some ways, to be sure, it did, for it abounds in changes of mood and a vein of sarcasm runs through it. Out of these he was certain to make the most that could be made. But Kean was drawn by natural sympathy to sharp, acid, active, double-dealing knaves, or to heroes who are possessed by tempest-like passions; therefore *Othello* above the rest of the Shakespearean repertory was by a double right his play. But Hamlet must be gentle, must be loving, must be a gentleman, and a gentleman moreover who meditates more than he acts. In these aspects of the character lay his difficulties. Yet if he could overcome them by the sheer strength of an intelligent will, his glory would be all the greater. With complete confidence in his ability to rise to his needs he faced the most crowded house that Drury Lane had seen since the opening night of the new theatre.

The result was not quite the triumph which he may have expected, but it was not far from it. It demonstrated that in the greatest of rôles he had qualities which, if they did not obliterate the memory of Garrick or throw terror among the Kembleites, fixed him more securely as an artist of genius. He proved, even to many of his enemies, that his range was not limited to the showy excitements of Richard, that he had depth as well as breadth. The *Times,* which would not have been sorry to damn him, gave him the same half-grudging praise it allowed his other rôles. It reviewed his defects—his undignified figure, his hard voice, his lack of grandeur in the graver passages, his overemphasis of sarcasm; it discovered too that he mistreated the text in several instances (a carelessness for which he was constantly to be reprimanded); he failed in the closet scene. But his scenes with the Ghost and with Ophelia were fine and he fenced well. His capital merit was to be always himself; hence he struck out many new beauties. "He is clearly a person of excellent good sense, and of a powerful discrimination." The *Post,* whose enthusiasm had grown with each new rôle, expressed an almost unqualified delight. The total effect was not perfect,

> but the faults we observed appeared to arise from want of physical means, not from any error of judgment, or deficiency of feeling . . . He possesses in a pre-eminent degree the faculty of speaking the language of Nature . . . His soliloquies in general are exceedingly fine—they are the workings of nature itself . . . Were we to sum up his extraordinary merits, and his occasional deficiency . . . and considering him already one of the most

splendid ornaments of the British Stage, a rich mine of wealth to the stock of our public pleasures and mental delights, we should feel ourselves justified in pronouncing his conception of his Author, his deportment and gesticulation, his varied expression of countenance, his natural and happily adapted flexibility of tone as perfect as we could desire.

Hazlitt in the *Chronicle* began by declaring that the general delineation of the character was wrong; it was "too strong and pointed," that is to say, there was too much of Richard in it. There is no line in *Hamlet* which should be spoken like any line in *Richard III*, but Kean did not always keep the two characters distinct. He gave his Hamlet a severity, "approaching virulence," which was never a property of that amiable prince. He put too much emphasis into common scenes, and in a few of the great moments failed to make the expected effect. But it was great acting. Parts of it were higher than anything he had done in Richard. Among the high spots were the scenes with the Ghost, with Ophelia, with Gertrude, with Rosencrantz and Guildenstern (except the last with these). Some of his best effects were gained by the natural ease of his manner, as when he took Rosencrantz and Guildenstern under each arm "under pretence of communicating a secret to them, when he only meant to trifle with them." The same natural ease, applied to his recitation, gave beauty to Hamlet's speech on his own melancholy, to the instructions to the players, and to the famous soliloquy on death. The critic's admiration for the actor mounted even higher than that which he had felt for his Richard.

The *Examiner*, among a stream of encomiums, had the bad judgment to exalt Kean by maligning Kemble. The new Hamlet, it said, is not likely to prove popular; it is

too good for the public, whose taste has been vitiated by the long-established affectations of the school of Kemble. That gentleman, in his representation of *Hamlet*, shewed an ignorance of the character which would have been scarcely pardonable in the first stroller picked up at a country-fair. *Hamlet*, whose sensibility is so keenly alive, that every trifle administers fresh pangs to his distress, was converted by Mr. Kemble into a dry scholastic personage, uttering wise saws with a sneer, and delivering his ironies with a spruce air and a smart tone, such as is used by forward boys and girls on their introduction into the world, when they wish to excite attention to their abortive bon-mots and unfledged sarcasms.

KEAN AS HAMLET

In taking such a line as this the *Examiner* did more harm than good to the man it wished to serve. It did not, to be sure, create the two-party division of Kembleites and Keanites, which was bound to come and had already begun to take alignment; but such vehemence in detraction could not help but give to partisan argument a deadly rancour which, under wiser leadership, might not have entered. There was room in London for both Kean and Kemble, but the radical critics would not have it so; they rashly attempted to kill off the conservative leader, who, firm in public respect and drawing toward the close of a long, honorable career, was not in the least hurt by them. But Kean suffered, because the enemy opened a counter attack whose weight fell almost entirely on him. He was made to pay not only for his own sins but for those of his champions, which, in the world of journalism, where the *Examiner* had a bad name, were accounted heavy. Blackwood's *Edinburgh Magazine,* which in 1824 published a virulent attack on him, referred then to his coterie of friendly critics as the "Cockney School," and characterized them as a "knot of numsculls," who exercised "the most conceited, insolent, filthy, and ignorant dominion" over the dramatic world. Moreover, there is reason to suppose that the warfare promoted by the "Cockney School" not only injured Kean's professional reputation but led him to adopt ways which did him further ill service. To be the center of a quarrel and still to keep oneself out of the mud requires a greater magnanimity and more common prudence than Kean possessed. One unfortunate result of the attacks made on him was the shady activities of the Wolves Club.

But to return to *Hamlet.* Of the many new "readings" which he introduced into the part, two in particular impressed the critics of both parties as having peculiar beauty. In addressing the Ghost, at the line "I'll call thee Hamlet, Father, Royal Dane," he breathed the word "father" with such melting pathos as to throw the audience into a commotion of sympathy. It was felt to be an intuition of noble truth, one of those "flashes of lightning" which astonished Coleridge. But it was at the end of the scene with Ophelia in Act III that he made his happiest point. After the words "To a nunnery, go," as he was on the point of leaving the stage, he suddenly returned, caught the hand of Ophelia, kissed it, and hurried off. The business was new and it took enormously. To Hazlitt it was "the finest commentary that was ever made on Shakespeare."

Of the many notable persons who for one reason or another now sought out the stage's darling, probably none brought a more flattering homage than the widow of David Garrick. This lively lady, still lively in spite of her many years, lived in a museum of her husband's relics, loyal to his memory as the greatest of actors but keeping still an interested eye on the pageantry of the theatre. In Kean she found the first worthy successor to her David, the first man to show his kind of genius. She was always finding that Kean delivered certain speeches and handled certain pieces of business as *he* had done. She had him to dinner, set him in David's chair, told him of these happy coincidences, gave him the jewelry that Garrick had used as Richard, and admonished him like a fond but critical aunt. To be approved by Garrick's widow, to be acclaimed as the true heir, must have been in the highest degree grateful to the young star. But what was sometimes a little trying, she undertook to school him in the points where he fell off from the model. In this she was entirely benevolent, but quite unsuccessful. Her involuntary pupil is reported to have tried, in one or two instances, to meet her wishes, but he could not wear his borrowed clothing with any grace. He could not give up being himself, even to be Garrick.

Following what may be called a triumphant début in *Hamlet*, Kean entered upon a weekly routine of his three plays, appearing on Mondays, Thursdays, and Saturdays. The receipts for all performances were very strong, averaging around £550, but it soon became patent that *Richard III* held up the best of the three, assuming from the beginning a leadership which it maintained throughout his career. He is still remembered chiefly as Richard. During Holy Week, as was the rule, all theatrical performances were suspended. His reappearance was further delayed a week by another illness. But when on April 18 he took up Richard again his popularity seemed undiminished. *Hamlet*, however, and *The Merchant of Venice* were losing ground. They each brought in close to £470, which was in itself a very satisfactory intake but which, in comparison with his best nights, suggested that it would be well to whet the public appetite with a new piece. On Thursday, May 5, therefore, the new piece appeared. It was *Othello*. Pope, a mediocre actor, played Iago, and Miss Smith, a newcomer of talent, Desdemona. The appearance of Kean in a new rôle was by now an event of prime importance. Some anonymous gentleman who has left us a handful of reminiscences visited the star's dressing room during the run of *Othello* and found it filled with "the first wits of the day," who stood in a semicircle of adoration while the object of their devotion practiced attitudes before a cheval glass and the dramatist Reynolds, raising a cautionary hand said, "Hush! do not disturb him!"

In view of the circumstance that Othello was destined to be one of Kean's most admired rôles, the reception of the play by the press showed less enthusiasm than one would expect. The *Post*, which had so warmly greeted *Hamlet*, gave *Othello* a single cold paragraph. Mr. Kean, it said, is not qualified personally to play the part, nor has he the physical powers. His performance in consequence did not enhance his reputation; yet it was not unworthy of him—it was "highly respectable." Hazlitt, although enthusiastic as one could wish over certain moments, was disappointed in the total effect. "His voice and person were not in consonance with the character, nor was there throughout that noble tide of deep and sustained passion, impetuous, but majestic, that 'flows on like the Propontic and knows no ebb,' which raises our admiration and pity of the lofty-minded Moor." But there were "repeated bursts of feeling and energy which we have never seen surpassed." In other places, however, where he expected equal satisfaction he did not get it, and in the common scenes the actor's manner, as in the case of *Hamlet*, had an emphasis which was out of keeping.

The failure of the critics to appraise Kean's Othello at its true value may raise a slight wonder in the reviewer of these events, but it had no significance. It did not in the least affect the general admiration and it was more than corrected by subsequent encomiums. Hazlitt himself soon came to the point where he could declare Kean's Othello to be "the finest piece of acting in the world." His feeling that Kean did not sufficiently exhibit "a noble tide of deep and sustained passion" may have been induced by Kean's treatment of the first two acts of the play. There being nothing in them upon which to exert his peculiar powers, he played them rather negligently, creating at the start a disappointment in the expectant eulogist. But in the great third scene of the third act he let himself go, with what extraordinary effect has been recorded time and time again. Here, among the elemental storms, he was at home. Through the gamut of uneasiness, suspicion, anguish, rage, recovery, renewed anguish and intenser rage he ran, again the unequalled virtuoso, the Paganini of the stage, whose bravura passages startled his hearers into a succession of raptures. From there on to the end of the play he was great. "Points" fell from him like rain, too numerous to record. Most of them, as was usual, came with the delivery of simple phrases, to which he knew how to give a penetrating force—"I felt not Cassio's kisses on her lips," and "Not a jot, not a jot." Of the longer passages we do not hear so much; Othello's narrative of his wooing, for example, that fine piece of grave declamation, was in no way remarkable. But the apostrophe in which Othello bids farewell to arms was given in haunting cadences which lingered in the memory beyond, it would seem, any passage in that or any other rôle. Hazlitt compared it to "the swelling notes of some divine music." George Vandenhoff, the actor, who could only have seen Kean in his later years,[6] expresses a professional admiration for the master's technique. "His delivery of Othello's 'Farewell' ran on the same tones and semitones, had the same rests and breaks, the same *forte* and *piano*, the same *crescendo* and *diminuendo*, night after night, as if he spoke it from a musical score. And what beautiful, what thrilling music it was! the music of a broken heart—the cry of a despairing soul!"[7]

The failure of the critics to appreciate Kean's Othello may also be due in part to a divided interest, for it had been announced that on the second night Kean would play Iago, and thereafter alternate the rôles. It is probable that they looked toward Iago with a greater anticipation of pleasure, just as it is certain that they found therein a greater satisfaction. In some ways this expectation was justified, for

[6] John Vandenhoff, the father, made his début at Covent Garden in 1819.

[7] Crabb Robinson (*Diary*, May 19, 1814), wrote of this passage: "I could hardly keep from crying; it was pure feeling."

KEAN AS OTHELLO

there was every reason to believe that Kean would be a supreme Iago. To be sure, the tempests of Othello promised well for him, but Othello is not eminently intellectual; he does not govern, but is governed; he might even be compared to a mad bull led by the nose. But Kean, by now, had established his reputation as an intellectual actor; he had appeared in rôles marked by strong intelligence and had excelled in situations where he dominated over the wills of others: he had given abundant evidence, moreover, of being a master of cutting irony and of hypocrisy. His passionate crises had been associated principally with frustrations of a controlling will. His intensities had been chiefly the intensities of will. From these considerations was born the expectancy which looked toward Iago, a part wherein the master's peculiar excellences would have ideally their home.

The expectancies were felt to be fully justified. From all sides arose a chorus of praise. The *Times,* which had neglected the Othello, declared the Iago to be a masterly performance from the outset. In the third act Kean was at the top of his powers.

> Fear, anxiety, sudden exultation, checked by the dread of the fierce and turbulent mind which he was deluding,—sudden variation of face and manner, as he saw that eye gleaming on him with reliance or hesitation,—solemn sincerity where he laboured at his proofs,—indignant patience where he retorted the suspicions of his fidelity,—and at the close, the deep and collected devotedness with which he knelt and declared his friend *Cassio* to be "no more for this world," completed a tout-ensemble of theatrical excellence which promises a new æra to the stage.

Hazlitt called it

> the most faultless of his performances—the most consistent and entire . . . The preservation of character was so complete, the air and manner were so much of a piece throughout, that the part seemed more like a detached scene or single *trait,* and of shorter duration than it usually does . . . It was the least overdone of his parts, though full of point, spirit, and brilliancy.

Kean conceived Iago as a "lighthearted monster, a careless, cordial, comfortable villain," whose odiousness was glossed over by "the extreme grace, alacrity and rapidity of the execution." A little too much so, the critic felt; he would have preferred a greater weight of villainy. "We have before complained that Mr. Kean's *Richard* was not gay enough, and we should now be disposed to complain that his *Iago* is not grave enough." But the execution was so dazzling that his head whirled; he was not sure but that the actor was right; it might not be true Shakespeare, but it was glorious. The *Examiner* echoed Hazlitt's praise. Kean's Iago was "the most perfect piece of acting on the stage . . . the most complete absorption of the man in the character. He looked so thoroughly self-possessed, so completely at home in his assumed qualities: he played upon Roderigo with such a contemptuous and condescending familiarity; he watched *Othello* with such an earnestness, and at the same time appeared so careless and honestly indifferent about the issue; he rubbed his hands, aside, with such a cordial satisfaction as his plot thickened, that we found it difficult to persuade ourselves that he was merely a young man who had put on a soldier's coat to play the villain for an hour or two."

This occasion, so happy for Kean, was unhappy for the obscure mummer who played Othello. He was a person by the name of Sowerby, a dull, literal plodder who no doubt did the best he could, but did it so badly that the audience took offense and in the frank manner of the day let him know it. The poor fellow's every entrance was received with contemptuous tumult: at the end of the play, says the *Post*, "all was dumb shew and noise." He never had the part again. It was given usually to Pope, occasionally to Rae, once or twice to Elliston. We may wonder with what feelings Kean stood opposite the Little Napoleon of Wych Street, his recent tormentor, whose trail he had hunted from one side of London to another only a few months before. But Elliston, who was a politician if he was anything, would be all graciousness and flattery, and Kean was no doubt content to wash old grudges out with an air of magnanimous good-fellowship. These two were to meet in a closer relationship, not many years hereafter, when Elliston should become the lessee of Drury Lane. All in all, they would be friends from now on.

Othello and Iago were the main diet of the Kean bills from now to the end of the season, playing to strong houses and proving nearly equal in favor but with a slight advantage for Othello. *The Merchant of Venice* and *Hamlet* were given occasionally, *Richard III* more frequently, for it still drew the most money. On June 16 Kean played Othello to the largest house of the season and one of the largest of his career, the performance being graced by the presence of the Emperor of Russia and the King of Prussia. It was a grand occasion which no doubt raised the tragedian's pride a notch higher, but no particulars have come down about it.

In view of the extraordinary success of his Iago with the press, one may wonder a little that it fell off so quickly, as it did, in popularity. The chief reason probably is that his Othello was so much the better liked. For all Iago's brilliance he is a hateful personage, much more hateful than Richard; one cannot thrill to him or weep for him. And whenever the public has choice in the matter it will always vote for that character which can make it thrill and weep. It never tired of Kean's Othello, of his tormented gestures, his anguished glances, his rages and his despairs; it never tired of hearing the "Farewell" chanted in those heart-wringing tones. Someone has said that Kean grew to be careless in his Iago. Perhaps he did, but it was because he saw how the tide ran. Eventually he abandoned the part. But Othello remained to the end one of his stoutest rôles, in which, along with Richard, Sir Giles Overreach, and Shylock, he is most remembered.

On May 25 he took his benefit, choosing for his play an adaptation of Massinger's *City Madam* by Sir James Bland Burges called *Riches*. Since neither this play nor its original is much known today, a brief statement of the plot may be permitted. Sir John Traffic, a rich merchant of London, is so bullied by an ambitious, extravagant virago of a wife that he bequeathes all his property to his brother Luke and feigns death. This Luke, a ruined libertine living on his brother's bounty, subject to the insolence of Lady Traffic and her domestics, has so well studied a pious, reformed manner that he has imposed not only on Sir John but on everybody. But as soon as he feels the reins of power in his hands he bares his fangs, turns his brother's wife and daughters into servants, oppresses debtors, sneers at all goodness, and riots with his new-found wealth. The reappearance of his brother, alive and angry, cuts short his courses. Luke, now completely beggared, slinks off with a snarl, while Sir John receives into his arms a repentent wife.

The character of Luke, it may be seen from even so brief a summary, had in it materials attractive to Kean. There are the sharp contrasts between the plausible hypocrite and the savage libertine, the double meanings, the caustic railings, the fawnings, the sneers, the sardonic laughter, and at the end the paroxysm of baffled rage. It is a part of no subtlety in execution, but boldly drawn and essentially actable. It was a part to please any actor, in an age which liked strong effects. Probably Kean liked it too because there was no sentimental mush in it. It fitted him like a glove.

His reception was good, but because the play bears no comparison either as literature or as life to the four which had preceded it, the critics had little to work on, except to praise some passages of acting merely as acting. There were no problems of interpretation to argue. There was no line of eminent Lukes on which to base comparison, for the play had come into being only so recently as 1810.[8] Inasmuch as Kean was the first man of genius to play the part, he established over it a recognized proprietorship, but it did not add many leaves to his bays.

Reluctant to bring their amazing prosperity to an end, the Drury Lane committee held their theatre open long after the usual date of closing. Finally, with a performance of Richard on July 16, the curtain was lowered for the last time that season. The treasurer's books showed a total from tickets sold of £68,329.1.6. Against the £75,598 of the season before this does not at first glance seem remarkable, especially in view of the fact that the previous season was one of 204 nights against 235 for the present year. On that basis, the average nightly receipts had dropped from £370 to £290. But to understand matters rightly one must consider what the present season would have amounted to without Kean. The following table will make this clear.

Total receipts for 235 performances	£68,329[9]
Total receipts of Kean nights, 68 performances	£32,940
Nightly average for Kean	£484
Nightly average for the rest of the season	£212

[8] It was produced by the Drury Lane Company at the Lyceum Theatre on February 3, 1810, with Raymond as Luke.

[9] In these and similar figures shillings and pence are disregarded. The total of receipts given here does not include subscriptions for private boxes, amounting to about £1,700.

On the basis of the last figure, the season's receipts without Kean would have been less than £50,000 (£49,820, to be exact). The value of Kean to the house, then, was exactly £18,509, and this in spite of the fact that nearly three good months had passed before he began active service.

It is no wonder, accordingly, that on July 16 Whitbread wrote Kean a letter of thanks and praise, informing him that the management had voted him five shares in the theatre, and that at the annual shareholders' dinner in the following September Whitbread declared that Kean had saved the theatre from bankruptcy. He had—for the moment.

The following analysis[10] will show the place of his various rôles in the whole scheme.

Play	*Performances*	*Average Receipts*
Richard	25	£502
Shylock	14	351
Hamlet	8	512
Othello	10	476
Iago	8	465
Luke[11]	3	457

Meanwhile the Keans were living such a life as Edmund even in his cups could never have dreamed. Pounds were commoner stuff than pence had been to them. A gentleman who called just before the benefit, found money scattered all over the room, bank notes in heaps on the mantlepiece and Charles on the floor playing with guineas. A stream of fashionable folk knocked hourly at their door. Invitations came with every post. Great persons linked elbows with Edmund, made him flattering speeches, and gave him presents. Lord Essex, one of the Drury Lane committee, gave him a sword and took him under his especial protection. Lord Byron, it is said, followed him about like a small boy after a cricket hero. The Grenfells had them down to their country house for Passion Week. Ladies called on Mary as on a princess, to gaze with hushed admiration at the marvellous man's marvellous wife. And Mary, no doubt pinching herself

10 Copied from the Drury Lane receipt books, Add. MSS, 29,711, in the British Museum.

11 Not including the benefit performance.

frequently to see if it could all be true, played the hostess, planned great things for her family and friends at home, worshipped Edmund, bustled, shopped, and was inordinately happy. Thomas Colley Grattan, who turned up in London about this time and renewed the acquaintance he had begun at Waterford, has left a charming sketch of the new Mary.

> She was, in her own house, and surrounded by everything that might dazzle the mind's eye, and dizzy the brain of almost every one, a fair specimen of natural character. Her head was evidently turned by her husband's fame, and the combined consequences were bodied forth with exquisite naiveté. But there was withal a shrewdness, an offhandedness, and tact quite Irish; and, what was still more so, a warm-hearted and overflowing recognizance of ever so trivial a kindness, or tribute of admiration offered to "Edmund" before he became a "great man."

On Edmund, however, the new life did not sit by any means so comfortably. At the first, and for a year or two, he bore himself modestly in his position, gave dinners and went to them, made conversation with eminent people, and in general did his best to live up to the social duties of his position. But it was too foreign to him, his training had been too one-sided.[12] The man who had lived all his life

[12] In the company of gentlemen not of his profession he felt awkward and constrained. On February 25, 1816, Crabb Robinson, having spent an evening with him, put down the following impression:

> "At eight I went to Rough's, where I met Kean,—I should say to *see* him, not to hear him; for he scarcely spoke. I should hardly have known him. He has certainly a fine eye, but his features were relaxed, as if he had undergone great fatigue. When he smiles, his look is rather constrained than natural."

Even with his brother actors, although at his ease, he did not become convivial until he was a little flown with wine. Macready, who supped with him during this first season, has left an interesting account of the meeting:

> "The mild and modest expression of his Italian features, and his unassuming manner, which I might perhaps justly describe as partaking in some degree of shyness, took me by surprise, and I remarked with special interest the indifference with which he endured the fulsome flatteries of Pope. He was very sparing of words during, and for some time after, supper; but about one o'clock, when the glass had circulated pretty freely, he became animated, fluent, and communicative. His anecdotes were related with a lively sense of the ridiculous, in the melodies he sang there was a touching grace, and his powers of mimicry were most humorously or happily exerted in an admirable imitation of Braham; and in a story of Incledon acting Steady the Quaker at Rochester without any rehearsal,—where, in singing the favourite air, "When the lads of the village so merrily, oh!" he heard himself to his dismay and consternation accompanied by a

in the theatre and for the theatre, among the draggle-tails of his profession, who had met only such gentlefolk as were amateurs of the stage, and whose club had been the tavern, found no common ground on which to meet the London fashionables. He knew nothing of politics, sport, literature, fine arts, economics, foreign policy, or scandal. He knew only the theatre, and when they turned to that they talked nonsense. "I can't sit down at a lord's table with comfort," he said, "when they expect every word that comes out of my mouth to be wonderful." For him the tavern was still the place where he could best expand and relax. So after many a dinner he slipped off to a private bar, and sometimes he went there when he should have been dining elsewhere. Life, which had so suddenly packed the cards for him, had kept an evil trick up its sleeve. It had opened to him the companionship of fine gentlemen, and had given him the tastes of a pothouse boozer.

---

single bassoon,—the music of his voice, his perplexity at each recurring sound of the bassoon, his undertone maledictions on the self-satisfied musician, the peculiarity of his habits, all were hit off with a humour and an exactness that equalled the best display Mathews ever made, and almost convulsed us with laughter."—Macready, *Reminiscences*, ed. by Sir Frederick Pollock. London, 1875. I, 96.

CHAPTER VI

THE FRUITS OF TRIUMPH

IMMEDIATELY after the close of the London season the Keans set out for Dublin—a most natural move, because for one thing Dublin was first among provincial theatre towns, but especially because Ireland was Mary's home, which she was impatient to revisit, as a wealthy prodigal, so that she might dazzle and comfort those who had grieved for her distresses. Her warm heart was enchanted at playing the part of Lady Bountiful. And her letters had set the Chambers family atwitter with excitement. On March 29 Susan had written to Miss Roberts of Waterford:

On Saturday I received a letter from *Her* and more like enchantment than reality. They have *so wonderfully* found the key to all Hearts, & from the utmost misery and poverty found riches absolutely (unlooked for Riches) pouring in on them dayly. The Earl of Essex has made Kean a present of his share in the theatre . . . and Kean has settled it on little Johnny[1] *your godson.* The prince Regent sent him a present of a Hundred guineas, and another Hundred was sent in an anonimous letter, besides the various other presents they daily receive. They go by Holly Head to Dublin. He remains there, she, and your little godson, comes to Waterford, and she wants to know whether she could lodge at your House. I told her I would ask you. I know she would rather be with *you* than any where else. She says she only comes for two days, but it may be a week, according as she finds Herself better or worse. Has my mother got lodgings, or what? Did she get the money? She will be as rich as a Jew. She tells me I must get 30 or 40 pounds worth of clothes—the richest and best *all from you,* and when she comes she will pay, as well as all other debts.—[Her mother, she adds, is also to be rigged out at Mary's expense.][2]

And so, in a shower of silks and satins, Mary Chambers came home.

Edmund's benevolences to his own relations were, as may be supposed, neither so spectacular nor so heartfelt. His mother was still about, among the provincial theatres—she was reported in October, 1814, to be playing at Peckham—and doubtless lost no time in reminding her prosperous son of her existence, but he cannot be blamed

[1] This is Charles, of course.

[2] From W. J. Lawrence's MS copy. Not hitherto printed.

if he received the news without enthusiasm. Nor can he have had much fraternal feeling for his half-brother Darnley, or for who knows how many other half-brothers and sisters who may have been revealed to him. Yet he was not lacking in a sense of filial duty, which was satisfied by settling on Ann Carey an annuity of £50, without, however, intimating that he wished her to live with him. Quite possibly one of the terms of the annuity was that she should not. We do not know when the allowance was settled upon her, but it was paid until her death, which came a few days after his own. Some six months before he died, when he was alone and ill at Richmond and she was ill and alone somewhere else, he called her to him. But we may doubt if he ever saw much of her between his childhood and his death.

His own son, Charles, was of course to have the education of a gentleman. When Edmund burst in upon his wife after the performance on the famous twenty-sixth of January, he is said to have cried, "Mary, you shall ride in your coach, and Charlie shall go to Eton!" And both promises came true. Although Charlie was now still too young for schooling, he was in due course of time sent off to various private institutions which prepared young gentlemen for Eton, and in the further course of time enrolled in that famous school. He was not, his father decided with emphasis, to be an actor.

The celebrated Edmund Kean of the Theatre Royal, Drury Lane, opened at the Theatre Royal, Dublin, on Monday, July 25, with *Richard III*. He had brought with him from London his friend and huge admirer, Pope, and thus was assured of something like adequate support in those plays, such as *Othello* and *Venice Preserved,* which require two male actors of great ability. Until the thirty-first of August he played in Dublin, presenting for the most part the rôles in which London had known him, but adding three more from his provincial repertory. These were Reuben Glenroy (in Morton's serious comedy *Town and Country*) on August 6, Macbeth on August 22, and Jaffeir (in *Venice Preserved*) for his benefit on the thirty-first. At this time the Dublin theatre possessed two actresses of quality, between whom a bitter rivalry was in progress. Miss Walstein was the *prima donna assoluta* by virtue of time and long favor, sometimes described as the "Irish Siddons." The epithet was too partial, as such epithets usually are, but until recently she had been vastly admired by all Dublin. Then about three years ago the theatre had acquired, more by accident than foresight, a Miss O'Neill, daughter of a strolling player, who happened to be in town during one of the favorite's excesses of temperament, and who had been called on hastily to fill her shoes. The new actress swept the town. She was young, beautiful, appealing, and possessed of remarkable talents especially in the line of pathos. Miss Walstein, returning when the fit had passed, to her duties, found a rival against whom she must exert her utmost powers, always a heartbreaking task when the rival has the odds of youth, beauty, and talent. Their contest was the more interesting in that it duplicated the one which had been going on in London between Kean and Kemble. Miss Walstein had not won her flattering sobriquet for nothing; she was of the Kemble-Siddons school, aiming at the grand style without, unfortunately, having quite the soul for it. Her majestic movements, pauses, declamations, were almost the genuine thing. Miss O'Neill, on the contrary, belonged by instinct to the new school of which Kean was the grand patriarch. She was all spontaneity and nature.

With both these ladies Kean played, with O'Neill in *The Merchant of Venice* and *Town and Country*, with Walstein in *Richard III*, *Othello*, and *Macbeth*. Fortunate Dublin, to see the new hero thus supported! Fortunate Drury Lane, if it had secured O'Neill then and there. It needed a tragic actress badly. Was it stupidity which let slip the chance of getting the finest actress since Siddons, or had the astute Harris already snapped her up for Covent Garden? At any rate, she went to Covent Garden the next October, took London by storm, and flourished in favor for a few years until, to the great loss of the stage, she married a gentleman who became a baronet. But Drury Lane, ironically enough, took over the Irish Siddons, who turned out to be rather a shabby copy of the great original and after a few unhappy months at London went back to her Dublin admirers. Thus Covent Garden scored heavily over Drury Lane. It may have been luck. But when one considers that during Kean's London years not one important tragic actor or actress was brought out at Drury Lane, whereas Covent Garden produced, not counting Young who was al-

ELIZA O'NEILL

ready established, Macready, Booth, and O'Neill, besides cultivating in Knowles the best tragic dramatist of the day, one's suspicions are aroused that the cause lies deeper than luck or even negligence. Kean was no lover of divided honors, especially in his own field of interpretation. We shall see later what he did to poor Booth.

After a very successful engagement in Dublin, where he made a great deal of money, was lionized as much as he would permit, and drank quantities of Irish whiskey, he returned slowly towards London, playing on the way at Gloucester and Birmingham. His second London season began on October 3 with the inevitable Richard and continued with repetitions of the other familiar rôles. The houses were full, the enthusiasm undiminished. On November 5 came the first new offering, *Macbeth*, with Pope as Banquo, Rae as Macduff, and Mrs. Bartley as Lady Macbeth. The quasi-operatic version which had long been in vogue was used, based on the original music of Matthew Locke and augmented by "a New Overture and Act Symphonies composed and arranged by Mr. Horn." The production was sumptuous—new scenes, new armor, new machinery, decorations, and dresses—for *Macbeth* (alone among the Shakespearean tragedies) had evolved into a theatrical show which, by the aid of choruses of witches and flying ballets of hobgoblins, took on some of the aspects of a Christmas pantomime.

A curious restraint hangs upon the stage history of *Macbeth*. Not that it has lacked productions, for there have been plenty of them, but that so few of the productions have made a noise. One does not reckon the famous male actors in this play, as one can reckon the famous actors in *Hamlet* and *Othello*. A similar restraint, in fact even more noticeable, hangs over *King Lear*, but this we can easily comprehend—the title rôle is almost beyond human power, as Charles Lamb has pointed out. But *Macbeth* reads so superbly, and is so compactly stage-trimmed, that it seems as though it ought to play itself. And yet it does not, or rather—for the play is indeed so theatric that it can never quite fail—it contrives somehow to baffle very excellent actors. Is it because Lady Macbeth is so much more interesting than her husband? Does not our curiosity, when the play is announced, leap first to inquire who will play *her*? Or is there something in the primitive simplicity of the Thane of Cawdor which eludes the artist? However that may be, many a stout actor has grappled his five rounds with the Thane and come lamely off.

In presenting this play Kean encroached more than hitherto on the property of the Kembles. For a generation it had been their play. True, that authority had been vested chiefly in Mrs. Siddons, whose Lady Macbeth was undoubtedly the grandest in the history of the stage. It was to her contemporaries an epitome of what high tragic action ought to be, the *ne plus ultra* of histrionic magnificence. Kemble's Macbeth, on the contrary, was admired rather than idolized; it did not ravish, but it was strong, sound, effective, and it was deeply respected. The two parts sustain each other so harmoniously that either is diminished if the other is weak. The Kembles had made such a pair as one may hope to find only once in a century.

Attended by the pomp of act symphonies, choral witches, and dissolving scenery, attended also by a Lady Macbeth of very ordinary capacity, Kean made his bid for honor in this most tricksy tragedy. The result was not failure, but neither was it triumph. It was a patchy performance, very great in a few moments, but for the most part, ineffective. The critics all agreed that his best scene was the one after the murder. The *Times* declared that "his remorse and terror—the repentant agony and sudden subduing of his mind—the contrast between the innocent sleep of his victims, and the fearful and wretched watchings of their murderer, uttered in a voice broken by terror, inward torment, and hopeless despair, were among the most masterly performances that the English stage has ever witnessed." The death fight with Macduff was also very fine, blazing with that concentration of rage, horror, and despair which Kean beyond all competitors was able to delineate. But of memorable interpretations of passages, flashes of lightning, there seem to have been few or none, and there were dead reaches. The general opinion of the reviewers is summed up in the judgment of the *Post*, that "his general conception of the character is good, his execution in many parts equally vigorous and correct, but several of the most interesting scenes are but sketched—the filling up being left to future study."[3]

[3] Crabb Robinson wrote (December 1, 1815), "In no other respect [i.e., than in the two scenes mentioned above] did he impress me beyond an ordinary actor."

As a whole the production was quite successful, though how much of the popularity was due to Kean and how much to the spectacle we cannot certainly tell. It was given twenty-four times during the season and produced the best average of any of his rôles. From now on it remained in his repertory, without ever attaining (except possibly in Edinburgh) especial prominence.

On January 2, 1815, he came out as Romeo with Mrs. Bartley as Juliet and Elliston as Mercutio. Report has it that he did so to oblige the committee and against his own will, which is easy to believe because Romeo is not a part to attract the mature tragedian—his passions are too juvenile, especially for a man of Kean's bent, but what damns the play sufficiently for the male star is that the major interest attaches to Juliet. Furthermore, Kean disliked sentimental rôles; he had nothing of the lover in him. Still, he had advantages in the way of youth, suppleness, vivacity, and intelligence, which, if he had chosen to throw himself into the part, would have made him the best Romeo of his day. Paired with O'Neill, an enchanting Juliet, he might have established a lasting popularity, but even if O'Neill had been available he would never have sunk himself in a mere partnership. That was one of his weaknesses, which cost him much and his theatre much more. It is very probable that the production of *Romeo and Juliet* was inspired by the success of Miss O'Neill in that play at Covent Garden, where she was reaping triumphs in every rôle. But if the desire of the Drury Lane committee was to bring forward a Romeo who would outshine her Juliet they were grievously in error.

If it is true that he took the part reluctantly, if he actually told his wife that "he would be damned if he did not disappoint the committee," he nevertheless hid his distaste remarkably well. The *Times* was impressed: "We have seen no delineation of this actor more strikingly sketched than his *Romeo*; and yet we do not recollect to have ever seen him more at his ease, with more of that happy security which is probably the last result of matured talent, or more of that dextrous skill, which, artless itself, is yet the sum of art." The *Chronicle*[4] singled out for especial praise the scenes in Friar Lawrence's cell

[4] No longer represented by Hazlitt, who had left its staff in May of 1814. He was now writing for the *Champion*.

and the tomb, of which it said that "after a pretty constant attendance at the Theatre for near forty years, we have only to say that we never witnessed so much affecting interest excited, or the sympathetic emotions of the auditory so forcibly aroused by this character." In fact the reviewer found no fault with Kean's Romeo at any point, but only with the Juliet, whose deficiencies moved him to urge the management to try out all the Juliets at command until they found a suitable one. The management was evidently of the same opinion, for at the fourth performance, of January 31, they substituted a new actress, Miss L. Kelly. But her charms were unable to stimulate a public which found Kean insufficiently exciting as Romeo. The play was given for a total of nine nights, to steadily diminishing receipts, and then was dropped from the repertory.

On February 13, Kean appeared as Reuben Glenroy in *Town and Country*, by Thomas Morton. This is a serious and well-forgotten comedy about a noble-hearted young Welshman who loves his fellow man, rescues travelers from storms, befriends villagers, reforms a scapegrace brother, persuades a society matron to nurse her child, is sublimely generous in love, and never, from the first to the last, utters a natural thought in natural language. It is all the most insipid trash imaginable, yet it had some vogue for a number of years,[5] and imposed its fustian heroics on the bad taste of Kean. He entertained the town with it for eight nights, with fair success, but thereafter kept it mainly for his provincial repertory.

His next enterprise was far more worthy of him, namely, a revival of Shakespeare's beautiful but infrequently acted *Richard II*. Of those undertakings which may be called departures from the accepted canon of the tragic actor this does him the most credit. He was not moved to vie with any famous rival in the part, for there was none; the play had never been popular; we may suppose him, therefore, to have been moved by genuine admiration for a fine work of art, all the more laudable because he must have realized how difficult it would be to make the town like it. That he was ambitious to make them like it, there can be little doubt. He felt that he could, with his new ways of interpreting, disclose unrealized beauties. To the proponent

[5] First produced at Covent Garden in 1807.

of nature in action, Richard has much to offer that is attractive: his moods and tempers, his vacillations, his indignations and abasements, his irony and pathos are drawn in phrases of penetrating, natural beauty. On the debit side there is, of course, the lack of engrossing interest, of that strong-fibred, insistent interest which makes the success of a play on the stage. The action is unheroic; Richard is weak and even at times irritating. If he is to be made interesting, therefore, it must be through the sincerity with which his all-too-human incapacities are delineated. Although he cannot be invested with grandeur he can at least be invested with a touching poignancy.

The play was produced on March 9, with Elliston as Bolingbroke, Pope as John of Gaunt, Rae as Norfolk, Holland as York, Wallack as Aumerle, and Mrs. Bartley as the Queen. "Considerable Alterations and Additions" were made by Richard Wroughton,[6] chiefly consisting of retrenchments. Thus one looks in vain on the playbill for the names of the Duchesses of York and Gloucester, whose functions, so far as they were kept at all, were transferred to the Queen and Bolingbroke. The tournament scene was omitted, Aumerle's conspiracy likewise; the Queen's part, however, was considerably augmented and she was permitted to lament over the corpse of Richard in language borrowed from Lear's lament over Cordelia. The result of these and many other lesser changes was, in Mr. Odell's opinion,[7] a very respectable stage version, which drew the action closer together and strengthened the interest on the female side, where it needed strengthening most.

In his conception of the character of Richard, Kean showed an originality which surprised and, in some instances, troubled his critics. The representative of the *New Monthly Magazine* confessed to his readers that he had supposed from reading the play that Richard was a weakling, even an imbecile.

> How were we surprised then to find the Richard II of Mr. Kean, a vigorous and elevated mind, struggling like a king; greater beyond comparison in his dungeon than Bolingbroke on his throne! The modern stage has exhibited nothing of temperate dignity equal to the speech in

[6] An actor in the company, then playing his last season.

[7] Odell, G. C. D., *Shakespeare from Betterton to Irving*. N. Y., 1920. II, 75.

which Richard compares his return to that of the sun . . . nothing of majestical anger equal to his rebuke of Northumberland on the "deposing of a king"—nothing of deep and exquisite pathos, approaching the look and action accompanying the words, "My eyes are full of tears," when he tries to evade the charges made against him.

The critic seems to have been delighted as well as surprised, but inasmuch as he evidently had thought little about the play his approval is of small consequence. What he has left us is a reflection of the turn given by Kean to the character of Richard toward the noble and heroic, a turn which, however captivating it may have been, one must pronounce to be alien to the conception of Shakespeare. There are no "majestical" angers in his Richard. It is clear that, either distrusting the effect on the audience of a delineation of Richard's full weakness or else rebelling against such a delineation from his own instinct, Kean tried to make of him a man of mettle, to win admiration for his energy and pity for his unmerited downfall. The conception was brilliant rather than just, so brilliant indeed that it won from the *Chronicle* the opinion that "in no one of the characters which [Kean] has hitherto acted has he approached in excellence to his masterly delineation of the character of King Richard II." The reviewer even professed to receive that succession of breath-taking shocks which was Kean's special glory. "During the last three acts," he declared, "the flashes are so brilliant and so frequent, that the mind is actually lost in the splendour which surrounds him."

But Hazlitt, writing now in Leigh Hunt's *Examiner*, was of a contrary opinion. "It has been supposed that this is his finest part: this is, however, a total misrepresentation. There are only one or two electrical shocks given in it; and in many of his characters he gives a much greater number." His conception was wrong, for he made of Richard "a character of *passion*, that is, of feeling combined with energy; whereas it is a character of *pathos*, that is to say, of feeling combined with weakness." Thus he erred at frequent places, as in dashing the looking-glass violently down instead of letting it fall from his hands, and where he should have been melancholy and thoughtful, he was fierce and heroic. Hazlitt had by now decided that Kean was an actor of great powers but limited range—"he expresses all the violence, the extravagance and fierceness of the passions, but not their misgivings, their helplessness, and sinkings into despair." In the reviews of this and subsequent years he frequently found fault, sometimes acrimoniously expressed, with his hero; but he still admired him above all others, partly for his unbounded energy, but chiefly because he was "food for critics," because "there is no end of topics he affords for discussion—for praise and blame."

The *Theatrical Inquisitor*, appearing near the end of March, stated it to be "the general opinion" that in *Richard II* Kean had excelled over all that he had done before. But his support, with the exception of Mrs. Bartley and Holland, was wretched. Pope, the *fidus Achates* of Kean who went to Dublin with him, was impossible. "Pope, as usual, raved and whined alternately, by turns ludicrous and by turns annoying. He is, in fact, a sort of monster upon the stage, a pantomimic elephant, who is entirely out of his proper sphere, and comes on solely for the amusement of the galleries." Poor Pope! He has been represented as a toady to the popular tragedian, but can he have been, in addition, as bad as all that? One hates to think so.

Kean played Richard consecutively until March 16, after which he took a short vacation in the north, playing four nights at Newcastle from the twenty-seventh and visiting Glasgow (according to the *Theatrical Inquisitor*) in April. He resumed at Drury Lane on April 8 with *Richard II*, repeating it during the season for a total of thirteen performances. On the twenty-second, for the first time in his life since the days of Ann of Swansea and Sheridan Knowles's *Leo*, he created a rôle in a new play. The play was *Ina*, a tragedy in blank verse by Mrs. Wilmot, the scene of which is laid in eighth-century England. In order to cement a truce between the hostile kingdoms of Mercia and Wessex, Edelfleda, the Mercian princess, has been betrothed to Egbert, the prince of Wessex, but Egbert has secretly married Ina. Edelfleda, who calls to mind (with notable differences) the Hermione of *Andromaque*, burning with injured pride, throws the two countries into war. While Egbert is engaged in defeating the Mercians, his father, abetted by Edelfleda and the wicked abbot Baldred, condemns Ina to death for *lése Majesté*, but she wins him over by displaying his infant grandson, Baldred is killed, Edelfleda commits suicide, and the wedded lovers receive the king's blessing. It is, in the words of the Honorable William Lamb's Prologue,

> A tale of secret love in generous youth,
> Uncompromising honour, dauntless truth;
> Faith, which sore-tried nor change nor doubt can know,
> And public danger mix'd with private woe.

But the modern eye, unfortunately for Mrs. Wilmot's fame, is jaundiced to themes of uncompromising honor, dauntless truth done in early-nineteenth-century blank verse. Tom Moore, whose sly Epilogue is a witty discourse on Blue Stockings, while he politely excepts *Ina* from his satire, pointed in exactly the right direction. This is a Blue Stocking tragedy, if there ever was one.

Why Kean should have been attracted to the rôle of Egbert is not easy to understand, for it offers little besides ardor and high principles, and the best opportunities, so far as there are any, go to Ina and Edelfleda. Certainly Mrs. Wilmot could not complain of the casting. With Mrs. Glover as the Mercian princess, Mrs. Bartley as Ina, Kean as Egbert, and Rae as the villainous Baldred the play was furnished with the best talents that Drury Lane could afford. Its complete damnation and withdrawal after a single performance was proof for once at least of Elliston's great maxim that "the public is always right."

The collapse of *Ina* made it necessary to turn elsewhere for novelty. The play chosen, none too judiciously, was Cumberland's sentimental comedy *The Wheel of Fortune,* first acted in 1795 and written for Kemble. It is a play which, although mawkish in its premises and deserving of the neglect into which it has fallen, is nevertheless, so spiritedly written, with so close an approximation to truth of character, that it can be read without pain and is altogether superior to *Town and Country.* The leading part, which suffers the name of Penruddock, is that of a misanthrope, who in his youth had loved a girl and been cheated out of her by his best friend, and who as the play begins has settled into a solitary life of morose study. The inheritance of a fortune, coinciding with the bankruptcy of his treacherous friend, puts him in command of the means of revenge; the action of the play is concerned with the experiences through which his hard heart is softened into mercy. Though he is but a middle-class, conventionalized Timon, though he expresses the commonplaces of the sentimental school in regard to natural and artificial life ("'Sdeath! can a man that has looked Nature in the face, gaze on these fripperies?"), though the later scenes melt into a surfeiting tenderness, there is stuff in the part into which an actor may set his teeth. Kemble had played it to perfection; the dry, formal, melancholic style of his action in common passages was fitted to the bilious moods of Penruddock, for which Kean was quite unsuited. Wherever the tough shell of Penruddock's misanthropy is broken by eruptions of passion, he was successful, as he was also in passages where the new tenderness is shown at war with the old hatred; but in all scenes where Penruddock is at his normal level he fell below Kemble. The challenge was unwise.

The Wheel of Fortune was produced on April 29 and repeated six times in all. On May 24 Kean took his benefit, choosing Zanga in *The Revenge* and, to give London a taste of his quality in comedy, Garrick's *Tobacconist,* an afterpiece adapted from Jonson's *Alchemist.* Edward Young's tragedy (produced in 1721) had in recent years enjoyed a considerable popularity under the leadership first of Mossop and later of Kemble. It is a story, obviously reminiscent of Othello, of the Moor Zanga, captured in battle by Don Alonzo and treated by him more as a friend than a slave, who nevertheless harbors an undying lust to be revenged. This purpose he accomplishes by utilizing the rivalry in love between Alonzo and his dearest friend Carlos for Leonora, by poisoning Alonzo's mind as Iago poisons Othello's, and by contriving the murder of Carlos and the suicides of Leonora and Alonzo. The tone of his character is struck at the outset, when we see him pacing the castle battlements on a stormy night and exhorting the weather:

> Rage on, ye winds; burst, clouds, and waters roar!
> You bear a just resemblance of my fortune,
> And suit the gloomy habit of my soul.

Hung about with the funeral crêpe of high tragedy, incredibly proud, baleful, unrelenting, he stalks through his manifold deceits, a kind of African Lucifer in Spanish exile. Though he is never for more than a moment at a time in contact with life, and though his unrelieved spleen grows toward monotony, the artificial energy of his pursuit makes an effect. It is not hard to see why the part should have appealed to an actor, or why Kean, the specialist in criminal passions, should have felt that he could do more with it than John Kemble, or the half-forgotten Mossop. He was supported by Rae as Alonzo, James Wallack as Carlos, and Miss L. Kelly as Leonora.

As to the success of the undertaking opinions are remarkably divergent. Hawkins celebrates in a characteristic panegyric "the overwhelming splendor of his Zanga, in which at one stroke he deposed Mossop from his traditional supremacy, and deprived Kemble of one of his oldest and most valued possessions." But the contemporary press seemed to be unaware of such a stroke. The *Times*, after calling the play "a grand composition . . . unquestionably the most glorious monument that its author has left behind him," complained that the part did not suit the actor; his face could not be seen for the blacking on it, and his voice could not compensate for the loss of facial expression. But the *Theatrical Inquisitor*, while agreeing that the performance missed fire, laid the fault to a quite opposite cause.

> It is not strange that Mr. Kean should not equal expectation in such a character; the very excellence of his system destroyed the part, for it shewed, in glaring lights, its absurdity; his action and utterance were those of a human being: but Zanga is not a human being, and no better mode could have been devised to make that fact evident to common apprehension, than that of natural acting; it was like the jarring effect produced on the ear by musical discord . . . Having completely routed the Kemble school in the legitimate drama, why not leave them in quiet possession of their Rollas, Zangas, and Octavians?

The difference in judgment is irreconcilable, as irreconcilable as the differences between the Kemble party and the Kean party. But in the end it amounted to this, that many in both parties were dissatisfied with Kean in the rôle,[8] which probably accounts for the fact that it never became one in which he was a favorite. Nevertheless, it con-

[8] Hazlitt however was pleased. He opened his *Examiner* review by saying: "We have seen Mr. Kean in no part to which his general style of acting is so completely adapted as to this, or to which he has given greater spirit and effect."

tained at least one of those explosions which have passed into history. The best account of it comes from Procter, who was a witness.

His grand blow was in the discovery of himself, and all that he had done, to Alonzo. *"Know then—'Twas I."* Here the effect was appalling, beyond anything that we ever witnessed. Rae, who played Alonzo, seemed to wither and shrink into half his size. It is a positive fact that he appeared less than Kean in this overpowering scene; although he was considerably the larger man. As we ourselves contemplated the dark and exulting Moor standing over his victim, with his flashing eyes and arms thrown upwards . . . we thought that we never beheld anything so like the "archangel ruined."

"We ourselves" prefer, to Procter's Miltonic admiration, the terse comment of his neighbor in the pit: "By God! he looks like the devil!"

As to Kean's success in the part of Abel Drugger in *The Tobacconist*, or in comedy generally, one finds some difference of opinion. A few liked him—some even insisted that he was a master of the comic art, that he had a rich fund of humor, that he was too subtle for his detractors, and so on. But the general voice denied him the true *vis comica*. In view of the positive statements of responsible men, we must suppose that he had no mean ability in the line of comedy; but whereas in his style of tragedy he had no competitors, in comedy he had a legion, headed by such natural side-splitters as Munden, Dowton, and the great Liston who could throw an audience into spasms by merely cocking his eye. Kean had plenty of humor; he could tell stories well and he excelled at mimicry, particularly among friends after the third bottle. But he was unwise in attempting stage comedy, which he coveted not from impulse so much as from ambition to play the Admirable Crichton in all branches of his art. Of his Abel Drugger there is nothing to relate except the possibly apocryphal exchange of notes with Mrs. Garrick. "Dear Sir: You can't play Abel Drugger," wrote the widow of the world's greatest Tobacconist. "Dear Madam: I know it," replied Kean, with more gallantry than true modesty, considering that he kept the piece in his repertory for more than ten years after.

On June 20 he appeared again in comedy, as Leon in *Rule a Wife and Have a Wife*, by Beaumont and Fletcher, in which, despite some praise from his admirers, he did not stir the town; on June 21 he gave readings from *Richard III* at Oxford; and on July 4, in aid of the Theatrical Fund Benefit, he played a part which had been a favorite of his strolling days, Octavian in *The Mountaineers*. This play was to have been repeated July 6, but on that day Samuel Whitbread died and the theatre was closed. Kean gave his last performance of the season, as Octavian, on July 7.

On reviewing his second season one is struck, first of all, by the number of new rôles. To the six of the previous season he had now added ten. But more striking, and more significant, is the rapid decline in nightly receipts. Indeed this second phenomenon is no doubt the main cause of the first. As one surveys the figures taken from the theatre records he sees a steady deflation, from the autumn months when £500 and £400 nights are the rule, through the winter nights which run persistently in the three hundreds, into the spring months which, save for an initial spurt in *Richard II*, dwindle through the two hundreds until, on June 26, one finds him playing Romeo to a paltry £128. He had, it is true, a packed house at his benefit, but to offset that, his name could draw to the Theatrical Fund benefit no more than £217. Whereas during the first season he played to an average of £484, his average had now fallen to something like £350. In the one hundred and sixteen nights of the present year he had taken in only a few thousand pounds more than in the sixty-eight nights of the last. With his services nearly doubled, the total sale of tickets for the season (£67,296) was slightly under the last year's total; whereas Covent Garden (thanks, it is true, mainly to Miss O'Neill) had done business to the sum of £90,000.

These figures are eloquent with meaning. I do not, of course, mean to put Kean on a pair of banker's scales and weigh his genius by the sums of money he drew in. But ticket sales are an infallible test of popularity, according to which we see, taking the present year as a fair index to his fortunes, that in the phenomenal success of Kean there was a certain lack of sinew, so that it was continually sagging between times of inflation. It could not, of itself, maintain a level. The times of inflation resulted from various causes—from new rôles (but these instances were rare), from association with rival actors (as

KEAN AS "THE THEATRICAL ATLAS"

in the cases of Booth and Young), from visits to new territory (especially the United States), or from scandalous notoriety. The fact is that for all his brilliance and for all the very genuine admiration that was entertained for him, he palled. Whether the fault was mainly his or mainly Drury Lane's is a matter of some doubt. Certainly Drury Lane, in failing to build up a competent support for him, was to blame. If it felt, as there is reason to suppose it did, that his presence in a play was a magnet of sufficient strength, it relied on a policy that was as ineffective as it was stupid. But there is also good reason to believe that Kean himself was the main abettor of such a policy, so that the division of responsibility cannot be made with any precision. Certainly it is true that Drury Lane had neither an adequate company on the tragic side, nor an adequate policy. And equally certain it is that had Kean been directed by an astute management, which built its productions around him instead of flinging him on a bare stage, he would have shone with a brighter and steadier luster. Nevertheless, in the light of his whole career, I am inclined to believe that as an artist (quite apart from his fleshly failings) Kean lacked sustaining power. The first acquaintance with him was exciting—but curiosity had a way of being quickly satisfied.

All this, however, had little effect in dimming his glory, which maintained itself even though people stayed away from his theatre. Through all the coming vicissitudes of life—through illness, debauchery, failing powers, the hisses of indignant moralists or insulted audiences—he continued to be the pride of the British stage, he became in fact an institution, battered and soiled indeed, but honored. And of course he continued to receive his twenty or his fifty pounds a night. If the people stayed away from his theatre, his pockets at least (whatever his withers may have felt) were unwrung.

I know not how the managers of Drury Lane viewed the season of 1814-15, with its rapid fire of new rôles and its steady decline in receipts. But Kean himself was living on the top of the world. He had taken more commodious apartments in the Cecil Street house, where, as often as Mary could persuade him, he gave dinners and held court. Gifts flowed in continuously—a gold box and a sword from Lord Byron, a Spanish cloak from Sir George Beaumont, a lace tippet formerly belonging to Garrick from the actor Wroughton, and a lion from Sir Edward Tucker. This beast—of what sort I cannot say except that it was American and indolent—created a small sensation of which its owner was very proud. He paraded it in the face of the world, kept it frequently in his house, introduced it to his hesitant guests, and devoted himself to its education, with the unfortunate result that the animal died. To keep a pet lion was quite in tone with his way of life, which had come to be one of wildness and display. He developed a fondness for boating, or rather being boated, in wherries on the Thames, a genuine fondness out of which grew an annual boatmen's race for which he donated a prize wherry. He kept a pair of huge black horses, on one or the other of which he would gallop furiously, in the dead of night, through the adjacent country. He drank constantly and inordinately, in the company of his fellows of the theatre or worse. There being no club to his liking, he organized one, the notorious Wolf Club, whose assembly rooms were in the Coal Hole Tavern, Fountain Court, Adelphi. It was made up chiefly of theatrical people—Elliston, Oxberry, Jack Bannister, Liston, Pope, the dramatist Reynolds, and many more—no gentlefolk, all plain men with sound bellies and lungs. No doubt it was organized for conviviality, for that free, loose-girthed, tavernous bonhomie which Kean so preferred to the mannerly conviviality of the Cecil Street dining room. There, night after night, he drank, cracked jests, sang, argued, and beat upon the table. And from there, night after night, he was brought home and put to bed. In the beginning it was a harmless club of scallawags, a little too low for his station, a little too liquorous for his health, but still harmless enough. But within a year or two it had earned itself an unsavory reputation, as a kind of society for the suppression of all rival claimants. It came to be believed throughout London that the Wolves played a noisy, mischievous game of theatrical politics, going as an organized claque to the theatres, either to support their master or to down some other tragedian. How much truth there was in this cannot now be determined, but as I have said it was generally believed, frequently asserted, and it cast an ill shadow on Kean's reputation. Where there is much smoke there is probably some fire. At any rate, things came to such a pass in the course of years that Kean thought it wise to dissolve the club and to publish the news of his housecleaning in the press.

No doubt in the picture I have drawn of Kean's way of life I have confused perspective by anticipating the developments of a few years later than the time of which we are now speaking. To find him entering upon the full tide of licence one should move, say, to 1817 or 1818—it is hard to tell just how rapidly he gave way to his various lusts. For the first few years he seems to have made some effort to live in the way that was expected of him. That is the testimony of Colley Grattan, who saw a good deal of him just after he came out at Drury Lane. Grattan visited frequently at Cecil Street, where the dinners were excellent without extravagance, there was a great deal of good music, and the evenings were very pleasant. Among the habitual guests he saw Miss Anne Plumptre (translator of Kotzebue and author of a *Tour of Ireland*), a Miss Spence, novelist, a Miss Benger, "a woman of higher talents," and Captain Glascock (author of *The Naval Sketch Book*)—very small literary fry for a man who might have dined Hazlitt, Byron, and Lamb. He saw there likewise, and regularly, Alderman and Mrs. Cox, the fatal woman of Kean's life, of whom Grattan says that "she was so little remarkable in any way that I can scarcely remember her appearance." Mary Kean was ambitious to have people of quality, and when possible, of title. These Edmund "seemed to endure, rather than take pride in them." He behaved well enough during their presence, but as soon as the house was cleared he slipped off to the Coal Hole. He once took Grattan to the Wolves Club, but his guest was received so forbiddingly that he stayed only a short while, and Kean seemed ever after to be ashamed of having taken him. Among Kean's favorite amusements at this time was prize fighting, which, along with his lion and his midnight gallops on black chargers, may be counted as part of his Byronism. He was not only a patron but a distinguished amateur, visited the matches and had sparring bouts in his dining-parlor with Mendoza and Richmond the Black. According to another reminiscent friend, the bouts were not always in his parlor; he once quarreled with a noted professor of the "fancy," fought him in the streets, and was lodged in St. Dunstan's watch-house to cool off.

Towards all persons of title, save one, he developed an unreasonable hostility, based, thought Grattan, on an exaggerated resentment of their rank. Because he felt that they condescended to him, expected him to fawn on them, he despised and shunned them. He had none of John Kemble's social good sense, or of his ease in all kinds of society. The one Lord whom he tolerated was Byron, who admired and pursued him and whom he for a time admired and accepted. The influence of Byron, thought Grattan, was bad. His example fostered in Kean a similar love of display, of eccentricity, of unconventional affectations, such as prize fighting, black horses, wherry racing, and lions. But their association was factitious; there was no real community of interest between them and the difference of their cultures was always a barrier. There could be no place at the Coal Hole for Byron, and the society which he frequented bored Kean. The thin cement of their friendship cracked when the actor failed to attend a dinner party of the poet's in favor of the Wolves Club. He was seeking his own level. It is too bad that Kean, who embodied so perfectly in the theatre the dominant feeling of his times which Byron embodied in poetry and Hazlitt in criticism, should have been unfitted to play, in all its phases, the part for which he was created.[9]

[9] Grattan's reflections on Kean, Byron and Napoleon are both interesting and suggestive:

"Who will refuse to see an analogy in character between Byron and his avowed archetype, Bonaparte? It must be sympathy which leads to imitation. And what Byron was to Bonaparte, Kean most assuredly was to Byron. My readers must not be startled by the *rapprochement*, nor think that the greatest conqueror of the age is degraded by forming one in the trinity of fame with the greatest poet and the greatest actor of England. And, after all, which was most a stage-player of the three? Was not the political world the great theatre of Napoleon's deeds—the social world of Byron's doings? Did not both act a part from first to last? and was not Kean more an actor in the broad gaze of London life than on the narrow boards of Drury Lane? The generic signs of genius were common to them all; and they were undoubtedly of the same species of mind. Had their relative positions been reversed, their individual careers had most probably been the same, or nearly so. Reckless, restless, adventurous, intemperate; brain-fevered by success, desperate in reverse; seeking to outdo their own destiny for good; and rushing upon dangers and difficulties, which they delighted first to make, and then to plunge within . . . The grand distinction in favour of Napoleon was, all through, not that he was an emperor, but that he was an original. Byron was an extravagant copy; Kean an absurd one."—Thomas Colley Grattan. *Beaten Paths; and Those Who Trod Them.* London, 1862. II, 195.

CHAPTER VII

INSOLENCE AND WINE

On the close of the London season in July, 1815, Kean returned to Dublin, where he played an engagement of three weeks and over, closing Monday, the fourteenth of August. Where he went then I do not know, but in September we find him at Liverpool for two weeks, opening on the fifteenth. If we can believe the *Theatrical Inquisitor*, not always reliable in its notes on the movements of actors, he went early in October to Rouen, where he gave public readings in a theatre. "His interesting countenance," we are told, "together with his touching manner, so affected the Frenchmen, that although they did not understand a word he said, they were all moved to tears." Perhaps!

On his return to London he moved from the Cecil Street apartments into a house formerly occupied by Lady Rycroft, in Clarges Street, Piccadilly. This was more suited to the dignity of his position and to the social projects of Mary Kean.

The death of Samuel Whitbread in July had resulted in an important change of management, for instead of selecting a new manager-in-chief the general committee of subscribers had most unwisely appointed the whole subcommittee as a kind of collective manager. This subcommittee was composed of the Earl of Essex, Lord Byron, the Honorable Douglas Kinnaird, the Honorable George Lamb, and Mr. Peter Moore, M.P., five upright and interested gentlemen to do the work of one and do it very badly, to whose number should be added as manager *extra ordinem*, Edmund Kean. With these six different intelligences working, for the most part, at cross purposes, the affairs of Old Drury were bound to be at sixes and sevens. But the time has not yet come to narrate their decline and fall.

Kean reopened at Drury Lane on October 16 with the inevitable *Richard III*, following it with *Othello, Richard II, Hamlet, Macbeth,* and *The Revenge*. Allowing for the greater strength which October always has over June, he picked up the thread of his success exactly where he had left it—apart from the first night his average receipts were slightly under £250. Then on November 6 he offered a new part, that of Bajazet in Rowe's forgotten tragedy, *Tamerlane*. This rôle, even more noisy than Zanga and without the saving drop of humanity which Zanga has,[1] interested the town but mildly. He opened at £383, ran for seven consecutive performances, and closed at £187. Another unprofitable experiment. Much less profitable was another excursion into comedy, with the part of Duke Aranza in John Tobin's popular *Honeymoon*. The town endured it for two performances. His next venture had better luck. This was a new play by the Honorable Douglas Kinnaird, of the managing committee, called *The Merchant of Bruges*, or rather a revamping of *The Beggars' Bush* by Beaumont and Fletcher. It is a dramatic romance, laid unconvincingly in Flanders, dealing with a usurping duke, the rightful duke in disguise as a beggar, his heir in disguise as a merchant prince of remarkably virtuous character, his daughter disguised as a beggar lass, a kidnapped princess of Brabant, a comical burgomaster, villainy, heroism, and a chorus of comic-opera beggars. Through the uninspired changes of Kinnaird gleams momentarily the salty vigor of old Beaumont and Fletcher. There is constant action, a sprinkling of competent humor, and an engaging zest in the telling of the incredible story. It would make a good libretto for a light opera, as indeed Kinnaird must have felt, for he put into it as many songs and glees as he could make room for. Kean was of course Florez, the hero-merchant; Holland was Gerrard, the deposed duke; Munden played the comic burgomaster, and Miss L. Kelly the musical beggar-maid, Jaculin.

The play opened dully, on December 14, to a poor house of £209, striking evidence that a new part for Kean was no longer an attraction. But as it ran on the receipts mounted. This is a phenomenon common to all the successful productions of the present year and making a significant contrast with the past two years. The people through experience had grown so distrustful of Kean's new rôles that they waited to be convinced of their worth before venturing to the

[1] "Kean performed that character throughout under the idea of his being a two-legged beast. He rushed on the stage at his first appearance as a wild beast may be supposed to enter a new den to which his keepers have transferred him."—Crabb Robinson (November 22, 1815).

theatre. *The Merchant of Bruges* crept, by the eighth performance, past the £300 mark, where it remained pretty consistently up to the eighteenth and last performance. From December 14, with only three interruptions, it was given continuously to January 12, a run indeed, but a run so to speak in the lower register, showing how sharply Kean's valuation had fallen since his first season and that the management was now thankful for what it could pick up.

On January 12, however, the former days of frantic adoration suddenly returned with Massinger's *A New Way to Pay Old Debts.* The character of Sir Giles Overreach was one to attract Kean, having all the harsh traits of character strongly etched, suggesting a little of Richard, a touch of Iago, and a good deal of Luke. Overreach is an upstart commoner, crude, base, conscienceless, who has amassed a fortune by dirty practices, has ruined his nephew, and means to wed his daughter, against her will, to a nobleman. By the aid of his treacherous bailiff, Marall, the representatives of decency succeed in unmasking and frustrating his villainy. Through this highly theatrical part Kean marched like a conqueror, underscoring in his unequalled manner the monster's crassness, duplicity, spleen, and remorseless will. But his great moments came in the final scene, where Overreach, cornered and exposed, lashes out in ungoverned fury at his pursuers, goes mad in fact from his own rage, foams, curses, and falls into a catalepsy. Here Kean was transcendent; no scene of a similar nature that he had previously exhibited came anywhere near it. The effect was prodigious. The pit rose bellowing, Lord Byron, as is well known, fell over in a convulsion, and what is more remarkable, even the actors were affected. We may discount the over-colored picture imagined by Hawkins, of Mrs. Glover fainting, Mrs. Horn breaking into hysterical tears, and Munden, stiffened with terror, dragged off the stage by his armpits. But there is sufficient testimony to the effect that the actors were visibly astonished and that Mrs. Glover had suddenly to find a chair. This in itself is sufficiently impressive.

Again the theatre-going public was startled into activity as fervently as it had been at the first showing of Richard. The press teemed with discussion, appraising the high lights, arguing over the interpretation of passages. One of the most debated questions was whether Kean was or was not in character when he made Overreach throw a contemptuous slur on every mention of "lord" and "nobility." Hazlitt found it peculiarly just that a vulgarian, though from ambition he had acquired a title for himself, should feel a vulgar scorn for title. Perhaps he was right: but we may, nevertheless, suspect that the first cause for this happy effect was rather Kean's own prejudices. He was entirely at one with Sir Giles on this point.

After a cautious start on the first night the play leaped into a furious popularity. The second night drew £528, successive nights increased until by the sixth night the admission sales amounted to £584. It was the good days again, of *queus* blocking the streets, of trampled feet and bruised sides, of "no orders admitted." Interspersed with the dying cadences of *The Merchant of Bruges* and a performance each of *Macbeth* and *Richard III*, the play ran steadily until the ninth of March.

The excitement and the glory of these days are reflected in a letter of Susan Chambers, living then with the Keans, to Margaret Roberts at Waterford: [2]

London, Jan 20

. . . I know you will be delighted to hear such *a great* account of Him in Sir Giles Over-reach. It is I think greater than any he has yet appeared in. Three hundred pounds was turned from the door last night that could not get room, tho' the third night of performing. The gold cup is making for him.[3] Hamlét the jewelor at the end of Lester square offered to make it without charging for the work. There is near three Hundred pounds collected already, & the work, if paid for, would be half of that. Mrs Garrick was with us yesterday. She says he is greater than ever. My dear Margaret I wish you were here to see the numerous letters of congratulation & visits on the same that is pouring in every day. The house is quite a fair! I believe I sent you off six or seven papers, one to-day. To see him in the last act I think you never would get over it. Mrs Glover got into strong histericks & many ladies fainted. It has brought 2 thousand pounds to the House tho' but three nights played. He dines to-day at Mr Renard's to meet the Duke of Sussex, and to-morrow we all dine at Mrs Bushes in the Citty. She is sister to Mrs Utterson, & there we meet a large party. We

[2] From W. J. Lawrence's copy. Never printed.

[3] The complimentary cup presented by the Drury Lane actors and managers in honor of Sir Giles Overreach. See below, page 162.

got a present of a Hare & two pheasants from Lady Elizabeth Whitbread yesterday & to-day Mr Maxwell send us a Hare & Brace of partridge, which we keep for tuesday when Mr & Mrs Grenfell, Mr & Mrs Utterson, Mr & Mrs Bush and Miss Brown, Mr Blackman, Mr Dinman, Mrs Plumptre & a Miss Maxwell dine here . . . Lord Biron is enchanted with Edmund, and is like a little dog behind the scenes, following him everywhere . . .

Your affect Friend,

S. Chambers

The story is told that after the first-night performance Kean drove home to Clarges Street, much as he had run home to Cecil Street after the opening of *The Merchant of Venice*, to bring the joyful tidings to Mary. "Well, Edmund," said she, "and what did Lord Essex say?" "Damn Lord Essex," cried he, *"the pit rose at me."* History or legend, the exchange is beautifully true of both parties.

According to the logic of the theatre which believes that because one play by X has made a hit another play by X will also make one, the star and his managers decided to revive Massinger's *Duke of Milan*. The logic, as usual, broke down. *The Duke of Milan*, although a good tragedy for Massinger, proved not to be a good tragedy for Kean. It was given seven performances at steadily decreasing receipts. The only noteworthy event of its run occurred on the night of March 26, when the actor failed to appear at the theatre. No word having come to the management of his intentions or whereabouts, Rae was obliged to announce baldly that he could not be found; would the audience take *Douglas* instead? No, they preferred to wait. Half an hour later Rae offered *Fortune's Frolic* and *Ways and Means*, which were at length accepted, but were done very badly. The audience was not pleased. The next day Kean gave out that in returning to London from Woolwich, his gig had been overturned by his horse starting at a flock of sheep. This caused some public uneasiness, which he allayed by a letter stating that his physician countenanced his appearance on the following Monday.

But rumor meanwhile was abroad with a different story, to the tune that Kean had got so drunk at Deptford that he was unable to proceed to London. As to just what happened, although there are many accounts, there is no reliable report, but it seems likely that rumor was in the main true. At any rate, Kean's excuse was not generally believed. The *New Monthly Magazine* of May 1, 1816, after declaring that "we shall not pretend to question the truth of this statement" (viz., the gig story), proceeded evasively to deliver a warning lecture.

Too often we have had to lament that men, exalted by their genius, should suffer themselves to be precipitated from it by failings and vices which degrade them to the level of the lowest of their species. With the striking example of Cooke before his eyes, we trust that Kean will have the prudence to avoid the fatal rock on which the former perished [that is, drink]: nay, we think that a more friendly office could not be rendered by those who value him than to have a starling taught to sing in his ears every hour of the day the emphatic admonition: "Remember Cooke!"

When Kean appeared as Shylock on April 1 he was greeted with a mixture of applause and hisses. According to the established custom of that day, an actor who had offended must apologize to his audience at the first opportunity. A considerable portion of the present audience evidently felt that an apology was due. But Kean, who never apologized if he could help it, got round them by a speech which neither apologized nor explained.

For the first time in my life I have disappointed the expectations of a London audience; for the first time in this theatre, out of two hundred and sixty-nine nights, as the public will acknowledge and the managers will attest. To your favor I am indebted for the reputation which I enjoy, and I throw myself on your candor as a shield against unworthy prejudices.

The appeal sufficed to an audience which was not very angry. They applauded and forgave. But the incident, had they known it, was big with prophecy. It was the first of a series of similar offenses which was to grow thicker in time until the public patience was fretted to breaking. The descent had begun.

During most of April Kean was away in the provinces filling engagements which included Glasgow. On his return he entered into rehearsals for a new tragedy, brought out on the ninth of May. This was *Bertram*, by the Rev. R. C. Maturin, a gifted but over-charged disciple of the Gothic School, whose lurid imagination had already given to the world *The Family of Montorio* and who was some years later to execute his *chef-d'oeuvre* in *Melmoth the Wanderer.* Scott recommended *Bertram* to Byron, and Byron recommended it to the committee, who for once acted on his advice. Maturin was one of the most satanic of the Satanists; his imagination lived on night, storms, forests, haunted ruins, tolling bells, withered hearts, blasting eyes, damnation, and hell. His play is a symphony of crime, rage, vengeance, despair, played *fortissimo* throughout. It begins with an appalling storm and ends with shrieks of madness. Bertram himself is Robber Moor, seasoned with Manfred. Maturin, as a dramatist and a poet, had powers of no mean order, though limited to the treatment of passionate emotions; but he had not that control over them by which they might have come to something really good. His dialogue is strained beyond all decorum, yet in the building of speeches, in the turns and variations of impassioned discourse, he showed a true dramatic instinct. His poetry, likewise, though surcharged with the *clichés* of his school and of his times, shows gleams of murky power through the smoke. It is not much to say of him that only two lines may be quoted with admiration:

> Have we not loved as none have ever loved,
> And must we part as none have ever parted?

Yet to find two such lines in the verse tragedy of the period (excepting, of course, Coleridge and the other poets who were not dramatists) is something of an adventure.

The play opened hesitantly, hung for two performances in the balance of public favor, then swung sharply upward and settled into a run which not only carried it into June but preëmpted most of the acting nights of the theatre. It was most definitely a success, being given twenty-two times before the close of the season. The leading female rôle, Imogine, was announced on the first bills as taken by a Young Lady ("being her first appearance on any stage"), whose name turned out to be Somerville. She had both good looks and talent, which gave her the foundations of a fairly successful career, first as Miss Somerville and later as Mrs. Bunn.

The last novelty of the season was *Every Man in His Humour,* produced on June 5 for Kean's benefit, and repeated once thereafter. The part of Kitely, the jealous husband, had been in the general repertory since the days of Garrick, who had done much with it. Therefore Kean's choice is understandable enough, particularly as the humors of a jealous man were such as he might be expected to handle with effect. But the effect turned out to be nothing remarkable. The second performance, which drew only £149, showed that the public was not amused.

On June 25 the committee presented him, amid the proper ceremony of speeches, with a large silver cup costing three hundred guineas in commemoration of his performance of Sir Giles Overreach. The cost was borne by a subscription raised among the committee and players of the theatre. Their names were cut on its sides, showing a complete roster save for the two leading comedians, Munden and Dowton. The former withheld from parsimony, the latter, who never liked Kean, from spleen. "You can cup Mr. Kean if you like, but you don't bleed me," is his reported *bon-mot*.

On June 27, with a repetition of *Bertram*, the season closed. So far as Kean's end of it is concerned, it was stronger than the last. Seven new parts were presented, of which three were decided successes and two were to stay permanently in his repertory. In fact, out of one hundred and four performances, sixty-six were divided among these three. The old successes appear sparsely—seven performances of *Richard*, four of *Othello*, two of *Macbeth*, one of *Hamlet*, none of *The Merchant of Venice*. All in all, thanks chiefly to Overreach and Bertram, it was a good season for Kean, particularly as his salary had been raised to £25. But the management counted a total of receipts which amounted to but £58,017, more than £9,000 under the last year's total. Covent Garden took in over £78,000.

During the summer Kean, as usual, was reaping money in the provinces. Between June 29 and July 12 he played a season at Bath, where his Overreach made a great sensation. Genest[4] tells that on the second presentation the curtain was called down at the point where Overreach is dragged from the stage, the audience being unwilling to hear

[4] *Some Account of the English Stage*. VIII, 565. Genest's dating of the Bath season is unquestionably correct. Yet Harvard possesses a Bristol bill of Thursday, July 11, citing Kean as Othello for his benefit and the last night of the season. Mrs. W. West, who was also in the Bath company, played Desdemona. Unless there is some mistake we must suppose that Kean was alternating Bath and Bristol.

anything that might take away from the impression they had received. It was one of the common phenomena of star-worship in those days. He then went to Liverpool, Exeter, Plymouth, Taunton (early in September), and in October played his first season in Edinburgh—first, that is, unless we can believe the tradition that he visited there in his early 'prentice days. His success was quite as great as it had been elsewhere, although the public of Edinburgh, devoted to the Kemble family and the Kemble manner, were a little slow in adjusting themselves to the new style. But he moved them as Richard, convinced them as Shylock, and swept them off their feet as Overreach. Thereafter they were his, and their critics were pleasantly occupied with making room for him beside their adored Siddons.

On July 7, 1816, Richard Brinsley Sheridan died. Drury Lane, desiring naturally to celebrate in some fitting manner the man who had been their most famous governor, the author of *The School for Scandal* and *Pizarro*, planned a memorial series of his plays, to open early in September with *The School for Scandal* and the recitation of a monody. To this end Douglas Kinnaird wrote Kean requesting him to recite the monody and to play Joseph Surface for the one night only. The tragedian instantly and haughtily refused. For one thing, he had made engagements for early September in various towns. For another, he would not hear of Joseph Surface. "Mr. Kean returns to the committee the character of Joseph Surface which he has with surprise and mortification received this day." He "submissively" reminded them of his material services rendered to their theatre, and declared that "he will never insult the judgment of a British public by appearing before them in any other station but the important one to which they have raised him." This indignant rejection of a comedy rôle sounds a little hollow from a man who delighted in playing Abel Drugger: the real motive lay in his inveterate determination never to play second parts under any circumstances. The committee, with a sigh, resigned the struggle. Wallack played Joseph, Mrs. Davison recited the monody, and Sheridan was honored without the assistance of Kean.[5]

[5] This episode has been wrongly placed in 1819. The letters of Kinnaird may be found in the *Athenæum* of April 30, 1836.

The season of 1816-17, save for one notable event, was the dullest that Kean had thus far endured. A glance over the receipt list shows a depressing array of figures, the majority between two and three hundred pounds, but descending frequently below one hundred and fifty, and rising only ten times above three hundred. None of the new parts won anything but an indifferent success. *Timon of Athens* (October 28) was given seven times running and then dropped forever; Colman's *Iron Chest* (November 23), which had been a prosperous vehicle for Kemble, was given seventeen times, to houses varying from middling to poor; Southerne's old tragedy of the Noble Savage, *Oroonoko* (January 20) ran for nine nights; a new tragedy by Maturin, *Manuel* (March 8), from which much was expected, proved to be feeble stuff and lasted four performances; *The Surrender of Calais* (May 17), by George Colman the younger, barely lasted two. For his benefit he chose Dr. John Browne's *Barbarossa* and the sentimental afterpiece *Paul and Virginia,* the latter because he could sing nicely and liked to exhibit his voice. The benefit was crowded, but at the single repetition of *Barbarossa* the public showed that it cared little for Kean in that rôle. And so the season came to an end, showing on the treasurer's books an intake of only £41,060. It was calamitous. The notes which, in the playhouse record books from which I have taken my data, follow the entries for the season, are full of gloomy consideration. The largest receipt was £500 (to which should be added that no other receipt came above £400); ten houses were under £100; nearly six hundred free tickets were distributed nightly; the average receipt was £197.

The woes of the committee of management were augmented by signs of revolt among the shareholders. The *Morning Post* of February 15, 1817, carried a letter from "An Old Subscriber" in which he stated that the dissatisfaction of the shareholders with the mismanagement of the theatre had been steadily increasing, that early in the season the committee had half-agreed to resign in favor of a more experienced single manager, but had subsequently changed their mind and had refused to furnish a list of subscribers so that a general meeting might be called. The only thing now to do was to call a general meeting by public announcement at the earliest possible date. It had been alleged, he added, that the theatre was saddled with a debt of £40,000 and that £100 shares had dropped to £20. This meeting was held and was reported in the *Times* of March 21. Mr. George Lamb bore the brunt for his fellow managers of a hot attack, denying that the committee had been proved to be incompetent or that the finances of the theatre were in the state represented, and complaining of the many abusive anonymous letters he had received. The only action taken was to adopt Mr. Grenfell's motion to let the theatre on lease, provided adequate rent and security could be obtained. The committee, accordingly, was left in control, but with its back to the wall.

Within the Kean family, also, things were not going too well. The following letter from the Earl of Essex, of the Drury Lane subcommittee, to Mary Kean is but vaguely allusive, yet it reflects clearly enough a condition which had begun to make itself felt uncomfortably and which would grow worse as the years passed. At its base were those wildnesses of conduct which were beginning to give Kean a scurrilous notoriety about town; the immediate source of worry lay evidently in certain unpleasant and quite possibly calumnious stories which had come to Mary's ear; and to top off there is a hint of the ominous Miss Tidswell's undying hostility toward the wife of her Edmund. All this probably weighed little on Edmund, but it troubled Mary. She was now learning that the life of prosperity had its thorns, as well as the life of poverty.

Lord Essex's letter follows:[6]

When you have lived as long as I have, you will find out, my dear Madam, that half the world is made up of *envy*, *hatred*, and *malice*. I have heard many idle stories about my friend Kean; and being interested, as I am, in his welfare, and the prosperity of both of you, I always endeavoured to disprove what I knew originated in falsehood and malevolence . . . I do not know anything of Miss Tidswell myself, and am sorry she should wish to be an enemy to those who, I am sure, will always act with gratitude towards her. Kean cannot do better than follow the advice, *upon all occasions*, of two such excellent men as Mr. Whitbread and Mr. Grenfell; and I am also certain, that your mind and heart towards him has the right bias, which ought to regulate it. Depend upon it, I never

[6] Printed in the *Athenæum*, April 30, 1836.

will believe idle stories. I wish you both happiness and comfort, which, I am sure, is in store for you, and which it is impossible either of you should be so unwise as to sacrifice . . .

I am yours ever faithfully,

June 11th, 1817. Essex.

The unhappy season of 1816-17 was enlivened by only one episode of note, but that was so full of color that it set the town agog for many days. On February 12 Covent Garden produced a new tragedian in the person of Junius Brutus Booth, who had been gathering bays in the provinces and had come up from the Brighton Theatre. He chose *Richard III*. The first-night audience found him to be a small man of more than common talents, but what struck them most forcibly was that his style seemed to be based on a close study of Kean. There were his manner, his energy, his pauses and sudden transitions. All the press commented on the resemblance. The *Chronicle*, with a few other papers loyal to Kean, snubbed him as a mere imitator. But the *Morning Post* voiced the majority opinion in discovering a degree of excellence, even of genius, which more than offset the regrettable resemblances. He was, it seemed, almost a duplicate Kean, not perhaps yet on a level with his master, but possessing a better voice and showing an original force that bade well to make a great star of him. In reviewing his second performance of Richard (February 13) the *Post* found that "to all the principal scenes he gave most forcible and masterly effect, and may be said to have already established himself at the height of his profession." The audiences were in no doubt about him; they applauded him with a fervor which recalled the first nights of Kean himself.

That gentleman was suddenly faced with a most unexpected and disquieting phenomenon. The popular acclaim of any new rival, of whatever school, would be painful to his ears, but how sharp, how alarming, must have been that pain when the rival proved to be his double! Were the disloyal multitude to be suffered to pour into Covent Garden in order to hear *his* accents in another mouth, to applaud *his* gestures in another's person? Yet what could he do except possess himself in outward patience and wait? He did not have to wait long. Before his third performance Booth had quarreled with the Covent Garden management over the primal root of evil. Booth wanted his salary fixed at a certain figure (£15 a week for three years, the newspapers said); Harris, the manager, offered him a much lower figure (reported to be £5) with the likelihood of increases according to his deserts. Almost as soon as the dispute was broached news of it traveled to Drury Lane, where the alert intelligence of Kean sensed that his opportunity had come. Ordering out his chariot he drove to his rival, plied him with compliments, extended a benignant hand, and told him to "jump in—he had got an engagement for him."[7] At Drury Lane Booth was flatteringly received by some members of the committee, including Lord Essex and Mr. Lamb, and cajoled into signing an agreement to play there at a salary substantially larger than had been offered by Harris. He protested afterwards that he had been carried by storm, without being allowed time for reflection, which may be true but is immaterial. What is more material is that he was welcomed in the most loving manner by the princes of Drury Lane and that Covent Garden found itself suddenly lacking its brightest star. The wrath of the cohorts of Harris was unbounded. They issued broadsides accusing the rival managers of gross breach of faith, citing an agreement drawn up between the two houses in Sheridan's time and later ratified by Whitbread and Lord Essex, that in case either theatre had been in treaty with an actor within a year the other theatre would not engage him until it had ascertained that all negotiations were ended. The fact of this agreement was indisputable: Mr. Douglas Kinnaird, who disapproved of the action of his committee, admitted it to be so, in the press. But the committee, unabashed, sat tight. They had their man.

On Thursday, February 20, they billed *Othello*, with Kean as the Moor and Booth as Iago. For the first time that season Drury Lane was filled to the roof. Public expectation, sharpened by the squabble and by the opportunity of seeing the two Keans on the same boards, rode high. Nor was it disappointed. The fortunate attendants at this spectacle saw a performance that none of them ever forgot. They

[7] So related by Booth's daughter in her *Passages, Incidents, and Anecdotes in the Life of Junius Brutus Booth*. N. Y., 1870. The account is substantially correct, inasmuch as Kean admitted that he was instrumental in drawing Booth to Drury Lane.

probably did not realize at the time the full meaning of what took place; the designs of Kean, masked behind his generous cordiality, were understood only upon reflection in the light of subsequent events. What they understood for the moment was that Kean played as he had never played before. He was possessed by a demon, he topped his best effects, he lifted them out of their seats, he played Booth off his feet. That wretched young man essayed his best, but he appeared to many present to be half stunned. Stories, for whose truth I cannot vouch, were later current of his distress—how he fled to the green room after one of the scenes and declared he would not face that fearful man again, had in fact to be coaxed back to the stage. The audience was hypnotized. Although they had welcomed Booth on his first entrance with loud applause, he lost ground with them after the great scenes of the third act had begun. Soon they were sitting with "a most appalling calm" when he had reason to expect the most approval. "When he ceased to speak," reported the *Post*, "he was lost among the subordinate characters, and it required an effort of memory to recognize him as the chief attraction of the night." There is no possibility of misconstruing Kean's motives on this occasion. Had he really meant well to Booth, had he really meant to play the patron as he pretended, he would have so conducted himself as to throw his protégé's abilities into as favorable a light as possible. But he never gave him a chance. As the *London Magazine* put it several years later, "They met—and Kean wrung the neck of his rival's glory forever!"

Between the acts he was all benevolence, leading forth his bewildered Iago by the hand, smiling like a happy father, by his gestures inviting the audience to share in the delight he felt for his friend's success.

On Saturday, February 22, *Othello*, with the same assignment of parts, was posted again, but as the time for performance came, Rae, as stage manager, appeared before the curtain bearing a paper in his hand and conveying by his presence the assurance that something had gone wrong. The paper was a letter from Booth received that afternoon, in which he regretted that owing to the agitation to which he had been subjected during the past week he had become too unnerved to play and had gone out of town to recuperate. Immediately on receipt of this message, Rae went on to say, he had gone to the actor's house, where Mrs. Booth had reported that her husband did complain of feeling unwell and had gone out—"but if he was out of town it was more than she knew." Rae then desired of the audience permission to act in Booth's place, which, after some opposition, was granted. Late that night another letter arrived from the truant, announcing that he repented of having left Covent Garden, where the most eligible situation was open to him, that at Drury Lane he found that every character he desired or was fitted to play was already in possession, and that he had returned to the forgiving arms of his first masters. In conclusion he begged the committee not to "persecute or molest a young man just entering into life, and who cannot afford either to be shelved (according to the theatrical phrase) at Drury-lane Theatre, or to be put into such characters as must infallibly mar all his future prospects."

By this letter, the essential fact of which is repeated in his daughter's memoir, Booth revealed the true purpose of the Drury Lane kidnapping. He was to be tied up in a three year's contract and then smothered with second line parts; to Kean's Richard, Hamlet, Macbeth he would play Richmond, Laertes, Macduff. No wonder the poor fellow was ill.

The theatres meanwhile were waging a broadside warfare in which each accused the other of bad faith. Drury Lane waved in the air its three-year contract. Covent Garden bore hard on the gentlemen's agreement sponsored by Sheridan. Of the mutual recriminations one deserves special notice because it was directed at Kean.

The Proprietors of Covent-Garden have received a notification from a person, who states that he was at a place called the *Coal Hole* on Sunday last, where a Club called *"The Wolves"* are accustomed to assemble, and that he heard the whole party pledge themselves to drive Mr. Booth from the Stage. If such a conspiracy exists it is severely punishable by law.

This charge, which was reprinted in the *Morning Post* of February 25, drew a reply from Kean in the issue of the twenty-seventh.

Sir,—I think it my duty, in justice to a society of which I once had the honour of being a member, to refute a most malicious piece of calumny.

The *Wolf Club* seems to have been the foil, with which the friends of the *rival theatre* have, for the last two years, parried the public censure against their unsuccessful candidates. I wish, therefore, through the medium of the public prints, to inform their *fears*, that such a society is no longer in existence, has not been for the last nine months, and, when it was, the principles of the institution were founded in integrity and *universal philanthropy*. The misrepresentations, with regard to this Society, laid before the public, rendered it, unjustly, an object of reprobation, and in acknowledgment of my duty to the public, I resigned it.

With regard to Mr. Booth, that I have the highest opinion of his talents I gave proof when I recommended his engagement to the Drury-lane Committee. If any one should assert that I would, individually or accessorily, do anything detrimental to the interests of Mr. Booth, I should be happy, in person, to tell the propagator of such a report that it is a falsehood.

I remain, Sir, etc.

The retort was unanswerable.[8] Hereafter Kean's name was left out of the quarrel.

The quarrel itself died quickly away. On February 24 the committee of Drury Lane filed a bill in Chancery against Booth and the Covent Garden proprietors for an injunction to restrain the actor from appearing anywhere but at Drury Lane. On the next day, however, following wiser counsel, they themselves petitioned to have their bill dismissed out of court, which was done.

But the public, which seldom remained neutral in cases like this, waged a little war of their own. The audience at Booth's first reappearance at Covent Garden, Tuesday, February 25, were made up of partisans and enemies. The partisans predominated, but so stout was the enemy campaign that the whole evening was a hubbub, nothing of the play was heard, neither Booth nor Fawcett, the manager, would be listened to, and fist battles were numerous. Even after the farce a considerable number stayed on, crying "No shelving!" "No wolves!" "Booth forever!" On the following Saturday he played Richard to as great a tumult as before. He tried to speak, apologized abjectly by mouth and by placard, but could not be heard. The opposition, however, rapidly wore itself out. By March 6 he was playing Richard

[8] It was backed by the landlord of the Coal Hole, who issued a circular on February 25 declaring that the Wolves had ceased to exist many months ago.

with all possible success, and when he essayed Overreach, on March 8, he was, says the *Post,* greeted by "thunders of applause, shouts, waving of hats, and every symptom, not only of sincere reconciliation, but of growing popularity."

Yet the victory remained with Kean. With one terrible stroke he had broken his rival's back, and the victim knew it. Booth played on into the spring, but with knowledge that the game was up. The public lost its interest in him. The press, on closer inspection, decided that he was no more than a talented copy. At the close of his engagement he drifted about for several years none too successfully, played again at Drury Lane during Kean's first absence in the United States, then followed him across the water, where he gained reputation and died, leaving a son who was to kill Abraham Lincoln and another son who was to be America's greatest actor.

The same season which saw the rise and fall of Booth saw also the first London appearance of an actor who was to prove a more formidable rival to Kean and a more lasting thorn in his flesh. This was William Charles Macready, son of a well-known provincial manager, who after winning great favor in the provinces was called to Covent Garden and came out there on September 16, 1816, as Orestes in Ambrose Philips' *Distressed Mother.* His reception was warm enough to keep him on as a permanent member of the company. By slow degrees his reputation grew until as Rob Roy and later as Virginius (1820) he obtained such success as to place him among the two or three leading actors of Great Britain. But not until then did he become a person of special note to Kean.

On June 23, 1817, John Philip Kemble celebrated the end of his active career by a farewell performance at Covent Garden, playing Coriolanus before a house packed with worshippers. He retired, as he deserved, in glory, to the accompaniment of speeches, dinners, odes, and a memorial vase. Leaving behind the irksome duties, the petty jealousies, the unremitting labor, the manifold crosses and the exaltations of theatrical life, universally respected and regretted, he withdrew to a villa near Lausanne where, on the twenty-sixth of February, 1823, he died. With him closed that important chapter of stage history which, aided by his matchless sister, he had written. His departure left the field clear to his rival, who from now on could, without fear of serious challenge, call himself the king of the British stage.

Early in April Kean played at Glasgow, and later, April 8-14, at Edinburgh. The last night of his Glasgow engagement (April 14) was marked by misadventures of an ominous cast. *Bertram* was the play; the house was packed. All went well until the middle of Act III, when Kean failed to enter when he should and Imogine was obliged to leave the stage in order to fetch him. On his appearance he was hissed. "Mr. Kean," so runs the report in the *Times,* "with that irresistible turn of feature, looked at the audience—moved his lips in silence—his countenance and manner spoke more than a thousand apologies—he was forgiven and huzzaed." All went well again until the audience conceived that the fourth act had been cut, whereupon they grew angry and demanded that it be repeated. On this being refused, they kept up such a noise that the fifth act passed in dumb show. In the midst of it Kean advanced, motioned for silence, then with a look of "ineffable disdain" directed towards the gallery, demanded, "What is *your* wish, *gentlemen?*" Whereupon the pit applauded loudly, but what the gods did we are not told, though we may feel sure they did not sit quietly under the rebuke. According to the Glasgow *Herald,* cited by the *Times,* the audience had a right to be disgusted; the piece was mangled by cuts, the acting was bad, Kean's performance was careless. In fact an early suspicion that he was drunk grew, as the evening advanced, to a certainty. The scene is typical of many that were to follow, in increasing numbers.

During the summer Kean was, of course, on tour. One finds him in Dublin in July and at Manchester September 20 (for one night only).

The season of 1817-18 produced nothing astonishing. From November 24 to December 15 Kean was ill, from what cause I know not. His previous illnesses had been slight affairs of a few days or at most a week; this looks like a more serious matter. Grattan tells of visiting him one night in his dressing-room after the play (as nearly as one can tell it was in 1816-17) and finding him, "as was usual after the performance of any of his principal parts, stretched on a sofa, retching violently, and throwing up blood." Something within his body was in a bad way, perhaps more things than one. He was already, at the age of thirty, in decay.

His first new play, offered December 22, was *Richard, Duke of York,* a tragedy arranged by J. H. Merivale from the three parts of *Henry IV* and designed to reawaken the interest in Richard of Gloucester which many repetitions of Shakespeare's play had dulled. It did not prove to be attractive and died after the seventh performance. The succeeding novelty had more interest. This was an arrangement of *The Bride of Abydos* made by William Dimond. Much was expected from a collaboration of the most-talked-of poet and the most-talked-of tragedian, and something indeed was realized, for the play ran continuously from its beginning (February 5) for twelve nights. But the run was thus prolonged less by the public demand than by managerial puffing. By the twelfth performance the play had so nearly exhausted its welcome that it appeared only twice more and then dropped. On April 24, at Kean's insistence, Marlowe's *Jew of Malta* was revived, and though coolly received was squeezed through eleven performances. In addition to these new parts, he acted Young Norval in Home's *Douglas* (May 6, four performances), Alexander the Great in an alteration of Lee's *Rival Queens* (June 8, benefit and single performance), and Shakespeare's *King John* (June 1). In choosing the last rôle he was decidedly in error. *King John* had grown to be the peculiar property of Kemble, partly from his own excellence and partly from the superb Constance of Mrs. Siddons. But Kean had no special fitness for his part and for Constance he had nothing better than Miss Macauley, a recent and unprofitable recruit from Dublin, so that far from ousting the memory of Kemble he languished through three performances whose combined income would scarcely have furnished a bumper house in his first year. With £87 in the house on the third night, he struck the lowest depth to which he had yet fallen.

Late in December he played an engagement at Ipswich, on January 7 he played *Othello* at Windsor, and during parts of March and April he was in Scotland, playing Edinburgh twice (March 16 to 24 and April 7 to 9), and Dumfries (April 10 and 11).

CHAPTER VIII

MANAGERS AND MISMANAGERS

In June of 1815 Lord Byron wrote to Tom Moore:

> I wished and wish that you were in the Committee, with all my heart. It seems so hopeless a business, that the company of a friend would be quite consoling . . . All my new function consists in listening to the despair of Cavendish Bradshaw, the hopes of Kinnaird, the wishes of Lord Essex, the complaints of Whitbread, and the calculations of Peter Moore, all of which, and whom, seem totally at variance. C. Bradshaw wants to light the theatre with *gas,* which may, perhaps (if the vulgar be believed), poison half the audience, and all the *dramatis personæ.* Essex has endeavoured to persuade Kean not to get drunk; the consequence of which is, that he has never been sober since. Kinnaird, with equal success, would have convinced Raymond that he, the said Raymond, had too much salary. Whitbread wants to assess the pit another sixpence,—a damned insidious proposition,—which will end in an O. P. combustion. To crown all, Robins, the auctioneer has the impudence to be displeased, because he has no dividend. The villain is a proprietor of shares, and a long-lunged orator in the meetings. I hear he has prophesied our incapacity,—"a foregone conclusion," whereof I hope to give him signal proofs before we are done.

Six years later, in his *Detached Thoughts,* Byron turned in retrospect to the committee days at Drury Lane, sketching good-humoredly the tribulations caused by authors, actors, and his fellow managers. He is speaking now of the time, after the death of Whitbread, when the subcommittee ruled:

> Then the Committee!—then the Sub-Committee!—we were but few, but never agreed. There was Peter Moore who contradicted Kinnaird, and Kinnaird who contradicted every body: then our two managers, Rae and Dibdin; and our secretary, Ward! and yet we were all very zealous and in earnest to do good and so forth.

To Byron, who took his duties lightly and was reproved by his colleagues for levity and "buffooning with the histrions," it was all very amusing. But to the rest of the committee, to the actors, and to the theatrical world at large it was no laughing matter, this attempt at management by a handful of gentlemen amateurs. Let them be as zealous and as earnest as possible, they could not, in the very nature of things, conduct a business so temperamental as a great theatre. And in the three years since they had gone into power Mr. Robins, the auctioneer's, prophecy had been amply verified, for every year the receipts fell off and every year the value of the shares dropped lower. Something, the proprietors thought, had to be done.[1]

It will be remembered that the continued losses of the theatre had been the subject of a meeting of shareholders in March, 1817, when the subcommittee had received a heavy fire of criticism. It will also be recalled that on Whitbread's death in July, 1815, the management had been vested in the subcommittee, which then consisted of George Lamb, Douglas Kinnaird, Peter Moore, Lord Essex and Lord Byron. At the time we are speaking of Byron had left England, and Kinnaird had resigned from the committee in October, 1816. Of the remaining members, the most active were Moore, as treasurer, and Lamb, as general-in-chief. During 1816-17 Rae served as stage manager, and he and Lamb ran the theatre, choosing all plays without having the necessary judgment (if we may believe the *Authentic Statement*), and mounting them lavishly. Although the subcommittee made futile gestures of interference and Moore wrote urgent letters on economy, Lamb overrode all objections. Before the season of 1817-18 Rae ceased to be stage manager. The subcommittee wanted to replace him with Stephen Kemble, the fat brother of John Philip; Lamb wanted, and got, Raymond,[2] with H. Johnstone as his assistant. Raymond dying on October 20, Lamb appointed Johnstone to his office. Then Kean, who disliked Johnstone, issued an ultimatum that he would not serve under the new manager or obey any order of his. Instead of resisting this act of insubordination, the committee weakly compromised, by allowing Kean to be the manager of his own plays. The result was to add another source of expense and failure, for Kean chose *The Duke of York*, *The Jew of Malta*, and *King John*, all expensive and

[1] The material for this account is drawn mainly from *An Authentic Statement of Facts Connected with the Interior Management of Drury-Lane Theatre, for the Last Three Seasons*. London, 1818. See also S. J. Arnold, *A Letter to All the Proprietors of Drury Lane Theatre*. London, 1818.

[2] Formerly stage manager, dismissed in the summer of 1816.

all losses. Meanwhile the committee, stirring itself to action, had issued an edict on November 7, that no new piece should be produced without their collective approval. Lamb then promptly resigned, with disparaging remarks on that kind of mismanagement in which everyone had a voice and no one authority. Shortly thereafter the committee appointed Stephen Kemble.

Just as the Honorable George Lamb figures as the villain of the *Authentic Statement*, so figures the Honorable Peter Moore in Arnold's *Letter to the Proprietors*. The treasurer of Drury Lane is there scored for his "mean and narrow policy," by the exercise of which, it is true, he has reduced the expenses of Drury Lane by some £27,000 a year, but only through depriving the theatre of its prime attraction, "a powerful phalanx of combined talent." In the interests of budget, fine performers have not only not been recruited, but have been actually driven away.

One gets a pretty clear idea from all this of the state of affairs indoors at Drury Lane. On one side is Lamb, playing the dictator with infinite zeal but little judgment, on another is Moore, striving so conscientiously to save, that in catching at pennies he loses sight of the problem as a whole, on still a third side is the independent principality of Kean, and between are a dissatisfied group of actors and other servants of the house. There is no discipline. In three years, counting assistants, there have been six stage managers. Meanwhile things grow steadily worse. In 1816-17 the expenses are more than £5,000 above income, in 1817-18 more than £4,000.[3] Nothing could be more badly mismanaged.

The basis of the security with which Kean was able to flout the discipline of a playhouse and impose his will on that of his employers is perfectly clear. They did not dare to displease him because he was their one source of income. It is true that the source was running sadly dry, that night after night he did not draw enough money to pay the running expenses, but one glance at the ledger of the nights when he did not play was enough to tell them how much worse off

[3] From a report of the subcommittee rendered in August, 1818. The precise figures are:

Date	*Income*	*Expenses*
1816-17	£43,926.10.9	£49,223.1.4
1817-18	£43,068.13.0	£47,715.11.10

they would be without him. Then, too, he was even more a possible than an actual asset—one could never tell when he might strike gold again—there was Overreach, for example. If he should go over to Covent Garden!—what orphans they would then become! So they clung to him, petted him, spoiled him, gave him his head in everything, let him play Barabas and John, and went on into debt.

On May 29, 1818, a meeting of the subcommittee and actors was held for the consideration of ways and means. Peter Moore, grown blind as a miser through poring over his ledgers, proposed that all actors whose salaries exceeded £4 should consent to a reduction proportioned to the amount they were paid, but they all protested vehemently. Dowton, offering at the same time to lend the treasury £500, declared with passion that he would never degrade his profession by degrading his salary. A special committee was then directed to ascertain the financial status of the theatre. Their report, submitted on June 8, showed the following debts:

Old claims	£ 3,718.5.11
Bond holders (principal)	24,416.5.0
Bond holders (interest)	4,871.0.8
New renters' annually due	12,812.11.3
Dividend arrears	1,280.5.8
Duke of Bedford's arrears	1,333.2.1
Tradesmen and authors	31,849.2.10
Total	£80,280.13.5

They recommended two principal measures of reform: (1) An important reduction in salaries and personnel; although, they acknowledged, any hope of liquidation must come rather from increased attraction than from decreased expenditure. (2) That the system of management be changed, and the theatre be put in the hands of a single qualified manager.

The committee no doubt discussed both measures at length, but for the moment they adopted neither.

Compared to these woes the affairs of Miss Macauley were a very small thorn. That lady was a turbulent personage, of the kind which is a perpetual trouble to herself, her friends, and her enemies, inordinately vain, never satisfied, driven by a demonic restlessness from post to post, and forever suspecting the presence of cabal. In an unguarded moment Drury Lane had been persuaded to bring her over from Dublin. She came out as Lady Randolph in *Douglas* on May 6, 1818, made a favorable impression, was cast as Constance in *King John* and failed. Oxberry says that she was so full of bile against Kean, whom she had known as a ragged trooper and whose success she found it hard to forgive, that she set out to play Constance as badly as possible. However that may be, she played it in such style that her services were then and there relinquished. In her usual way, she saw herself as the victim of persecution, denounced the managers, denounced Kean, denounced everybody to anyone who would listen to her, and when she had told everyone whom she could reach verbally, she had recourse to print. Her *Theatric Revolution, or, Plain Truth Addressed to Common Sense* appeared in 1819. It is mainly an attack on Kean, who by now had become the whole cause of her troubles.

> Mr. Kean stands in general estimation, as the enemy of his profession, and the public; as one, who to raise himself to a climax of theatrical grandeur, has bartered the best feelings of human nature; as one who has endeavoured to sacrifice the feelings, fortunes, and even hopes of Actors, and Authors, unless they made themselves subservient to him; as one who repayed the generosity of the public, by keeping from them all prospects of amusement but what centred on himself.

From Drury Lane she passed, for a brief moment, to Covent Garden, from which she was as quickly dropped. In 1820 she pleaded her larger case in *Three Questions to the Public*. As late as 1824 she was still inveighing against the patent theatres in *Facts against Falsehood*. She was a most persistent protestant.

So notorious a trouble maker would not be worth quoting here if there were not a grain of truth in her charges. Whatever her own rights and wrongs may have been, she did but repeat what others, with better authority, were saying of Kean. We have seen what he did to Booth. Oxberry, whose anecdotes of Drury Lane rest on his own connection with the acting staff, gives us his word for it that after Miss Somerville's most promising début in *Bertram*, Kean would have nothing to do with her in another part—"She is too big for me," was the reason he gave, but everyone knew that he meant, "She is too good, she will stand in my light." For this reason the poor girl was given only secondary rôles, so that at length she moved dispiritedly into the provinces. Other unpleasant stories were current, as, for example, that he gave up *Manuel* because Rae, as De Zelos, far outshone him. One does not, however, need to go to green room gossip to know that Kean was very jealous of his fellow artists. He has left a sufficient record of that in his own utterances. Of his behavior to authors we shall have occasion to speak later on.

During the summer of 1818, for the first time in his life, Kean took a vacation. Accompanied by Mary he went first to Paris, where he was received with all honors by his brother potentate, the great Talma of the Comédie française, given a banquet, introduced to the members of the Comédie, and presented with a gold snuffbox by the manager. Pursuing his travels he went south in a chaise, visited Lake Geneva, sang to the monks at St. Bernard, and climbed Mount Blanc—or so he said when he reached home, but the books which record ascents do not contain his name and modern skepticism holds that his climbing was wholly cerebral.

He arrived in London full of enthusiasm for a new part, namely, Orestes. In Paris he had seen Talma play sad Electra's brother in the *Andromaque* of Racine, with such effect, especially in the close where Orestes after the murder of Pyrrhus and the suicide of Hermione, breaks into a fine flight of madness, that he could scarcely wait to show his public what *he* could do with it. For his vehicle he revived a play better left dead, *The Distressed Mother*, an anaemic variation on Racine's fine tragedy composed by Ambrose Philips.[4] The production came forth on October 22, but far from being wrought on by the expected pity and terror the audience seemed to be only mildly interested in the distraught son of Agamemnon. After six presentations the play was dropped. Then a little later, on December 3, he did what the committee was always hoping he would do—he struck gold.

John Howard Payne, the American actor, dramatist, and poet of *Home, Sweet Home*, had been in England for some time plying his mystery where he could find engagements about the provinces and

[4] The play chosen by Macready for his London début in September, 1816.

offering his plays to managers who put them away on their shelves. To Drury Lane he had sent a verse tragedy entitled *Brutus, or, the Fall of Tarquin,* which he had manufactured chiefly from plays on the subject by Cumberland and Dowman, and it had been accepted. There has always been something not quite accountable about the success of this entirely mediocre play. Perhaps its subject was attractive to a public which had long admired the high Roman fashion of Cato and Coriolanus. I am inclined to think they had a weakness for togas and fasces. Perhaps their liking was wholly due to Kean, who, although he had little of the Roman in his microcosm, seems for once to have found a part of that kind to suit him. At any rate, the play ran as no play of his had run before or would run again, for thirty-nine consecutive performances and for a total of fifty-two before the end of the season. It must be admitted that, from the point of view of cash return, it was not a high-powered run, because the receipts of all but a few nights lay under £300, but in the aggregate they lay well over the line between profit and loss and the total income was better than £10,000. This, in the present state of Drury Lane, was almost prosperity. From now on *Brutus* kept an important place in the repertory of Kean.

The next important event was the production on February 15, 1819, of *Switzerland,* by Miss Jane Porter, a minor episode in the Kean annals which nevertheless throws considerable light on the tragedian's artistic *mores.* The story of what occurred may best be told as the authoress understood it.[5]

Having set up with considerable success as a novelist through *The Scottish Chiefs* and *Thaddeus of Warsaw,* Miss Porter had not thought much about the fascinating art of playwriting until Whitbread at one time requested her to write a play for him in the style of her romances. She had then declined, but in talking later with a confidential friend of Kean, she was much struck at hearing that the tragedian longed to have some one write for him a part of heroic virtue, so that he might "shew the world, he had talents for something besides villains." All her strong moral impulses kindled at the idea, and she

[5] Taken from a letter of Miss Porter to Mrs. Whitelocke, Clifton, near Bristol, April 23, 1819. Harvard Library.

set to work immediately on a Swiss theme. At the beginning of the present season Kean pledged himself to give his utmost powers to the part, he met the author daily at rehearsals without hinting the slightest objection, and often rehearsed so finely as to draw applause from the manager.

Think, then, my astonishment, when on the night of Public Representation, the Curtain drew up, and discovered all this promised energy, transformed into an almost motionless Automaton! He appeared to have lost his memory, and his power of action: The other Performers became disconcerted in their parts: and the confusion on the Stage, being now answered by an equal confusion amongst the audience, the whole became a chaos of uproar. "Shame!—Shame Kean!"—burst from every part of the House; contending with the vociferous yells of a set of wretches, who could only have come from the lowest orgies of the Western Hustings of that day . . . When the Curtain dropt, (though stunned by the cool, deliberate act of—I will not give it a name—I had just witnessed;) I yet sufficiently possessed myself, to insist on *withdrawing the Piece totally*; though urged by a member of the Committee, to permit a second representation, and with a new Performer. I had been betrayed, by the actor in whose honour and talents I had trusted!

One thing the unhappy author failed to perceive was that her play was in itself a dull thing, a tiresome sequence of conversation without action. Consequently part of the opposition arose from her own dramatic shortcomings. But she was right in insisting that her play did not have a fair trial. All the newspapers expressed indignation. The *Morning Herald* surmised that even the scene shifters were in the conspiracy, because two scenes fell flat during the performance. But the head and front of offense came from Kean, who, as the *Theatrical Inquisitor* said, "did not in one single instance condescend to display his powers." Many in the audience cried out "Shame!"

And what were the motives behind all this? Miss Porter believed that her tragedy had been the pawn of a struggle for power between Kean and the committee. She had been informed, by some one, that the committee had wished to bring out *Switzerland* in the previous year but had been met with a counter proposal from Kean to do *The Jew of Malta*. The committee were obliged, unwillingly, to yield. A year later they again brought up *Switzerland*, meeting this time no opposition from the actor, who was all compliments and compliance. But underneath his smiles lay a dark purpose, to show that he meant to be master of all his field of action, that no play could succeed without his suffrage. "I do not like to dwell," lamented the unfortunate authoress, "on the features of the dark scene . . . —that my Play, was to Lead a kind of Forlorn-Hope, against a sort of theatrical usurpation!—to mount a breach, beneath which a mine was laid!"

In the absence of any testimony from the parties of the defense, one cannot say how exactly Miss Porter's interpretation of things agreed with the reality; at least their silence in the face of general censure tends to her support. She was admittedly influenced by another and similar quarrel, of much larger proportions, which had been going on under cover for more than a year and had at length burst into notoriety. In the autumn of 1817 one Charles Bucke had offered to Drury Lane a verse tragedy called *The Italians*; it had been accepted and its author voted the customary freedom of the house. But with the death of the Princess Charlotte, which occurred at this time, undertakings of the theatre were suspended for three weeks. On the reopening Kean read the tragedy, approved it enthusiastically, and it was announced in the bills for immediate performance. But first it had to yield to *The Bride of Abydos*, which had a prior claim, then to a comedy (*The Castle of Glendower*) in which Kean was interested, and still later to *The Jew of Malta*. By this time Bucke was growing impatient. He consented, however, to give way on the solemn assurance of the committee that his tragedy should be produced immediately after, and, in accordance, as soon as the *Jew* was out of the way, work was begun toward fitting *The Italians* with scenery and music. All was thus apparently going well, "when, one evening, that I chanced to be in the Green Room, it was hinted to me by Mr. Kean, that 'the character of Manfredi was too much in his line;'[6]—'that the Blind Man was too good;'—'that the Page would excite too much interest;'—and 'that no one should write a Tragedy for that House, without making the entire interest centre in the character *He* should perform.' "

[6] Kean was to play Albanio.

Much disturbed by these pointed remarks he made inquiries from which he learned disquieting news. One of the Drury Lane officials admitted that Kean's jealousy was well known; a literary friend, who had submitted a tragedy, received a letter from Kean to the effect that "unless the entire interest centered in the character, designed for him, it would neither suit his reputation, nor the interests of the Theatre, that it should be accepted." And he was still more disquieted by the receipt of a letter from Peter Moore, suggesting that his play be laid by. To this he vehemently objected; a rehearsal was called; the performers were invited to express their opinions as to the probable success of the play. They were manifestly cool—the play was beautifully written, they said, but they questioned whether, in the present unsettled state of public favor—and so on. Their coolness was attributed by members of the committee, "to the strong feeling of opposition, which had so frequently been expressed to all the measures they had proposed for the benefit of the Theatre." He was advised to pay no attention to it.

Nevertheless, such a state of confusion existed, such open hostilities between committee and performers, that Bucke at length withdrew his play. Yet he did not give up hope of production during the next year, because Moore had promised him his support. Accordingly, in January of 1819 he wrote a letter to Kean, reciting the whole story and asking for an interview. To this he received a brief, cold reply: Mr. Kean does not need to be instructed as to his duty to the public; he has nothing to do with the management of the theatre; if the committee chooses a play he will act in it to the best of his ability.

Meanwhile the *Switzerland* fiasco took place, the effect of which on Bucke was to make him withdraw his play at once and print it, with a preface retailing the history of the past year. So great was the public interest in the quarrel that by May seven editions had been printed, report of progress being added to the prefaces of the third, sixth, and seventh. Kean was forced to reply, in a haughty letter to the press of March 18; various gentlemen rushed to his defense in hasty pamphlets, impugning the merits of Bucke's play and the ethics of his campaign; but a considerable portion of the public and the press felt that an injustice had been done. The *Morning Herald*, for example, advised all literary men: "Never write for Drury-lane Theatre, so long as the present system continues: you but waste your noble energies; and subject yourselves not only to disappointment, but to insult."

Meanwhile *The Italians* was again put in rehearsal, this time with Rae in the rôle which Kean would have taken, without consulting the author or heeding his protests. As a matter of fact, a proceeding which might seem to be unwarrantable was justified by the copyright laws of the day, because a play once printed became free to any manager who wished to produce it. On April 3 the subject of all this controversy was presented to a full house in which every person was a partisan of one side or the other. The result, as might be expected, was riotous. The play was damned. After one more performance on April 12 to a thin house, it was dropped. When the aggrieved author applied for royalty he was told that by printing his play he had forfeited all claim.

Again we may decline to pronounce a final judgment on the charges brought against Kean. In this case, as with *Switzerland*, his position was strengthened by the fact that the play was weak and would have failed in any event. We may also discount as unproved Bucke's solemn belief that he was booed down by an organized claque, although it is quite true that with feeling running as high as it did his play was not judged impartially. But so circumstantial and so well documented is his story that one cannot refuse to accept its main features, which draw a picture of anarchy within the walls of Drury Lane, of a harassed, incompetent committee at odds with itself and with its company, and of an autocratic tragedian whose sole policy might be expressed: L'état, c'est moi. "Every person . . . knows," wrote Bucke in his first preface, "and knows well, that though Mr. Kean is saving that establishment with his right hand, he is ruining it with his left."

The effect of this episode, as of the *Switzerland* one, was bad for Kean—that is, with all persons who liked modesty in a popular actor. With others it made him something of a hero, but this was because of the unpopularity of the Drury Lane management.

On March 9, 1819, Kean adventured as Hotspur in *Henry IV* to the Falstaff of Stephen Kemble. He repeated it only once. On March

13 he displayed the quality of his judgment in plays by presenting a piece of trash from the pen of George Soane called *The Dwarf of Naples*, of which the *Theatrical Inquisitor* remarked that "the present production seems to us, an attempt to try what monstrous excess of absurdity an audience will tolerate." It lasted six performances. On May 13 he brought out for ten nights a very inoffensive dull play by Horace Twiss called *The Carib Chief*. And for his benefit (May 31) he revived Sheridan's famous *Pizarro*, with the farcical afterpiece, *All the World's a Stage*. The season closed on June 7 with a repetition of *Pizarro*, but for reasons which are not clear to me the company moved to the Haymarket for a short season of one month. I suspect that this was a benefit affair, designed to raise money for the debts of the theatre. One finds, for instance, that Kean "liberally offered" his services for a performance of *Richard III* on the eighteenth of June. The proprietors were direly in need of help, for the last season had been the most disastrous they had yet experienced. Despite the phenomenal run of *Brutus* the treasurer was able to show receipts amounting only to £34,337. Kean's salary had been advanced to £30 a week.

At Easter and again during the summer Kean was on tour, but I have not succeeded in tracing him anywhere except in Edinburgh, which he visited in April. He was in Liverpool some time in the autumn, and at Dumfries from October 25 to 29.

In June of 1819 the subcommittee of Drury Lane, perceiving at last that the inevitable is always inevitable, decided to resign their powers into the hands of a competent lessee-manager, who should pay a flat rent for the theatre and be free to make what he could of it. Kean was one of the first to apply. "The public," he said, "has witnessed the mismanagement that has brought this magnificent theatre to ruin: its restoration can only be achieved by a popular professional man! I now stand forward to devote my property, reputation, and experience, to this great cause—to cleanse the Augean stable, and 'raise a new Palmyra.' " For rent and taxes he offered £10,000 a year, but the printed articles of agreement which were drawn up to settle the relations between lessee and proprietors he rejected *in toto*. "I shut my door against all committees, expecting an immediate surrender of their keys and all privileges in possession. I select my officers, my own performers, 'my reason's in my will;' and can only be accountable to the proprietors for payment of the rent, and to the public for their amusements."

Such a cavalier proposal was not likely to meet with favor from the committee. Instead they listened attentively to another applicant, who had entered the ring almost before the bell had ceased ringing, that redoubtable captain of industry, Robert William Elliston. He came forward with many ingratiating words and an attractive proposal—to spend £7,000 on redecorating the auditorium, to pay £8,000 rent for the first year, £9,000 for the second, and £10,000 from then on for a total period of fourteen years—and he offered good security amounting to £25,000. On August 7 the committee accepted him. He strutted all over town, proud as Punch.

Kean was deeply vexed. The committee, he felt, had played him another low turn; he was not to be allowed to build the new Palmyra; the pleasant task of cleansing the Augean stables was intrusted to—of all persons—that officious busybody, his quondam plague, the ex-Napoleon of Wych Street. I cannot feel sure that Kean resented the selection of Elliston more than of any other person, but I think so. He seems to have harbored feelings toward his colleague which were always ready to break into hostility. At any rate, he promptly declared that he would never serve under his authority at any time or in any place. And having spoken vaguely in his proposals to the committee of going to America should he be rejected, he now reaffirmed that intention with public vehemence.

But Elliston was all concern, respect, and brotherly love; he extended his arms, he cast his eyes to heaven, and his tongue dripped honey. We find him, on August 28, writing in a tone of affectionate remonstrance.[7] He beseeches Kean not to go to America. Has Elliston offended him? Anything that can be done to make the terms satisfactory will be done, only let him name them. Does he imagine that Elliston will resume any part which is in Kean's repertory? "If," he continues in his inimitable manner, "if my L'Amour propria could urge me to such folly prudence would restrain me . . . I . . . think it

[7] This and the next two letters are at Harvard.

ROBERT WILLIAM ELLISTON

no degradation to perform Cassio to your Othello—I write currente calamo . . . Think of me as a friend."

Kean replied, on September 1, in a vein of studied insolence.

I congratulate you and the public on your accession to the diadem of Drury Lane, wearied and disgusted, as all sensible people must have been, with the stultified dynasty of the last two seasons. The lovers of the drama will hail with rapture a minister to their amusements so transcendent in his art and so mature in experience as Robert William Elliston.

As for his own humble affairs, he let it be known at the end of the last season that if he failed to get the Drury Lane managership he would go to America. The plans are all made; he leaves England early in November. He will be happy to treat with Elliston on his return, "but you must allow me to observe that even then it will not be consonant with my feelings to act in any Theatre, where I have not the full appropriation of my own talents & this I am aware can only be obtained by *nightly* engagements."[8] He will not trouble Elliston to pursue the correspondence further; he has prepared Mrs. Kean to answer any inquiries that may come in his absence. "Richards and Hamlets grow on every hedge & I doubt not but I shall shortly hear of some Dramatic Meteor, whose refulgence shall shrink into insignificance the twinkling Capacities of yours, Edmund Kean." To this he added a truly feline postscript: "If I shou'd go by water to the next world I should certainly relate to our great Master you thought it no degradation to act his Cassio!!"

Although still under contract with the theatre, at £1,000 penalty for breaking, Kean nevertheless declared that he would rather pay the forfeit than serve under Elliston. In fact he directed his solicitor to tender the fine, but it was refused. On September 24 Elliston wrote him again at length, reminding him of the contract but not threatening. He had, he said, posted Kean's name in the list of performers for the coming season; should he refuse to play, it would rest with him to explain to the public the reasons for not doing so. After all that Elliston had said and done, if Kean should not return it would look as though there were some personal feeling. If Kean indeed

[8] Engagements, that is, for a stipulated number of nights, instead of for the season, the salary of course to be on a nightly, instead of weekly, basis.

wished a year's leave to travel in America, he might have it at the close of the approaching season.

This was all very tactful. But underneath the soft Ellistonian glove was a mailed fist, about which little was said but whose existence was becoming painfully real to the rebellious actor. It was not simply the £1,000 fine. On the day after Elliston's last letter Kean wrote to a friend—a "Jack" somebody—saying: "I am staggered by legal opinions, they all agree, that Elliston can come down upon me for damages beyond the forfeiture, to the amount of ten thousand pounds, if this is the case it wou'd be madness to embark for America." In the face of this prospect he gave up the fight. And on the twenty-seventh of September Mary Kean wrote to Winston, of Drury Lane, that on the advice of friends her husband had consented to return into the fold, and would the eighth or twelfth of November do for his opening?

Having already sent to the press a denial that he was to take part in the new season, as the advance bills of the theatre had said, and his dispute being no longer a private matter, he felt it necessary to lay his grievances before the public. This he did in a long letter to the *Sunday Monitor* of October 3, in the course of which he revealed other sources of annoyance than those we have been dealing with. Inasmuch as it is a most characteristic document, I shall quote it almost entire.

For the last two years my situation at the Theatre has been highly embarrassing. I have been considered responsible for circumstances over which I have no controul, and even the press has attached blame to me for occurrences I could neither foresee nor avoid. It would be perhaps indelicate for me to enter into particulars, but you, Sir, seem yourself to be aware, that I have been an innocent sufferor upon occasions when I should have been held blameless. When the Theatre fell into the hands of Mr. Elliston, I understood that he had made such arrangements as were a virtual breach of my articles, and I was unwilling to embarrass an undertaking of such risk and importance by returning to claim their fulfilment. The former reason still operating powerfully on my mind as an inducement to withdraw myself, for a period, I thought it would be equally advantageous both to Mr. Elliston, and myself, to take upon me the responsibility of breaking with him. Under the circumstances, too, which had come to my knowledge, I thought that Mr. Elliston would himself consider the thousand pounds penalty, which I offered to pay, a full equivalent for my services; and I, even now, doubt whether he would not prefer this arrangement. By my articles I must be manager on the nights on which I play, and this must necessarily embarrass Mr. Elliston, if he has not provided for it. By another clause in my articles, which I only mention by the way, since I have a right to demand their fulfilment to the *very letter,* to shew that Mr. Elliston could not have contemplated my return, my name must still continue as large in the bills as the Committee first chose to advertise it. Should I insist upon my right in this point, Mr. Elliston will be forced to break with an actor (in his line) of the first importance in his profession—I mean Mr. Dowton, who has in his articles, I understand, stipulated that my name should be advertised like others. This matter, though a trifle in appearance, must lead to the question whether I am to yield to Mr. Dowton, or Mr. Dowton to me. Now Mr. Elliston has provided against the alternative, had not my submission to public opinion obliged me to forego my first intention of retiring to America. He has engaged Mr. Vandenhoff, of Liverpool, an actor of the first consequence, and a gentleman whose high talents deserve the first place, and whom it would be therefore degrading to make secondary to anyone. This Gentleman's walk in the drama is the same as my own, and he has established a high reputation by his performance [of] *Brutus, Sir Giles Overreach, Sir Edward Mortimer,* and all those characters in which I have been in any way distinguished. What place then is there for me at this House? I still cannot help thinking, that to withdraw for a time would be only fair towards my compeers, and an advantage to Mr. Elliston. But since the public voice demands my return, I shall obey it as I have always done, and obey it cheerfully.

Edinburgh, September, 1819

An extraordinary justification, which offered no more grounds for his actions than a row with Dowton and a jealousy of Vandenhoff! Dowton, who was himself no saint in respect to envy, had stipulated with Elliston that no name was to be printed on the bills in larger type than his own, meaning thereby to direct a thrust at Kean. But Kean's articles of January, 1818, provided that "his name shall be continued in the bills of performance, in the same manner as it is at present." Dowton was obliged to yield. "If the *little gentleman,*" he wrote Elliston, "has really an article with the old committee, in which it was stipulated he should be seen in *big letters,* I should suggest *great A*, to be the fittest character. I agree with you, that you are in honour bound to insult the whole profession by obeying the articles already entered into by the committee." Later on Elliston tried to sooth him by an elevation to the big-letter rank, but he was not to be appeased. "I am sorry you have done this," he grumbled. "You know well what I mean—this cursed quackery; these big letters!—there is a want of respectability about it; or rather, a notoriety, which gives one the feeling of some absconded felon, against whom a Hue and Cry is made public." Whatever assurances of sympathy, complete agreement, and regret Elliston may have made to his indignant confrère in respect to this important issue, and we are certain that he was voluble, he kept his tongue in his cheek, for he was from ingrained habit a big-letter man. Hitherto Kean's name had appeared only sporadically in large type; beginning with the summer season of 1820 and lasting until the arrival of Young, Elliston made it a custom.

During a visit to Edinburgh in October-November of 1819, a group of admirers, headed by Sir John Sinclair, presented Kean with a sword of state, as a testimonial of their high regard for his talents, but especially for "the very superior manner in which [he] performed the character of Macbeth," expressing a desire that he should wear it when he appeared in that tragedy as the crowned king of Scotland. It was inscribed,

To
EDMUND KEAN, Esq.,
As a tribute of admiration of his splendid talents,
From his friends at Edinburgh.

On November 8 Kean began his season at Drury Lane under the new management, as Richard to the Richmond of Elliston. The combination of these two, together with the public airing of their differences, drew a bumper house of £561; but immediately thereafter Kean relapsed into that ambling pace which had become usual. On January 25, 1820, he came out as *Coriolanus*, but the contrast with Kemble was so disadvantageous that he laid it down after four performances. March 2 saw the appearance of *The Hebrew*, an arrangement of Scott's *Ivanhoe* made by George Soane, in which Kean played Isaac of York. It was a poor thing and deservedly failed. The death of George III (January 29) released for the stage *King Lear,* which had been shelved for some time in deference to the king's state of mind. Covent Garden came forth with it first, on April 13, with Booth as Lear; Drury Lane followed on April 24. Kean's assumption of this rôle must count as one of the major achievements of his career, an act that goes far toward recompense for the many bad plays, the follies, and the arrogance of his recent years. With it he completed his account of the four master tragedies of Shakespeare, in the other three of which he had exhibited what was most truly noble in his genius. His Macbeth was the least remarkable of the three rôles, yet it had its times of great power; his Hamlet was, all in all, very fine indeed; as Othello he was admittedly preëminent. It is gratifying to know that as Lear, the almost superhuman old man whom Lamb said no one could act, he gave one of the most impressive performances of his career,[9] in spite of natural drawbacks which must have worked sorely against him—his stature and his voice. One imagines Lear built after one of Michael Angelo's prophets, vast in his ruin, grand in his outpourings as the tempest which lashes him. But what Kean lacked in physique he could supply by the inward fire which, in his best moments, sprang into hot, communicable flame. It was not a perfect performance, it did not please all critics (Hazlitt among them), it did not please in all parts, but it had enough moments of greatness to give it memorable quality, and it was by far the best Lear that the contemporary stage could produce.[10] Booth, the only other who might be expected to make a flash in it, had failed miserably.

King Lear was given for twenty-six consecutive performances through to May 27, and twice again before the end of the season. Its run was broken off to allow the production of *Virginius,* which

[9] I am taking account of his American success in this rôle, which seems to have been rather greater than in England.

[10] "Kean delighted me much in Lear, though the critics are not satisfied with him. His representation of imbecile age was admirable. In the famous imprecation scene he produced astonishing effect by his manner of bringing out the words with the effort of a man nearly exhausted and breathless, rather spelling his syllables than forming them into words. 'How sharp-er-than-a-serp-ent's-tooth-it-is,' etc., etc. His exhibition of madness was always exquisite. Kean's defects are lost in this character, and become almost virtues. He does not need vigor or grace as Lear, but passion—and this never fails him." —Crabb Robinson (April 26, 1820).

demands a word. I have already told, in an earlier chapter,[11] of how on one of his Glasgow visits Kean renewed his friendship with Sheridan Knowles, how he asked the poet for a tragedy, suggesting the story of Virginius, and how Knowles in three months finished a play on that subject. But when he submitted the play to Drury Lane he was told that another Virginius play, by George Soane, had already been accepted. He then succeeded in placing it at Glasgow, where it was acted by Cooper and Mrs. Lovell; Tait, a friend of Macready, saw it there, wrote Macready about it, it was asked for at Covent Garden, accepted, and produced on May 17, 1820. Knowles's son, who gives us these details, mentions no dates, so that one cannot be sure just when these transactions took place, but it is clear that many weeks at least would be required for the refusal, the production at Glasgow, and the transmission to Covent Garden. When, therefore, we find Drury Lane breaking off its long run of *Lear* to push forward their *Virginius,* it is certain that they were prompted solely by the remarkable success which Macready had made at Covent Garden. In fact, the two houses were indulging in that most foolish game of duplication. Macready's Coriolanus had been followed by Kean's, Booth's Lear, by Kean's, on the same night which introduced *The Hebrew* Covent Garden had put on their own arrangement of *Ivanhoe.* In this absurd contest, thanks to *King Lear,* Drury Lane had slightly the advantage, but with *Virginius* they were soundly beaten. Soane's play was so bad that it lasted only three nights and was never revived or printed. Knowles's play held the stage through the nineteenth century, became a stock piece in the repertory of all the tragedians, and made the reputation of Macready. There is no doubt that it fell into the hands best able to exploit it, but Kean, nevertheless, had missed a chance at one of the most effective plays of the century. Hereafter the talents of the leading dramatist of his times were to be devoted not to him, but to his most dangerous rival.

No other new parts were taken by Kean this season except at his benefit, on June 12, when he played Jaffeir, in *Venice Preserved,* to the Pierre of Elliston and the Belvidera of Mrs. MacGibbon. A crowded house of nearly £700 attended this popular tragedy. The

[11] See above, page 61.

most curious part of the evening, however, was the afterpiece, which recalls certain indulgences of Kean's provincial days and which supplied wonder and mirth to the participants for years afterwards. It consisted of a farce, "written for the occasion," called *The Admirable Crichton,* in which Kean promised to give a taste of his versatility in singing, dancing, and imitations of celebrated actors. He would also impersonate Harlequin and with Mr. O'Shaugnessy give a display of the *assaut des armes.*

In the front row of a box was an intelligent young gentleman, John Hicks by name, who was so struck by the Admirable Crichton vaudeville that on his return home he wrote out a full account of it. Many years after, his son published it in *Notes and Queries.*[12] Kean, he said, began by singing to his own accompaniment on the piano; his voice was deep and sweet, such as would be accounted excellent in an amateur; this was much the best thing in the whole performance. Upon that followed a bout with the fencing-master, O'Shaugnessy. They began by

> thrusting *carte* and *tierce,* in the salute of which they did not keep time, Kean being behind hand; they then thrust the *contres* (sometimes, as is usual, doubling), first *contre carte* and then *contre tierce.* Little, if anything, more was done, and in the course of this O'Shaugnessy *twice* fixed his point. Kean in the *riposte en seconde* missed and passed by O'Shaugnessy, but drew back his point (which is not allowable) and fixed it, and then the rabblement shouted. This exhibition concluded by Kean disarming O'Shaugnessy while he remained in the lunge . . . To say the least, it was trifling.

Dancing followed, first Miss Valancey alone, then "Kean likewise danced alone with considerable activity, but without elegance." At the end of this movement instead of being at the back of the stage by Miss Valancy he was close to the lamps. They were then to dance hand-in-hand, but Kean only walked till he quitted her hand, when he danced again a little, "but apparently unable (as he had also seemed while holding her hand) to keep time." The young spectator attributed this unsteadiness to drink, until, after the curtain fell, Russell came forward to apologize for the omission of Harlequin,

[12] Seventh Series, VII (1889), 341.

Kean having sprained a muscle in his leg while dancing.[13] As a consequence of this accident all of the second act was dropped except the imitations, for which Kean appeared with a blue ribbon tied around his calf. The imitations, Hicks thought, were so-so; Kemble as Hamlet was bad, songs in the manner of Braham and Incledon were better, Munden was fair but then anyone can take off Munden.

"This display," added the critic mildly, "will certainly not raise his reputation." We are glad to learn that Kean was afterwards ashamed of himself.

The season closed on July 7, 1820, with *Othello*. The total of receipts showed a little better than £44,000, a gain of nearly £10,000 over the last year, for which Elliston could take the credit to himself. He was a popular manager and also a popular actor, although not always a good one. Still, aside from his general notoriety, he was an addition of considerable strength to the company. It is noticeable that except for a few opening nights in new parts, Kean's best receipts came from playing in combination with Elliston. His Richard was a better box-office attraction by £150 when Elliston played Richmond, and together they crowded the theatre for *Venice Preserved* as it had not been crowded for many a year. From this it might be inferred that what Kean needed to maintain the public interest in him was support on the stage. He never could see it, but Elliston did.

It will be remembered that Elliston had promised Kean a year's leave of absence for his American visit if he would not secede from Drury Lane. But now the idea of a year ago had become a certainty. He was to sail in September, and accordingly he set out on a summer tour which was something in the nature of a farewell. July 18 to 29 he visited Edinburgh. In August he returned to London for a special season at the Haymarket, at which he reviewed a dozen or more of his rôles for a public supposedly distressed at his parting. Actually there was a good deal of interest shown. The houses were for the most part not strong, but they were quite up to his winter average and there-

[13] A malicious story, included by Leman Rede in his *New Monthly* recollections, told that when Kean appeared to dance, clad in white satin tights which threw into prominence his paunchy stomach, a titter broke forth, upon which he immediately drew up his leg and taking Miss Valancey by the hand limped off. Hicks's account is in disagreement.

fore unusually good for summer. One observes with some surprise that Booth was engaged from Covent Garden for a few performances; there is no evidence that the two who had met and parted so dramatically only four years ago did not play in this occasion with perfect harmony. But the public showed they had not forgotten by giving their best attendance on the nights when the two rivals played.[14] The season closed on September 16 with *Richard III*, at the conclusion of which Kean addressed to the audience a characteristic valedictory:

> It is with pain I announce to you that a long period must elapse before I can again have the honor of coming before you, and when I reflect on the uncertainty of life, the sentiment will obtrude itself that this may possibly be my last appearance on these boards. (Cries of "No, no!—We hope not!") I cannot but remember with gratitude that this is the spot where I first enjoyed the welcome of public favor. I was then a wanderer, and unknown: but received here shelter, and, I may add, reputation. During six years your favor has been my protection and encouragement; my present enjoyment and future hope. It has been to me a shield against the shafts of calumny to which I have been exposed; it is the cargo that freights my venture to another clime; it is the star to which my thoughts, when I again direct them to my native home, ultimately turn. After nearly seven years of anxious endeavor to deserve your favor, I have now to bid you farewell. My recollections will be gratifying, for they will remind me of that honorable rank in my profession to which your kindness elevated me. If at any time I have forgotten the dignity of that position, it should be imputed to the delirium which your favor inspired, and it is to you alone that I need apologise. With the deepest sentiments of esteem and gratitude, I respectfully bid you farewell.

To these sentiments the audience replied with loud huzzas.

It may seem heartless to quote, in juxtaposition to such proper gestures of a formal leave-taking, the following paragraph from the July *Theatrical Inquisitor*, but the truth must be told that whereas a goodly portion of London wished him at least a formal godspeed, there were others whose feelings toward him might be digested into: "Go, and be damned."

There [i.e., in America], if fortune be propitious, may the bubble repu-

[14] These were: August 15, *Richard III*; August 16, *Venice Preserved*; August 19, *Othello*; August 21, *Lear* (with Booth as Edgar); August 28, *Othello*.

tation remain entire much beyond the period which our Admirable Kean has at present fixed for returning; and if the vessel which carries out the arts, the ignorance, and the effrontery that have given success to his career, can only be stocked with a moderate portion of the public dulness to which Mr. Kean has appealed, we will guarantee the same stupid admiration on the part of our Yankee friends, by which the idolaters of Mr. Kean in this country have been disgraced and degraded.

There often comes a time in the affairs of actors when a little absence is the surest way of all to make the hearts at home grow fonder. Kean's American tour was altogether wise.

As soon as his Haymarket engagement was over he traveled north, scattering I presume farewell appearances on the way, until he reached Liverpool. There he played his last stand, from September 25 to October 6, closing with *Othello*. The next day he sailed westward on the packet "Martha."

Before going on to his American adventures I must pause here for a moment to speak of a side of his character to which hitherto I have paid little attention and which it would be most unjust to omit. The account I have given of him, particularly in the latter years of his London residence, has dealt so much with his shortcomings as to lead the reader to suppose that he was compounded wholly of arrogance, deceit, and dissipation. But there was another, more attractive side which has been the subject of scores of anecdotes, picturing him as a prince of boon companions, a puck in humor, a lovable spendthrift, with a hand ever held out to the fellow actor in distress. I must confess that it has been something of a problem, to know what to do with these anecdotes; most of them are trivial; few can be substantiated; many are doubtless apocryphal or unproved; they are too many and too long. For these reasons and also from the exigencies of space I have decided to make a general clearance of them, although I am aware that in so doing I am sacrificing much that gives life to the character. But as insecure as they are individually, the general tenor of them cannot be wrong, nor must they on any account be left out of consideration in forming a judgment of the man.

I venture as my own opinion, that Kean was not, in the truest sense, either just or benevolent. That he was liberal with his money, that he had many generous impulses, that he performed many kind acts which do him a deal of credit, cannot be denied. But his liberality was mainly waste, and his kind acts arose more from his feelings of the moment than from a benignancy of temper. His memory both for slights and favors was good, but rather better for slights than for favors. To all those who had done him a kindness in his days of want he cherished a gratitude which often showed itself in astonishing feats of requital, but these displays were not of equal force. Leman Rede, for instance, says that to a man who lent him half a guinea on his wedding day he returned just half a guinea, but an actor who once breakfasted him when he was starving he later fitted with clothes and a three years' engagement. His generosity flowed most consistently toward the needy provincial mummer, whose distresses he had himself known so intimately. Many stories are told of his coming upon some wretched company faced with disaster in some stolid town and pausing long enough to offer them a free benefit as Richard or Othello. He was kind also to country managers whom he had known and liked. Grattan tells of his playing in Brussels for Penley, who maintained an English theatre there. Another story (not so well authorized) tells that when filling an engagement at Brighton, and after playing on the manager's benefit night, he would not accept his due share of the proceeds—"I'll have none of it, for you have nine children and I only one." It is also said that he did the same for Butler, the manager of a company in Northallerton and the son of the manager under whom Kean was serving when called to the Haymarket in 1806, because the father had given him the money with which to go to London—a return of £80 for perhaps £5. There can be little doubt that in many of these benevolences was mingled an element of harmless vanity. He enjoyed the rôle of Prince Fortunatus. He liked to play Richard in a barn before an astonished concourse of provincials; he liked to drink in the tavern afterwards with his protégés of the night, to shake them all by the hand and wish them good luck; and as he climbed into his carriage the next morning and rolled away from their effusive thanks, he liked the warm feeling that came from a good deed. Yet the vanity may easily be pardoned him; it *was* a good deed.

Toward the humble and the poor in his profession he was often a fountain of help. Toward his equals, especially in his own line, he could be suspicious, crafty, and mean. Enough has been said on that score in previous pages. His liberality was spontaneous, but utterly unregulated. Many have expressed astonishment that a man who earned, for more than sixteen years, upwards of £10,000 a year should have left no vestige of it at his death. He did not go in for charities. He did not gamble.[15] He could scarcely drink it all away. What then? No one knows. It simply went, thrown away for the most part, probably, on the bloodsuckers that infested him, on Ophelia (whom we shall meet later) and her like. I strongly suspect that some of it went to Aunt Tidswell, but this is merely an ill natured guess. Certainly Mary Kean had little good of it, or Charles either, although he at least got an Eton education. In the face of such waste the tale of ten guineas tucked into a poor mummer's hand loses some of its lustre.

Among persons who were congenial to him he was a good companion. That such company was not always low we know from his friendship with a few men like Grattan and Dr. Francis of New York. But he was not really at home except in a tavern, and with men of his own calling. Leman Rede says that when quite sober he was modest and unassuming, but that when drunk he was noisy, quarrelsome, and overbearing. He loved to sing, to exchange stories, to tell untruthful anecdotes of his early struggles, and to take off in imitations the popular actors of the day. He liked, however, always to be the center, and he seldom took a thrust at himself with a good grace. Occasionally he did. The story is told that on the night before sailing from Liverpool, while he was expatiating on his intention of raising a monument to George Frederick Cooke and after he had asked for suggestions for an epitaph, one impudent wag offered the following:

> Beneath this stone lies Cooke interred,
> And with him Shakespeare's Dick the Third.

The great disciple of Cooke read and smiled: "*Dum lego, assentior.*" He must have been in an amiable frame of mind that night.

[15] Unless it was in investments in country theatres. I suspect that a good deal of money went that way.

Leman Rede is the authority for a story which might be taken as an epitome not only of Kean in relaxation, but of a great many of his kind. Though it belongs to a period a few years later in his life it applies equally to any part of it. Phillips, Kean's secretary, is supposed to be waiting while his employer makes merry in another room in the tavern.

Time, two in the morning

Phillips. Waiter, what was Mr. Kean doing when you left the room?

Waiter. Playing the piano, sir, and singing.

Phillips. Oh, come, he's all right, then.

Quarter-past two

Phillips. What's Mr. Kean doing now?

Waiter. Making a speech, sir, about Shakespeare.

Phillips. He's getting drunk; you'd better order the carriage.

Half-past two

Phillips. What's he at now?

Waiter. He's talking Latin, sir.

Phillips. Then he *is* drunk. I must get him away.

CHAPTER IX

THE UNITED STATES, 1820-21

In going to the United States Kean was tracing the steps of his great forerunner, George Frederick Cooke, who may be said to have discovered America as an annex to the British stage. He was not the first English actor to go there, but he was the first important one, his success was prodigious, and his entry marked the beginning of that immigration of theatrical notables which is so much a feature of the artistic annals of the United States. There can be little doubt that Kean's visit to the new world was prompted in part by imitation of that actor whom he most admired and over whose grave in New York he proposed to erect a monument; it was something in the nature of a pious pilgrimage. But the main impulse arose from the opinion, growing stronger in England with every year, that the American market must be attended to.

In those days, five cities scattered along the seaboard carried an important traffic in the drama—New York, Boston, Philadelphia, Baltimore, and Charleston. Each had its resident company or companies, each was actively concerned with the stage; through their journals they were kept aware of the latest English fashions in plays and actors; their managers imported the London hits almost as fast as they came out. The business arrangements of a visitor in 1820 were made easy through the enterprise of Stephen Price, owner of the Park Theatre in New York and soon to be lessee of Drury Lane, who had established an understanding with the managers of other cities by which he was able to sell to them any attractions that he might import. The plans of Kean's tour were therefore settled, at least in rough outline, before he left England. It was understood that he was to have so many engagements, with the probability of extensions, in such and such towns at a determined price. As to the last item, precise information is furnished by Kean's American diary, a portion of which (or possibly all) is now in the Widener collection at Harvard University.[1] For his New York engagement he received £50 a night for

[1] First used by George C. D. Odell in his *Annals of the New York Stage*. II, 582.

the first seven nights and half the clear receipts for the eighth (benefit) night, the same arrangement being repeated in the second octave, the total guaranteed engagement being sixteen nights. At Philadelphia, to which he went next, he was to perform fourteen nights, dividing the receipts with the management after charges (these amounted to £66) had been deducted for the first six nights, and dividing the seventh night without charge—that is, taking half of the gross receipts. The same agreement held for the second half of his engagement. This proved to be considerably more profitable than the New York terms.

He arrived in New York Friday, November 24, 1820, and was billed to open as Richard on November 29 with the Park Theatre company, then domiciled at the Anthony Street Theatre.[2] Public interest was alive, for his meteoric career was common knowledge. Every theatre goer in New York knew something about him; through reprints from the English press they had been informed of his sensational triumphs, of his failures, of the critical battles over him, even of his misdeeds. They were prepared for something new, something extraordinary. But, as he was soon to find out, the same division of prejudices that had torn the amateurs of London existed in New York and the other American cities. The Kemble ideal was embodied in Thomas Abthorpe Cooper, who for upwards of a quarter century had been the leading native tragedian and who had established a strong following, jealous of his honors, ready to fly to his defense. The situation was further complicated by George Frederick Cooke, who in the two years of his American residence had made a deep impression. Kean had, therefore, not only to combat the Cooperites but also to win over the Cookeites, who might be supposed to be sympathetic toward him but who were frequently as difficult as the others. The first guns in this war were shot on the eve of his appearance. The New York *Evening Post* had printed an essay by one signing himself "Crito" in which the artificialities of Cooper were severely dealt with. On November 29, the New York *American*, already ranged against Kean, rose to the challenge. The attack of Crito, it said, was evidently meant as a demolition preparatory to welcoming the new hero. "Mr. C. must

[2] Their own theatre had burned the previous May.

be believed to be *too* dignified and stately, before the pantomimic starts and lounging walk of Mr. K. can demand applause. Mr. C.'s commanding figure—clear . . . voice, and graceful gestures, must be destroyed, that he who wants them all, may be held up as nature's favoured child."

That so hostile an attitude should be taken when the actor had not yet been seen may well cause surprise. But it suggests what subsequent events proved, that American newspaper opinion had been pretty well made up before Kean reached the United States. The press in New York, Boston, and Philadelphia took on an instantaneous alignment which altered very little during the actor's two visits. The most that can be said of changes is that a number of papers which in the beginning were hypocritically favorable turned against him after the Boston "insult." On what grounds did this hostility rest?

Before attempting an answer to the question, a word must be said about dramatic criticism in the United States. There were no qualified, professional critics, but, as in English provincial towns, the newspapers depended largely on voluntary contributions. All the cities abounded in amateur critics of the most dogmatic sort. In many cases, however, where something of importance was afoot, the editors themselves covered the theatre, as they often did for Kean, using the editorial column for their expressions of opinion. The results were sometimes chaotic, as for example when an editor out of a momentary sense of impartiality opened his paper to an adverse contributor and then engaged in verbal fisticuffs with him. It must not be supposed, however, that all criticism was bad; some of it was remarkably perceptive. But too often it consisted of indiscriminate puffery or of indiscriminate abuse, revealing that its basis was prejudice rather than inquiry after truth. Not infrequently its tone was sharpened by a personal animosity existing between editors, with the result that Kean was exalted or cast down for reasons that had little to do with him.

I cannot pretend to have a full understanding of the editorial mind in regard to Kean, more specifically, the state of that mind prior to his arrival. But I think that the considerations which follow went into the making of it. There was, first of all, a passionate regard in certain quarters for the excellences of Cooper and the memory of

Cooke. Then undoubtedly a good deal of adverse feeling had been aroused by reports from England concerning Kean's behavior. Such charges as those made by Bucke, and such comments as that quoted on a recent page from the *Theatrical Inquisitor* must have had an effect. The impression, which might easily be got from reading certain of the English journals, that Kean was a pretentious, arrogant fellow who laid dogmatic claim to being the greatest living actor would stiffen the backs of many Americans who, although dogmatic and arrogant themselves, had the most sensitive feelings in regard to those vices in an English visitor. There is no doubt that such an impression obtained. Mr. Odell quotes part of a letter written by Edmund Simpson, stage manager of the New York company, to a friend in Ireland soon after the opening of the first engagement: "We find him [Kean] extremely agreeable in the Theatre & are agreeably disappointed in finding him in manner and conduct exactly the reverse of what we expected." Then too one should bear in mind a difference in bias between the English and American publics, namely, that whereas the provincial English towns were usually quite ready to follow the London verdict on the greatness of actors, a part of the American public was inclined to look on English labels with suspicion; it required to be "shown" and took a niggling pride in its independence of judgment. I suspect, moreover, that in many cases the bitter division of policies between newspapers carried through to all matters of opinion, however irrelevant to polities—that, for example, because the *National Advocate* declared early for Kean, the New York *American* declared against him. All this, however, is merely guessing at feelings to which no explicit statement was ever given. What we can see is the outward manifestation, and that plainly enough. A goodly part of the press were lukewarm if not actively hostile from the beginning; so long as the public furor lasted they held themselves in, but at the first slip which Kean made they gave free vent to their rancor.

A fashionable audience packed the Anthony Street Theatre on the evening of Wednesday, November 29, 1820, for *Richard III*. It tingled with excitement; it was prepared for something outside experience, it did not know just what; with all the conflicting reports about the new star one could hardly tell what to expect. This pleasant uncertainty is well expressed by the critic of the *Evening Post*:[3]

No actor, perhaps, has ever appeared in New-York, with such prepossessions in his favor, or such prejudices to encounter, and we candidly confess, we were among the number of those who entertained the latter. We were assured that certain imitations of him were exact likenesses; and that certain actors were good copies; that his excellences consisted in sudden starts, frequent and unexpected pauses, in short, a complete knowledge of what is called stage trick, which we hold in contempt. But he had not finished his soliloquy, before our prejudices gave way, and we saw the most complete actor, in our judgment, that ever appeared on our boards.

I shall not quote the rest of this long review, nor the equally laudatory one from the *National Advocate*. They deal, as did those of the *Chronicle* and the *Examiner* on Kean's first London appearance, with delighted appreciations of striking moments and fine readings, and they but repeat with variations of detail the ecstasies of Hazlitt and Thomas Barnes. The one most important fact is that Kean won his audience in the United States as he had won an audience nearly seven years before in London. Not quite instantly, because his method was so new (in spite of Cooke) that it took many people a short time in which to adjust themselves to it. Edward Simpson, in the letter recently cited, tells us that "the people don't know exactly what to make of him—his strange manner surprises them but his style gains converts every night & before he leaves us, I expect they will be unanimous in calling him as they express it the greatest creature they ever saw." But in spite of some bewilderment, the first night was unmistakably a triumph; the popular voice spoke out peremptorily in favor of the new tragedian. In the face of it even the unfriendly journals expressed a grudging approval. They solaced themselves with dwelling on defects and mannerisms. "Among the latter," said the *American*, "his delivery is new; every word comes forth as if it were measured in a slow method of speech he uses, which, as it was continued through all those scenes where it was possible to employ it, rendered it at length very tiresome." This is very interesting, because it shows that Kean had by now entered upon that change of style which be-

[3] Issue of November 30. Quoted by Mr. Odell, *Annals of the New York Stage*. II, 583.

KEAN AS RICHARD III (ACT I, SCENE 2)

came in time so marked as to draw forth the censure that he was "more artificial than Kemble."

The rest of the engagement was as follows:

December 1	*Othello*
December 2	*Merchant of Venice*
December 4	*Richard III*
December 5	*Brutus*
December 7	*Hamlet*
December 8	*A New Way to Pay Old Debts*
December 11	*A New Way to Pay Old Debts*
December 13	*Lear*
December 15	*Town and Country*
December 16	*Richard III*
December 18	*Hamlet*
December 19	*Iron Chest*
December 21	*Macbeth*
December 22	*Bertram*
December 26	*Richard II*
December 28 (for Simpson's benefit)	*Lear*

He was supported by Maywood, a capable Drury Lane actor who had preceded him to the United States by a year and who himself specialized in the Kean rôles, by manager Simpson, by Moreland from the York Theatre, but especially by Mrs. Barnes, charming and gifted actress, a great favorite, with whom Kean played frequently during both his American visits.

With each new rôle he strengthened his hold on the popular favor. Newspapers were rife with commentary and dispute. The *Evening Post* said its desk was piled with contributions for which it could not find room. On December 4 it admitted, with reluctance, a dissertation from the "Crito" who had a week before picked Cooper to pieces. This gentleman seems to have been a most impartial executioner, for now he turns to the chopping off of Kean's head with as much zest as he had given to Cooper. The new actor is full of specious mannerisms: Crito disapproves of his meaningless gesturing, his distortion of speeches, his slow articulation in soliloquies, his exaggerated pauses. "Yet," he allows at the end, "I admit that Mr. Kean has great powers of conception;—glittering gems of genius, sparkling amidst masses of error." This was too much for Coleman, editor of the *Evening Post*; he could, out of fair play, allow Crito to be heard, but he could not tolerate him without rebuke; and so on December 5 one finds a lively exchange of shots between them—Crito not caring to be lessoned by the *Post* and the *Post* not caring what Crito cares. On December 8 "A Philadelphian" entered the ring, decidedly for Kean but registering a protest against "a kind of hysterical, convulsive laugh" which Kean used to excess. A great deal was said about that laugh in the course of the year. The *American* critic of December 3 pitched upon Shylock, complaining that in place of the vaunted "naturalness" of Kean he found clap-trap. The scenes were all unequal: the famous one with Tubal was a "mixture of touching pathos and disgusting rant;" the trial scene excited both admiration and contempt. Kean, he found, had less "keeping" than any actor he knew.

After the New York engagement had closed, various summings up appeared. The *National Advocate* bore heavily on the superior qualities of the new school of Kean and Kean's superiority to his imitators.

> Instead of a cold, we have a vivid conception of character; instead of a lofty, studied style of declamation, we have all the transitions of nature and all the force of reality. In others we see the actor, in Kean we have the man; others describe the passions, Kean feels them; his style not only pleases from its novelty but from its truth.

The writer[4] added also his testimony to Kean's personal character.

> Although the private deportment of Mr. Kean may have no relation to his professional merit, it is still gratifying to know that he is a modest, unassuming gentleman—securing the esteem of all who have become acquainted with him—easy in manners—always accessible, refined and classic in conversation—and, when animated, the very life of the festive board.

In the *Post* of January 11-12 "A New Yorker" spoke out loudly for Cooper and the classical school. Kean's innovations, he insisted, were motivated by his defects; he could not manage the grand style and so he went in for naturalism.

[4] Certainly Major Noah, the editor, an ardent champion and friend of Kean.

Mr. Kean had little or no grace of gesture, therefore his predecessors were cold, stiff and stately. He had no voice (or, as the Examiner uncourteously says, one "between an apoplexy and a cough") and therefore their recitation was too measured and continuous . . . We contend that he has manifested, by the choice he has made, both a vicious taste and a bad judgment, and is therefore in no way to be classed with either of these gentlemen [Cooper and Kemble].

On January 12 "Knickerbocker" rose indignantly to Kean's defense. He closed with deep sarcasm:

From the celebrity which Mr. Kean has attained in New York, by means of his apoplectic voice, ungraceful action, diminutive figure and hysteric cough, one might expect, that if a dumb, clumsy, dwarfish idiot should make his appearance on our boards, he would certainly reach the very pinnacle of fame.

Particular occasion for these comparisons had been given by Cooper, who had most injudiciously chosen to play at the Anthony Street Theatre immediately on the close of Kean's engagement. His season was a complete failure—two hundred persons attended his *Othello*, less than one hundred and fifty his *Macbeth*, five hundred his *Richard III*. But his followers rallied to him in the press. On January 4 the *American* compared him to "the tragic muse in good health, and her sober senses," and Kean to "the same lady labouring under an attack of the palsy, or a visitation of St. Vitus," and censured the public for favoring "the superiority of fingers and feet over the voice and countenance" and "legalizing the most unnatural union between tragedy and farce."

These discords, however vigorously they were sounded, were more than covered by choruses of praise, in which the powerful voices of the *Evening Post* and the *National Advocate* dominated. The *Post* was particularly enraptured with Lear. "But no adequate conception can be conveyed, by words, of Mr. Kean's representation of this high-drawn and arduous character . . . When we lately . . . said upon seeing the second representation of Richard, that 'acting could go no further,' it was because we had not then witnessed his Lear."[5]

On December 27 a dinner was given at the City Hall, at which Mr. D. Lynch presided with Stephen Price as vice-president. Major

[5] Quoted from Mr. Odell, *Annals of the New York Stage*. II, 588.

Noah, the redoubtable leader of the *National Advocate* and one of the best-hated editors of New York, offered the toast to Kean. On the next night, for Simpson's benefit, he repeated Lear before a demonstrative audience which punctuated the play with cries of "Bravo, Kean! Huzzah, Kean!" At the close he was called upon for a speech and again they soundly cheered. So, with New York in his pocket and a great many American dollars also, he set out for the conquest of Philadelphia.

There he opened at the Walnut Street Theatre on January with the invariable *Richard III*. The following is a list of his performances, with the receipts as reported by his manager Wood:[6]

January 8 (Monday)	*Richard III* ($1178)
January 10	*Othello* ($837)
January 12	*Merchant of Venice* ($1260)
January 13	*Hamlet* ($718)
January 15	*Richard III* ($883)
January 17	*Brutus* ($897)
January 19	*A New Way to Pay Old Debts* (benefit, $1397)
January 20	*Macbeth* ($615)
January 22	*Lear* ($1351)
January 24	*Rule a Wife* ($699)
January 26	*Bertram* ($650)
January 27	*Town and Country* ($675)
January 29	*Lear* ($889)
January 31	*Othello* (benefit, $1199)
February 2	*Merchant of Venice* (reëngagement, $400)
February 3	*Iron Chest* ($727)

He was welcomed by a crowded house which, from fear of accident, held few women. Again the novelty of his style told momentarily against him; his reception was cordial but, says the *Aurora and General Advertiser*, the prevailing feeling was that "Cooke was the greater actor as well as in part the *model* of Kean." Apparently too he was not in his best form, at least such was the later opinion of the *Aurora* in comparing his opening performance with those which fol-

[6] Wood, William B., *Personal Recollections of the Stage*. Philadelphia, 1855.

lowed. That newspaper was soon caught into the whirl of immense admiration. On January 15 it was pronouncing that "all that has been said of Mr. Kean, in anticipation, was in his performance of Othello realized—we may safely say exceeded." On the eighteenth it printed a long criticism by "Moderation" which, although enthusiastic in the main, revealed a startling provinciality of taste: Kean's Richard is inferior to Cooper's, his Hamlet (ye gods!) to Duff's. On January 20 "Sophocles" entered the arena with two columns of undiluted praise of Brutus, in which rôle he discovered Kean to be "the genuine representative of nature, the chaste and classic tragedian, covered with the classic mantle of Greece and Rome." On January 23 "Sophocles" rhapsodized for a column and a half over Macbeth, while a more meticulous "Euripides" found fault with the toga of Brutus and the armor of the Scottish king. On February 6 "H" compared the natural manner of Kean with the artificial manner of Cooper. "Kean never recites, you perceive no blank verse, no rythm [*sic*] in his speeches, which are natural and *unencumbered by the trammels of an artificial imitative taste*—he never *thinks* of decorum—but he always acts decorously."

Other papers joined with the *Aurora* in praise of the new star, among them the *Democratic Press*, whose reviews were the longest, the most frequent, and the most gushing in Philadelphia. But as in New York, a party of opposition existed, who had this advantage over the Keanites that their chief organ, the *National Gazette*, was unusually well written. The *Gazette* carried on from the first a campaign of depreciation. Its first notice, of Overreach on January 20, is severe. The first four acts passed in a kind of apathy, during which the absence of Cooke was felt. In the fifth Kean exerted himself to effect,

> but at the same time the insufficiency and harshness of his voice, his *excessive* efforts, amounting to the wildest rant, the inordinate vivacity and irregularity of his gesticulation, destructive of all dignity and grace, gave absolute pain, and contributed to mar the efficacy of those sallies of genius and occasional excellencies of declamation, those magical evolutions of face and that deep sensibility, which all of us are willing to acknowledge and extol.

A sarcastic gentleman writing as "Cibber" now appears in the *Gazette,* whose chief delight is to ridicule the absurd flights of the *Democratic Press.* Thus on January 22 he accused the *Press* of having said that in the last scene of *A New Way* the audience was so enraptured that it could not keep its seat. True, says Cibber, it did stand up, but the reason was that Kean had thrown himself flat on the stage, the first rows of the pit stood up to see, and so the rows behind stood also. On February 5 "Betterton" wrote on Kean's popularity in Philadelphia, denying that he was especially well liked—he reaped less applause than Cooke, Wallack, or Mrs. Bartley; there was no general wish to renew his engagement; on Wednesday at the close of *Othello* there were some calls for Kean; he came out to know what they desired; a person in the gallery called out something about a reëngagement, whereupon Kean at once said that he would comply with the general desire as far as other engagements would let him. This transaction, thought Betterton, had the air of pre-concert and was so regarded by many; it is curious, in the face of things, that so few people went to the theatre on Friday.

This "Betterton" was no common criticaster, but a fellow of sense and experience whose identity I should much like to know. On February 6, 7, and 8 he printed in the *National Gazette* a summary of Kean which is not only the best American criticism I have seen but one of the most valuable descriptions of that actor's method to be found anywhere, valuable particularly because he sees the subject with fresh eyes and because he tells us what he *sees.* Most reviews of Kean, unfortunately, are of little aid to the historian because they are too subjective—they tell us more about what the critic feels than about what the actor does—and therefore some of the best glimpses come from cool foreigners, men like the German Tieck and the American "Betterton." The *Gazette* articles are too long to quote here and now, nor is this the place for a digression into Kean's manner. Therefore I shall give them in full in the Appendix, and make use of them when the time comes for a general consideration of that manner.

Notwithstanding the discordant notes, Kean's reception in Philadelphia was quite satisfactory to him. On February 4 he entered in his diary:

paid into Leroy & Bayards hands—the produce of my Philadelphia engagement—4444^{D}-44^{C}—making one thousand pounds sterling—for immediate remittance to Coutts & Co., London.

This was the substantial proof of public favor, but the more spiritual gratifications were also abundant, flattery, invitations, and constant attendance. Manager Wood tells us that the tragedian was beset every night with a crowd of idlers waiting after the play to carry him off to some supper party, to prevent which the manager used often to tire out the would-be hosts by waiting in Kean's dressing room, sometimes until three in the morning. He also testifies to Kean's good behavior in the theatre.

> He appeared among us . . . a mild, unassuming and cheerful man, wholly free from every affectation of superiority or dictation. His suggestions as to business on the stage, were always given with a gentleness of manner which secured their immediate adoption. The deficiencies of humbler performers were treated with indulgence, and created even in the most careless of them a desire to excel. His presence in the greenroom was always a source of enjoyment.

From Philadelphia he went to Boston, where he was looked for with the greatest impatience.[7] He gave the following performances:

February 12 (Monday)	*Richard III*
February 13	*Othello*
February 15	*Richard III*
February 16	*Merchant of Venice*
February 19	*Hamlet*
February 20	*Iron Chest*
February 22	*Macbeth*
February 23	*A New Way to Pay Old Debts*
February 26	*Lear* (benefit)
February 27	*Iron Chest*
February 28	*Othello*
March 1	*Brutus*
March 2	*A New Way to Pay Old Debts*
March 5	*Lear*
March 6	*Bertram*
March 7	*Distressed Mother*

[7] An excellent account of his visits has been left by W. W. Clapp in *A Record of the Boston Stage*. Boston and Cambridge, 1853.

So great was the demand for seats that before the sale opened it was announced that only one box would be sold to a person. This restrictive measure proved to be inadequate. Beginning with the performance of February 23 the management put into operation a new scheme, called forth by "the riotous conduct of the persons who surrounded the Box office, to obtain Tickets, solely for the purpose of selling them again, at an enormous advance." I do not know whether this was the first instance of "scalping" in the United States, but certainly it was the first on so large a scale. The thrifty New England minds of the managers were troubled by this private speculation. And so they ingeniously proposed to sell their boxes hereafter by public auction, the premiums to be distributed among charities. It was a brilliant idea. So reckless was the curiosity of the Bostonians that when the season ended $2,999.75 had been taken in this way, above the regular charge of one dollar for box seats. The charitable organizations were delighted; all Boston was pleased; the United States wondered and admired; and Kean basked in a general good will.

The Boston reviews, with exceptions like those we have met elsewhere, echoed this good will. The *Daily Advertiser* chanted his praises loudly. Speaking (February 16) of his Othello, it declared that "his action is the finest I ever saw. I will not call it graceful—it *was* graceful—but it was a thousand times more—it was eloquent with every emotion of the soul. We had been told the contrary of this." The *Commercial Gazette*, on February 19, burst into a rhapsody which I cannot forbear quoting:

> He is so strikingly blended, so exquisitely intermixed—so variently, yet so harmoniously mingled,—that he becomes imposing by contrariety;—and like the subtle radiation of the Iris, which by the very opposing combinations of its hues becomes at once a variegated arc of splendour and delight.

The *Columbian Centinel*, summing up the season on March 10, found that the reports from other cities as to Kean's objectionable mannerisms had proceeded from the myopia of ignorance. The Boston public "heard and saw what had been thus denominated, and they were satisfied they were the 'mannerisms,' and 'pauses,' and exhibitions of genius, and profound knowledge of human action in extraordinary cases."

Along with these resounding praises sounded the sharp bark of disapproval, the tone of which has already been well enough sampled to make extended quotation needless. A communicant to the *Daily Advertiser* (March 2) was indignant because in place of Shakespeare's noble Moor "we find only a diminutive person, ill bred hurry and hustle, a feeble, broken voice . . . and for heroic grandeur a cockpit style of taunting." The *New England Palladium* on March 13 and 20 printed a long attack of which the burden ran that Kean's reputation was tinsel, made up of the acclamations of mobs and an interested press. It is folly to compare him with Siddons, Kemble, or even that true natural genius, Cooke. His chief weakness is that he is all bustle.

> *Motion* is his true element, but it is a motion allied more to the corporeal than to the intellectual system . . . Mr. Kean's forces cannot act in detachments. The eye, the lip, the forehead, the voice, the step, the soul itself, have not in him each its own independent sway. Hence comes his acknowledged failure in Macbeth, and, we may add, in all such parts as require less bustle, than sustained dignity.

Furthermore, he is deficient in "keeping up" a character.

> He preys upon it as on a victim, instead of hugging it to his bosom, and wearing it in his heart.

On the authority of Clapp, Kean's receipts for his sixteen Boston nights were $5,454.26. He remitted £1000 to his bankers. A crowd of several hundred cheered him as he drove out of the city.

He returned to New York for a second engagement, playing as follows:

March 12 (Monday)	*Hamlet*
March 14	*Othello*
March 16	*Lear*
March 17	*Mountaineers*
March 19	*Riches*
March 20	*Brutus*
March 22	*Bertram*
March 23	*Richard III*
March 26	*Jew of Malta* (benefit)
March 27	*Lear* (reëngagement)

March 29	*Merchant of Venice*
March 30	*Macbeth*
April 2	*Othello*
April 3	*A New Way to Pay Old Debts*
April 4	*Alexander the Great*
April 5	*Lear*
April 6	*Venice Preserved* (benefit)

From there he went again to Philadelphia, where, as Wood's report shows, the edge of public interest had been taken off by his first visit.

April 9 (Monday)	*Richard III* ($613)
April 11	*Othello* ($528)
April 13	*Riches* ($523)
April 14	*Lear* ($412)
April 16	*Iron Chest* ($537)
April 18	*Venice Preserved* (benefit, $1005)

Of this and the New York return engagements there is nothing that needs be said, inasmuch as the press, according to their custom, paid little or no attention to them. He was received with all the favor that might be expected of repetition and the advancing season. He himself was perfectly satisfied. On March 19 he wrote to Douglas Kinnaird, "I am making money & fame by bushels;" he has asked Elliston for a year's extension of leave, which, if he gets it, will give him fifteen or sixteen thousand pounds to bring home—"& then farewell Critics Authors—Greasy Corps of Whistlers."

He went next to Baltimore, where the resident company was controlled by manager Wood of Philadelphia. As a theatre town, Baltimore was not of the rank of New York, Philadelphia, or Boston, but it did its best for him.

April 23 (Monday)	*Richard III* ($789)
April 25	*Othello* ($611)
April 27	*Merchant of Venice* ($799)
April 28	*A New Way to Pay Old Debts* ($696)
April 30	*Lear* ($929)
May 2	*Macbeth* ($630)
May 4	*Iron Chest* ($602)
May 5	*Brutus* ($430)
May 7	*Hamlet* ($652)

May 9	*Town and Country* ($633)
May 11	*Bertram* ($570)
May 12	*Riches* ($495)
May 14	*Othello* (benefit, $785)
May 15 (extra night)	*Richard III* ($654)

The critical reception of Kean in Baltimore, to judge from the *American*, was just what it had been elsewhere, resembling Philadelphia in this particular that an initial disappointment in his Richard was effaced by his Othello. I confess to some curiosity as to these lapses of Richard.[8] It may be that because his novelty of style was in this rôle especially accented, it troubled his auditors; or it may be that from excessive repetition he was falling into more mannerism than had as yet crept into his other rôles. One finds in the columns of the Baltimore *American* the familiar warfare of schools. A communicant signing himself "Many" is allowed, on April 27, to confess his disappointment: Kean is not only behind Cooper and Cooke, but also (good heavens!) behind Hodgkinson, Fennel, and Chalmers. His Richard is a piece of stage trickery, a thing "outrageous on nature—a *fretting* of her passion into tatters." But on May 9 an unsigned critique places him before every actor save Garrick; he is of the school of Talma (a curious nesting!), alike in genius and occasional descent into trickery; his Hamlet is far above Cooper's, his Othello is unimaginable. In Baltimore, as elsewhere, the discords are all but drowned in a general concord of praise.

His reception there was peculiar in at least one way. On the first two nights considerable annoyance was caused by unruly boys, who amused themselves by yelling "Fire!" outside the theatre and invariably set all the tocsins in the city to ringing.

Thus far the American tour had been all that Kean had hoped it would be. He saw everywhere about him, and felt with satisfaction, the enthusiasm of a nation; he was besieged with flattering testimonials; the public filled his theatre and shouted "Bravo, Kean;" journalists, professional men, writers, society folk, flocked about him, making amiable gestures; he was sending home a thousand pounds

[8] Kean entered in his diary, for the first Baltimore performance: "no applause—some hissing."

every month. He heard also, but did not feel, the ominous under-current, the snarls of detraction. He was accustomed to these at home, and he treated them here as there, with contempt. The journals that pleased him, that "understood" him, he read; the others his servant carried to the trash bin with a pair of tongs. He planned now to remain until the next February: he had made arrangements for thirty-five performances in southern cities and had engaged to play six nights at Richmond in October.[9] Then, by one unlucky error of temper, he wrecked himself.

Before the close of his Baltimore run he had written to the Boston Theatre proposing a second engagement. Manager Dickson, in view of the lateness of the season, tried to dissuade him, but yielded to insistence. Accordingly he was announced to reopen on Monday, May 21, as Lear, but actually opened on Wednesday, having been delayed by illness in New York. Manager Dickson's fears were realized; a thin house greeted Lear; on Thursday a still thinner house greeted Jaffeir of *Venice Preserved*; on Friday, for Richard, a mere handful were present. Kean was hurt and indignant; he looked through the curtain at the empty benches, declared that he would not play, and made ready to leave the theatre. Dickson implored, offered to release him from the rest of the engagement if he would keep faith with his audience, but the wounded tragedian could feel nothing but his own injuries. He stalked away, declaring he would leave Boston the next morning.

When the hour for performance arrived the house looked better, as the boxes had pretty well filled up. Dickson, angry in his turn, was in no mood to cover the face of things by a discreet managerial lie. He sent out Duff, the stage manager and the leading resident actor, to announce baldly that Kean, after many importunities to the contrary, had positively refused to play; should they go on without him? The audience replied with a loud affirmation; the curtain opened, but calls were raised for the manager, who again appeared. What did they wish? They wished to know Kean's reasons for leaving. Want of patronage, said Duff bluntly. At length the play was grudgingly al-

[9] From notices in the Charleston *Patriot* and Richmond *Compiler*, reprinted in the New York *Evening Post* of April 10, 1821.

lowed to continue with Brown as Richard. Kean left for New York next morning.

Boston was furious. Indignant cries went up from all the papers. One or two, like the *Advertiser*, kept a tone of reasonable disapprobation, but most of them fell savagely upon the truant. The *Commercial Gazette*, which three months before had compared him to the rainbow, headed its notice, "Kean—Decamped!" and characterized his action as "too foul and dishonoring to be overlooked—the actor too unprincipled not to be noticed with the finger of scorn." "Longinus," writing to the *Centinel* on May 30, declared that the collapse of the Kean bubble was just what should be expected; the common sense of the country had revolted at a tawdry, tricky style; the man so absurdly run after was "scarcely a second rate actor of the London stage." The *Galaxy* said: "They ought to have taken this insolent pretender, this inflated, self conceited, unprincipled vagabond by the nose, and dragged him before the curtain to make his excuses for his conduct himself."

Very shortly after the incident[10] Kean wrote privately to Dickson:

I much regret the occasion of my abrupt departure, but you must feel with me that my professional reputation must not be trifled with. An indifferent house to such plays as "Venice Preserved," etc. *however well acted*, may be found in the catalogues of histrionic events, but a total desertion of the public to that character which has been the foundation of my fame and fortune, requires a greater portion of philosophy than I am master of. I must lament to find that curiosity alone was the incitement of the apparent enthusiasm that attended my efforts on the first engagement I had vainly conceived the *talent* not the *novelty* had attracted. Be kind enough to pay into Mr. Tileston's hands my portion of the first night's receipts.

The howl of outraged majesty that was set up in Boston echoed through the press of the country. This immediacy of resentment, astounding and incomprehensible to the causer, even yet astonishes the modern observer. A good deal, of course, must be laid to the touchiness of American temper, that supersensitiveness to the behavior of foreign visitors which stirred the spleen of Dickens and Mrs. Trollope.

10 The letter is quoted by Clapp, *Record of the Boston Stage*, p. 191, without date; but it was evidently written immediately after the affair, and before the storm broke.

But, as Kean's friends in the press pointed out, Cooke had done the same thing more than once without causing an uproar—Cooke who, as the story went, had declared on being invited to play at Washington for the President, that he would be hanged if he would act for any "damned Yankee Doodle president." The sudden about-face of newspapers which had piled their praises on Kean's head leads one to believe that there existed a surly undercurrent of hostility which boiled to the surface at the first opportunity. The press seemed *glad* to be able to fall upon this man, who had until now conducted himself in the most decent way but who for some reason had not won their affection. Why was this? Why did so many persons, before and after the fall, proclaim with such heat that he was a charlatan, a second-rater, a harlequin in tragic clothes, a "mere mob actor?" The ordinary disagreements of schools would not engender such passion; the stoutest Kembleites back in 1814 did not claw the new pretender into tatters. There was a virus at work in the present moment which calls for explanation, but beyond the conjectures made near the beginning of this chapter I cannot go.

Mingled in the denunciations of Kean one finds now and then a wicked delight in the humiliation of Boston, the text for which was given by the actor, who in addressing the Boston audience at his first reception had expressed his pleasure at being in the "literary emporium of the western world." The phrase stuck in the memory of a people addicted to phrase making. Now it was pulled out with a relish. The Baltimore *American* (May 31) in an editorial headed "Mr. Kean *vs.* the 'Emporium'" treated the incident with sardonic amusement. Kean had made a fool of Boston and Boston has made a fool of Kean. The whole affair is ridiculous. "After lavishing encomiums where they were so little merited—and after squandering their money upon an individual who entertains not even common gratitude towards the bestowers, we think the Bostonians richly deserve all they have received of Mr. Kean." The Philadelphia *Democratic Press*, which had brayed extravagantly over Kean's marvelous art, found his behavior "superciliously insolent" and predicted that "assuredly he will never again be permitted to appear before an American audience." The New York *American*, after quoting from a Boston paper,

"I am heartily tired of Kean—he caricatures every passion, every emotion," expressed its complete concurrence: "In its justness we fully coincide, and . . . have not doubted that the ebb of fashion would leave the mock Roscius stranded on the shoals of thin houses, and sleepy hearers." Only a few newspapers treated the matter in a way commensurate to the facts and appropriate to their own dignity. Among these I am glad to find the *National Gazette* of Philadelphia, which, as it had been a severe but just commentator on the Kean furor of January, now became a severe but just commentator on his persecution. It perceived that offenses had been committed on both sides and thought they should be settled by mutual concessions.

We really wish to see this gentleman indulgently treated. It was fair to criticise his professional merit; it is not unjust nor harsh to make merry with his egotism, when thus displayed in a printed address: we may pity his weakness in sneering at the public who, he acknowledges, had treated him "with the greatest liberality."[11] But it is coarse and despicable to circulate lampoons on his person, and ridiculous to manifest resentment at his freaks.

In New York his two staunch friends, Noah and Coleman, stood by him. Noah in the *National Advocate* pronounced the whole stir to be "ridiculous."

Mr. Kean was wrong, no doubt, but that is an affair for him to settle with the Boston audience . . . At all events, his genius and wonderful powers suffer no diminution by his eccentricities.

Coleman took a graver, more reserved tone.

Unless something satisfactory should appear on the part of Mr. Kean, it may safely be predicted that his career in this country has arrived at a premature termination . . . We will not, however, be too precipitate in our condemnation; perhaps Mr. Kean's conduct may admit of explanation; if so, he has the opportunity to make it; if not, he cannot too soon bid a farewell, a long farewell, to his American popularity.—*"Othello's occupation's gone."*

Coleman's request for an explanation was instantly complied with. On June 1 the *National Advocate* printed a long letter which contained scarcely a hint of the expected apology but which, on the con-

[11] This editorial (June 6) appeared after Kean's letter to the *National Advocate.*

trary, showed that Kean had no understanding of the forces at work against him. It is the letter of an angry man, who feels that he has been gravely injured and whose resentment is not lessened by an underlying consciousness of having committed a tactical error. It was the worst possible letter he could write, because it expressed, or could easily be interpreted to express, that conceited arrogance with which he was widely credited.

He begins by saying that as a public servant he is amenable to public censure, and will apologize with due submission if he is shown to be in error.

> But, sir, is it not extraordinary, that the offence with which I am charged took place at Boston, with the concurrence of the managers; with the approbation of friends, with whom I spent the evening, gentlemen of fortune and literary acquirements; and that I should not hear any dissatisfaction expressed until I arrived in this city?

He had gone to Boston at great expense "and with all that additional cost which falls to the lot of a stranger," ignorant of the fact that

> Theatres were only visited in certain months of the year . . . I never could or would believe that the arts in this country were only encouraged periodically, or that there could be any season in which Shakespeare was diminished in value; but as I am now initiated into these mysteries, I shall hereafter profit by my experience.

He is a man who lives and supports a family by his exertions; he cannot afford to give his talents away.[12]

> I had performed two of my principle [*sic*] characters without hopes of remuneration in that town, where my efforts had, two months before, contributed largely to augment the public charities. I repeat, I had acted two characters to the very extent of my abilities without profit.[13] On looking through the curtains, at seven o'clock, on the night I was to represent Richard the Third, (that character which has been the foundation of my fame and fortune) I counted twenty persons in front of the theatre. I then decided, hastily if you please, that it was better to husband my resources

[12] The agreement on the occasion of his second Boston engagement was not for a fixed sum, but for a share in the profits.

[13] Evidently the receipts on the first two nights had been insufficient to pay more than the fixed charges.

for a more favourable season, and, in this decision, no disrespect was contemplated to the audience, slender as it was. The managers apparently concurred with me, deplored the unfortunate state of the times, and we parted in perfect harmony and confidence.

He has intended to leave America at the close of his southern engagements. Now, however, he thinks it his duty to return to Boston to vindicate himself at a season when the patrons of the theatre are assembled.

The public have treated me with the greatest liberality, and I shall ever acknowledge its favors with pride and gratitude.

But the present hostility is not the voice of the public;

it is that spirit of detraction ever attendant on little minds; a spirit which watches for its prey, and seizes upon transient and accidental occurrences to defame and destroy. That respectable presses in this country should have been influenced by such feelings, and denounce with such acrimony and bitterness, is to me extraordinary.

As to the reports of certain gentlemen that he has played to equally bad houses in England, they are simply untrue.

The present existence of the first Theatre in Europe is founded on abilities which they affect to despise. The provincial managers of England, Scotland and Ireland have thankfully rewarded my services with sums equal to what I receive from my friend Mr. Price. For the first three years of a career unprecedented in dramatic annals, I was in receipt of double that sum in every Theatre in which I acted,[14] and, even allowing a trifling diminution in the space of seven years, what am I to think of a city in which I have been received with equal enthusiasm, and witness a *total desertion* in the space of three months! But the public say I was too precipitate, and that I should have performed that evening, and then closed my engagement.—Granted. Our feelings frequently mar our better judgments, and from trifling causes, lead to results which we subsequently regret. The error was venal, for who is exempt from error!

He is now convinced that the fine weather was chiefly his enemy, and will return to Boston before leaving the United States.

I beg leave, sir [he said in closing], to submit this "round unvarnished tale" to the consideration and decision of the public; and I have too

14 He probably means to refer only to the provincial cities where he acted on a share basis.

exalted an opinion of their justice and liberality, not to anticipate a verdict in my favour.

The first result of this unfortunate epistle was to draw from Messrs. Dickson and Duff a joint denial of those statements which concerned their share in the events of the fatal night. They resented Kean's saying that they "concurred" in his withdrawal. "They, therefore, respectfully state, that Mr. Kean's refusal to perform the part of *Richard the Third,* was not only without their concurrence, but met from them all the opposition in their power, which they thought decorous and gentlemanly." One can scarcely doubt the truth of their statement, all the evidence supports it; they would not have conducted matters at the theatre after Kean's exit so tactlessly had there been a concurrence between the parties, and Kean's own letter to Dickson implies clearly that he is trying to smooth over a disagreement.

Kean's "apology" finished him beyond hope of recovery. From Boston to Baltimore the press yelped with anger. "His first fault might, after a suitable & humble apology, have been overlooked," said the Boston *Commercial Gazette* in tones comparatively mild, "but his disingenuousness in attempting to throw the fault on our Managers, and afterwards insulting the whole American public, by charging them with a want of taste for Shakespeare, as well as disinclination to patronize genius, has fixed the climax of contempt on his character in the United States." To this and greater severities Kean returned an answer in the columns of the *National Advocate,* in which he still protested his innocence and his injuries, declared his conduct had been such "as every man would pursue under the same circumstances in the country where Shakespeare was born and Garrick has acted," and said that, inasmuch as he could not feel sure that under the same circumstances he would not again act in the same manner, he "thought it proper to leave the theatre open to such compeers whose interest it may be to study the customs, and not offend them by his presence any longer." So, cancelling his southern engagements and bidding farewell to the little knot of loyal friends, he took passage on the same "Martha" on which he had come over.

Before he left, however, he completed the pious intent which he had brought with him, to erect a monument to George Frederick

KEAN AND DR. FRANCIS AT THE GRAVE OF COOKE

Cooke. It is still to be seen in St. Paul's churchyard near the Battery, a stone's throw from the turmoil of Broadway, a gray stone so worn that, although it has been restored three times, scarcely a trace of the inscription is decipherable. The reinterment of Cooke was the one religious act of Kean which history reveals. He was genuinely exalted in the presence of these mighty relics; he wept, recited Shakespeare, loitered in the churchyard communing with the past and singing his favorite song, "Those Evening Bells"; in his pocket he carried away a bone of the forefinger of his saint.

On Wednesday, June 6, 1821, the "Martha" sailed eastward through the beautiful Narrows and out past Sandy Hook. With the last mails taken off he sent a brief farewell letter to the *Advocate*, begging his friend Noah to persuade the American public of his high admiration and respect and promising to return at some future time. Behind him he left a press that wiped its hands with satisfaction over a thrashing well administered; behind him also boomed the stout voice of editor Noah, raised in the interest of common sense and common justice:

> Had he robbed the Banks; burnt all the books in the "Literary Emporium"; seduced all the women—and thrown all the Printers type into the river, he would not have been more roughly handled than for giving vent to vain feelings, and, in a moment of peevish fretfulness, refusing to play on a certain night, and disappointing a slender audience. Hodgkinson, Fennel, Cooper, and Cooke, have done the same many a time, and what was the result? Were they hooted, pelted, and abused? Did the audience forever forbid them to appear, and deprive themselves of the gratification arising from their acting? By no means: they explained—they apologized, or no notice was taken of it; but in the case of this unrivalled performer, no mercy was to be shown him; he was to be trampled upon; driven indignantly from the country; no apology was to be received; and even in this city, where he had fulfilled his engagements, a party was made up to hiss him from the stage.

With this *oraison funèbre*, rising above the noise of trombones, piccolos, and kettledrums, the first American adventure comes to an end.

CHAPTER X

HOME AGAIN

On or about July 19, 1821, Kean reached Liverpool, whence he wrote to Elliston:

> With feelings which an Englishman can alone understand, I have touched once again my native land. I shall be at the stage-door of Drury Lane at noon on Monday next. Do you think a few nights now would be of advantage to you? I am full of health and ambition, both of which are at your service, or they will run riot.

He found London in gala mood. George IV had been crowned on the day he landed; the town seethed with people and festivities, Drury Lane was keeping open house all summer, Elliston, furiously busy, was putting the finishing touches to a very gorgeous pageant reproducing to the smallest detail the coronation, in which he had reserved for himself the honor of impersonating the monarch. Flushed as he was with grandeur, he yet had room to feel the spectacular value of the great tragedian's return, and immediately issued handbills announcing the glad tidings. Kean reached London, as he had promised, at noon on Monday the twenty-third. He was escorted to the theatre (says Raymond in his *Life of Elliston*) by a fantastic bodyguard composed of six outriders in various costumes of the theatrical wardrobe, a troop of horsemen on the flanks, three or four carriages, the first of which bore the Great Lessee in solitary state, and an inquisitive rabble. At the theatre door he was ushered in as a king into his palace; the company crowded about; there were congratulations, speeches, and after the play a dinner. Elliston, who lived on pomp and circumstance, knew what was fitting to such an occasion.

That evening Kean played Richard to an audience of good size which welcomed him with every noisy token of affection. The London public, in its best humor, was genuinely glad of his return. On Wednesday he played Shylock, on Thursday, Othello, on Saturday, Richard again. Then he broke down. Far from being in that state of vigor which his letter declared, he came to London tired and ill. After struggling for a week he was obliged to give up, and rested until well into November. Meanwhile the mock coronation came out at Drury Lane in unprecedented splendor, gaped at by admiring thousands. Elliston was translated. As he strutted in his robes and crown, amid all the regal panoply and before a shouting populace, his brain reeling between truth and fiction, he lifted a benign hand and in accents that were more than make-believe blessed his happy subjects.

Kean took up his duties on November 12, with *Richard III.* But the quickening of public interest which his return had caused forthwith lapsed into apathy. He played throughout the season to poor houses, nor were his ventures into new rôles attended with the least success. On November 27 he revived Joanna Baillie's tragedy *De Montfort,* which had failed under Siddons and Kemble and promptly failed again. On December 14 he tried the part of Hastings in Rowe's *Jane Shore,* one of the successes of his early provincial days, but the town was completely indifferent. On January 28, 1822, came a new play, *Owen, Prince of Powys,* so insignificant a piece that the name of its author seems to have been lost. It lasted three nights. On March 17 he made another of those puzzling starts into the incomprehensible, this time picking on Sir Pertinax Macsycophant in Macklin's forgotten comedy, *The Man of the World.* Although forgotten now the comedy was famous enough in its own day, from the vogue given it by Macklin, the author and creator, and Cooke. But the dour, verbose, and sycophantish Gael whose characterization makes whatever is valuable in the play requires an interpreter of special physique and powers. This physique and these powers were possessed by Kean's two great forerunners; they were not possessed by him. He played it six times, on the last night to receipts of £83. On March 30 for the benefit of Russell, the stage manager, he played Osmond in Monk Lewis' popular *pièce d'épouvante, The Castle Spectre.* The house was good, thanks to Russell's friends, but when Kean acted the play twice more the combined receipts were only £225. On May 20 he tried again to pluck a pinion from the wing of Kemble, in *Henry VIII,* but when at the fourth try the house contained £60 he gave it up.

On May 21 Miss Tidswell, having trod the boards of Drury for upwards of forty years and being ripe now for retirement into private life, bade farewell to a public which cared little whether she went or stayed. She chose Mrs. Centlivre's vigorous old comedy *The Wonder*, in which her "nephew," as may be supposed, played Don Felix. A number of old friends paid their compliments to her: Munden acted in *Lock and Key*, Braham sang, Knight gave a Yorkshire recitation, Miss Tree danced. The lady herself took no part in either of the plays, for her repertory contained nothing worthy of such an occasion. The playbills said that after the comedy she would "*attempt* to take a respectful leave." One can imagine her entering on the empty stage with all appropriate agitation, curtseying to the good-natured applause, and reciting her carefully prepared lines, to be forgotten at once as she curtseyed herself off. This small, rusted piece slipped quietly from the machinery of Drury Lane.

On June 3 Kean chose for his benefit, *The Roman Actor*, Massinger's famous tragedy which offers so varied and attractive a rôle for the lead, *The Mountaineers*, and *The Waterman*, a musical afterpiece, in which he played Tom Tug. The whole proceeds of this entertainment, after the house expenses had been deducted, were to "be applied to the Relief of the Distressed Peasantry of the Sister Kingdom" (i.e., Ireland). It is sad to relate that the Sister Kingdom was little the better for this generous act, because in spite of the rich bill, the triple presence of Kean, and the good cause, the profits amounted to but £5.17.7.

The season of 1821-22, at least on the tragic side, was a poor thing. Elliston had done nothing to strengthen the company, save for the introduction of a certain Miss Edmiston, who was a good find and who with the veteran Mrs. W. West gave respectability to the female side. All of his energy seems to have been exhausted in the Coronation; tragedy was allowed to shuffle along in the old lax way, with the result that on Kean nights the theatre stood three-quarters empty, and the press was full of complaints. In speaking of the *Henry VIII* failures the *Theatrical Inquisitor* raised the question as to whether the public were getting tired of Kean. "There are many who argue . . . that he has lost all his attraction," an opinion in which the *Inquisitor* did not concur. Kean, it thought, was equal to what he was in the days of his popularity, indeed even greater, but one man alone cannot fill a theatre: the fault lies with the management for not supporting him. On June 15 the *Inquisitor* ruminated upon the "most disastrous season." As reasons for the general public neglect it suggested: (1) the state of the times, (2) poor actors, especially in the tragic line, (3) the objectionable form of the playhouse, and (4) its filthy condition. "Thus this Theatre, opposed to the more approved construction, sociability, freshness, expensive and happy combinations of dramatic art with musical, mechanical, and scenic talent, exhibited in Covent Garden Theatre, could not maintain the contest for attraction."

The critic of the *London Magazine* (January, 1822) took a similar view, but with more severity for the actor. He thought also that the main trouble was in lack of support, yet a good deal of it lay with Kean, who was growing lax and mannered—in his way as artificial as Kemble.

> Flattery before him, and weakness behind him, have swelled a proper self-appreciation into a dreaming security; he seems, generally speaking, to have composed a sort of off-hand, compendious theory of setting giddy palms in motion, lively and imposing, flashy and shallow, which though more affected than the graceful majesty of John Kemble, is termed nature by the parasites.

The critic returned to these thoughts in the July issue of the *London Magazine*, induced thereto by the striking fact that for the first time in his metropolitan career the actor had failed to draw a good house to his benefit. Kean, he said, is no longer a novelty or the fashion, "or if there be any fashion in regard to him, it is a fashion of dislike." The fault lies with him; though he cannot make himself more novel, "yet he ought to make himself more popular, not by paltry arts, or by becoming the mountebank of any society, but by a [illegible] and honourable discharge of his duty as an actor. Let him too be more chary of his good name; for the audience, whether right or wrong, will mix up the private with the public character." The critic then went on to a consideration of the benefit performances, his remarks on which, from their bearing on the present question, are worth repeating. Kean's Paris (in *The Roman Actor*) was exceedingly bad—"overbearing, familiar, sarcastic, pompous without dignity, and violent without energy." In the second act of *The Mountaineers* he was no better, "but in the cottage scene, both before and after the entrance of Floranthe, he was brilliant beyond the power of words to do him justice." His Tom Tug was "a still, beautiful piece of acting that only wants to be more known to become a subject of general admiration." In sum, then, the exhibition was a mingling of good with bad, in which the few great moments shone brilliantly amid a heap of rubbish. It demonstrated only too clearly (as indeed every one was saying) that the actor had grown lazy, careless, neglectful.

During the summer vacation Kean played through the provincial cities, including Birmingham (late in June), Dublin (July 15 to August 12), Edinburgh (August 19-31), Glasgow (September), Perth (October), Dumfries (early November). His popularity was stronger in these places than in London, to judge from Dublin, which (on the authority of the *Theatrical Observer*) crowded to his opening performance of *Richard III* in such numbers that box money was paid to gain access to the pit. At Glasgow he was obliged to cancel the latter part of his engagement (again on the *Observer's* authority) by an illness which required the care of two doctors. At some time during the summer, probably after his return to Scotland in October, he purchased an estate of some twenty acres and a house on the island of Bute, which lies at the head of the Firth of Clyde. I do not know whether this was the result of previous acquaintance or sudden impulse—probably the latter. The idea of a retreat in the bosom of nature, among the picturesque mountains and waters of western Scotland, took strong hold on his fancy, at least for a time. He no doubt imagined himself living, like Reuben Glenroy, free, healthy, and innocent, far from all the pain of thankless labor, rivalry, envy, and disappointment. So he entered with childlike zest into his domain of mossy bog, built roads, improved his cottage, meditated the pastoral life, and talked to his wife and son of finishing out his years in this primeval harmony. His wife, I should suppose, knew him too well to be deceived, but was glad enough to see him happy.

Meanwhile Elliston was enormously busy in London. Stirred by the constant plaints of journals and conscious himself that something drastic must be done to pull his theatre out of the slough, he was going about it in his large way. For one thing, the interior of Drury

Lane was entirely rebuilt, at a cost of £10,000,[1] and brightened with all the lustre that paint, imitation marble, and mirrors could give it. Also, he made a bold raid on Covent Garden, whence he took Young, Liston, Madam Vestris, and Miss Stephens and thereby added material strength to his own resources in tragedy, comedy, and operetta. He also acquired the diminutive Clara Fisher, vastly popular in romping farce. These purchases were costly. Liston, the first comedian of the day (whose coming must have put a crimp in Munden's temper), drew from him £50 a week. Young, who had been sulking at Covent Garden under £20 a week, was lifted to £20 a night. Clara Fisher drew £31.10 a week, and Vestris, on the threshold of her brilliant career, £30. Elliston did everything nobly.

In one direction, however, he saw trouble. The acquisition of Young, by which he broke up the powerful Young-Macready combination at Covent Garden and added a tragedian who had inherited the affections of the Kembleites, was a clever stroke—but what would Kean say? He cautiously addressed to the absent lion, through his treasurer, an impersonal, businesslike statement of plans for the coming season. The answer came hot from Dundee (October 13):[2]

Dear Elliston | Your Treasurer has written to me a letter so overcharged with *we* and *us* that it is with difficulty I cou'd extract the subject but the drift I find is—that as Mr. Young is engaged for *30* nights & my services are wanted—to act with him—now this I call exceedingly impudent, & I hope without your authority.—The Throne is mine I will maintain it —even at the expence of expatriation—go where I will I shall always bear it with me—& even if I sail to another quarter of the globe, no man, in this profession, can rob me of the character of the first English Actor. When I come to London Elliston I open in Richard the 3*d* my second character *Othello!! Hamlet—Lear*—& so through my general cast if Mr. Young is ambitious to act with me, he must commence with *Iago.*—& when the whole of *my* characters is exhausted we may then turn our thoughts—to Cymbeline, & Venice Preserved—at the same time I do not wish to influence your Dramatic Politicks, if you think Mr Young will answer your purpose better than me

Verbum sat Vale Edmund Kean

1 So the *Theatrical Observer.* Raymond, in his *Life of Elliston,* says £22,000.

2 This and the two following letters are at Harvard.

I shall be in the Highlands but a letter directed for me at J S Knowles Esq—Glasgow will find me.

To this burst of anger Elliston replied in his most disarming, persuasive vein, but letting it be clearly seen that he had no intention of altering his plans. Kean's next letter is more temperate and altogether sincere; he speaks, for once, directly from the heart, not without a trace of affectation in the latter part, it is true, but on the whole with an admirable frankness. I like him better in this letter, I think, than in almost any other.

Rothesay, Isle of Bute
23d October [1822]

Dear Elliston | I cannot according to the arrangements I have made, be in London till Monday, the *11th* You can if you please advertise me for Richard on that night—You must forgive my being jealous of my hard earned laurels. I know how brittle is the ground I stand upon—& how transient is public favor—Mr Young has many advantages that I have not a commanding figure, sonorous voice—& above all Lordly connexion—I had too much regard for my own happiness not to kick all such trash[?] to the devil. I am therefore coming to meet an opposition, made up of my own enemies (which like locusts—can almost darken the sun) Mr Youngs *friends*—& his very great abilities—with nothing but humble genius to support me, a mere ephemera—always at the command of caprice—& the same breath that nourishes the flame this day—to morrow puts it out. Aut Caesar, Aut Nullus, is my text. if I become secondary in any point of view, I shrink into insignificance, I shall not trouble the world longer than the two years I am engaged to you—I have taken a house in Scotland for the purpose of retirement with my family at the termination of my engagement & all I ask of you—is to let me retire with my reputation Undiminished, that I may enjoy the retrospection, when I am the world forgetting, & by the world forgot—as the Covent Garden Hero—comes upon my ground, the Challenger—I have doubtless my choice of weapons, he *must* play Iago!—before I act Jaffier I am told he is extraordinarily great in Pierre—if so—I am beaten—this must not be—I cannot bear it I wou'd rather go in chains to Botany Bay—I am not ashamed to say—I am afraid of the contest. will you take the *thousand pounds* & dismiss me—I shall be at Dumfries from the *28th* to the *30th*

Yours &c

E Kean

The character of Elliston's reply is shadowed in the next letter, which shows a temper swung round again to exasperation. It is dated "31st of October," postmarked "Carlisle, 1822."

My dear Elliston | I never doubted your ingenuity in composing a letter, but you must excuse me when I say, from the first moment of our acquaintance, I have questioned your sincerity. Your letter very cleverly—but not honestly evades the answer of a simple question is Mr Young to act Iago with me first or is Mr Kean to act Jaffier with Mr Young's Pierre—You tell me you are surrounded by equal talent in your department—I acknowledge this—but I do not see Mr. Dowton or Mr Munden or Mr Knight or Mr Harly or Mr ——— [*sic*] in for *Rover Ranger*—I see Mr Young's name for Hamlet!!! did Mr Young's Hamlet ever bring to the treasury the same Money that mine has. is there any Country Manager will give Mr Young *10£* for his acting Hamlet. I made *54* for playing it last night—

Why is Mr Young engaged for a certain number of nights, when Mr Kean is attached to the Property |

Elliston, My *dear* Elliston, I *know you*—I see the deep entangled Web you have extended for me but that Providence which has guided me through all the perils of worldly Chicanery—fights for me now & will defeat the plot [against me][3] though *Coutts Bank* flowed into the coffers of my enemy—& his Suite composed of *Lords* & *Auctioneers.* I am prepared for *war*—, you make some references in your letter.

I am tired of Pimps and Sycophants.

Yours Edmund Kean

Veritas vincit

However the lion might roar and lash his tail, Elliston had his way; he did not relinquish Young, or accept Kean's thousand pounds, or accede to his peremptory wishes concerning the order of repertory. He had steered his boat through worse storms than this. So in despite of thunder from the north, Young opened at Drury Lane on October 17 as Hamlet, his most admired rôle. For the next fortnight he played Pizarro, Macbeth, and Hamlet, to such attendance as Kean had not seen in years. Elliston's business sense was true. He knew that heat may ensue from the juxtaposition of normally cool elements. At Covent Garden Young was admired but not greatly run after, at

[3] Crossed out.

Drury Lane Kean was moribund. By housing these two antipathetic elements together he raised the caloric values of each several degrees. There was obvious economy in paying Young twenty pounds a night if the attendance was the better by one hundred and fifty or two hundred. Nor was their combined presence necessary to this blessed result; each profited by the mere imminence of the other. That subtle humor which nowadays we call *morale* and which at one time had leaped at the sole touch of Kean, now flowed again through the walls of Drury. Excitement was alive in the air, and that queer irrational animal, the public, which had not cared greatly for either when they were a few rods apart, now thronged to see Kean on Wednesday because they had seen Young on Tuesday.

Therefore, when Kean offered, on November 11, his shop-worn Richard of Gloucester, such an audience gathered for it as had been wont to gather when that character was the sensation of London. And when he played Othello on the fifteenth to the Iago of "a Gentleman," the house was again well filled. For a fortnight the two rivals kept apart, then came the anticipated union. On November 27 they played *Othello*, with Young as Iago, and on the twenty-ninth *Venice Preserved*, with Kean as Jaffeir and Young as Pierre. On both nights the house was crowded by a public which had not forgotten the spectacular duel with Booth; the *Morning Post* reviewer, anent *Othello*, said he had not seen such a determined striving for places "since that night of mighty expectation." If the audience looked for another slaughter, they were disappointed; their hero was no longer capable of exerting himself so mightily, he was tiring already under the strain of constant expenditure, the sinews of his will had lost their tautness. Yet though he did not play Young off his feet, as he had played Booth, he played better than he had done for a long time. He may have given a *finer* performance than on that other historic occasion, but not so electric; the time for demonic energy had passed, the time for finesse had come, for those rarifications of art which seek to replace the vigor of prime. He was not in his best voice, the *Morning Post* reported, and many sentences were spoken so low, in a tone little above a whisper, that only those near the stage could hear. It had not been a whispering Othello who vanquished Booth! But he played nobly, and the house was enchanted. How well Young acquitted himself is not altogether easy to determine, from the conflicting testimony of reviews. As the heir of Kemble and vested chief of the classic school he had inveterate enemies, who aggravated their dislike of his principles by a loud contempt for him as a weak imitation of his master. Hazlitt, for one, would see him as nothing but a dead simulacrum. Yet that must have been far less than justice, for aside from the impressive evidence of Kean's fear of him there is enough respectable opinion to show that, although not a great actor, he was many times a fine one. To the natural advantages of a handsome person and a melodious voice he added a respectable understanding of his characters, but he lacked the divine ingredient of genius. His line was dignity, grace, and fine diction. His admirers declared that he excelled Kean in the *keeping* of a character, that his compositions were wholes in which nothing was sacrificed to momentary display, by which contention they tacitly admitted that he never ravished by sudden flights. If Kean may be said to illuminate Shakespeare by flashes of lightning, Young's aim, and in the minds of many his accomplishment, was a steady glow. What is certain is that he neither reached the heights of John Kemble in his own line, nor had any of the peculiar brilliancies of Kean.

They played together through the season in *Othello* and *Venice Preserved*, adding on January 22, *Cymbeline*, in which Kean acted Posthumus and Young Iachimo, on June 18, Monk Lewis' *Adelgitha* (for two performances), and on June 23, *Alexander the Great* (once only). Of these *Othello* proved the strongest attraction, but all were well attended. In his solo passages Kean introduced no novelties, except that, for three performances, he restored the original ending of *King Lear*, in place of the "improved" version of Nahum Tate which had held the stage for over a hundred years. Tate in the interest of sentimental justice had preserved the lives of Cordelia and Lear, married Cordelia to Edgar, and thus had made "bearable" a play whose ending Dr. Johnson said no audience could endure. The restoration was made partly because of the protests of Hazlitt and other critics, partly, it is said, because of Kean's own desire; no one, he declared, could know what he was capable of until they had seen him over the dead body of Cordelia. But if Genest may be trusted, the experiment turned unhappily to laughter, for Lear staggered under the weight of Mrs. W. West, the audience tittered, and Shakespeare was lost. After two repetitions of the original ending during this season, Kean returned to Tate.

When the season closed on June 30 Elliston counted a total of receipts from all sources that passed well beyond £60,000. This was prosperity indeed. He was able to pay over £9,000 toward his restorations of the theatre, and nearly £4,000 toward arrears.

Kean's provincial engagements were as follows: Salisbury, six nights beginning December 30, 1822; Dublin, thirteen nights beginning March 31, 1823; Swansea, July 7 for a few nights; Cork and southern Ireland in August and September; Belfast in mid-October. The *Theatrical Observer*, from which these scattered items are mostly taken, reports that the Irish tour was prosperous to the sum of £4,000 and more. There are also references at various times to attacks of illness. Such notices become frequent in theatrical columns from now on.

The season of 1823-24 contained some matters of interest, none of which had anything to do with Kean. Miss Somerville, now Mrs. Alfred Bunn, whose husband was employed as stage manager, returned; Munden, winding up a long and prosperous career, took leave of the stage on May 31; Young returned to Covent Garden and Macready came over to Drury Lane. The exchange was not likely to please Kean, though no doubt he was more indifferent to Macready, whom he despised and did not so greatly fear. At any rate he was not required to play with him: the two stars revolved in their own orbits, each oblivious, so far as it was possible, of the existence of the other.

Beyond question the most sensational event was the production of *The Cataract of the Ganges*, which broke before an astounded public on October 27. This was another masterpiece from the mind of Elliston, who, believing that a theatre should be all things to all men and observing that horses were popular at Covent Garden and aquatic melodramas popular at Sadler's Wells, commissioned Moncrieff to write a play for horses and a cataract. The result was as sumptuous a piece of oriental pageantry as London had ever seen—Genest says that it was in fact the finest spectacle ever exhibited—and the cataract made a huge sensation. It roared with all the majesty of veritable water down the center of Drury Lane stage; on its shore the wicked Brahmin priest was preparing to burn Zamine, the Rajah's daughter; but in the nick her gallant lover snatched her to his crupper and galloped straight up the cataract! No wonder the piece ran for fifty-four nights.

While Macready and the Ganges were making their history at Drury Lane, Kean went into an obstinate retirement in his Scotch paradise, with an ear open toward London. Ill health was possibly a reason, but from two letters quoted by Procter it appears that ill health was only the excuse which covered a subtle defense against the new threat of Macready. Both letters are to his secretary, Phillips, and both are from Bute Island. The first is dated November 14, 1823.

> Mrs. Kean wrote to Elliston on the 8th, telling him that I have not above one week to live. All is well by my keeping away. Dam the Ganges, to prevent further overflow: send to hell the Prometheus that animated the statue:[4] set fire to Bun Row; and then I will return—at any time very reluctantly—for this is the most beautiful place in the world. Write and send me play-bills *every day*. How was the box-plan for the 17th?[5] I can get another doctor's certificate if it is necessary.

The second letter, dated November 18, shows that Phillips had been urging his return, to take up the gauntlet with Macready.

> I thank you for your prompt attention. I must differ with you, about my coming to London. Fabius Maximus conquered not by fighting a powerful enemy, but by avoiding him. He weakened his resources, and saved the city of Rome.
>
> I shall not move from this heavenly spot, till Caius Gracchus meets his fate,—till Weare's murderers are hung,[6]—the Christmas pantomime over,—

[4] Referring to Macready, who played Leontes in *The Winter's Tale*, November 3.

[5] The date (October 17) of Macready's first performance of *Hamlet*.

[6] Macready came out in *Caius Gracchus*, a new play by Sheridan Knowles, on November 18. The Weare murder, committed October 23, made a great sensation, and touched Kean especially because he had formerly been a close friend of the murderer, Thurtell. Thurtell killed Weare in the latter's gig: he was hanged January 9, 1824. On November 17 the Surrey Theatre (London) offered a play on this subject, which was immediately suppressed. The gig used was claimed to be the same in which Weare was killed. The

and a general stagnation of public excitement: and *then*—like a hawk I'll pounce upon my prey. Write and send bills, or those penny critiques, *every day*!!!

On December 6 Macready closed the first part of his engagement at Drury Lane and withdrew himself elsewhere. On the eighth, Kean reappeared as Richard. Whether because of his long absence, or because of a freshening of interest induced by the presence of Macready, the public welcomed him right heartily. One finds him repeatedly drawing over £350 to *Richard*, £422 to *The Merchant of Venice*, £420 even to *Macbeth*, £352 to *Hamlet*—quite in the good old way. His only novelty was that war horse of sentimental tragedy, *The Stranger*, produced for his benefit on April 6. This seems to have been his last performance. On May 19 Macready returned for the balance of the season.

Kean had played an engagement in Portsmouth in January. As soon as his duties at Drury Lane were over he retired into the provinces, and did not act again in London until the following January. We find him at Manchester, April 20-24; Lincoln, April 26—May 1; Derby in May. On May 10 he was billed at Drury Lane as Richard, but illness kept him at Derby and Macready had to be substituted in his place. Elliston probably intended to use both men through the rest of the season, partly in union, but Kean on the plea of ill health escaped to France and did not again play until August, at Dublin. By June he was on the Isle of Bute, supervising additions to his house and building roads. On July 25 he left with Phillips for Ireland, where he played in Dublin, August 2-30; Limerick and Galway in September; returned to Liverpool in October, and Glasgow in November; crossed to Belfast late in November.

Two letters which, though incompletely dated certainly belong here, show that he was in low spirits, dissatisfied with the conduct of affairs at Drury Lane, and determined to break away, either by going over to Covent Garden or by returning to the United States. The

newspaper *John Bull*, on February 15, 1824, affirmed that "Mr. Kean . . . performed the part of Weare the other evening at the Circus, and was driven over the stage of that Theatre in the identical gig in which the murder was committed," but this was probably a malicious invention. There is no evidence that the play was on the boards of any theatre after Kean returned to London.

first[7] is dated "Dieppe—Friday, 21st May," and is addressed to J. Hughes, at Crookes's Theatrical Reading Rooms, Brydges Street, Covent Garden.

Dear Jack | the closer they pursue, the further I shall recede—by the time you receive this Mrs Kean & myself are on our way to Paris—where I shall remain, till I see the last night advertised of Drury Lane Theatre, the day after you will see me in London. Settle all bills for me: I will discharge them on the instant I return—I shall then quit England for *ever* —but I carry with me the reputation of the first English actor. which if I had allowed them to have their way, I cou'd not have done, if I had acted—I know hundreds were prepared for hostility, & in the bad parts they were forcing me to play with Macready he must have skimmed the cream of my professional dish.—he may now take the whole.—& the Public may talk and be damned I shall be soon out of hearing—& change of Country—I hope will destroy every feeling, however it was not artifice. I was so ill, that if I had attempted to act I am convinced I shou'd have fallen on the stage.—Dunn was sent to Brighton & I immediately got into the Packet & sailed—I shall not act any where now, till August—my *Dublin engagement* & then—Vale Patria.

One can guess pretty clearly from this what happened. When Kean reached London from Derby he found Elliston proposing to link him with the despised Macready, in what plays we do not know but evidently they were such that he feared the encounter. Hence his sudden flight, in a black melancholy, to Dieppe and Paris.

The second letter[8] bears merely the address "Londonderry, Oct. 1st." It is evidently written to an official at Drury Lane, probably the treasurer.

Sir | as far as regards the twenty pounds per night[9] I accede to Mr Ellistons proposals. for the ensuing season, with the proviso—that he does not expect me to act in farce—interlude &c on the night of my benefit.

with the respect to the other points of your letter I shall only say—I hope Mr Elliston will not deceive himself in the belief of my renewal of engagement for Drury Lane Theatre. the frequent usurpations of my

[7] At Harvard.

[8] British Museum, Add. MSS, 27,925.

[9] I do not certainly know when Kean began receiving £50 a night in London, but it was not until his return from American soil in 1826, and I suspect that Price was the first manager to offer it.

right—the forgetfulness of my former Services. & above all the *violation* of *word,* must have excited disgust in a less irritable mind than mine—& I assure you Sir—no Galley slave—ever sighed for emancipation, more deeply than I. to bid farewell—to Elliston & his management. Novelty—is the weapon, which he teaches me to adopt—& by carrying my merchandise to the rival market—I doubt not but the novelty will excite a more than common sensation I shall now publicly avow my intention of closing my Theatrical career, at Covent Garden Theatre. by going through the whole routine of my characters. previous to my departure for America—the effects of this I am vain enough to believe—will require *very very novel* attractions in Mr Elliston to counteract but his is the speculation—not mine . . . [Postscript] As Mr Macready is occupying my Situation my Services will not perhaps be wanted so early as the—3d—I am making a vast deal of money in this country—I have no wish to give it up. while it chooses to flow your answer on *this subject* will oblige me

I stay at Londonderry—till the *11th*

In June, 1824, Charles Kean, now a boy of thirteen, was entered at Eton, on a generous allowance for board and education of £300 per annum. And there he remained for three years, doing well at boating and fencing and Latin verse, maintaining a decent gentlemanly scholastic average, and no doubt enjoying himself hugely.

CHAPTER XI

COX VS. KEAN

VEXED as he was by Macready, Elliston, and crumbling health, Kean did not dream that troubles were in store for him far worse than anything he had experienced even in the darkest days of his apprentice wanderings, that he was on the brink of an explosion which would shake two hemispheres, split apart his family, and hasten his steps to the grave. He knew before he left for France in May of 1824 that a long-smoking fuse had at length reached the powder, that his friend Alderman Cox was threatening to sue him for criminal conversation with his wife, but so blinded was he by vanity that he was more excited than alarmed. On the return from France, at Boulogne, he talked over the business with Thomas Colley Grattan. "He spoke of the affair," writes Grattan, "as one which gave him no uneasiness; said he had no fears for the result; and he seemed quite unconscious of the ruinous risk that awaited him. I was rather impressed with the idea that he did not dislike the approaching contest, which was to display him to the world as a man of gallantry."

The following account is derived chiefly from evidence submitted at the trial and from Kean's letters read there. The whole affair is so sordidly commonplace and Kean emerges from it such a very draggle-tailed Romeo, that the kindest act would be to pass lightly by it. But it bears too heavily upon his life.

In 1805 Robert Albion Cox, a banker of Dorchester, aged 33, married Frances Charlotte ——— (I do not know her maiden name), aged 21. In 1812, with the increase of business, they moved to London, but continued to visit Dorchester, near which lay Cox's paternal estate. As to the commencement of their friendship with Kean, the evidence at the trial slightly disagreed. Mr. Sergeant Denman said that while Kean was a stroller at Dorchester, Cox befriended him, and the acquaintance thus made ripened in London. Miss Ann Wickstead, Cox's niece, however placed the meeting at Taunton. It seems that Mrs. Cox had fainted at a performance of *Othello* (which would never have occurred if Kean had not already become a celebrated actor before whom ladies might be expected to faint), had been carried to the actor's dressing room, and there had received courtesies which had been returned in London.[1]

Cox was an amateur of the theatre, a shareholder in Drury Lane, and a member of the larger committee. Therefore the acquaintance was as agreeable to him as to his wife; they hung upon the actor, visited his dressing room frequently, entertained him and were entertained. Grattan, it may be recalled, met them constantly at Kean's table in 1817, without being much impressed with Mrs. Cox, whom he describes as having "nothing attractive about her, either as to person or manners." There is no telling as to just when criminal relations began; the prosecution said seven years before the discovery was made, which would put it in the spring of 1817, but the earliest letter submitted in evidence was dated 1820. At any rate, Cox did not discover the relationship, or professed not to discover it, until March of 1824. He left his house at once, she left soon after, he then returned, and found a "vast mass of letters, which were carefully, but most unaccountably, left packed up." The news got out at once; quizzical and but slightly veiled references began to appear in the press in April; on May 6 Mary Kean wrote to Attorney Sigell to know if anything had yet been decided with Alderman Cox and to say that she was very unhappy.[2] On January 17, 1825, before the Court of King's Bench, Cox sued Kean for £2,000 damages. The case excited the greatest interest; the *Times* on January 18 carried ten columns of summary out of a total of twenty; full reports appeared in the American papers.

Inasmuch as the charge of adultery was incontestable, the defense made its sole objective a mitigation of damages, by attempting to show that Cox was not, as Mr. Sergeant Denman represented, a hoodwinked husband but on the contrary was party to his own dishonor. In his letter of August 26, 1824, Kean wrote to his attorney:

[1] In a letter of August 26, 1824, to Henry Sigell, his solicitor, Kean wrote, "I imagine Mrs. Cox's age to be about 45 when she first flapped her ferret eyed affection upon me. I was about 27." The meeting was in or about 1814, but the lady was then only thirty. The whereabouts of this letter I do not know—it recently cropped up in a bookseller's catalogue—but extracts from it have been printed in older catalogues.

[2] A letter in the possession of Frederick King, of New York.

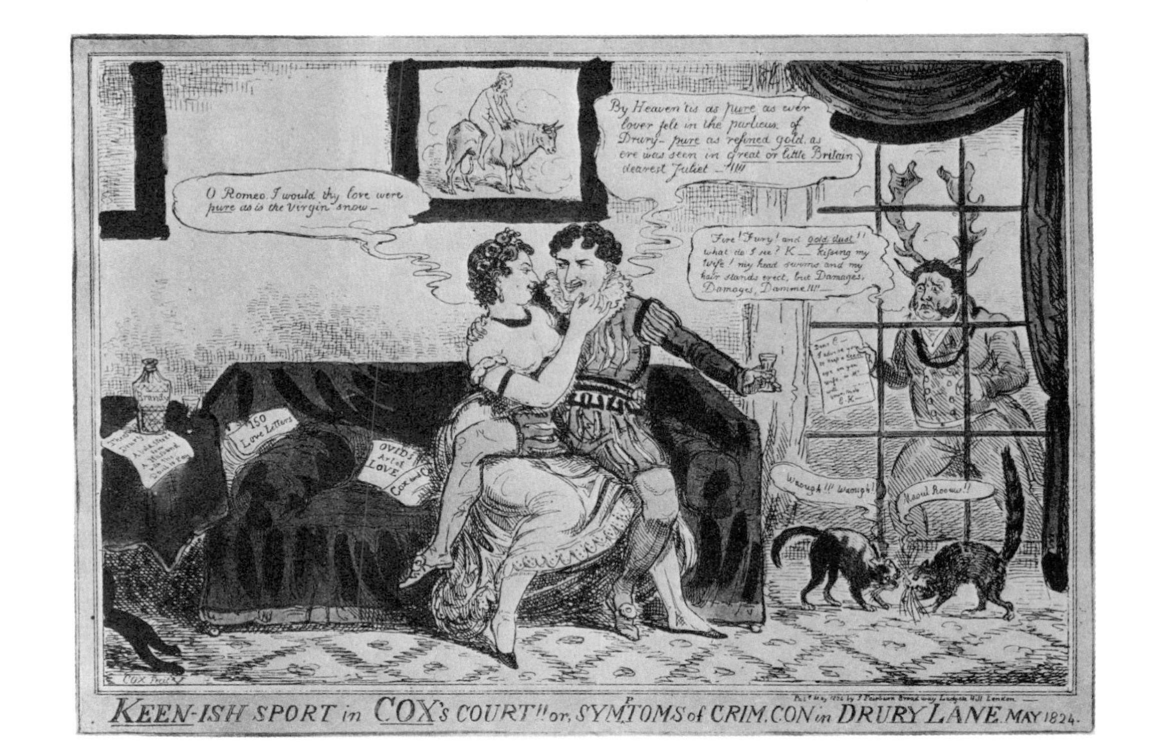

CARICATURE OF KEAN AND MRS. COX

The principal events for forming your defence I take to be what I wrote you before—Mrs. Kean's rejection of their acquaintance, his courting it after such circumstance, his continually pressing me to sleep in the house which, he must have been aware, was unknown to my wife, *forcing his wife and niece from their beds to accompany me in drunken excursions to Croydon &c., leaving her there with me while he went to settle business in London, and in short, living upon my exertions in many of my country engagements.*

Pursuant to these and similar instructions the defending barrister, Mr. Scarlett, attacked the credit not only of Cox but of his wife. He maintained that Mrs. Cox had some years before aroused her husband's suspicions in regard to another man, that she was in fact at the present moment living with Cox's secretary, Watmore, against whom a second action was pending; that Cox must have been cognizant of her affair with Kean because of several incidents of an eye-opening kind, as for example that on one occasion Mrs. Kean had protested against a continuance of the friendship, on another Cox had sent his son Robert to Birmingham out of suspicion that his wife had gone there instead of to Brighton and Robert had reported finding his stepmother living with Kean. Then at Salisbury, in January, 1823, Cox had been so suspicious of misconduct that he had flared into open accusation and had been quieted with some difficulty. But none of these precise accusations of connivance were proved except for the Salisbury quarrel, which as we shall see turned heavily to Kean's dishonor. The examination of witnesses brought out nothing of importance to either side, and nothing creditable. It revealed that the Coxes were constantly in the actor's dressing room, that he was constantly in their house, that he was sometimes drunk and noisy there, that he often came banging at their door late in the night and was sometimes admitted and sometimes not, that they went off on excursions together without Mary Kean, and that the whole association was noisy, vulgar, and impregnated with whiskey. Miss Wickstead was unable to recall anything more overt than Kean's once running up the terrace at Windsor with Mrs. Cox in his arms. "Mr. Kean's attentions to my aunt were very marked," she said, "but not in Mr. Cox's presence."

The defense was therefore not quite able to prove complicity, but it established a presumption of complicity which carried full weight in the popular mind and probably carried weight with the bench. How could a man be respected who pursued another as Cox pursued Kean, who turned a deaf ear to Mrs. Kean's remonstrances, who took money from him constantly, who accused him at Salisbury of seducing his wife and then borrowed £10 for his expenses to London? And what of Mrs. Cox, who after the exposure left behind her a packet of Kean's letters where her husband would be sure to find them? The judgment of posterity need not modify the judgment of contemporary London, that Cox was contemptible and that Mrs. Cox was a great fool and possibly worse. No doubt the Court was disgusted, but it could not help finding for the plaintiff. It awarded damages of £800.

The principal evidence submitted by the plaintiff was the packet of Kean's letters, which were read in full and then spread abroad, to the amusement and scandal of the Anglo-Saxon world. They do not make pleasant reading, pitted as they are with all the corruptions, both in manners and behavior, of a low intrigue. The best that can be said for the writer of them is that he seems to have been genuinely in love with this negligible woman. In spite of his hollow-sounding rhetoric, in spite of the coarseness bred of familiarity, she was as near as he could come to a great passion; she held him, by the most fundamental of bonds, for many years; she gave him a kind of sensuous exaltation; he dwelt on her in absence and hastened to her, through mean subterfuges, as soon as he returned; she made him jealous. Although their amour was of the least noble and most selfish kind, although it was little more than a prolonged heat, yet it was at least "*Venus entière à sa proie attachée*," and it deserves such compassion as may be due to any man enslaved by what all flesh is heir to.

We find him writing from the United States, February 6, 1821:

Oh, dear, dear, dear girl, if I had you in my arms, amidst the acclamations that attend my professional career, I should think this the promised Elysium.

April 5, 1821:

I have now, Charlotte, dispassionately and reflectively placed my whole heart and soul upon you! It may perhaps be burdensome to you, for I am jealous, very jealous . . . I have given up all the frivolities of my nature, rejected all correspondence that could interfere with your feelings. I have thought of you with the affection of a lover, and with the admiration of a friend.

August 2, 1822:

O God! Charlotte, how I love you. If such a feeling is a crime, why are we given it? I did not seek it. The power that will condemn has placed you in my way; the same inspiring hand that framed my better qualities pointed to you as the object of my love—my everlasting love. I must not doubt the justice of the great Being, and have little or no faith in the general Tempter. Whate'er it be, "You are my fate—my heaven or my hell."

He swears at one time that he could live twenty years in a cavern, in the hope of possessing her at the end.

His love does not always dwell on the high ideal plane; sometimes he speaks like a teamster to his doxy. "My dear, dear, dear, little B———, I do declare, when next I see you, I will whip * * * ." The immortal words are veiled forever behind asterisks. His favorite name for Charlotte was "Little Breeches." This caused much ribald laughter.

Amid the vexations of provincial duties he turns to her for comfort.

Bath, June 19, 1822

It is now my dearest girl I wish for you, now that I am suffering under the most painful sensations of wounded pride, and the evident dupe of determined scoundrels, my mind boiling with rage and grief . . . Indignation, resentment, and all the passions of the furies guides my hand while I tell you that in this infernal city, where I was a few years since the idol of the people, my endeavours are totally failing. I have not yet acted one night to the expenses; come to me, darling come to me, or I shall go mad.

Dublin, April 3, 1823

I am horribly tormented. Dublin, in which I had centered the most sanguine expectations, is completely failing. I really do not think I shall get £5 a night.

From Newry, Ireland, September 21, 1824, he complains that his return to London has been delayed by "Two damned quarreling managers . . . The fact is, two managers hold the Belfast Theatre, one has the keys of the Theatre, the other has me in written possession; neither will resign their pretensions, and so 'between two stools down falleth the dish.' "

He gives frequent glimpses of a life of lies at home, under the eyes of a suspicious wife.

Swansea, August 16, 1821

I cannot write fully to you till I get to Cork. Half of your letter has been found, and created a most terrible explosion. She leaves me on Saturday, the 19th; I shall then write about arrangements.

Hastings, August 18, 1821

You must be aware how difficult it is to get one moment to myself: the eyes of Argus may be eluded, but those of a jealous wife impossible, even now I am on tenter-hooks. I expect the door forced open, "and what are you writing?" the exclamation. Or, Susan,[3] to see if everything is comfortable, or Charles with a handful of endearments for his dear papa, all tending to the same thing,—what is he about?

(No date)

Some evil spirit has got into our house. I cannot see what is the matter. I dare not go out alone. She says, "she has as much right to pay visits as me," and is determined that Charles or herself accompanies me wherever I go, till I leave London.

(No date)

She has taken it into her head to accompany me to-day wherever I go, and I cannot shake her off. You must guess my mortification.

Carlisle, November 3, 1822

She left me yesterday for London; if that had not been the case, I could not have written you now. I am watched more closely than Buonaparte at St. Helena.

The letters are full of caution against detection and advice for their meetings. On August 28, 1822, he suggested that she take, in the name of Simpson, a small furnished house in a quiet suburb—Camden Town, Kentish Town, or the Surrey side. He makes appointments "close by the Diorama, Regent's Park," or for the saloon of the theatre, or says that he will "cross over Waterloo-bridge on Tuesday, between one and two o'clock." His letters are addressed to Mrs. Allen, in care of Mrs. Price, or to Mrs. Simpson in care of Miss Tidswell, 12 Tavistock Row, Covent Garden. Both his "aunts," then,

[3] Query, Susan Chambers?

August 12th

My darling Love/
You must be aware. how very difficult it is to get one moment to myself. the Eyes of Argus. may be eluded. but those of a jealous wife impossible. even now I am on tenter hooks. — I expect the door forced open & what are you writing. the exclamation on Susan — to see. if every thing is comfortable, — or Charles. with a handful of endearments for his dear Papa — all tending precisely to the same thing — What is he about — I shall therefore only say — here — there or any where — I love you — dearly love you — & so — forever — ever — ever

LETTER FROM KEAN TO MRS. COX

were go-betweens, but Miss Tidswell was the mainstay of the lovers. He bids Charlotte "tell Tidswell that had she no further claims on my affection but behaviour to you, I should hold her in my heart forever." He writes to aunt Tidswell from Shrewsbury, July 9, 1822, that he counts on her giving assistance to Charlotte—"I place her for a time under your protection;" he signs himself "your affectionate friend and nephew."

In occasional moments of exaltation Kean had reckless thoughts of carrying off his mistress in the face of the world, but more commonly one finds him shrinking prudently, even timorously, from scandal. "Indeed, my love," he writes from Portsmouth, January 22, 1824, "I adore you, and if it becomes your determination to proceed to extremities, you shall ever find in me, your lover, husband, father, friend:" but he adds immediately thereafter, "There is but one point on which I am firm; that is, my duty to my family; after that, I am all in all yours for ever." No wonder the Court laughed when it heard this.

After the almost disastrous quarrel at Salisbury in January, 1823, a tone of strain and anxiety enters the correspondence; he feels that they are treading thin ice, Charlotte is getting difficult to control, he takes frequent alarm, and his temper is ragged.

December 9, 1823

On my return from America all shall be as you wish, till then it is impossible. You must think for a man struggling to obtain competence for his family, which the circumstances of our connection must totally destroy. I feel for you most sincerely, on my soul, my heart is breaking, but any rash step would destroy our hopes forever. I long to see you, but will not come to your house . . . Our meeting last night was cold and distant, not as formerly.

(No date)

If you are determined to distress me continually with unnecessary accusations, on my soul I shall take you at your word—everything I have in the world is now at stake, and by God I will not be bothered.

And again, with brutal anger, "What is the matter with you, you little b———, if you do not be quiet I will kick your * * * ."

Towards the end his fears of scandal were aggravated by jealousy. From Southampton, January 21, 1824:

Six months ago, I was the only subject of your epistles. Every page gave assurances of your love, and your terminations the hope of passing your life with me. It seems now as if you had become weary of the subject, but think it necessary to fill the paper, that I may not too suddenly perceive a change of feeling. You now tell me of concerts, going to plays, give me long critiques of singers and actors, to whose merits or defects I am totally indifferent, and seem very clearly to have made up your mind to a circumstance, which once I was vain enough to think would have broken your heart—that of parting to meet no more . . . But above all, dearest, for I still must call you so, you have betrayed a littleness of mind, which, if I had not read under your hand, I never could have believed. Your rejection of his [query, my?] offers, upon the plea of giving up houses, servants, and society—is this my Charlotte? No, I will believe that some fiend has usurped her character; for if you can so coolly balance the world's enjoyments against your love for me, I have been mistaken in you, and think with uninterested observers, it was passion, not love.

On January 30 he is defending himself in his turn: he does not know what she means by "parties" last winter; she knows that he was with her all the time except when professionally engaged or ill; these suspicions are the hissing of a set of serpents "whom my hand has fed, my breast warmed, and name protected"; why has she accepted money from one who has lost his confidence and spoken ill of him to her?

The last letter (no date given, but evidently written in March or April of 1824) is full of panic:

My dearest little Love,—I am frightened out of my senses—what is this damned paragraph, the Actor and the Citizen? I do very much fear there is some evil design in hand. I am sorry I took you to that Tavern; it originates from that. My darling love, we must be more cautious—we must consider how many interests are involved in our destruction (for destruction is the word for discovery), wives, husbands, children, fortune.

I regret very much your not coming here: his being with you always lulls suspicion, that is, with a little prudence on your side. I shall be in Waterford, I fear, on your arrival.

Heaven bless you, my darling! I shall write again in a week, during which time believe that I love you—dearly, dearly love you.

Little Breeches!

Such were the letters which stripped a shoddy liaison of every romantic veil that imagination might have thrown over it. One may almost say that London was mortified beneath its indignation. Were these the loves of Hamlet, Othello, or Octavian? Granted that by now the public pretty well knew the mortal, ailing stuff of which their greatest tragedian was made, none the less a softening haze lay over the impersonator of ideal nobility, so that there was something particularly offensive in the discovery that his body was of such common clay. Then, too, all those whose sensibilities had been irritated by his previous conduct rushed forward jubilantly to proclaim that he was every whit as bad as they thought him to be. The fact is that almost no one liked him as a man; he was never able, as some have been, to draw people to his defense by the attraction of his personality; he held them, precariously, by art alone. When the howling mob was let loose upon him, men did indeed rally to his support, not from love, however, but from pity and a British sense of fair play.

In the persecutions which followed the trial there was much that sounded like the cowardly snapping of curs at a wounded bear, but one must recognize also the presence of a genuine feeling of moral outrage. The behavior of a man who is deceiving his wife is always deplorable, but it is not always ignominious. And ignominious is just the description which fits Kean, who jeered about his wife to his mistress and yet was full of pretensions toward his family which had a nastily hypocritical sound. And although no one wasted any sympathy on either of the Coxes,[4] nevertheless, his treatment of the alderman seemed more than ordinarily cynical, using him so callously as a screen behind which to hide. Particularly injurious to Kean were the two letters which he wrote on the day following his quarrel with Cox at Salisbury.

To the husband he said:

I must be the worst of villains, if I could take that man by the hand, while meditating towards him an act of injustice. You do not know me, Cox: mine are follies, not vices. It has been my text to do all the good I could in the world, and when I am called to a superior bourne, my memory may be blamed, but not despised.

4 The future history of the Coxes in brief is this. In June, 1825, he was suing her in the Consistory Court for restitution of conjugal rights, she having sued for maintenance. Probably they settled their disagreements—they would. He died in June, 1826. Subsequently she married a Charles Lamy, grocer, and died in 1846.

To the wife he wrote:

My dear little imprudent girl.—your incaution has been very near bringing our acquaintance to the most lamentable crisis. Of course he will shew you the letter I have written him; appear to countenance it, and let him think we are never to meet again, and in so doing he has lost a friend. Leave all further arrangements to me.

Treachery, as the *Morning Chronicle* pointed out, lurks in every adultery, but it is offensive to have it dragged so plainly into the light of day, to see it perpetrated with such nonchalance.

In the trail of this wretched affair sprouted a mushroom growth of pamphlets, ballads, and ribaldries.[5] The letters were reprinted and smuttily gloated over. Cartoons in glaring colors showed the actor dandling a smirking woman in his lap. Ballads were hawked about. As late as July two ballad mongers, singing on the same corner about Kean, got into a fight.

Meanwhile the press was acting its various parts as it thought best. The *Morning Post* maintained a dignified editorial silence, printing a report of the trial but making no comment. The *Morning Chronicle* was for fair play. "We do not think," it said on January 18, "the mere circumstance of the defendant being an actor, deprives him of the benefit of the rule to which others lay claim, that no man is amenable for his vices to the tribunal of the public." But the majority of newspapers gave way to loud, virtuous anger, especially on hearing immediately after the trial that Elliston had posted Kean on the Drury Lane bills for the twenty-fourth of January. This seemed like flaunting profligacy in the face of the public—as the *Theatrical Inquisitor* put it, "a tacit declaration of utter disregard for the feelings of the best

[5] For example: *Secrets Worth Knowing:Suppressed Letters: Cox vs. Kean; The Actor and the Alderman's Wife, or, Kean and His Little Breeches, A Farce in Three Acts. Written by Thomas Little, Esq.* (Pseudonym for Thomas Moore.); *Cocks and Cuckoldom!! Original Songs, on Kean, Cocks, and Little Breeches; The Poetic Epistles of Edmund: with Notes, Illustrations, and Reflections . . . Dedicated to the British People, as the Guardians of Virtue, Both Public and Private; An Appeal to the Justice and Common Sense of the Friends of the True Drama; wherein is compared the treatment experienced by Miss Foote, of Covent Garden, with that experienced by Mr. Kean, of Drury Lane, on certain late occasions; Kean Vindicated, or, the Truth Discovered; Kean versus O. P. What Can Be Said for Kean?*

portion of society." High above all the rest was heard the dreadful voice of the *Times*, working itself into a frenzy. For reasons best known to its editor (who, as other journals indignantly pointed out, was then known to be living in adultery) it pulled out all the stops of its organ of invective.

The conduct of persons who appear on the stage [it declared, January 18] has never been the most irreproachable; and it may be doubted whether such a mass of living vice as the actors and actresses but too generally present in their private lives is not more injurious to public morals, than the splendid examples of virtue which they exhibit in their theatrical characters are useful. It appears, however, that Kean . . . is advanced many steps in profligacy beyond the most profligate of his sisters and brethren of the stage . . . yet have the managers of Drury-lane Theatre the effrontery to present, or to attempt presenting, such a creature as this to the gaze of a British audience, on Monday next. It is of little consequence to the nation whether the character of *King Richard* or *Othello* be well or ill acted; but it is of importance that public feeling be not shocked, and public decency be not outraged.

Throughout the week which elapsed before Kean's public appearance the *Times* incited to riot. Friday, January 21:

If we had seen no intimation of Mr. Kean's immediate appearance on the stage, we should have made no comment on his private conduct; but when we see the very day se'nnight on which he is convicted of adultery, chosen as his first appearance after a long absence—when every person who can read knows that his offence is aggravated by the most shocking circumstances of indecency, brutality, obscenity, perfidy, and hypocrisy—we do say that the public . . . ought not to be insulted by his immediate obtrusion before them as a candidate for their applause.

On the same day the *Chronicle* issued a long and reasonable plea for common sense in morals, directed especially at the *Times*. It did not believe that the press should be an arbiter of conduct; it deplored especially the power which the *Times* and other papers assumed of making and breaking reputations at will, on the plea that this was one of the rights inalienable from the "freedom of the press." It thought the case of Kean an excellent one for illustration.

It is made a charge against Mr. Kean that he has himself said "I must be the *worst of villains* if I could take a man by the hand while meditating towards him an act of injustice."—Mr. Kean not only denied to the husband his guilty connection, but denied it with a solemnity which it is thought was by no means called for. But in ninety-nine *Crim. Cons.* out of a hundred, there is evidence of treachery, and black, long-continued treachery. The confidence of the husband is always abused, and the adulterer seldom scruples to add falsehood to his other sins, when the husband's suspicion leads him to accuse him of improper intimacy. Nay, we will go farther, we say distinctly, that so depraved is the moral sense of what is called good society in this country, that if the offender, on being charged by the husband with dishonouring him, were to confess, he would be in imminent danger of being cut by all his acquaintance as a poltroon, for not being prepared to defend the honour of the woman he had seduced at whatever expence of fraud or falsehood.

This view was also held by the *Examiner*, which, though it took a severe attitude toward Kean ("we deem [him] irreparably degraded by the late disclosures") was all against mob legislation.

For our own parts whatever opinion we may form of the prudence or propriety of so prompt an appearance on the part of Mr. Kean, we shall deem his expulsion from the stage, looking to the parallel cases in higher quarters which are passed over with perfect indifference, as one of the grossest instances of cant and oppression ever witnessed, in an age which affords but too many instances of their union.

Kean had approached his trial rather jauntily than otherwise—Grattan thought he was not displeased to appear in the rôle of conqueror in love. In writing to Sigell August 26, 1824, he had said: "I cannot understand your term of *better than we have a right to expect.* I think we have a right to expect everything, and the more I consider the matter the more I am convinced I shall turn the accusers to infamy and contempt." The issue of the trial then must have been a blow to him, but he scarcely could have gauged the strength of public feeling, when he allowed Elliston to post his name for Richard. Possibly if he had guessed it, he would still have braved the many-headed beast, for he was no coward. But it was a great tactical error, this appearance. If he had vanished quietly until the next October all would by then have blown over, but with a strange blindness he threw himself to the beast when it was most furious for his blood. Some may think that Elliston's imprudent haste was prompted by his inordinate respect for publicity; but I like to believe that in this instance it was warmth of heart, that the doughty little manager wanted only to show that he stood shoulder to shoulder with his persecuted friend and that Drury Lane was a loyal mother to her children.

On Monday night, January 24, 1825, the theatre was packed with a mob snuffing the air of battle. There was a strong Kean army, which the *Times* reported to be composed of bullies and prostitutes, but we must suspect the *Times's* candor. Yet it is true that, as one might expect, a quantity of scum was drawn in by the prospect of a riot, and no decent woman was there. In the *Examiner's* opinion the pit was chiefly for Kean, "and appeared to be partly composed of the description of animals called bloods, fancy men, &c."

A more comprehensive picture was given by the *Chronicle*:

It was somewhat amusing to notice the sort of persons who were most vociferous; young men of fashion in the boxes, who made good use of their hunting halloos, and young tradesmen & apprentices in the Pit, who went only for the sake of the disturbance; the friends of Mr. Kean, the friends of the Manager, & a few white-headed men scattered about the boxes, who seemed the staunchest supporters of the morality and suppression of vice side of the question.

The pack was in a mood of prurient hilarity; during the interval before the curtain rose it shouted, laughed, whistled, sang, and bandied dirty jests.

The play began amid a din that drowned all speech and never ceased. But it was like a drowsy murmur compared to the yell that went up when Richard advanced for his famous monologue. Friends and enemies met for the first real trial of strength; the walls of Drury trembled. Kean halted, took off his hat, made as if to address the house, but at this the clamor swelled even louder. So on went the hat, Richard became himself again, and moved his lips in what one might guess to be a resumption of the soliloquy. At this point a modern manager would have brought down the curtain and sent for the police, but in the old days it was the custom to fight these not uncommon battles to a finish, at least until the spectators began tearing up the benches. Had not John Kemble, back in 1809 when the patrons of Covent Garden were up in arms over an increase in prices, fought an angry public from September to the middle of December? So long as it was merely a question of noise the play would go on. And on it did go through the five long acts, which passed in dumb show, under a bawling tempest. One may wonder, in these more temperate and softer days, at the endurance of the actors, who must have suffered excruciatingly, and at the endurance of British lungs. For three hours the pandemonium kept up, not without personal encounters in pit, gallery, and boxes. From the upper parts of the house came showers of orange peel—fortunately nothing more solid. Through all this heart-sickening storm the hero-victim moved, to outward appearance at least, unfaltering and collected. Two or three times he advanced as if in appeal, but each time the storm rose all the louder. Once, when an orange peel fell close to him, he unsheathed his sword and with the point flicked it composedly away. "Mr. Kean," said the *Post*, "kept the stage with undismayed boldness to the end of the piece; nor was there any token of an abashed spirit discovered in his look or gesture throughout." The *Chronicle* representative, however, who went back stage, found him "extremely agitated, at the same time struggling to maintain the firmness which belongs to his character." Extremely agitated!—say rather, bewildered, bleeding, lacerated in every sensitive artist's nerve. Lucky for him that he did not realize that this was only the first of a score of similar battles, to be fought in two countries, lasting over a year and culminating in the Boston massacre.

On Friday, January 28, he played Othello. The *Times*, that morning, was venomous:

> That obscene little personage (Mr. Kean) is, we see, announced to make another appearance this evening. The ladies of the lobby, and the "Wolves" from the Coal-Hole, have undertaken to bear him triumphantly through his ordeal, and he—fit head for such a band—once more ventures to brave the indignation of the respectable and decent part of society.

The audience on this occasion was considerably smaller, and the volume of racket proportionately less, but the results were much as on Monday night—a play in pantomime. During the third act, where Kean was wont to be most enthralling, he almost captured the general attention, but the murder of Desdemona whipped up a frenzy.

The play was, under the circumstances, an unfortunate choice, because it gave incentive to libidinous applications, which the *Times* seized on with a fury beyond any it had shown before.

The character of persons [it said, January 29] who were employed to support Kean through the test of the theatre, may be judged from this fact,—that whenever the incidents of the play brought him into such a situation that he had to touch Mrs. West, (the *Desdemona* of the night, and we believe a respectable woman), the savage tribe roared as if in triumph at this insult offered to the innate feelings of female purity. It was like the yell of *Caliban*, when the prospect of violating *Miranda* occurred to his lascivious mind. "Would I had done it!" We ask Elliston . . . what women, who are they, and from whence do they come—what women, we again say, are THEY, whom Elliston WILL bring forward on the stage, to be fawned on and caressed by this obscene mimic? . . . Is it not shocking that women should be forced to undergo this process with such a creature, for the sake of bread, before an assembled people?

At the conclusion of the performance calls were raised for Elliston, who came forward and explained, amid constant interruptions, that he had engaged Kean in July for twenty nights, from January 16 to March 16, and could not be so unfriendly as to scratch his name from the bills. When he had retired Kean appeared in ordinary clothes. In the lulls between hisses and applause he made a short speech: He was not there, he said, to justify his private conduct, for he could not do so—"I stand before you as the representative of Shakespeare's heroes,"—his case had been tried before a legal tribunal—he could, if decency had not forbidden, have given evidence that would have gone far toward shifting the blame to his accusers—he could not help feeling that he was a professional victim—"If this is the work of a hostile press, I shall endeavor with firmness to withstand it; but if it proceeds from your verdict and decision, I will at once bow to it, and shall retire with deep regret, and with a grateful sense of all the favors which your patronage has hitherto conferred on me."

On Monday, January 31, came *A New Way to Pay Old Debts*. Although the *Times* declared that "uproar lorded it during the whole night" and described the evening as filled with the howling of Wolves and the "indecent applause of women of the town," more impartial reports showed that the victory was swinging to Kean. There was a good deal of disturbance, but on the part of isolated die-hards. The leaders of opposition, so the *Chronicle* said, were two dandyfied youths in a side box, who were able by their own efforts to make a pantomime of the first two acts. Then the whole pit rose, demanding their ejection. They merely sneered, and when two young men from an adjoining box threatened to put them out, they went on bawling, "Off! Off!" Whereupon they were promptly dragged away. The sentiment of the house was prevailingly for Kean, who received nine cheers at his entrance and was mightily cheered again at the end. The gallery displayed signs reading "Kean for ever" and "Forget and forgive," and threw orange peel not on the stage but on the puritans.

By February 4, when *Macbeth* was given, the fight was practically over. A smallish audience made considerable noise, but it was predominantly friendly, and from then on no opposition raised its tongue. The *Times*, which had sent two correspondents to cover the proceedings independently, was patently annoyed that the rioting had ceased. It contented itself perforce with sneering at the pit filled "chiefly, we should imagine, with Mr. Kean's friends, 'the wolves,' judging from the howlings that people in it made, and the Witney coats, dirty handkerchiefs, and 'milling crops,' of which they were ostentatious," and promising that the managers will find themselves mistaken if they think that "such adherents as Jews, bullies, brothel-keepers, and prize-fighters, can . . . enable them to quash the feeling of a community, or to resist its expression." It was an empty threat. Within two weeks even the *Times* had surrendered, and was reviewing *Masaniello* quite in its usual dispassionate vein.

Kean repeated *Macbeth* on February 7 to a half-filled and peaceable house. Then, for some reason, with *The Merchant of Venice* (February 11) public interest awoke, and until he closed on March 26 in *Othello* he had strong houses, averaging well above £400, with £578 in the house for *Brutus* (March 24). Sympathy, I suppose, and admiration did it; he had made a good fight, taken his punishment manfully; he was forgiven. No doubt the virulence of his enemies in the press worked for him; the public conscience, having spent its overcharged energy, subsided into reason and found that he had been ill used. A touching scene marked the farewell speech after *Othello*;

after alluding to the *Times* as "a most powerful engine placed for my destruction," and thanking the public for its generous support, he spoke with gratitude of the staunchness with which Elliston had stood by him: "The Manager has acted towards me in the hour of adversity with the affectionate kindness of a father, a brother, and a friend." With tears in his eyes Elliston hastened forward, embraced him, and amid deafening cheers led him from the stage.

In spite of his distresses Kean created a new part, on February 17, that of Masaniello in a poor play of the same name by Milner. It was damned, on its own deserts, and died instantly.

Kean was victorious, but victory may be won at too great a cost. Whatever front he might put on before the world, inwardly he was a wreck; he would never be the same man again. His wife had left him, not divorced but living in permanent separation on an income of £200 which he assured her and which, be it said to his credit, he paid till his death; his son Charles, still at Eton, was alienated; his mistress was gone; he was alone, except for those friends who would always booze with him and fawn upon him. His sensibilities were cruelly lacerated; each of those interminable nights through which, like a condemned man on a scaffold, he had postured before a congregation of yelling fiends had drained from him the vital essence of self-respect; he ate his heart in unceasing resentment against the cruel injustice of man to man. Aching with a hundred wounds he turned to anything that would assuage his pain—to drink, women, and the flattery of sycophants.

From London he went to Brussels, where Smithson was manager of an English company, under an engagement made in London and under the impression that he was to appear in the Theatre Royal. But on arrival he found that he was booked for a small theatre holding only £70, and indignant at the insult to his position as the first English actor he broke his contract and returned to England. He then traveled the provinces, playing at Chichester (April 9 and following), Manchester (April 18-20), Lincoln (six performances beginning April 26), Glasgow (May), Dublin (May 31), and Liverpool (June 18). At all of these places he was made to pay again for his offenses to British morality; at his first night in Chichester there was not £20 in the house; Glasgow and Manchester hooted him; only Dublin seems to have given him a decent reception. These continued assaults stung him to fury; more than one witness has expressed the belief that his mind was unhinged. Leman Rede declares that he was "certainly insane"; that he harangued his audiences on his private affairs; that at Cheltenham, as Sylvester Daggerwood, he carried a whip, saying, "I keep this little instrument to punish cheating aldermen and lying editors"; that in the same character he would say, as he turned a handspring, "I may as well practice, for I suppose I must go back to this." When Grattan called on him shortly before his departure for the United States, he was shocked at his appearance. "I never saw a man so changed; he had all the air of desperation about him. He looked bloated with rage and brandy; his nose was red, his cheeks blotched, his eyes blood-shot; I really pitied him."

From June 20 to July 9 he played again at Drury Lane, to very moderate receipts, and then started off on another provincial tour before setting sail for America. He was still seething with bile, paraded his injuries before the world, treated the public of Manchester and Liverpool to impromptu harangues, lost to all sense of dignity, drunk with rage and liquor. From August 22 to 26 he was playing at Liverpool what he announced to be his last engagement in England, and proclaiming that he was being "driven from England by the machinations of scoundrels, by a combination of ruffians who seem determined to destroy me." Yet he lingered on through September, playing no doubt in the north of England and making a professional visit to the Isle of Man. Finally, late in September, he sailed on the "Silas Richards."

CHAPTER XII

THE UNITED STATES AGAIN

WHEN Kean spoke of his departure for the United States as an "exile" he might have been reminded that the intention to revisit had lain in his mind for two years. Yet under the stress of circumstances old ideas take on a new coloring, so that it is easy to understand how the thing which had formerly been merely an act of business now appeared to him as an act of renunciation. At various times, when he had been particularly troubled by crosses, he had expressed a vehement wish to retire from England, into some peaceful refuge, but these had been the impulses of ill humor and low spirits which he forgot the next day or the next hour. Now, however, filled as he was with rancor, believing that his career at home was irretrievably ruined, he may really have felt, as the "Silas Richards" dropped into the West, that he had seen his native land for the last time, that like another Byron he would withdraw himself proudly among an alien people, there live and there die. He would punish his faithless country by absenting himself from it. Had he known his Dryden as he knew his Shakespeare he might have murmured with approval the lines from the *Conquest of Granada*:

> Where'er I go there can no exile be;
> But from Almanzor's sight I banish *thee*.

If he thought to find across the water a people aloof from the passions which had bruised his head, who would shrug their shoulders at the late rumpus as none of their affair, look upon him merely as an artist, and give him respite in which to heal his hurts, he was completely wrong. The United States had followed every move, with passionate attention; they knew all about the Cox trial, they had read the damning letters, they had been informed of the riots at Drury Lane and of his tempestuous course through the provinces, and they had felt all the moral indignation of the English public, along with their own personal and still unappeased resentment. The Boston affair had been neither forgotten nor forgiven, at least by a determined minority, although the memory of it might have been less vehement if the new scandal had not come to show men that Kean was even worse than they had thought him to be. It must be admitted that the United States has never been generous toward the sins of its visitors from abroad, which have frequently seemed to it more dangerous than those grown at home. In the old days, before the national security had been assured by Ellis Island and before the resistance to moral turpitude had been vested in societies for the suppression of vice, the duty of protection was assumed hortatively by the press and practically by the mob. So when Kean, a very blackened sheep, returned to America he found that many an editorial sword was being sharpened for his slaughter. Every paper was agitated over the question, how was he to be received. Nearly every one looked toward him with severe disapproval. His old friend Coleman of the New York *Evening Post* had turned against him, with the expressed opinion that the famous letter to Cox was "certainly the basest attempt at deception we ever met with." On November 1, 1825, he refused to publish a letter in defense of Kean because "we have come to the determination to admit of nothing to be published in the Evening Post relating to this actor." His policy of condemnation by silence was followed pretty generally by papers in and out of New York, which consistently omitted all comment on Kean's performances and took no share in the arguments over him. To others, however, it was more pleasing to speak out, particularly in Boston. The *Courier*, November 5, said ominously: "People in other American cities are looking to New-York for their cue in regard to this infamous tragedian. It is wrong." The *Commercial Gazette*, November 21, explained: "We were amongst those who opposed Mr. Kean—not that he was much worse than others that we have seen, on the stage at times, and have applauded too, but the defiance he bore to public opinion at the discovery of his guilt was not to be countenanced." By the *Daily Advertiser*, November 2, he was described as "a man, who has not only grossly insulted the Boston public, and done all in his power to subject them to derision abroad, but who comes among us, whom he has thus disdainfully treated, merely as a refuge from the indignation of the British public, for his violation of the decencies of private life." The *Courier* reminded its readers that in a letter to Mrs. Cox, Kean had written, "I wish to forget everything connected with America, and do not desire the acquaintance or friendship of any American."

In New York two voices were stoutly raised for his support, those of Major Noah, his former champion, in the New York *National Advocate*, and of James Gordon Bennett in Snowden's *National Advocate*.[1] But, as Tom Dibdin might have said, these were about the only real *advocates* he had.

The press then, with rare exceptions, was mostly silent and cold, or violently hostile. Yet one may easily draw an unbalanced conclusion from such evidence as this. A good many papers were silent not because they cared much one way or another, but because it was the more prudent course. And the majority feeling among the people, as events showed, was for Kean. Moral demonstrations are nearly always a minority affair; most people, confronted with a case such as Kean's, are either indifferent to the moral question altogether, or take ground that private life is no concern of art. On his first visit the tragedian had given to thousands of persons a pleasure such as they had never experienced and which they did not mean to relinquish at the command of self-imposed rulers of conduct. Ultimately, because they were the more numerous, their numbers would prevail; but unfortunately a single hiss has a more penetrating quality than the clapping of twenty hands, and a knot of men in a gallery can render an effect of judgment out of all proportion to their numbers.

On Monday, November 14, 1825, some two thousand persons crammed themselves into the Park Theatre, filling all the seats and standing wherever a foothold could be got. The play was *Richard III*. Pit and boxes were friendly or at least inclined to peace, but in the slips and gallery was lodged a committee of opposition, estimated by the *National Advocate* to be composed of not more than a hundred men. These protestants kept up a hullabaloo which, joined with the

[1] The *National Advocate*, of which Noah was editor and publisher 1820-24, lasted from 1820 to 1829. In 1825-26 Thomas Snowden became the publisher and Bennett the editor; it was called at this time "Snowden's Advocate" to distinguish it from the other paper of the same name. In 1829 it united with the New York *Statesman* to form the *Morning Herald*.

On leaving the *National Advocate* Noah founded the New York *National Advocate* (1824) which he edited till July 6, 1826, after which it was edited by E. J. Roberts.

racket of friends to the house, made the evening a replica of January 24 at Drury Lane. One theatrical riot is much like another: it is needless, therefore, to go into the details of this one—the roar which greeted the entrance of the actor, the cat-calls, the hisses, the shower of missiles, the vain attempts to plead for a hearing. In the wooing scene a piece of rope nearly hit Mrs. Hilson, the Lady Anne, which so alarmed the leader of the orchestra, that he jumped to the stage and led her off. Later an orange struck Kean on the breast; he picked it up, walked forward, tried to speak but was not permitted, and then tossed it contemptuously into the wings. None of the play was heard, but towards the end the force of opposition grew less, and the curtain fell to shouts of applause. When Lee announced *Othello* for Wednesday he was lustily cheered. It was evident that the public vote had a clear majority for Kean. "We are positive," said Snowden's *Advocate*, "when we say that his reception was most enthusiastic."

A significant fact, and one which no doubt hastened Kean's victory in New York, was that the hostile party was alien, or was at any rate taken to be so by most of the people there—specifically, it was Bostonian. "The hissing characters," said Snowden's *Advocate*, "were noted to be nearly all strangers, & the audience hallowed frequently 'put the Bostonians out'—'away with the noisy Bostonians'—'away with Buckingham'—'off with his head,' and such like exclamations." The *National Advocate* made the same observation: "It was evident that the rioters did not belong to the city, for they constantly vociferated *Boston*—send him to *Boston*." By the Boston press these accusations were generally resented as being merely New York slander, but confirmation was given by the Boston *Commercial Gazette*:

> We have understood from a Bostonian who was present, that the most inveterate enemies that Kean had to encounter on the above occasion, were either persons belonging to this city, or those who had left it within the last four years and settled in New York. Their forces were regularly organized, and they were determined not to give Mr. Kean a hearing on his first night.

Such interference in their own affairs was naturally displeasing to the New Yorkers, who had no intention of being dictated to by the Emporium, and so Kean profited by the jealousies of cities. "We hope," said the *National Advocate*, "that on the second night officers will be stationed to protect *New-Yorkers*, and place the disturbers of the peace in the place allotted for them by law."

The unhappy subject of dispute, meanwhile, was unaware that fortune had decided in his favor; he came from the appalling din of the Park Theatre completely broken in spirit. Was it all to be gone through again? Had the whole world let fall its horrible displeasure upon him? Was he to be hissed from every corner where he fled for refuge? In such a despairing frame of mind he threw himself on the public mercy by means of a letter to the *National Advocate*. "With oppressed feelings," he began, "heartrending to my friends and triumphant to my enemies, I make an appeal to that country famed for hospitality to the stranger and mercy to the conquered." He is not conscious of ever having thought or done anything to show disrespect to the inhabitants of New York. The public voice has convicted him of error, but justice must allow the delinquent to make reparation in that place where the offense was committed. "My misunderstandings took place in Boston; to Boston I shall assuredly go to apologize for my indiscretions."

I visit this country now under different feelings and auspices than on a former occasion. Then I was an ambitious man, and the proud representative of Shakespeare's heroes; now the spark of ambition is extinct, and I merely ask a shelter in which to close my professional and mortal career.

The Park Theatre managers took prudent steps to forestall disorder at the performance of *Othello* by closing the fourth tier of boxes, the slips, and the gallery. None the less there was some hissing, but no real disturbance and the friendliness of the audience was beyond question. From then on he had no troubles in New York. The roster of his plays at this first engagement is as follows:

November 14	*Richard III*
November 16	*Othello*
November 17	*Richard III*
November 18	*Merchant of Venice*
November 21	*A New Way to Pay Old Debts*
November 23	*Lear*
November 24	*Brutus*

November 28	*Othello*
November 30	*Macbeth*
December 1	*Iron Chest*
December 2	*Lear* (benefit)

Not many reviews were printed, either now or at any time during his American engagements, but it is interesting to note that in the opinions of some critics he had improved his style since his first visit. "Thespis" in the *Evening Post* found him "more chaste and natural." Bennett in Snowden's *Advocate* made the same observation. "He has less stage trick—there is more calmness, moderation, and just design in his delineation." I suspect, however, that these changes were due less to intention than to weariness. The machine was running more slowly.

From New York he went to Albany, where he had not played before and where he was engaged for six nights. Albany had no bones to pick with him, either for Boston or for the general cause of morality, so that his engagement was mutually quite satisfactory. A full house received him Monday, December 5, as Richard, with loud and prolonged cheers, listened to him with every mark of pleased attention, and drew from him a speech in which he assured it that "the American people had revived, resuscitated and invigorated the spirit of a poor, broken-hearted man." He appeared, thought the *Argus and City Gazette,* both exhausted and embarrassed.

The engagement at Albany, otherwise quite unimportant, is given a special interest by the fact that the descendant star of Kean touched for a few days the orbit of a young and rising star. Edwin Forrest had been working out his apprenticeship in the American theatres and had risen to such a degree that he was serving under manager Gilfert as leading tragic actor of the resident company. In Philadelphia, in 1821, he had watched Kean and admired him. Now he was to play Iago to that famous Othello. As the great man did not come to the theatre for rehearsal, Forrest called on him for instructions. They were what Kean always gave on such occasions: "My boy, I do not care how you come on or go off, if while we are on the stage you always keep in front of me and let not your attention wander from me." Then he sat down to the piano and sang Moore's "Farewell, but

Whenever You Welcome the Hour" so movingly that they both wept. To the young, impressionable American actor, still almost a boy, it was an unforgettable experience. He worshipped Kean. And Kean, it is said, thought well of him, so well that at a dinner in Philadelphia he prophesied a brilliant career. They never met again, at least, on the same stage.[2]

A full and fashionable house on December 16 at Kean's benefit, *Brutus,* bade him godspeed on his way to Boston.

As he approached that angry city he waved a flag of truce, in the shape of a letter to the *Columbian Centinel*:

I take the liberty of informing the citizens of Boston through the medium of your journal of my arrival, confident that liberality and forbearance will gain the ascendance over prejudice and cruelty. That I have erred, I acknowledge; that I have suffered for my errors and indiscretions, my loss of fame and fortune is but too melancholy an illustration. Acting from an impulse of irritation, I certainly was disrespectful to the Boston public; calm deliberation convinces me that I was wrong. The first step toward the Throne of Mercy is confession—the hope we are taught, forgiveness. Man must not expect more than those attributes which we offer to God.

But Boston was not in a placable mood. It was watching his approach like a great crouching cat eyeing a reckless mouse, with bristled fur and twitching tail, uncertain yet whether to strike the intruder down or disdainfully let it pass. The temper of the press was summed up in a *Courier* editorial of November 19:

For his ungentlemanly deportment he says he means to apologize. Let us then hear his apology. If it be satisfactory, let him play; if not, insist upon another. For his vices and crimes committed in Europe, it does not belong to us to inflict any other punishment than neglect. He sets up no claim to innocence, to purity of moral character. He asks not to be admitted to our dwellings; he solicits no social intercourse. To such privileges he is no doubt conscious that he has forfeited all claim. But he asks an asylum. No one can sincerely respect him; no one can love him. But every one can pity while he condemns, and no one can carry his resentment so far as to drive from the face of the earth the wretched fallen creature on whom the Almighty seems to have set the seal of his displeasure.

[2] The anecdote above is told by W. R. Alger in his *Life of Edwin Forrest.* Philadelphia, 1877.

The least that Boston expected from Kean was abject abasement. Had he beaten his breast, knocked his forehead on the ground, and cried his *mea culpa* in the proper accent of grief, I think it might have let him play. But the apology was not at all the right thing; the obnoxious tone of protest in it rang out louder than the confession of fault. "So far from being an apology," cried the *Courier* angrily, "it is an additional insult . . . 'Acting from the impulse of irritation,' he says, he 'certainly was disrespectful to the Boston public.' *Disrespectful,* indeed. Does he acknowledge so much? Was he not insolent, impertinent, arrogant, ungrateful?" The cat's eyes flashed. It was no longer in doubt as to what needed to be done.

Richard III was posted for performance at the Boston theatre for Wednesday, December 21. For several days beforehand, the coming riot had been foreshadowed at the box office, where men clawed each other, hats were lost and clothing torn. The temper of the audience that night was ugly.[3] In the street outside a large crowd was gathered. Inside was pandemonium. Manager Finn came out before the curtain to say that Kean would apologize, but could not make himself heard. Kean then appeared in street clothes, pale and dejected, to be received with cries of "Off! Off!" and a shower of nuts, pieces of cake, and other harmless but insulting missiles. Then Kilner, in the dress of King Henry, tried to say that an apology would be made, but was sent off. Various gentlemen in the boxes now addressed the house, with like success. Kean came back, was roared down, retired to the green room, and wept like a child.

A placard was next borne upon the stage, asking if the play should go on without Kean. The answer being equivocal, the attempt was made and the first act performed in dumb show. Then Finn, who had taken the part of Richard, announced that Kean had left the theatre. At that the mob, balked of its vengeance, fell upon the playhouse. The mob in the street outside, hearing the yells and the crash of furniture, stormed the doors, the pit fled across the stage, and the upper boxes took to the windows. A gallant band of gentlemen defended the stage and scenery, but the auditorium was lost to the

[3] I have drawn upon the excellent account in Clapp's *Record of the Boston Stage.*

rioters. Mr. Justice Whitman twice read the riot act, but no one listened.

Kean, meanwhile, in actual fear of his life, had escaped into the house of a Mrs. Powell which adjoined the theatre. Where he went from there is not certainly known; one account says that he slept at the Lamb Tavern, another that he was driven to Brighton and caught the stage for Worcester: at any rate he fled from Boston to the safe haven of New York.

On the day following the riot an inquisitive correspondent of the *Courier* viewed the damaged theatre.

> The doors of the lower tier of boxes on the *south side only,* are torn off and broken; most of the seats in the front portion of the *third row* are taken up, and thrown into the pit. A few of the seats in the pit are a little shattered at the edges. The stoves are overturned, and part of the funnels have fallen with them. The lamps with which the Theatre was lighted are missing . . . The iron railing of the lower boxes and third row, is torn off. The lower windows on the *south* side are broken. This is all of the perceptible injury done to the interior.

He considered it "trifling." Possibly it was, for Boston.

Safely arrived in New York Kean played Lear on January 4, 1826, for Mrs. Hilson's benefit. A crowded house did what it could to show him that he was now among friends. The words,

> I am a man
> More sinned against than sinning,

evoked a great burst of applause, partly from their general application but more no doubt from their commentary on the recent event down east.

Kean was under contract with manager Wood to open in Philadelphia on January 11, but he shrank not unnaturally from another trial by ordeal, and asked to be released. The Philadelphia papers therefore carried a brief notice that his engagement was to be deferred for the present, to which the *National Gazette* added the bald explanation that "Mr. Kean declines appearing in this city for the present." Probably Wood himself was uneasy over the turn affairs might take and was not too unwilling to save his theatre from any "trifling" damage. But the public wanted Kean, and made its want known in the usual manner, on the night of June 9, while Cooper was playing William Tell, by calling loudly for an explanation. Feeling that the interest was friendly rather than hostile, and perceiving also that since the Boston affair Kean was rising in public sympathy, Wood ventured to reopen and to conclude the matter of an engagement.

So on January 18 Kean girded on the sword of Richard for another doubtful encounter. One must admire the man's courage, and one cannot but wonder that when he was saluted by another uproar he had heart enough to go on. With Boston so fresh in his memory I think his vitals must have frozen; nevertheless, he moved forward and made a vain attempt to speak. Then all the friendly portions of the house rose and cheered him. That put some heart in him; he went on, and as the play progressed the opposition gradually died away—it was after all not much of an opposition, nothing like Boston, or even New York, and consisted only in hissing.

The rest of the engagement went off prosperously and undisturbed. I quote manager Wood's figures:

January 18 (Wednesday)	*Richard III* ($1,165)
January 20	*Othello* ($941)
January 21	*Merchant of Venice* ($786)
January 23	*Lear* ($751)
January 25	*A New Way to Pay Old Debts* ($720)
January 26	*Othello* ($501)
January 27	*Iron Chest* ($642)
January 28	*Town and Country* ($570)
January 30	*Macbeth* ($650)
January 31	*Brutus* ($636)
February 1	*Richard III* (benefit, $1,254)
February 2	*Hamlet* ("by particular desire," $574)

After Philadelphia he returned to New York for a second run. It was a brilliant season for the Park Theatre, because in addition to Kean it was housing the first Italian opera to visit the United States. This was the famous Garcia troupe, a very family affair in which Signor Garcia, his wife, son, and daughter controlled the principal parts. It is enough to remind the reader that Signorina Maria Felicita Garcia was none other than that glorious singer known better as Mme. Malibran. She had made her début in New York on November 29, just before Kean ended his first run, and had become the rage. With her and her family of song birds Kean alternated in February. What an opportunity, to hear him on Monday and the Signorina on Tuesday, or to match the Otello of Garcia with the Othello of Kean! Lucky New York!

He opened on Monday, February 6, in *Richard III* to an overflowing house which contained many ladies, a sure sign not only that his sins had been forgiven but that all danger of violence was over. He continued:

February 8	*Othello*
February 9	*A New Way to Pay Old Debts*
February 10	*Hamlet*
February 13	*Lear*
February 14-19	No performance because of illness
February 20	*Richard III*
February 23	*Bertram*
February 24	*Barbarossa* and *Paul and Virginia* (benefit)

The benefit was hugely successful, according to the *Evening Post*; the audience was fashionable and the *clear* receipts were estimated at $1,800.

On February 25 the *Evening Post* welcomed back an old correspondent on theatrical matters whose voice had been heard during the first Kean appearances in 1820—"Crito." Then he had been most difficult to please; now he was remarkably sweetened. He was in a reflective mood. All this season, he said, the theatre had been poorly attended—Conway, Cooper, and Hamblin had played to empty benches—only Kean and the Garcias had drawn uniformly good houses—why was it? Certainly it was not due to enmity for Conway or the others.

> The secret of [Kean's] success here may, I think, be fairly ascribed to two great and powerful causes; his transcendant merits as an actor, and that generous reaction which spontaneously arises in our minds when we think of the bad—even brutal treatment he had experienced. He comes before us as an ill used and persecuted man, and our sympathies are even involuntarily enlisted in his favor. So far Mr. Kean is lastingly indebted to the Bostonians.

From New York Kean sailed, appropriately enough on the ship "Othello," for Charleston, South Carolina, where he arrived March 12. With him went Mrs. Battersby and Lee of the Park Theatre company.

In some newspaper, at some time long after these events,[4] was printed a most interesting reminiscence of the "Kean riots in Charleston," by one John Carboy. We are there told, with much circumstantial plausibility, that when Joe Cowell, the manager, went on board to welcome his guest he found him wretched from anxiety. "For God's sake," he said in broken tones, "I entreat you not to let me play if you think the audience will not receive me. I have not strength of mind and body . . . to undergo a continuance of the suffering and persecution I have already endured." The house for *Richard III* (March 13) was packed with men, who received the play with stony silence. "A grand performance," said Cowell. "And wasted upon a mob of dolts," answered Kean. "Hear them moving out—how they would like to fall upon me like a pack of famished wolves!" At *Othello*, the next performance, the house was again sold out, but this time the storm broke. Oranges were thrown; Cowell gathered them up, bowed, retired, applause broke out; then Kean led Desdemona forth by the hand, the house rose at him, cheering madly. From then on he was made much of. This story is also found in Molloy's *Life of Edmund Kean*, evidently from the same source.

Well, it is too bad to discredit so picturesque a legend, but unless the Charleston papers were all in a conspiracy one must accuse John Carboy of inditing a pure romance. It seems to be another case of Guernsey. Actually Kean's reception at Charleston was most favorable—there was no silence and there were no oranges. "Mr. Kean's reception last night," said the *Southern Patriot* of March 14, "was in the highest degree flattering—an overflowing house testified by repeated plaudits its sense of his great merits in the character he personated." So also said the *City Gazette and Commercial Daily Advertiser*:

The reception of Mr. Kean last evening, must have been as flattering to his feelings, as it was creditable to the decorum and liberality of the

[4] I regret that I cannot tell when or where, because my information is derived from one of those clippings which collectors never date.

Charleston Audience. The Theatre was filled to overflowing; and altho' not graced by the presence of ladies generally, (who were doubtless deterred from going by the fear of a disturbance,) it was alike respectable from the character and standing of those who attended..

As to the *Othello* performance, the *City Gazette* gives no hint of disturbance: "A brilliant, fashionable and numerous audience crowded the Theatre last evening, and attested, more by their attentive silence, than by noisy plaudits, the powerful representation by Mr. Kean of the character he had assumed." All through his Charleston engagement Kean received warm and discriminating praise from the press; as early as March 17 "Roscius," in the *Southern Patriot*, was calling him "a great and original genius."

He played as follows:

March 13 (Monday)	*Richard III*
April 3	*Merchant of Venice*
April 5	*Brutus*
April 6	*Iron Chest* (Lee's benefit)
April 7	*Othello*
April 10	*Richard III* (benefit)
April 24	*Bertram* (benefit of Mr. and Mrs. Cowell)

At his benefit he had said: "I regret I cannot gratify that portion of my patrons who wish a renewal of my engagement. My health is much impaired, and a cessation from my professional duties is absolutely necessary for its resuscitation." From then until the twenty-fourth he had rested as a guest on an estate near Charleston, and I suspect that after playing for the Cowells he lingered on a short while.

During this visit reports appeared in the New York papers that Kean meant to settle permanently in the United States and was negotiating for a house in New York. That is altogether likely. Certainly he counted on staying through the next season, and was corresponding with Caldwell for a spring engagement at New Orleans.

During May he was again playing in New York, with Mrs. Barnes and Lee, sharing the Park Theatre as before with the Garcias.

May 11 (Thursday)	*Richard III*
May 12	*Othello*
May 15	*Lear*

May 18	*Bertram*
May 19	*A New Way to Pay Old Debts*
May 22	*Merchant of Venice*
May 25	*Hamlet*
May 26	*Henry VIII* and *Sylvester Daggerwood* (benefit)
May 29	*Iron Chest* (three day renewal)
June 1	*Stranger*
June 2	*Richard III*

He received no attention from the press, and I do not know how well he was patronized.

On June 7 he opened as Richard what was meant to be eight nights in Baltimore. But here, quite unexpectedly, history repeated itself in the Boston manner. Again the play broke up in riot, again Kean fled in terror through an adjoining house. There is some doubt that the hostilities were really as dangerous as they sounded. The Baltimore *Patriot* thought that if it had not been for the obstreperous zeal of friends the house would have been quieted by the second act, but the noise made by ejecting the rioters brought a large crowd outside the theatre, which flung stones against the windows. No doubt the scene was alarming enough, what with the shouts inside, the commotion in the street, the crash of windows and the screams of women. Manager Wood was not present, having been called back to Philadelphia. When he returned next day a council of war was held; some were for going on, but as threats of further violence had been made and Kean's nerves were in pieces, Wood thought it more prudent to cancel the remainder of the engagement. So he returned to Philadelphia with Kean, who had volunteered to play there in remuneration for the losses in Baltimore.

June 12 (Monday)	*Richard III*
June 14	*Othello*
June 15	*Merchant of Venice*
June 16	*A New Way to Pay Old Debts*
June 17	*Stranger*
June 19	*Lear*
June 20	*Iron Chest*
June 21	*Brutus*

June 22	*Mountaineers*
June 23	*Bertram*
June 24	*Stranger*
June 26	*Henry VIII* and *Sylvester Daggerwood* (benefit)

Neither Wood nor Kean profited much by this second Philadelphia season, for the houses averaged under $300. The newspapers gave him little attention, not out of hostility but because he had ceased to be "news." On June 23, however, the *Aurora and Franklin Gazette* paid its compliments both to him and to the two intransigeant cities:

This highly gifted tragedian has effected a revolution in the dramatic taste of our city, for even those who were the most severely critical upon his style of acting, now acknowledge his numberless beauties, and freely award to transcendent talent its just meed of praise . . . The Baltimoreans and Bostonians are railing against each other for the reception they bestowed upon Mr. Kean. If a leather medal were to be awarded upon this occasion by a society for the suppression of vice and immorality, it would be a knotty point for our friend of the Commercial Advertiser to decide, which of the *par nobile urbes* should receive it.

The movements of Kean after his Philadelphia engagement and before his appearance in Canada have been lost to view. What he meant to do is told in a letter of June 24 to Caldwell, the New Orleans manager:

The next month I devote to my body's recreation, and to my mind's improvement, by visiting the Falls of Niagara, and savages of Buffalo, for the purpose of analyzing character and distinguishing between the aboriginal savage and the exotics of Boston and Baltimore. I then professionally visit Montreal, Quebec and Halifax, return to my engagement at New York in November, Philadelphia in December, and shall sail for the capital of the south the end of January.

It is not likely that he visited the falls of Niagara, or he would certainly have spoken of it afterwards; but he did go up by way of Albany and Rochester, for the Montreal *Herald,* July 29, tells of his performing gratis at the latter town for the manager of the theatre there, who was, as so often happened, in distress.

He opened an engagement of five nights at Montreal on Monday, July 31, at the Theatre Royal, playing Richard to the Richmond of

Lee (perhaps the same Lee who went to Charleston with him), the Lord Mayor of Placide, the Tressel of F. Brown, and the Anne of Miss Riddle. His coming aroused considerable excitement. People drove in from the countryside; some minor injuries were sustained at the opening of the box office and still more at the opening of the pit; the large audience was in a mood of elated expectancy—it insisted that the orchestra play "Rule, Britannia," and felt for some reason extremely patriotic. When the great actor at last appeared he was received with a "thundering acclamation" that lasted several minutes. The *Gazette de Quebec*, viewing with approval this loyal demonstration, hoped that it "will be a salutary lesson to our fellow subjects on the other side of the Atlantic, how they ought to treat the first actor of the age, and how they ought to receive him when he again presents himself before them. It is to the honour of Canada that it has been the *first* of British subjects to redeem the character of Englishmen in everything that regards the first of her tragedians." At the end of the performance he was too exhausted to appear, and sent his apologies by the manager.

On August 2 he played Shylock, on the third, Othello, on the fifth, Sir Edward Mortimer, on the seventh, Overreach, and on the ninth, for his benefit, Lear, to houses which on all occasions were "nearly full." The Montreal *Herald* commented at length on most of these performances, liking him enormously as Othello, extolling him with reservations as Richard, but not caring much for the famous Overreach. It hastened to explain, in the last case, that its objections lay not so much against the actor as against the play, whose "inconsistencies and absurdities must have hung as heavy on Mr. Kean, while acting, as did the injured widows on the sword arm of the remorse-struck Sir Giles. This may account for some instances of forced passion, which were evident in his acting."

The engagement was then considerably extended by these performances:

August 12	*Richard III*
August 14	*Macbeth* (to the Lady Macbeth of Mrs. Gilfert, newly engaged)
August 16	*Brutus*

August 17	*Hamlet*
August 21	*Henry VIII* and *Sylvester Daggerwood*
August 23	*The Stranger* (Lee's benefit)
August 24	*Bertram* (Miss Riddle's benefit)
August 28	*Alexander* (Mrs. Brown's benefit)

So amid general applause and a shower of benefits he filled out the month. The *Herald* had nothing to say about most of these performances, but it wrote at length on *Brutus* with the enthusiasm of discovery, dismissed *Alexander the Great* as unworthy, and developed its theory of *Hamlet* at such length that it had time only to remark of Kean that he was "most admirable."

On Tuesday, August 22, he was banqueted at the Masonic Hall Hotel. He made a speech, of course, even more flourishing than was his custom, the tenor of which was that Canada had poured the water of life into a dying man—

> a waif upon the world's wide common, I expected nothing more than to drag out the remaining portion of my existence in those hard exertions of my public duties; how then shall I thank those beings who have rekindled the social spark, almost extinct, and have lighted up my heart again to friendship and esteem? It is as dew drops to the parched—as sunbeams through the prison gate—the key unlocking the barriers to society —the symbol that I have not *wholly* lost the affections of my countrymen . . . More than on my own account, I hail this day hallowed—fast as the winds can bear these tidings to the British shores, it will enliven those who in spite of my inconsistencies and errors, watch with anxious eye my progress, and whose grateful hearts will beat like mine at the receipt of that friendship which restores me again to the rank of a gentleman!

On Monday, September 4, he revealed his Richard to Quebec. Some doubt existed as to whether the towboat "Hercules," by which he was voyaging, would arrive in time, but at six he was in the city, at seven the house was full, and after a delay of two hours due to necessary alterations in the scenery, the play began at nine o'clock. It was enthusiastically applauded. By good fortune Mr. and Mrs. Barnes, of the Park Theatre, New York, had been playing in Quebec during August. Kean was thus able to have the support of that excellent actress, most luckily for Quebec, whose resident company was execrable.

On September 5 he played Shylock, and on the eighth Othello. After the last performance he was taken ill; on Sunday, September 10, he suffered "a most violent inflammatory attack," and he remained in bed all week. Mrs. Barnes also fell ill, so that it seemed doubtful if she would be able to play again. Nevertheless, she ventured out on Monday, September 18, for *A New Way to Pay Old Debts,* although it was evident that she ought to have stayed in bed. At *The Stranger* on Tuesday she was better. The performances then ran:

September 22 (Friday)	*Lear* (Kean's benefit)
September 23	*Iron Chest*
September 25	*Richard III*
September 27	*Macbeth*
September 28	*Mountaineers*

On Wednesday, October 4, he said farewell. The play, "by special request," was to be *Hamlet.*

> The performance however [said the *Gazette* the next day] proceeded no farther than the commencement of the second act, when Mr. Kean finding it impossible longer to contend with the gross errors and inattention of some of the performers, who marred his acting in the finest passages, and being also apprized that the absence of others of the Company would stop the progress of the piece in a future scene, came forward and, after briefly stating these circumstances, claimed the indulgence of the public for himself and Mrs. Barnes, and complained of the neglect of the person entrusted with the stage management for not having made proper arrangements for the business of the evening.

Spiller, the acting stage manager, then came forward to explain that he had not the power of compelling attendance at rehearsals, which was doubtless true but did not help matters. Kean then proposed that, inasmuch as it was impossible to go on with *Hamlet,* he and Mrs. Barnes go through some scenes from *Venice Preserved.* This they did exquisitely, then retired amid great applause. Some of the audience now went home, but others remained and as the ballet began showed their displeasure by tearing up the benches. It is a pleasure to record one riot of which Kean was not the victim.

This disgraceful affair has the aspect of a mutiny, but what caused it I cannot say. According to the *Gazette* the company was undisciplined, and the actor who caused most trouble was aggrieved because he had been "cut up in the newspapers." But the disaffection seems to have been general.

On Friday, October 6, a complimentary dinner to Kean was given at Paine's Hotel and on Saturday he returned to Montreal.

One experience during his Quebec visit made a profound impression on him. It seems that four Huron chiefs were introduced to him, each of whom he presented with a medal, dated October 5, in return for which courtesy they adopted him into their tribe. His account of it a year or so later to Grattan is evidently colored too much by imagination:

> He told me he had been *mad* at Quebec for several days, and related an incident which proved it, namely, his having mounted a fiery horse in the full costume of the Huron tribe of Indians, of which he had been elected a chief; and, after joining them in their village or camp, haranguing them, parading them, and no doubt amusing them much, being carried back by some pursuing friends to the place whence he came, and treated for a considerable time as a lunatic.

This is pure fiction. His adoption must have taken place between Wednesday, when he played Hamlet, and Saturday, when he left for Montreal. He was perfectly sane at this time and during his Quebec visit. The brief notice in the *Gazette*, October 12, states clearly that the adoption took place *after* the giving of the medals (which evidently was done on October 5) in the presence of Captain Sir William Wiseman of H.M.S. "Jupiter," Commissioner General Turquand, and several naval officers and friends. Had anything eccentric happened it would surely have been noticed.

Nevertheless, Kean was enormously, childishly proud of the honor. Apparently he had the average European's romantic notions about the Noble Red Man, soured as he was on all the works of civilization, and he was wondrously exalted at being taken into their companionship, at being spiritually baptized in the waters of a primitive and uncorrupted savagery. He loved the name they had given him, Alanienouidet, which rippled like some wild Canadian stream. He never tired of dressing in the costume of a Huron chief, paint, war whoop, and all: he used to receive his friends in it, and had his picture made.

Dr. Francis tells of one such masquerade. He had been summoned to Kean's hotel in New York to meet an Indian chief, and went obedient, but mystified.

> I entered, aided by the feeble light of the room; but at the remote end I perceived something like a forest of evergreens, lighted up by many rays from floor-lamps, and surrounding a stage or throne; and seated in great state was the chief. I advanced, and a more terrific warrior I never surveyed. Red Jacket or Black Hawk was an unadorned, simple personage in comparison. Full dressed, with skins tagged loosely about his person, a broad collar of bear-skin over his shoulders, his leggings, with many stripes, garnished with porcupine quills; his moccasons decorated with beads; his head decked with the war-eagle's plumes, behind which flowed massive black locks of dishevelled horse-hair; golden-colored rings pendant from his nose and ears; streaks of yellow paint over his face, massive red daubings about the eyes, with various hues in streaks across the forehead, not very artistically drawn. A broad belt surrounded his waist, with tomahawk; his arms, with shining bracelets, stretched out with bow and arrow, as if ready for a mark. He descended his throne and rapidly approached me. His eye was meteoric and fearful, like the furnace of a cyclops. He vociferously exclaimed, Alantenaida! . . . He was wrought up to the highest pitch of enthusiasm at the Indian honor he had received, and declared that even Old Drury had never conferred so proud a distinction on him as he had received from the Hurons.

He also said that he was uncertain what to do—whether to seek happiness by taking up his abode with the tribe, or to win renown in London by enacting the Noble Savage.

He did neither of course, although on some few occasions he addressed his English public in full Indian regalia. It is just as well that Forrest should have had the fame of creating Metamora.

Grattan also, calling one day at the Hummums Hotel, Covent Garden, found Alanienouidet, propped up in bed, wrapped in a buffalo skin, decked in horsehair and feathers, a scalping knife in his belt, a tomahawk in one hand, a glass of grog in the other, sitting for his portrait.

We had left Kean setting out for Montreal on October 7. Mrs. Barnes went with him. This time he was engaged not by the Theatre Royal but by Blanchard of the Royal Amphitheatre, although after

KEAN AS ALANIENOUIDET

the first performance the company was moved to the Theatre Royal.

October 19 (Thursday)	*Othello*
October 21	*Douglas*
October 25	*Macbeth*
October 30	*Romeo and Juliet*

This second course was run much less gloriously than the first. A thin house greeted *Othello*, from the fact that the performance was uncertain until shortly before it began; it appears that he had been announced for Monday the sixteenth and for some reason had been delayed. The *Herald* found that he played "in his usual matchless manner" but was hoarser than when he had been there before; it praised Mrs. Barnes also and Messrs. Brown and Spiller as Iago and Cassio, but the rest of the cast was wretched—"the representative of Roderigo could not speak two lines to an end." Incidents both pleasant and unpleasant marked a decline in the morale of the audience. Before the play began a tipsy gentleman in the pit caused vast amusement by auctioning off the curtain and other appurtenances of the theatre. During the performance a country visitor made a scandal by shouting "Mrs. Cox!" but was promptly suppressed by his neighbors. "We heard it alleged," commented the *Herald*, "that he had been set on to this conduct by some people in a noted American tavern in this city, and that several bottles of wine were to be the reward of his manly exploit." This was the last faint echo of Cox.

The last word from Montreal concerns the *Macbeth*, which turned into an ignoble fiasco.

On Wednesday last [said the *Herald*], the Tragedy of Macbeth was murdered at our Theatre, and we are sorry to say that Mr. Kean was one of the perpetrators of the "horrible deed." Never did we see a play worse performed. The representative of the King resembled nothing connected with authority, save that useful personage, a sheriff officer, and the greater part of the Thanes seemed worthy of their monarch . . . Never was Royalty so caricatured. Kean himself, accustomed as he must be to command his countenance, laughed in the sovereign's face. This was bad enough, but while he was endeavouring to depict the remorse felt by Macbeth, after the murder of Duncan, the propensity to laugh got the better of his self command. While he was striving to gain composure, a dog made its appearance from the room where the murdered Duncan was supposed to be lying, and looked up in Mr. Kean's face, commenced howling and barking, and was followed by several others in various parts of the house. This addition to the *dramatis personæ*, completely got the better of the Tragedian, and the scene being nearly over, he left the stage laughing. Through the whole piece he was inferior. Mrs. Barnes seemed to be the only one who took an interest in the piece.

It is really too bad to find the expedition to the Canadas ending thus ignominiously. We may hope that *Romeo and Juliet* fared better.

During the summer affairs at Drury Lane had taken a turn which persuaded Kean to change all his plans. In July of 1825, while Kean was still ramping through the English provinces, Elliston had been seized with a paralytic stroke, the product of years of dissipation, overwork, and mental eccentricity, which in a moment reduced the Great Lessee to a useless bundle of complaining nerves. Yet, though he was exiled to the seaside under a doctor's care, with hands so paralyzed that he could not even write his name, the plucky little captain of industry refused to give in, but made over the management of Drury to his son and set about reorganizing his bodily forces, which in time he partly succeeded in doing, but only to meet fresh troubles. For by now his personal affairs had got into a sad way, he had spent his fortune on the theatre, he was deeply in debt, his creditors pressed him, so that scarcely was he out of bed than he was forced to take refuge in the rules of the King's Bench prison. After some weeks of comfortable durance, in the course of which he entertained half of London at his tea parties and cracked innumerable puns on his misfortunes, he was enabled by the aid of friends to compound his debts and return to duty, but he was only half the man he had been. His will was indomitable, but his body was broken; he began to act again, and fainted during a performance. Meanwhile the theatre, under the mismanagement of his lieutenants, was going badly, he was £5,500 in default in rent, and the committee, alarmed, decided not unreasonably that he was in no fit state to carry on the business. So in May of 1826 they held a meeting at which they voted, in cruel haste and in spite of frantic efforts from poor Elliston, to call for his resignation if the arrears were not paid within three days, knowing very well that they demanded the impossible. So, infirm and beggared, this extraordinary man retired from the theatre which had crowned his ambitions, went into bankruptcy, moped for a few months, saw that the Surrey Theatre was for rent, scraped together a bit of capital, leased it, and within two years had started out again, boiling with enthusiasm and plans, to rebuild his fortunes. Absurd, admirable man! Among the kings of trapdoors and tinsel, Elliston ought surely to rank as Emperor.

The vacant lease of Drury Lane was taken up by no other person than Stephen Price of New York, thus working out a destiny which might seem designed for the special purpose of restoring Edmund Kean from his voluntary exile. Price had a strong conviction that Kean was necessary to his success, and Kean liked Price, who had done much for him; the removal of Price to London put a new aspect on affairs in both countries: therefore it was not hard to persuade Kean that the path of wisdom lay in the direction of London. He told Grattan a story of his being lured home by false promises of the managership of Drury Lane, of his indignation at the deceit, and of being conciliated with a fee of one hundred guineas a night, and indeed there are passages in his Canadian speeches which indicate that he had some such belief.

He had, of course, to break with Caldwell. The New Orleans manager took it very badly; he had lost $6,000 on his last season and counted, I suppose, on the English star to make it up. But there was nothing he could do except protest indignantly through the newspapers—and publish the letters he had received from Kean.

On returning to New York, Kean found an evil smell of Macready in the air. Opening on October 2 as Virginius to a crowded house and tumultuous approval, the rival tragedian had played out a most successful engagement and was now, as Kean prepared for his last New York season, throwing Boston into ecstasies. That impenitent city was again auctioning off boxes. With Macready the lion of the hour, himself an old story, Kean no doubt felt still more clearly that the path of wisdom led in the direction of London.

On Monday, November 13, he played Richard at the Park Theatre, with Mrs. Barnes. But he was not himself, he was evidently feeble, many people could not hear him, his best scenes lacked their customary brilliance. On Wednesday he played Othello, on Friday, Shylock, on Monday, November 20, Lear. He was to repeat Richard on Wednesday, but suffered a spasmodic attack soon after reaching the theatre and was unable to play again until the following Monday.

From then on he played:

November 27 (Monday)	*Richard III*
November 29	*Hamlet*
December 1	*Bertram*
December 4	*De Montfort* and *The Waterman*
December 5 (Tuesday)	*Richard III*

On Friday, December 8, 1826, he sailed for England.

CHAPTER XIII

DISINTEGRATION

On January 8, 1827, Kean once more faced a London audience, as Shylock; but now it was an audience that had forgotten every grievance in its joy at having him back again. "A rush so fearful, an audience so packed, a reconciliation so complete, acting so faultless and a dramatic enjoyment so exquisite, I have never experienced," wrote Dr. Doran,[1] ". . . and I have heard no shout since as that which greeted him." It must have been good to come home to such a welcome, to hear those hearty English huzzas roll through the expanse of Drury Lane, the quick hush that followed as he opened his lips on the "Three thousand ducats," to look out again at those tiers of intent, adoring faces, to know that once more as of old he was king of kings in his own tragic world. Outside was the fog, the drizzle, the mud, the homely smell of the only city on earth. Screwing himself up to the top notch of his powers, he became for two hours the great master he had once been and had ceased to be; Shylock was never more alive, more lambent, more authoritative. No one who looked on could guess that the tragic Jew of compelling eyes and eloquent hands was projected by sheer will, and that his beard and gaberdine hid a mass of protesting bodily ailments.

All next day, says Doran, he lay in bed at the Hummums Hotel, Covent Garden, where he had taken residence, playing moodily with the trappings of Alanienouidet and dosing himself with cognac. He was very ill, ill in mind as well as in body. His conquest of the United States, his reconciliation with his own people, conferred only a restless, flickering pleasure, because he was in the fullest sense of the phrase, out of sorts. No amount of panegyric or huzzaing could disguise the fact that his life was ruined, his integrity and peace of mind gone forever. He would always be spotted by the Cox scandal; men might be friendly with him, but no decent matron would have him at her table again, not that he had ever much cared for her table, but there is a difference between staying away and being shut out. He

[1] *Their Majesties' Servants.* London, 1888. III, 406.

had no home—his wife lived in hostile retirement in Westminster and his son at Eton was against him, too. He was alone, cut adrift, with his thoughts for company, and those thoughts bore constantly on the harassments of the last two years. Every savage invective of the *Times*, every sneer, every knowing look, every snub, every yell during those countless hours when he had been flogged in the public theatre by public scorn, had left its wound. As an artist he had beaten down his enemies, but as a man, in all the capacities of friend, lover, husband, father which give a man self-respect, they had stripped him bare. His self-respect was gone to the last shred, and with it whatever authority he had over himself. From now on he drifted on the current of his animal desires, sodden with drink, consorting with harlots, preyed on by sharpers, seeking nothing from life but a deadening of the unending pain in mind and body.

Grattan, who saw him immediately after his return to England, said that he "presented a mixture of subdued fierceness, unsatisfied triumph, and suppressed dissipation." His face was blotched and bloated, his eyes bloodshot. He drank unceasingly.

Ordinarily he drank strong spirits. Once when Grattan called (finding him propped up in bed in the costume of Alanienouidet) he had only a negus of white wine, but this was by the order of Dr. Carpue, who had prescribed "the strictest regimen." By nursing himself for two days together, he was able to play three times a week. As Grattan left he encountered two veiled and equivocal ladies, who, Kean said, were a clergyman's daughters, in love with him. The scene is characteristic of so many like it—the dishevelled room, the odor of spirits, the unmade bed, the complaints of gout (or what he preferred to call gout) and a head aching from last night's debauch, and in a back room the flurry of some clergyman's daughter beating a hasty retreat from the visitor.

Through January and February he played at Drury Lane,[2] usually twice a week, but sometimes only once. He closed the first part of his engagement on February 27 as Sir Giles Overreach. He then went to Manchester for four nights beginning March 1, and afterwards

[2] As the Drury Lane receipt books are lacking after 1825 I am unable to determine his patronage in these later appearances.

crossed to Dublin, where he played from March 12 to April 2. At the close of his benefit performance there (*King Lear* on April 2), he recited "a farewell address, written expressly for the occasion by a gentleman of this city,[3] in the character and costume of Alanienouidet, Chief of the Huron Indians, which name and title were conferred upon him by a full assembly of the tribes at Quebec in 1826." On April 16 he opened an engagement in Edinburgh after an absence of five years, closing on April 25 with *The Iron Chest* and Alanienouidet.

At all these places his reception proved that his sins had been forgiven.

By May 7 he was back again at Drury Lane for another two months, playing his usual round of characters (which now consisted mainly of Richard, Shylock, Overreach, Brutus, Othello, Lear, Macbeth, and Hamlet), and preparing for a new play.

Immediately after Kean's triumphant reappearance at Drury Lane in January, Thomas Colley Grattan had carried to him a tragedy called *Ben Nazir*, which the actor had read with warm approval and selected from among half a dozen or more that had been submitted. He felt that a new rôle was expected of him, that the flood of renewed favor was auspicious for it, that it was the one thing needed to consolidate his position, to prove to the world that he was still the undefeated champion of the tragic ring. A tragedian cannot live long on conquered rôles, he must be always adding new conquests or he will be looked upon as a man whose best days are over. Therefore Kean seized eagerly on the part of Ben Nazir, studied it, kept it under his pillow, carried it away on his provincial travels, was sure it would serve him as well as Bertram had and play a hundred nights, ordered a portrait of himself in the part, named his newest wherry after it, and paid fifty guineas for a costume.

He arrived in London still full of enthusiasm and, he assured Grattan, letter perfect. He attended only two of the earlier rehearsals, it is true, but at both of them he exhibited so much energy that the author was filled with the most delighted expectations. From later

3 The author was one William Kertland, a perfumier; so says W. J. Lawrence, who writes on "Edmund Kean in Dublin" in the *Weekly Irish Times*, June 1, 1907.

rehearsals he excused himself on the rather curious plea that he did not wish to take any time away from the close study of his part; and every day he drove to Kensington Gardens or had himself rowed on the river, where he recited speeches all afternoon with impressive effect, but always from the book. He was a pattern of diligence; he was in bed every night by eleven, and always sober. On the morning of the performance he strutted about the drawing room of his lodgings,[4] in his magnificent clothes, as confident as ever, declaiming favorite passages—but still from the book! The author went to his private box on the night of May 21, 1827, feeling more than a few qualms of uneasiness. The house was crowded with an audience full of anticipation, who looked impatiently to the appearance of their hero and greeted him with loud cheers. Let the unhappy author of *Ben Nazir* tell us what then happened.

> The intention of the author, and the keeping of the character, required him to rush rapidly upon the stage, giving utterance to a burst of joyous soliloquy. What was my astonishment to see him, as the scene opened, standing on the centre of the stage, his arms crossed, and his whole attitude one of thoughtful solemnity! His dress was splendid; and thunders of applause greeted him from all parts of the house. To display the one and give time for the other, were the objects for which he stood fixed for several minutes, and sacrificed the sense of the situation. He spoke; but what a speech! The one I wrote consisted of eight or nine lines; *his* was of two or three sentences, but not six consecutive words of the text. His look, his manner, his tone, were to *me* quite appalling; to any other observer they must have been incomprehensible. He stood fixed, drawled out his incoherent words, and gave the notion of a man who had been half-hanged and then dragged through a horse-pond . . . I had all along felt that this scene would be the touchstone of the play. Kean went through it like a man in the last stage of exhaustion and decay. The act closed—a dead silence followed the fall of the curtain; and I felt, though I could not hear, the voiceless verdict of "damnation."

The rest of the play dragged through in the same ghastly way. Of the several hundred lines in his part Kean spoke, thought Grattan, scarce fifty, and but few of these correctly; he left out entirely the

[4] He had by now moved to Duke Street, Adelphi.

soliloquies at the conclusion, and during all the last act made almost no effort to speak a line of the text. As the curtain fell at the end Wallack, the stage manager, offered Kean's apologies for his failure to know his lines, pleading bodily illness and distress of mind, but they were none too well received. The audience was frankly disgusted. Going back stage now for the first time Grattan met Kean being led away to his dressing room; the actor hung his head, waved his hand, and muttered some expression of deep shame.

The blow was worse for Kean than for Grattan, although the latter probably did not think so at the time. Poetic tragedy was not his line, and certainly no harm was done either to him or to literature by the snuffing out of his first invention, however painful the experience may have been. But Kean was irretrievably exposed in all his weakness, as a man half dead who could never hope to live again, as a man condemned henceforth to be a mere reflection of himself. His mind had suddenly hardened; it could retain what it had acquired while it was alive, but it could add nothing more. The realization must have appalled him.

Nevertheless, he went on through the routine of his parts until June 28, the only incident worthy of note being that on June 7, for the first time in six years, he played Iago, to the Othello of Wallack. At the close of his London engagement he went on tour, playing Newcastle, July 2-7, and Leeds, July 9-12. According to the *Theatrical Observer* he toured elsewhere in the north, and then went (or was to go) to Bute for a rest. In September the *Observer* reported him to be at Cork; and he began a short engagement at Liverpool on October 1.

Though Charles Kean, still at Eton, had stood by his mother in the division of the family, his father had not lost his interest in the boy or in his future. He was now sixteen, he had nearly finished his preparatory schooling, and as there was apparently no thought of his going to a university it became necessary to cast about for some occupation. Early in 1827, soon after his return from America, Edmund received an obliging offer from Mr. J. Calcraft, member of Parliament and formerly of the Drury Lane committee, to find Charles a cadetship in the East India service. Kean was pleased; it seemed to be as good a thing as the boy was likely to meet; he indicated as much to Charles. But to Mary Kean, alone, disconsolate, and ill in her lodgings, it seemed far otherwise. Charles was the one thing left to her out of her ruined life, her only comfort, and her only reason for continuing to live. So in a panic of fear at the thought of losing him she implored him not to go, and he obediently promised. Among the various accounts of the ensuing quarrel between father and son, mainly imaginary, I suspect, we may select Procter's as probably derived from Mary Kean and therefore most nearly authentic. Charles, then, carried an ultimatum to his father, that he would accept the cadetship on condition that his mother's annuity be increased from £200 to £300. The ultimatum was angrily countered with another—Charles must either accept the cadetship or expect no more help from his father. But the boy, who had stuff in him, refused to yield, so the matter was left at this, that he might finish the present half year at Eton and then must shift for himself. As to how an immature boy, trained for no occupation and softly nourished, was to shift for himself, the father did not inquire. So Charles went back to school with a troublesome bee in his bonnet.

Not long afterwards, for reasons which nobody has stated,[5] Kean quarreled with Stephen Price and entered into contract with Charles Kemble, then manager at Covent Garden, to play there during the next season. Price, aggrieved and indignant, looked about for means of vengeance. No doubt the break between father and son was known to him; probably also he knew that Kean was energetically set against having a son of his follow a stage career. Therefore, if he could persuade Charles to Drury Lane, he would not only provide a sensation for the next season but stick a thorn into Edmund's side that would rankle mightily. Accordingly Wallack was dispatched to Eton, interviewed Charles with honeyed words, promising him £10 a week for the first year and £11 and £12 for the two succeeding if he prospered, and had no difficulty in winning the boy, who had already determined that the stage was the only occupation which he could possibly fill and who was dazzled by so grand an offer coming so opportunely to the relief of his necessity.

[5] But which may be guessed if it is true that Price had promised Kean the managership of Drury Lane.

When, therefore, the month of October, 1827, arrived it astonished London with the double spectacle of Edmund deserting to Covent Garden from the theatre with which his name had been linked for thirteen years, and of Charles making his bow on the stage which had been sanctified to his father's use. Price, with canny showmanship, had titillated the public curiosity by promises of a "great unknown" to replace Kean; when the identity of the great unknown was revealed it stirred the town to such a pitch that the *Theatrical Observer*, on the morning of Charles's appearance, was moved to remark, "We never recollect so much interest being excited in the theatrical world, as by the first appearance of Mr. Kean, Jun., this evening."

Charles came out October 1, 1827, as Young Norval, in Home's *Douglas*, the rôle among all serious plays best suited to his tender years. Norval is a lad of Charles's own age; lost in infancy and believed to be dead, he has been reared by a peasant as his son, and as a peasant boy, but clad in heroic thoughts, he chances to pass the castle of Lord Randolph, saves that nobleman from a murderous attack, is brought into the castle, meets his mother, now Randolph's wife, speaks the piece once lisped in drawing rooms by thousands of infant spouters—

My name is Norval: on the Grampian hills
My father feeds his flocks; a frugal swain . . .

and through the ensuing scenes of recognition, suspicion, treachery, and death behaves like a boy of spirit and a true son of Douglas. Such is the adolescent hero whom Charles, fresh from the Eton cricket fields, a raw cub hastily licked with a little coaching, essayed before the eyes of London's expert critics and of a house packed to the roof.

The house was friendly enough—it applauded every actor as he appeared, under the mistaken impression that he was Norval. When Charles finally came on in the second act he was visibly atremble and had to support himself with his sword, but he quickly recovered and launched into "My name is Norval," which he spoke as though he had a cold, or was pressing his finger against his nose. His resemblance to his father, especially in profile, was at once noticed; in figure he was well made, light, and graceful. But he revealed nothing that one might not see in any school theatricals, and his voice was childish. "With respect to his voice and style," reported the *Times*, "we can say nothing favourable. The former is weak, unmusical, and puerile; the latter better adapted to the conventicle than the stage. It is tedious, drawling, and monotonous, such as well-whipped boys occasionally at Christmas exhibit before their delighted parents." At rare moments a well-delivered line or a well-conceived piece of action flashed forth and drew applause, but they were few and they were all copied from his father; Charles, it was clear, had nothing of his own to give. The friendly audience showed its disappointment by the quick diminution of applause; yet at the end it called him out, and the poor lad quite unaware of the true verdict beamed as though he had really made the triumph he dreamed of.

The next day's reviews disillusioned him. They considered him at length, dissected his voice, his style, his by-play, laid all his immaturities cruelly bare, and judged him sternly or leniently according to their moods. The *Times* advised "the young gentleman" to take his cadetship in the East Indies, and opined that if he had been any other man's son he "would most assuredly have been driven from the boards with at least as much precipitancy as that with which the American manager has forced him on them." The *Examiner,* a shade more kindly, recognized "a clever youth, struggling manfully with a strong natural defect (the voice), quick at imitation, and that equally of defects and beauties . . . This may bespeak ability, but clearly not of the first order. We can therefore imagine this young gentleman becoming a respectable, but scarcely a great performer." The *Morning Post,* still more lenient, found that he had "evidently considerable capabilities for the stage," and hoped that time and a provincial education would perhaps lead him to eminence.

Miserably disappointed, Charles was for throwing up his contract then and there, but Price urged him to stay on at least a little longer. And so he did, repeating *Douglas* and trying the parts of Selim in *Barbarossa,* Frederick in *Lover's Vows,* and Lothaire in *Adelgitha,* to constantly thinning houses and growing indifference. Discouraged, heartsick, but still determined to make an actor of himself, he turned his face, as spring came on, to the great school of actors and chastener of spirits, the provinces. The boy had stuff in him, such as his father had. Without any of Edmund's genius, he had his self-confidence and his dogged persistence, and though he never made a great actor of himself he made a most highly respectable one. We may glance a score of years forward to see him prosperous, established, wedded to the delightful Ellen Tree, never failing, never doing anything in the least disgraceful, an upright, conscientious gentleman. But no one who saw the boy go out to his training field in the spring of 1828 would have guessed the outcome.

From Liverpool, where he was acting at the time of Charles's first flight, Kean watched with interest the doings of his boy. Hawkins prints a letter from an unnamed correspondent, giving the father a first-hand account of the son's behavior and enclosing the damning *Times* review. It is precise and merciless. "I have given you as near a report as is in my power," this informant concludes, "and I will add that, even with this well-mustered audience, he would have left the stage forever but for the name he bore. He will draw one or two more good houses, and then, I fear, sink into nothingness." There is no report on how Edmund took this news, whether with grim satisfaction or a twinge of disappointment.

The Covent Garden bills of October 4 announced that Mr. Kean was engaged for a limited number of nights, "having determined to leave the Stage at the conclusion of the present Season." From now on he was always leaving the stage at the conclusion of the present season, and I find more pathos than absurdity in these reiterated promises: he wanted to stop, but he could not, for he had nothing laid by to live on. He must work or starve. There is something both heroic and pitiable in the sad spectacle of these last five years of daily war between infirmity and will. One can see where Charles got the stuff of which he was made.

Edmund came out at Covent Garden on October 15 as Shylock to the Bassanio of Charles Kemble, the Antonio of Egerton, and the Portia of Miss Jarman. On the twenty-second he played Richard, on the twenty-fifth, Overreach, and from then on through November alternated these latter two rôles. The change of scene, the combination with a different company, the support of such excellent actors as Kemble and Miss Jarman, gave such a spur to public interest that Covent Garden was filled as Drury Lane had been in his best days.

From November 22, when he repeated Shylock, to December 17 he was ill, dangerously ill the newspapers said. Apparently he went to Brighton for treatment, for the Brighton *Gazette* (quoted by the *Theatrical Observer*) declared that his condition was alarming—he had two ulcers on his face and his nose was sunk considerably from erysipelas. Nevertheless, he was back on December 17, with Shylock; he played Overreach on the nineteenth, and on December 21 he acted Othello to the Iago of Young, the Cassio of Kemble, and the Desdemona of Miss Jarman—a superb cast that brought a great crush of people to the theatre. Dr. Doran, who was present,

> saw strong men clamber from the pit, over the boxes, to escape suffocation, and weak men, in a fainting condition, passed by friendly hands towards the air, in the same way. I remember Charles Kemble, in his lofty, bland way, trying to persuade a too-closely packed audience to fancy themselves comfortable, and to be silent, which they would not be till *he* appeared, who, on that, and some after nights, could subdue them to silence or stir them to ecstacy, at his will.

Doran then draws a picture, not circumscribed to this night, but as more than one eyewitness agrees, a common spectacle through these latter years, of Kean waiting back stage for his cue, "a helpless, speechless, fainting mass bent up in a chair," a glass of strong hot brandy-and-water in his trembling hand; when his time comes he looks about as in a dream, sighs, drags himself painfully to his feet, totters toward the stage, and by an extraordinary conscription of his forces, walks strongly on, plays his scene with a simulation of energetic brilliance, and collapses again.

He did not act again until January 7, 1828, when he played *Richard III*. On the tenth he played *The Iron Chest*, and on the fourteenth was to repeat Richard, but another "alarming illness" seized him, *Hamlet* with Kemble was substituted, and Kean did not reappear until February 14. From then until the Easter holidays he played regularly twice a week.

His state of mind, his health, and his interest in the Bute property are reflected in a letter of March 12 written to a Mr. Corkingdale of the Bute Arms, Rothesay.[6]

[6] Owned by J. S. Dodd of Brooklyn, N. Y.

Dear Corkingdale | The multiplicity of business I am at present engaged in prevented me from answering your letter on the instant. it was my hope to have visited the Isle of Bute at the termination of my engagement at the Theatre Covent Garden, which takes place March the 30*th* but I find it impracticable, My engagements are numerous & must be fulfilled, on my return from France, which will be about the end of June. I shall repair to the happy Isle, as fast [as] Horses, & steam boats can carry me, You will oblige me therefore by acting as my agent during the interval of absence, & direct Reed, to let me find the grounds on my return precisely as I have been accustomed to see them, I do not understand Gardening technicalities, but they always looked very beautiful & beautiful I wish them to remain. My health is very fast improving. & the public favour greatly increasing, & yet I do not know how it is, amidst the blaze of popularity that is the natural attendant upon the favourites of caprice, I cannot help envying, the poorest peasant that doffs his cap to the visitor of Rothsay—however if the world, & my profession prevents my living there, it remains with myself the power of dying there & even that, I look forward to with gratification—You will do me a favour, if you will enquire of the Housekeeper & Read whether or [not] I am in arrears; if so, he had enough to pay them, & I will send you the amount by return of Post. Direct for me, as usual Theatre Royal Covent Garden. Entre nous If I had known Mrs. Clarke[7] had been inclined to bring dirty children with her, I shou'd have invoked the shades of *Herod* before they had polluted my Temple Your very truly

E Kean.

To the rôles previously exhibited, Kean added Lear, March 10 and 17 (to the Edgar of Warde, the Edmund of Diddear, the Kent of Fawcett, and the Cordelia of Miss Jarman), and repeated Othello on March 18, 20, 22, 27. On March 29, for Fawcett's benefit, he took part in a mixed bill, playing the third act of *Richard II*. His engagement, which was to close at Easter, was renewed, and he gave eight performances from April 11 to May 1, five of them being of Othello. He then left for Paris to join the English company playing there.

This famous enterprise belongs more to the history of the French stage than of the English. We have no occasion here to repeat the familiar story of the determined battle waged through the second decade

[7] Possibly, even probably, the same Mrs. Clarke who befriended Kean in his childhood. If so, what a change in relationship this remark discloses!

of the century by the French romantics in favor of Shakespeare. The translation of the plays by Guizot in 1821, the publication of the first part of Stendhal's *Racine et Shakespeare* in 1822, *Un Voyage historique et littéraire en Angleterre et en Écosse* of Amédie Pichot in 1825, the letters of Eugène Delacroix from London praising the English stage in 1825, the founding in 1824 of the *Globe* newspaper with its systematic campaigning for better translations of Shakespeare and more public exhibitions, had bred a huge curiosity as to the great English master of tragedy and as to the English manner of presenting him, which was described as being impressive in ways unknown to France. Though all this, and the subsequent fertilization of the great and little romantics—Hugo, Dumas *père,* de Vigny, Mérimée, and others—falls outside the scope of our study, we may afford to pause for a quick review of the theatrical end of these remarkable activities, for an undertaking so fruitful of results to the drama not only of France but of Europe, and one in which Kean had a share, deserves more than casual treatment.[8]

In 1822, Merle, director of the Théâtre de la Porte-St.-Martin, had brought up from Brussels the mediocre English troupe which acted there under Penley, and for whose benefit, it may be recalled, Kean played at Boulogne in 1824. They failed disastrously. Merle, not discouraged, still cherished the idea of Shakespeare in Paris, and was planning to bring over a company from England in 1826 when he lost the direction of his theatre. The enterprise, as it fell from his hands, was seized by Émile Laurent. On December 15, 1826, he obtained permission from the ministry of the interior to establish an English company by subscription. Frederick H. Yates, a London manager, organized the company for him. Then came the difficulty of finding a theatre. Laurent applied to the Département des Beaux-arts for permission to use the Salle Favart, alternating with the Italian Opera established there, but was denied from fear that if his company proved to be successful it would injure the opera. Then he proposed to build a theatre, but was again refused permission. Finally he arranged to be accommodated at the Odéon for a rental of fr.1,400 a night.

[8] The following account is drawn from J. L. Borgerhoff, *Le Théâtre anglais à Paris sous la Restauration.* Paris, 1913.

The permanent company was made up of the following artists from various theatres:

Covent Garden: Abbot, Egerton, Grey, Mason, Spencer, Mrs. Bathurst.
Drury Lane: Burch, Mrs. Smithson, Harriet Constance Smithson.
Haymarket: Bennett, Brindal, Mrs. Brindal.
Theatre Royal, Dublin: Chippendale, Latham, Reynolds, Mrs. Vaughan.
Theatre Royal, Bath: Burnet, Dale, Mrs. Gashall, Mrs. Russell.

With the exception of Abbot, who was also manager, and Miss Smithson, it turned out to be a pretty poor assortment. Moreover, the productions were badly equipped. Merle complained, in a pamphlet, *Du marasme dramatique*, 1829, that Richard held his court in Othello's palace, Jane Shore died in Rome, and Shylock was tried in Juliet's bedchamber. Apparently the French were subjected to such performances as might be given in a minor provincial English town by some company of barnstormers, except for the two actors mentioned above and the visiting stars. These latter were chosen from the best that the London stage had to offer—Liston, Charles Kemble, Terry (director of the Adelphi), Wallack, Macready, Kean, Miss Foote, and Mrs. W. West.

The season opened September 6, 1827, at the Odéon with *The Rivals*.[9] The French cared little for English comedy, even when such a native darling as Miss Foote came late in September to play in *The School for Scandal* and *The Belle's Stratagem*—they found it much like their own but not so good. They cared only for tragedy, particularly Shakespeare. On September 11 Kemble impersonated Hamlet, on the fifteenth Romeo, in both of which he was eminent, and on the eighteenth, Othello, in which he was not. But he suffered badly from the kind of support given him, so that his success was but moderate. The troupe moved to the Salle Favart October 4, Laurent having conciliated the Département des Beaux-arts by taking over the direction of the Italian Opera and its financial risks. On October 8 Abbot and Miss Foote performed *Romeo and Juliet*, in which she scored better than she had done in comedy, although Paris generally preferred Miss Smithson. This latter actress, who had been well liked at home but had never caused much excitement, had an enormous

[9] So Borgerhoff. The London *Morning Post* (Sept. 11) gave *The School for Scandal* and *Fortune's Frolic* (with Liston).

success in Paris, comparable to that which Miss O'Neill had had in London and which Fanny Kemble was soon to have. The Parisians found in her Juliet, Desdemona, Jane Shore, and Belvidera all the piercing sweetness in sorrow, all the sublime simplicity of nature, which they had hoped to discover in English tragedy. She was beyond cavil authentic, beautiful, touching; they wept and adored.

The government permit expired December 10, but there was no difficulty in getting an extension. Early in February Miss Smithson played the closing scenes of *Jane Shore* at the Théâtre français in a benefit for Baptist *père*. The *Theatrical Observer* (February 5), which like several other English journals followed the invasion of Paris with great interest, quoted a French critic to the effect that "Miss Smithson's splendid acting in the closing scenes of the tragedy, produced its usual effect—tears, sobbings, faintings, and peals of applause, that sounded as if they would last forever." Her own benefit, on March 3, was an extraordinary occasion: Mlle. Mars came over from the Comédie with several others to play *Le Manteau,* the Italian Opera sang *The Barber of Seville,* and the English company performed *Romeo and Juliet.*

With spring came the two great leaders of tragedy whom Paris was most eager to see. Macready was first. The *Theatrical Observer* of April 7, printed a letter from a correspondent:

> Our press attacks Macready before his arrival—instead of appearing as *Virginius* or *Tell,* which he has made his own, he persists, it seems, in commencing with *Macbeth,* and our good natured Paris critics have already selected every line of censure which their London brethren have bestowed on his performance of the "ambitious Thane"—merely, they say, to give the public time to "*think* before they *pay*"—the fact is, they are angry at Macready's preceding Kean, about whom there is great anxiety; they are afraid he'll die before they see him; his name is in everybody's mouth as the "*only Shakesperian.*"

Macready did in fact prove disappointing at first sight as Macbeth, but on further acquaintance, and especially after he had revealed his Virginius, he quite swept Paris off its feet. Within a month of his opening he was being acclaimed as "simple, grand, impassioned," and, as ultimate proof of admiration, compared with Talma.

On May 12, 1828, Kean at last appeared as Richard.[10] The Parisians, well informed of his vast reputation at home, thronged the theatre in such numbers that the orchestra was cleared for more stalls. They were prepared for something as astonishing as it was unprecedented. But they were disappointed. They saw a tired, haggard, debilitated man struggling with a rôle that was evidently too much for him, gasping forth broken lines in an asthmatic voice, laboring at effects that failed because of sheer exhaustion. In the level passages, where the voice had not to be forced and he could make the most of what the *Journal des débats* called "his profound and skilful pantomime," he played with all his wonted effect, but he could not electrify; and because they wanted above all to be electrified the audience grew cold. They were interested, but they looked on him more as a curious transpontine phenomenon—so *this* is the "only Shakespearian," they thought, with a slight lift of the eyebrows. Many looked on with a sympathetic compassion, feeling with the critic of the *Réunion* that they were seeing a ghost, though "a ghost which still had grandeur, of which one could imagine what it was during its life."

At one point, however, Kean was able to communicate something of the electric thrill—the death of Richard, that famous pantomime of menacing, weaponless hands and furious eyes in which he concentrated the demonic spirit of Gloucester, and in which he could never quite fail. Here, at any rate, was the unprecedented and the astonishing. "Sa mort, surtout, a été sublime," said the *Journal des débats*;

> his glances, half extinguished but still furious; the last sigh of life, or rather of vengeance, exhaling from his pale and trembling lips; the rage with which he gnaws the dust, had all of it a frightful veracity, and it is particularly in this series of pictures that one recovers most completely the great actor, the tragedian indeed worthy of the fame which had preceded him among us.

On May 16 he played Othello to the Iago of Chapman, the Cassio of Abbot, and the Desdemona of Miss Smithson. The *Journal des débats* found that it suffered from the same physical weaknesses and showed the same order of beauties as the Richard. Kean, it thought,

[10] The fictions that have been told of this visit by the biographers of Kean are amazing.

was admirable in his pantomime, in the brief flashes of jealousy, and in his death. It suggests that he would do much better as Iago, a part calling for less force and one to which the temper of his acting would be perfectly fitted. The real star of the evening was Miss Smithson, whose Desdemona was "always beautiful, touching, and pathetic." He repeated *Othello*, May 19. On May 21, 23, and 26 he played Shylock, a rôle which, because it made few demands upon his physical energies, had suffered least through his decay. Consequently he made a much stronger impression than before; the *Journal des débats* conceded that Shylock lay wholly within his powers and was brilliantly done; the press in general expressed a sincere admiration. On May 28 he played *Brutus*, which the critics thought poorly of as a play but which won him some fresh plaudits. His season then ran:

May 30	*Merchant of Venice*
June 2	*Brutus*
June 4	*Lear*
June 6	*Lear*
June 9	*A New Way to Pay Old Debts*
June 13	*A New Way to Pay Old Debts*
June 16	*Othello*
June 20	*Merchant of Venice* (benefit)

His Overreach made something of a sensation, although here again he must have failed in giving to the last scene the energy which used to be so appalling. His Lear was mostly ignored by the press. By the time of his benefit he had in considerable measure won back the ground he had lost at the beginning, but as a popular success he was never in hailing distance of Macready, and his benefit was but scantily attended.

Three days after his departure Macready was welcomed back with open arms. From then until the theatre closed a month later he was enthroned in public favor beside the adored Smithson. As Othello, in the last performance of July 21, he did what no male actor of the company had been able to do—aroused the audience to a tumult of enthusiasm. They demanded his appearance before the curtain; when it was explained that a French law forbade it, a group of young men carried him into the orchestra and thence to the stage, where he was crowned with a wreath of flowers, to much shouting. Fortunately for Kean he was busy at home during these unpleasant scenes, but reports must have drifted over to him. Doubtless he laid them to the deficiency of French taste.[11]

After his return from France, Kean spent the summer partly in fulfilling engagements, partly in resting at Bute. I have seen bills for *Othello* at Exeter, July 17 (last performance but two), and for *The Merchant of Venice* and *Othello* at Liverpool, August 27 and 29. Early in September the *Theatrical Observer* reported that he was at Bute, his health quite restored; later the issue of September 18 stated that he had concluded an engagement of four nights at Douglas, Isle of Man.

Meanwhile, the breach with Charles had been healed. Most accounts say that Charles visited him during the summer and exchanged the kiss of peace, but this happy reunion may have come about earlier, for on February 15 the *Theatrical Observer* had announced a reconcilement and had further stated that the elder Kean was then preparing the younger for Romeo. During Edmund's skirmishes with the French public Charles had been touring on his own account, not too unsuccessfully. One of his first engagements on leaving Drury Lane was at Dublin, where he acted young *Norval* on April 28 to an audience disposed to be friendly and indulgent. To his unbounded surprise they called for a speech; the embarrassed youngster clapped his hand to his breast, blushed, stammered, and finally uttered a number of incoherent remarks something to this effect: "Ladies and gentlemen, I am deeply sensible of your being quite unprepared—no, I don't mean that—I mean, of my being quite unprepared—over-

11 A letter in the Theatre Collection at Harvard, of no great interest, shows that the Paris engagement had its internal disagreements. It is dated simply "May 29th" and is addressed to "L Laurent Esqr":

"*My dear Sir*

You have already broken the former contract made in London—I am at a considerable loss by coming to Paris—and further protraction I will not submit to. I must make up in England what I lose in France. I have already conceeded too much and must tell you plainly—I have yielded one point to you—and if a single *Ioto*, of the last regulation is broken—*I play no more* in Paris

Yours &c

Edmund Kean"

I do not know what the trouble was.

whelming kindness—incapable of thanks—totally unmerited—never to be effaced—when time shall be no more—" "That will do, Charley," cried a friendly voice; "go home to your mother!" And as the laughter subsided and poor Charles stumbled into the wings, another voice roared, "Three cheers for Charley Kean's speech!"

By September Charles had got round to Glasgow, where a public and striking evidence was given that the old lion was friends once more with his cub. In October, Edmund came down from Bute to play for his son's benefit, taking the part of Brutus, in John Howard Payne's tragedy, to Charles's Titus. The house was crowded, as well it might be. In one highly emotional scene, when Brutus fell on Titus' neck and cried, "Embrace thy wretched father," loud applause broke forth. "Charley," whispered Edmund in the ear of Charles, "we're doing the trick!"

During the season of 1828-29 Kean's health seems to have improved. Opening at Covent Garden on October 13 as Richard, he played regularly at least twice a week until January. From November 17 to December 3 the theatre was closed for the installation of gas, an adventure which aroused no end of curiosity and considerable fear of asphyxiation. During the interval the company played at the Theatre Royal, English Opera. On December 15 Kean gave proof of his physical recovery by performing successfully—that is to say, without loss of memory—the rôle of Virginius in Sheridan Knowles's tragedy. It was repeated twice. On January 12 his health broke again. While dressing for Richard II he was taken with a violent ague and the play had to be cancelled.

He then left Covent Garden for the remainder of the season. In February he was reported to be resting in Bute:[12] during March he was still too ill to keep an engagement in Dublin, so that Charles was commissioned in his place. By April, however, he had so far recovered that we find him playing with Charles in Cork. The *Theatrical Observer* records another breakdown at that place on April 9; he collapsed in the middle of *Macbeth* and Charles had to piece out the evening with *Douglas*.

[12] The *Theatrical Observer* reported a Bristol engagement of three nights, either late in January or early in February.

The attack was a serious one, if we may trust the *Theatrical Observer*, which reported on April 30 that for the last ten days Kean had been laid up at Gresham's Hotel, Kingstown, with a paralysis of his legs. On Friday, April 24, he was so ill that the surgeon-general was sent for, and for some hours his life was despaired of. At the time of writing he had partially recovered, but there was good reason to fear that he would never act again. By May 2 the *Theatrical Observer* was able to say that he had left his bed, but that it was feared he would never recover the entire use of his legs.

After his Cork engagement, he was to have begun at Dublin on April 20, but as he was still confined to his bed, Bunn, the manager, had again to send for Charles to fill in. By May 4 he was miraculously on his feet. On that night father and son appeared as Shylock and Bassanio.[13] Edmund must have been in a bad state, for the critics found he had much fallen off. Further illness[14] delayed his second appearance until May 18, when he was able to play Overreach. He played Othello to the Iago of Charles, May 21, on May 23, Brutus to Charles's Titus, and on May 25, Macbeth, which was, probably, his last performance in Dublin. He had been billed as Lear for Miss Paton's benefit on May 30, but between Monday and Thursday he suddenly left for England and the lady thus unexpectedly jilted had to substitute *The Belle's Stratagem*. A day or two later manager Bunn published a letter full of wrath and grievance.

Owing to the state of inebriation in which Mr. Kean appeared on the Dublin stage last Saturday in the character of Brutus, and the inefficient and enfeebled manner in which he attempted Macbeth on Monday last, the lessee caused an intimation to be made to him on the subject, as a circumstance highly infringing on the respect due to the public; and at the same time (having paid him already a very large sum in advance on account of his engagement), the lessee stipulated for the appointment of trustees to

[13] The fullest account of Kean's engagements in Dublin is given by W. J. Lawrence in the *Weekly Irish Times* for May 25 and June 1, 1907. The present account is drawn from the second article.

[14] So said the *Theatrical Observer*, which reported that Edmund was taken ill on Monday, May 11, just before going on as Sir Edmund Mortimer in *The Iron Chest*, and Charles had to be substituted. Mr. Lawrence lays these various failures to drunkenness, on what authority I know not. Certainly the evidence is in favor of illness, although one should be willing to admit that Kean was probably drunk too.

receive whatever balance should eventually be due to him on the completion of his contract; upon which, without giving the management the slightest intimation of his purposes, he embarked last Thursday night on board the Erin steam packet for Glasgow. The lessee trusts that this plain statement of facts will be a sufficient apology to the public for the disappointment thus occasioned them, by a proceeding without any parallel in the annals of the stage.

To this plain statement the *Northern Whig* gave an answer which was most probably inspired by Kean himself, alleging that Bunn's version of the case was quite wrong, and that the tragedian had been the victim of annoyances which had acted on a mind already irritated by illness. The exact nature of these vexations is exposed in a letter from Kean to his solicitor:[15]

Dear Stock |[16] June 13 1829

I am still miserably ill & the calumnies of that rascal Bunn, is increasing my disorder. it is as much as I can do to put my pen to paper. Mr Phillips has left me. & I am left alone a waif upon the worlds wide common. But he has most scandalously asserted a lie, with regard to the night of Macbeth—can be proved by my Son, Mr Phillips & my Servant—Brutus was so miserably acted by his wretched Company that it was impossible not only to perform my own character with effect but without the assistance of Charles Kean the curtain must have dropt at the end of the second act, the engagement was for 12 nights, he paid me but for four. employing his villainous mind to traduce my character, & injure my professional reputation

he owes me now *50 £* for the performance of Macbeth is not this enough to establish an action, blended with the infamous calumny if so proceed with it instanter, I can write no more. My nerves are quite destroyed, if your leisure wou'd serve you to take a trip to this vale of enchantment I need not say how happy I shou'd be to see you, let me at all events hear from you by return of post.

Your very Sincere but Unhappy friend

Edmund Kean

Mrs Kean[17] desires her best regards, & joins with me in the invitation to Paradise

[15] Forster Collection, Victoria and Albert Museum.

[16] Uncertain, but apparently "Stock."

[17] Not Mary Kean, but the lady of the next paragraph but one.

There the matter rests, with no means of assessing the greater blame, though as between the word of Bunn and the word of Kean I know no reason for preferring Bunn. The *Theatrical Observer* on June 13 reported that Bunn had lodged suit against Kean; on June 25, that eleven actions, including one by Kean, were pending against Bunn, but whether they came to anything I cannot say.

From Dublin Kean went to his retreat in the Isle of Bute. And there, within a few days of his arrival occurred a disgraceful incident which cost him the friendship of his devoted secretary Phillips. The cause of it was Ophelia Benjamin, an Irish trollop, whose existence is casually mentioned in the lives of Kean but of whose antecedents or history nothing seems to be known. When or where he picked her up I cannot say; the earliest mention of her occurs in a postscript ("Ophelia's compliments") to a letter of April, 1828. It is possible that he acquired her during his visit to Dublin in 1827; it is certain that she stuck with him till his death. The Forster Collection at the Victoria and Albert Museum, South Kensington, contains a sheet in Kean's writing headed "Edmund Kean's last will"; it begins: "the Villainy of the Irish strumpet Ophelia Benjamin, has undone me & though I despise her, I feel life totally valueless without her I leave her my curses." We may guess her to have been a bold, handsome wench, high-tempered, brazen, and vulgar. In 1829, probably late in the year, was printed a scurrilous piece of verse entitled *Ophelia Keen!! A Dramatic Legendary Tale,*[18] setting forth how Kean, having dismissed his mistress, was in the midst of a convivial party to celebrate his freedom, when Ophelia broke in upon them drunk, engaged in a battle royal with the guests, and had to be placated with a gift of £50. This was the virago who ruled over Kean's domestic life for upwards of six years, the successor to Mary Chambers and Charlotte Cox—a genius shockingly fitted to preside over the decline and fall.

What happened at Bute early in June, 1829, is not recorded, but it is plain from the following letter that Ophelia's conduct had taken

[18] London: John Cumberland, 19 Ludgate Hill. 1829. The author was George David. The British Museum copy bears a manuscript note by him, declaring that the incident "absolutely" took place in 1829 at Kean's house in Mornington Place, Hampstead Road. It must have been in the autumn or later, because Kean was not in London from January on. The Phillips incident may have been at the bottom of it.

some manifestations so outrageous to Phillips that he had fled precipitately from the place. The hastily penned note[19] that Kean dispatched after him is touching in its pain, its humiliation, and its helplessness.

Friday Morning
Dear Philips | 5th June

I am shocked but not Surprised. in error I was born in error I have lived in error I shall die, that a *gentleman* should be insulted under my roof, creates a blush that I shall carry to my grave, & that you are so in every sense of the word is unquestionable. from Education, Habit, & manners. it is too true that I have fostered a worm till it has become a viper but my guilt is on my head, farewell

Your [illegible]

Edmund Kean

Phillips' place was taken soon afterward by John Lee, who remained with Kean until his death, serving him with devotion, and, we may hope, giving some protection against the vultures which hovered about his master.[20]

During July, according to the *Theatrical Observer*, Kean was playing in Belfast. He played in Liverpool August 3-8, Miss Smithson being of the company. Later in the month he is reported to be playing vigorously at Manchester. From there he swung up to Scotland, playing at Paisley either late in August or early in September, and opening

[19] British Museum, Egerton MSS, 2,159, fol. 89.

[20] The place was first offered to Tom Cunningham, an actor then playing in Dublin. Molloy prints the following letter, without date. It belongs in August.

"Dear Tom.

I have read the Dublin Theatre is to be sold, and I suppose the greater part of the company left to starve or rob, according to their inclinations. Off with his head—so much for Berkley Bunn. Phillips has left me, and I feel quite at a loss for a friend and man of business. If you would like to spend the remainder of your days with me, correspond with the damned managers, and take care they don't swindle, I should be most happy to receive you. I would give you the precise terms I did Phillips—£50 a year, and as much bub and grub as you can stow in you, and the non-play days we will over pipe and glass laugh and defy the villainies and falsehoods of this world. I play next week in Manchester, from that to Edinburgh.

Yours, dear Tom,

Very sincerely,

Edmund Kean.

Ophelia sends her respects, and, like myself, would be very happy to see you."

Friday Morning
5th June

89

Dear Philips/

I am shocked but
not surprised, in error I was born
error I have lived, in error I shall
i.e. that a gentleman should be
insulted under my roof, creates
a blush ~~that~~ I shall carry to my
grave, & ~~that~~ you are so in every sense
of the word is unquestionable. from
Education habit. & manners.
it is too true ~~that~~ I have fostered
till it has become a viper
a worm. but my guilt is on my head. farewell

[illegible]

Edmund Kean

LETTER OF KEAN TO R. PHILLIPS

an engagement of six nights at Edinburgh on September 24; the *Scotsman* reported no falling off in his vigor. I have seen bills for Newcastle of October 15 (*Othello*, last night), Scarborough of October 19 (*The Merchant of Venice*, first of four nights), and the Shakespeare Theatre, Stratford, of November 16 and 17 (*The Merchant of Venice* and *Richard*, two nights only). The *Theatrical Observer* reported him to have been at Derby on November 4. He must have recovered amazingly from his desperate illness in Ireland. On November 22 he was back in London.

Since his return from America—in fact since the winter of 1825—he had signed no yearly contracts with either of the London patent theatres, but had engaged himself, after the manner of performers in provincial theatres, for a stipulated number of appearances, at a salary which seems to have varied from fifty to sixty pounds a night. But on his return in November, 1829, he had not yet announced his intentions for the winter, a circumstance that gave rise to various rumors during the summer. On August 6, for example, he was "confidently reported" in the *Theatrical Observer* to be engaged for a few nights at the Surrey, over which Elliston was now presiding. On August 10 this was curiously denied as "one of the many inventions of his enemies." A week later Elliston was reported to have offered him £700 for one month. On September 26 the *Theatrical Observer* mentioned a rumor that Price had secured him for Drury Lane, adding:

> We do not believe this report, because when Kean left Covent Garden so abruptly last year, he wrote to the manager, pledging himself to complete his stipulated number of nights at that Theatre, previous to accepting an engagement at any other metropolitan Theatre; nor do we think he is the man to desert the concern, in its present state of embarrassment.

He had no sooner got to London than he plunged into a quarrel involving both the great theatres.

We must go back a little into the recent history of Covent Garden. Since 1822, Charles Kemble had been the lessee and manager, but like Elliston he had succeeded only in piling up debts, which by 1829 amounted to more than £20,000. In August the crash came; a warrant of distraint was issued for parish rates and taxes, the theatre was seized and plastered with bills advertising it for sale. Friends, of course, came to the rescue: various persons subscribed money, the King's Theatre gave a benefit, and several leading actors offered to perform gratuitously for certain numbers of nights. Among these was Kean, who wrote down from the north offering three appearances. In this way the theatre was given sufficient relief to clear itself of its legal impediments.

This is not the place to tell in detail the pleasant story of how Charles Kemble's nineteen-year-old daughter, Fanny, came to the rescue. She had no intention of becoming an actress, she did not want to, and indeed never liked acting, in spite of her great popularity, but when, one day in September, her parents decided that she must venture as Juliet, the obedient girl could not protest in the face of their distresses. Charles grasped at her like one who will try anything in an emergency; nothing but desperation could have moved him to pitch this green girl, who had never acted a part in her life, headfirst on the stage of Covent Garden. He felt there was a chance—she was lovely, she was fresh, she had beautiful eyes, and she came of a famous theatrical family. And so, after some three weeks of rehearsals, she was offered to the London public on October 5, the opening night of the season. Abbott, the same Abbott (or Abbot) I suppose who had played with Miss Smithson in Paris, was her Romeo; Charles played Mercutio, Mrs. Kemble, her mother, came out of several years' retirement to be Lady Capulet, Mrs. Davenport was the nurse. The events of that extraordinary night have been told in vivid detail by Fanny Kemble in *Memories of My Girlhood*—the suppressed anxiety of everyone behind the curtain, the panic of the girl in her dressing room weeping off her rouge as fast as her aunt Siddons put it on, the awful moment when she was pushed on the stage, in a mist, the green baize floor heaving beneath her feet, deafened and bewildered by the friendly roar that went up from a packed house. Then her inheritance took hold upon her—something from her father, her mother, her uncle Stephen, her uncle John, her aunt Sarah—stiffened her, taught her limbs to move, her eyes to sparkle, her lips to sing, and before she knew it she was caught up into Juliet and was delighting her audience as no woman had delighted them since the autumn of 1814 when the great O'Neill had swum into their ken. Two hours later Charles Kemble was assuring them of his infinite satisfaction and promising that *Romeo and Juliet* would be repeated every Monday, Wednesday, and Friday thereafter.

And thrice a week, all through October and November, Fanny Kemble played Juliet to a public which could not get enough of her. In one night she had made herself famous, adored, the toast of all the bucks of town. And what was more urgent to her father, by the end of the season she had put the theatre in the way of paying off £13,000 of its debt.

Into the midst of this furor Edmund Kean casually dropped, late in November, with the intent of fulfilling his promise to give three performances in aid of the theatre. But instead of aid he brought confusion. The order of events, as subsequently published in various affidavits and letters, went as follows.

On November 22 "a person" called at Covent Garden to say that Kean had arrived in town and that the "Drury Lane people" were already about him. George Bartley, the stage manager, then called on him the next day to arrange for the three nights, and was told with characteristic authority that they would be the following Monday, Wednesday, and Friday (November 30–December 4). Bartley said it was impossible—those nights were reserved for Miss Kemble; to which Kean replied, "I cannot act on the off nights, that would let Roscius down indeed!" Bartley then made an appointment for Kean with Kemble on the following day, which the actor did not keep; instead he sent a letter reiterating his wish to play on the nights he had indicated and adding, "I give the Management to understand that I play on no other nights but those I have been accustomed to in both the London Theatres." Bartley replied November 24 by letter, insisting that the nights in question were not available and promising that the management would do everything else in its power to meet Mr. Kean's wishes. To this no answer was made. Instead, the Drury Lane bills of Friday, November 27, carried the announcement that "Mr. Kean has kindly volunteered his Services in Aid of the Establishment which first fostered his Talent, and will act Richard the Third, on Monday."

Kemble was angry. He believed that he held Kean under contract to play nowhere but at Covent Garden, and he forthwith secured an injunction which prevented Kean from playing on November 30 but did no further service because on a hearing before the Vice-Chancellor in December, it was dissolved. The only recourse was an appeal to the public. Bartley's letters, affidavits by Kemble, Bartley, and Phillips, counter-affidavits by Kean and others, appeared in the press.[21] The real quarrel was then seen to be concerned with what had been said and done in the previous January.

Kemble's story was that Kean had agreed to play an engagement of twenty-four nights at Covent Garden between October 1 and Christmas of 1828, at £50 a night. Owing to the gas installation he had been able to act only sixteen of the agreed number before January; Kemble then proposed to cancel the former agreement and enter into a new one, for twelve nights after Christmas. To this Kean consented, and played January 5 and 8, but was then taken ill. Shortly thereafter Phillips, Kean's secretary and business agent, called on Kemble with the request that Kean be allowed to retire for rest and study of new rôles, as he felt that his attraction in the old ones was diminishing. To this Kemble sent a hearty acquiescence and the outline of still a new agreement, to the effect that Kean was to suspend performances at Covent Garden until season after next, study two or three new rôles, and be ready at the commencement of the winter of 1830-31 to complete his ten nights; in the meantime it was to be understood that he was not to act in London. Kean replied with a formal statement that he accepted these proposals. His letter had no date, but Phillips called later and affixed the date "January 22, 1829," with the notation "the date added by B. [should be R.] Phillips by Mr. Kean's authority."

Kean's affidavit, made December 1 before the Vice-Chancellor, declared that Phillips had no authority to propose anything regarding the season of 1830-31 or to add a date to his letter; that when he (Kean) replied to Kemble's proposal he was ill in bed, too ill to give attention to business, and believed, and continued to believe until early in the last November, that the proposal related to 1829-30.

21 See, for example, the *Morning Post* of November 30, December 1 and 2.

An affidavit submitted by Phillips stated that he called on Kemble by Kean's request, that the terms of agreement as drawn in Kemble's letter were explained to Kean, who understood clearly what season was in question, and that Kean wrote an acceptance with those terms correctly in mind. Against which a certain Cooper swore that Kean first became aware of the 1830-31 clause on November 7, when Cooper pointed it out to him; whereupon Kean appeared much surprised and declared he had never agreed to it knowingly.

The Vice-Chancellor was spared the labor of sorting out the truth of these contradictions; he interrupted the arguments of counsel in full tide to say that the terms of the agreement were so loose, in any case, that they never could be enforced by a Court of Equity.

Thus Kean was released from all obstructions on the part of Covent Garden. But there remained an aspect of the matter which would weigh far more in public estimation than a contract with a manager —his cavalier behavior toward the innocent and adorable Fanny Kemble, which had drawn unfavorable comment from the press. Here was probable danger. Mobs have hooted an actor for less cause than this. So he went again before the public tribunal with another of his characteristic letters, in which he sought to placate opinion by means of insolence, conceit, and lack of candor.

To the *Times*, December 1, 1829:

Sir,—Men are usually influenced in their dealings with one another by two paramount principles,—friendship or interest. Now, with reference to the letters of Mr. Bartley, as sanctioned by Mr. C. Kemble, it will doubtless be obvious to many, that the intention aimed at was chiefly the securing my services, at a sacrifice of those paramount conveniences that are considered, by the profession, as usual concessions to gentlemen who are indulged with any particular share of the public favour. That I enjoy this enviable satisfaction is, and ever was, a source of pride to me. But, that I ever wished to encroach, in the ungallant manner represented in the journals, on the special nights devoted to the performance of Miss Kemble, I positively deny. Seldom I notice newspaper tirades, but I feel myself bound in this instance to disclaim the remotest intention of depriving the public of the services of Miss F. Kemble, for one night even. More I do not choose to add at present, as the ulterior of this unpleasant proceeding will be discussed in a place more fitting than that of the columns even of the *Times*.

So ended a piece of behavior characterized in every part by petulance, selfishness, and arrogance. It is at any rate the last discreditable quarrel we shall have to record, which is some comfort. That he suffered no manifestation of public resentment at his insulting letter or the conduct which preceded it, I lay to the fact that the Drury Lane patrons were indifferent to what passed at the other house; but it is somewhat remarkable that Covent Garden sent over no retributive delegation.

He reappeared at Drury under the wing of Stephen Price on Wednesday, December 2, as Richard, before a crowded house that welcomed him tumultuously. He was given an ovation on his entrance, and at the end the pit rose and cheered. The *Theatrical Observer* remarked that he seemed to be stronger and was in better voice than last year. On Friday he joined forces with his old enemy, Young, in *Othello*. This drew, said the *Morning Post*, as crowded a house as ever assembled in Drury, and more noisy demonstrations. He went on through December and January playing his usual repertory in evident good health, for he appeared regularly three times a week and omitted the vacation which he ordinarily took at Christmas. He varied the round of *Richard*, *A New Way to Pay Old Debts*, *Othello*, *Brutus*, and *The Merchant of Venice* by reviving *Riches* on January 25. From February 3 to 15 was a gap, due, so the bills said, to illness; but I find him closing an engagement at Sheffield on February 11 (*A New Way to Pay Old Debts*) and 13 (*Town and Country*).

FANNY KEMBLE

CHAPTER XIV

DEATH

ENCOURAGED by his success of the previous year in memorizing Knowles's *Virginius*, which had erased the unhappy memory of *Ben Nazir*, he was venturing now on another new rôle, Shakespeare's Henry V. On his return from Sheffield the play went into the final rehearsals, and was scheduled for February 22, 1830, but illness again intervened, and it had to be withdrawn at the very last moment. When Wallack made the announcement the audience took it badly, crying "Apology! Apology!" and "Kean's drunk," and someone in the gallery threw oranges at the aggrieved stage manager. Finally on March 8 it came to production, with Cooper as Exeter, Browne as Fluellen, Wallack as Williams, Harley as Pistol, and the charming Miss Faucit,[1] who had joined the company this season, as the princess Katharine. A great deal of money had been spent on getting up the play.

But it was *Ben Nazir* all over again. Kean had no sooner acknowledged the cheers of reception and begun to speak when it was plain that he knew nothing of what he should be saying. Soon he was being hissed at every exit. By the fifth act the noise was so great that the first scene passed in dumb show. Kean then spoke:

"Ladies and gentlemen, I have for many years shared your favor with my brother actors, but this is the first time I have ever incurred your censure. (Cries of "No!") I have worked hard, ladies and gentlemen, for your amusement, but time and other circumstances must plead my apology. I stand here in the most degraded situation, and call upon you as my countrymen to show your usual liberality."

This was received with mingled cheers and hisses. The play went on, but so mangled that it was finished in ten minutes.

Crushed by this second catastrophe, the stricken tragedian apologized to his public through a letter in the *Times* of March 10. We need not quote the whole of this epistle, chiefly filled with grandilo-

[1] Sister, I believe, of Helen Faucit, the author of *The Girlhood of Shakespeare's Heroines.*

quent references to past favors and declarations of undying gratitude; some phrases express a mournful acceptance of the unavoided doom of destiny: "I find too late that I must rest upon my former favours. My heart is willing, but my memory has flown. All that I have done I can and will; what is to do I leave to a rising generation . . . Let me once more have to say, that the old spoiled favourite is forgiven . . ." A clearer sight into his despair is furnished by a personal letter to the editor of the *Star*:[2]

Dear Halpin,

Fight for me, I have no resources in myself; mind is gone, and body is hopeless. God knows my heart. I would do, but cannot. Memory, the first of goddesses, has forsaken me, and I am left without a hope but from those old resources that the public and myself are tired of. Damn, God damn ambition. The soul leaps, the body falls.

Edmund Kean.

Yet with magnificent courage he faced the task of keeping what he though could be kept. On March 15 he nerved himself to meet his public again as Richard. Fortunately the ordeal was made easy by an audience which felt more sympathy for him than resentment. He was painfully agitated as he entered the stage, perspiration covered his face, but a good-natured salvo of applause restored his self-possession instantly. He was bent on showing them that he was not all spent, and he did. "To us," said one of the reviewers, "it is a matter of doubt if he ever played Richard better than last Monday . . . His exclamation, 'Richard's himself again,' was heartily cheered by the audience, a compliment which he seemed to feel deeply."

He played past the middle of May, but sparingly, averaging less than a performance a week.[3] On May 17, for Farren's benefit, he revived *The Iron Chest* with a fine cast—Wallack as Wilford, Farren as Adam Winterton, and Mme. Vestris as Blanch; on May 21, for Cooper's benefit, he played Wolsey in *Henry VIII* to the Henry of Cooper and the Katherine of Mrs. Bunn.

[2] Quoted by Molloy.

[3] I have seen a bill of the Shakespeare Festival, Stratford, for Saturday, April 24, announcing Kean as Richard for that night, for Monday as Hamlet, and for Wednesday (his last performance) as Rolla in *Pizarro*. But he was billed at Drury Lane on Monday, April 26, as Brutus. I am unable to resolve this conflict.

Depressed by his infirmities and with the *Henry V* calamity still weighing on him, he now made up his mind to pay a farewell visit to America and then retire from the stage. Accordingly, in order that so important an event might be staged with the proper ceremonies, he arranged a farewell season at the Haymarket, as he had done in 1820 before his first visit to the United States, announced as "positively his last appearance on the London Boards."

These performances were given:

June 16 (Wednesday)	*Richard III*
June 21	*Othello*
June 25	*Merchant of Venice*
June 28	*Othello*
July 2	*A New Way to Pay Old Debts*
July 5	*Merchant of Venice*
July 9	*A New Way to Pay Old Debts*
July 12	*Lear*

He was supported by Cooper, Mrs. Glover, and Miss F. H. Kelly, but the quality of production seems to have been less than respectable. One reviewer complained that "whatever our admiration of Mr. Kean, tragedy at the Haymarket is but a melancholy farce dressed from Rag Fair, and acted, in too many instances, as if it were at Bartholomew." The *Theatrical Observer* noted a huge crowd at the first *Othello*; Kean himself was in fine form, but Cooper, as Iago, cut a poor figure, and Miss Kelly was hissed. Nevertheless, the short season was well attended, and *Lear* drew a packed house that manifested a good deal of excitement. The *Theatrical Observer's* comments are interesting:

> The whole of Kean's performance was marked by the utmost care, but were we to select a single part from a perpetual triumph, we should take that when after killing two of the assailants of *Cordelia* he throws away his sword and exclaims "I am old now;" the pathos with which he utters these three words was one of the finest triumphs of the actor's art we ever witnessed; the house burst into uncontrollable enthusiasm, and one lady in the boxes aided the effect by hysterical screams.

One remarkable phenomenon of the latter end of Kean's career is that in spite of his disabilities he should still be able, on occasion, to rouse his audiences as he had done in his great prime. The lightning could flash still, and I suppose it struck all the more thrillingly on the beholder as the stretches of darkness became longer. There must have been something peculiarly moving in the spectacle of that inert mass galvanized suddenly into intense life.

Because the Haymarket was too small a theatre, he took his benefit on July 19 at the King's Theatre, also in the Haymarket, a huge building occupied by the Italian opera. For this purpose he borrowed from various theatres a company of notables and gave a variorum bill consisting of high lights from five of his best plays: the fourth act of *Richard III*, the fourth of *The Merchant of Venice*, the fifth of *A New Way to Pay Old Debts*, the second of *Macbeth*, and the third of *Othello*. There was, said the *Theatrical Observer*, a terrific crowd, which paid £1,370 for admission—quite the largest audience that Kean ever played before. The *Times* reviewer, who was in the crush at the pit door, could remember nothing like it; for a scene comparable in the suffocation, the heat, the fetid odor, the screams of women, the outcries of men, the faintings, and the actual fear of life, he could think of nothing but the Black Hole at Calcutta. Inside, the crowd not only filled the orchestra space but overflowed into the stage wings, where they pushed and peered to the annoyance of the people everywhere else. The orchestra was obliged to play its overture from the stage.

At the end of the performance Kean made his farewell speech, in the course of which he hoped that the English people would always select a "proper person to fill the theatrical throne; for however some individuals may deem it a matter of no moment, as compared with other things, I think it one of very great importance to the intellectual character of this country; for that character the theatre will do more than all the conventicles that ever existed." Then he wished his public "a long—a last—farewell."

Directly thereafter he set out on a formal leave-taking through the provinces, "previous to his departure from England." He played at Brighton July 21 and 22, at Liverpool later in the month, then joined Smith's Norwich company for a tour of the circuit. I find him at Manchester August 2-6, at Norwich August 9-13, and at Yarmouth August

16-19 or later. The *Theatrical Observer* on September 15 published a statement which gives a vivid picture of the dreadful physical handicap under which he was now laboring.

Kean, while in Manchester, had a most dreadful attack of "purulent ophthalmia." So alarmed was he that he dispatched a messenger to London to bring down his friend and medical adviser, Mr. Deuchez, who, on arriving at Norwich, on Monday evening, found Kean acting *Richard* so blind, as not to be able to distinguish *Lady Anne* from his "Cousin of Buckingham," except by their "sweet voices."

He recovered, after a fashion, and went on to Peterborough, but he fell ill again (September 2) and had to cancel performances there and at Spalding. But by September 17 he was on his feet again, playing Lear on the last night of an engagement at Cheltenham. Late in September he played five nights at Bristol. On October 8, as Othello, he played the next-to-last performance of a farewell engagement at Plymouth.

Extraordinary man! Since the previous December—indeed since the July before that—save for intermissions caused by illness, he had not laid off his harness. For curiosity's sake I have counted the performances for the period from August 4, 1829, to October 8, 1830, crediting only performances for which I have seen bills. There are eighty-five, which, at £50 apiece, comes to £4,250. And when one takes benefits into account, and the fact that my provincial record is only a portion of the whole, the sum total may safely be placed at very nearly double. What indomitable spirit!

By the end of October the London journals reported him to be at Rothesay, in good health. He deserved to be.

I know not what motive led him to give up the idea of an American tour, unless it were the altogether likely one that he knew himself to be too ill. It was still his intention when he visited Plymouth in October, but between then and December the plan evaporated, along with his intention to retire from the stage. By the end of December he had put on the harness again and was playing at Bath, where he closed December 30. Then we find him at Hull (January 10-14, 1831), and Leeds.

On January 31, 1831, he reappeared at Drury Lane as Richard. That theatre was now under new management, for Price had laid down his burden the previous March, sadly disillusioned as to American enterprise in London, and Alexander Lee was now hopefully ruining himself. Kean, it may be noticed with wonder in passing, had been an applicant.

The present engagement was short and quite unremarkable. He played ten times, from January 31 to March 7, leaning on the five plays which were now his rod and his staff with a single performance of *The Iron Chest*, February 5. From London he went, in March, to Woolwich and Birmingham; on April 10 he was finishing an engagement at Boston; and May 10-14 we find him in Edinburgh.

He returned to London in May for a venture quite different from anything he had undertaken before. A couple of years earlier some foolish fellow had converted into a theatre a disused chapel standing in Milton Street, which lies north of the Guildhall and close by Moorgate Station, remote from the ordinary haunts of theatregoers. In 1831 a certain J. K. Chapman, after dabbling in various minor theatrical enterprises and getting expelled from the Tottenham Court Theatre for infringing on the holy prerogatives of the patent houses, took over the management, probably thinking that he would be too far away for either monopolist to bother about. He was, I suppose, a friend of Kean; anyway, he cunningly persuaded the actor to take out an interest in the theatre, thereby gaining not only financial support, which he doubtless needed badly, but acquiring the services of England's greatest tragedian. The incident perhaps throws some light on the dark problem of what became of Kean's immense income—he had also, it is known, shares in Irish theatres. There was no easier way, in those days, of losing money than by investing it in such enterprises. And so, as part owner of the City Theatre, as it was called, Kean astonished London by carrying his Shylock and Othello to that small minor playhouse hidden in the east.

He opened on May 23 in *The Merchant of Venice*, during which he made a speech, reported in substance by the *Tatler*, in which he alluded to "the declining state of the large theatres and their monopolizing spirit," and declared his "determination to try and make the little theatre in which he then addressed the patrons of the drama, the rival of the large ones in talent, though not in size."

I can only guess at the circumstances which lay behind this, and my guess is that he had taken offense at Alexander Lee, whose policy at Drury Lane ran strongly to farce, opera, melodrama, spectacle, pantomime, interlude, and in fact anything but tragedy. Feeling that he was not rightly valued there, and knowing that the doors of Covent Garden were closed to him, he had been captivated by the idea of leading his own little insurrection against the patent theatres, which now appeared to him as odious monopolists. It should be remembered that the performance of Shakespeare, or of any legitimate drama, elsewhere in London than at Drury Lane, Covent Garden, and (in the summer months) the Haymarket, was illegal. Therefore Kean and Chapman were breaking the law, and had they been anywhere within the theatre district as it was commonly understood they would certainly have been stopped; in fact an action was brought against them by Drury Lane, but whether from their remote situation or for some other cause it seems to have come to nothing. Therefore the experiment of building a refuge for Shakespeare in Moorfields was given full liberty of trial, at least for a short time.

From May 23 to June 20 he played every Monday, Wednesday, and Friday. The theatre then closed for a fortnight. When it reopened on July 4 he was announced as in prospect, but he never played there again.[4] During his run an amusing incident occurred. On June 7 Kean gave his services to Drury Lane for a benefit for three of his friends, Barrymore, Bedford, and Hughes, playing Sir Edward Mortimer in *The Iron Chest*. The bills of this performance carried the announcement after his name, "By permission of John Kemble Chapman, Esq., of the City Theatre," which not only insulted the dignity of the proprietors but was doubly ironical because Chapman was then defending a suit for violation of monopoly.

On June 27 he appeared at another minor theatre, the Coburg on the Surrey side (later called the Victoria), a place which from more respectable beginnings had sunk to the rawest kind of melodrama

[4] The City Theatre struggled along until 1836, when it was sold and converted into a warehouse.

and was frequented only by the rabble who lived in that unsavory neighborhood. This was the theatre at which the murder of Weare had been staged in 1823, and where Kean was reported to have driven about the stage in the notorious gig. A possible explanation for his condescending to this most unfashionable place is offered by a statement of Barton Baker[5] that in 1831 the Coburg and City theatres came under one management, the performers being conveyed from one to the other in hackney coaches. But he does not say just when the coalition took place. I may suggest, however, merely as a guess, that the closing of the City Theatre in June resulted from the action brought against it, and that its reopening in July was under the new Coburg management.

Besides the opening bill of *Richard III* for June 27, I have seen one other Coburg bill of *King Lear* for July 4, being Kean's fourth night. He therefore played more than the two performances heretofore mentioned, but how many more I cannot say—probably few, if any. The hazards of the Coburg are revealed in an anecdote relating to the performance of *King Lear*, which has been hitherto wrongly attached to *Othello*. We may let the *Theatrical Observer* tell it:

> On Monday night (July 4) Kean was playing *Lear* at this Theatre, when the gods conducted themselves very uproariously and one man threw a piece of orange at his feet. After the curtain had fallen, there was a general call for Kean. He came forward, evidently in great anger, and said that, whatever talent he possessed, he considered himself degraded in being obliged to appear before such *things* as those, (pointing to the gallery). Cheers issued from the pit, which the gallery, not knowing what had been said, re-echoed.

To the spring or early summer of 1831 must be assigned another and more important undertaking. For years Kean had hankered, strangely, after the managership of some theatre. Since the fall of committee rule at Drury Lane, and with every change in management, he had been an applicant for the position there, unsuccessfully as we have seen. Early in the present year the need of moving out of London into some rural spot which would benefit his health had led him to Richmond, where he found not only a charming, quiet village but a theatre for rent. Here was the opportunity for rest and

[5] Baker, H. Barton, *The London Stage*. London, 1889. II, 250.

KEAN'S THEATRE AND HOUSE, RICHMOND

amusement at one and the same time. Accordingly he leased the King's Theatre on Richmond green and settled in a cottage adjoining it.

Probably he turned to the business of organizing and equipping a company as soon as his Coburg engagement was over. On August 9 the *Theatrical Observer* noted that "a promising young actress, incognita," had made her appearance at Richmond under his management. He played there himself, of course, and frequently. The first occasion I have found was on July 29, when he gave *A New Way to Pay Old Debts*. On September 1 he played *The Merchant of Venice*, and on September 14, *Hamlet* (with Miss Faucit). The *Theatrical Observer* of Monday, October 24, stated that he had realized £240 during the last week, and was billed for Overreach, Shylock, and Macbeth on the coming Wednesday, Thursday, and Friday, and Lear for his benefit on Monday next. On November 5 the same paper had heard that he had made a successful speculation with his Richmond theatre; he had engaged Mr. and Mrs. Wood (popular singers of ballad opera) for *Love in a Village*.

As if this were not enough, he appeared in Birmingham, August 2-5, and entered into a six week's engagement at the Haymarket. This latter act would seem to confirm rumors which went about London at this time concerning a break between Kean and Chapman of the City Theatre and which were further confirmed by the circumstance that just as Kean opened at the Haymarket, Moss began to play his rôles at the City.

Kean's Haymarket season started on Monday, August 29, with *Richard III*. Thereafter he played Fridays and Mondays: September 2, *Othello*; September 5, *A New Way to Pay Old Debts*; September 9, *The Merchant of Venice*; September 12, *Hamlet*. At this last performance he was taken ill again, having to surrender his place to Cooper at the end of the first act. The *Theatrical Observer* assured its readers that his indisposition was not due to drink (which seems to have been the general opinion) but to cholera (which is far less plausible). By Wednesday, September 21, he had recovered sufficiently to take part in *The Surrender of Calais*, which he had not played for years. Thereafter he played thrice a week until October 15. He then returned to his affairs at Richmond for a month. In November he was on the road again, playing at Manchester on November 12, being ill in North Wales a week later, and commencing a twelve nights' engagement at Bristol on November 28.

If we may trust the *Theatrical Observer*, he played at Dublin during the latter part of December. Mr. W. J. Lawrence, who has made a special study of Kean in Dublin, says that his last appearance there was on May 25, 1829; but as reported by the *Observer*, January 7, 1832, he had been playing there when he was taken ill on Thursday, December 29, then recovered sufficiently to play Reuben Glenroy on Saturday the thirty-first.

In February he was in Edinburgh, announced to open an engagement of seven nights on February 13, 1832. Illness prevented his beginning on schedule, but I suppose he filled his engagement, because he took his benefit on February 27 with the same mixed bill that he had used at the King's Theatre, Haymarket, in July of 1830. This was his last appearance in Edinburgh.

We hear little of him during the spring, a circumstance which is to be laid, I feel sure, on his growing infirmity and the interruptions of illness. On April 19 he is reported to have recovered sufficiently to resume playing. On May 16 he returned to Drury Lane for a single performance, playing Shylock at the benefit of Russell, Bedford, and Hughes. On June 4 he began an engagement of three weeks at the Haymarket with the very considerable support of Miss Smithson, playing Mondays, Wednesdays, and Fridays, and closing on July 20. He seems not only to have completed it without mishap, but in the week of June 25 to have added three performances at Windsor for the races. Of this Haymarket engagement the *Theatrical Observer* (not, it may be cautioned, to be relied on as to terms of contract) said that it was nominally for £50 a performance, but that as he played twice as often as his contract called for he really received only half as much.

After the Haymarket he was reported as scheduled for a short provincial tour. On July 25 the *Theatrical Observer* carried this notice:

The Richmond Theatre, or as it is now styled "The King's Theatre Richmond," will open on Monday next, under the management of Kean, who is to perform there three times a week, at Windsor twice, and at the

Haymarket every Monday during the season; pretty sharp work that for a man with a shattered constitution.

Pretty sharp work indeed. I cannot say how faithfully he carried out the Richmond and Windsor ends of this killing program, but he did play at the Haymarket on four Mondays from July 23 to August 13, besides adding a Friday performance on August 3. I have seen one Windsor bill for this summer, for *Richard III* on Tuesday, August 21, and one Richmond bill for *Hamlet,* on Monday, September 3.

Of his life in Richmond during these last two years several first-hand accounts have been preserved, particularly from Dr. James Smith, a resident physician who served the actor and from whom Hawkins obtained several reminiscent letters which he prints in his biography. On fair days he might be seen walking, or rather hobbling, on Richmond green or in the park, muffled in a fur coat and cap; more often he was driven in his carriage or rowed on the Thames. He still loved the water, and he still gave his annual wherry. Helen Faucit, when a little child, met him once on the green—"a small pale man with a fur cap, and wrapped in a fur cloak. He looked to me as if come from the grave. A stray lock of very dark hair crossed his forehead, under which shone eyes which looked dark, and yet bright as lamps." He spoke kindly with the child, in a hollow voice which "seemed to come from far away—a long, long way behind him." Miss Tidswell now lived with him and was generally to be seen by his side in the carriage, or supporting him on foot, a tall, erect, gray-haired woman. The life was quiet, almost peaceful; he spent much of his time in his cottage, reading and singing to himself at the piano; the poor of Richmond had frequent occasion to bless his generosity. His family, too, was not forgotten; Ann Carey had received her £50 yearly, and he seems to have done something for his half-brother Henry Darnley and his children. Gone were the old days of nightly carousal, because he could no longer endure them—not, however, the drinking of strong spirits, on which, in fact, he lived. Dr. Smith said that he "did not take an ounce of solid food for weeks together," that his stomach was "entirely gone." He subsisted on the residue of what must be considered a remarkable vitality, burning himself up with brandy and water, dying day by day, yet rousing himself for one more performance at his own theatre, or to be driven to Windsor or to the Haymarket.

Impressions of him on the stage at this period have been left by Talfourd and Dr. Doran. Talfourd[6] found that in one part, Shylock, he was still as fine as he had ever been, if not indeed more harmonious. "We used to think the trial scene in the fourth act languid, compared with the rest of the performance; but now it seems quite worthy of all that precedes it; and the close—where generally no effect has been produced—is marked by a mild and peculiar beauty." His Overreach was less terrible than it used to be when it could throw Byron into convulsions, "but it is sustained by a quiet consciousness of power, and superiority to principle or fear, and the deficiency of physical force in the last scene is supplied with consummate skill." His Othello had altered greatly for the worse, although preserving some fine moments. But of all parts the one now to be avoided was, alas, Richard; it had, especially in the last act, grown "pitiably feeble." "He whispers when he should shout; creeps and totters about the stage when he should spring or rush forward; and is even palpably assisted by his adversary to fight or fall. Yet his last look at Richmond as he stands is fearful."

Doran saw him for the last time as Richard at the Haymarket in 1832.

The sight was pitiable. Genius was not traceable in that bloated face; intellect was all but quenched in those once matchless eyes; and the power seemed gone, despite the will that would recall it. I noted in a diary, that night, the above facts, and, in addition, that by bursts he was as grand as he had even been,—that though he looked well as long as he was still, he moved only with difficulty, using his sword as a stick . . . In the scene with the Mayor and Buckingham, he displayed talent unsurpassable;—the scarcely-subdued triumph that lurked in his eyes, as he refused the crown; his tone in "Call him again;" his acceptance of the throne, and his burst of joy, when he had dismissed the petitioners, were perfect in their several ways; but he was exhausted before the fifth act, and when, after a short fight, Richmond (Cooper) gave him his death-wound in Bosworth Field, as he seemed to deal the blow, he grasped Kean by the hand, and let him gently down, lest he should be injured by the fall.

[6] Writing for the *New Monthly Magazine,* March, 1831.

Early in September he received a letter from Ann Carey, written September 7:

Dear Edmund,

I wrote to you the first of last month, my quarter's money being due the 1st of September. As I have had no answer, I fear you did not get my letter. I am in great anxiety till it comes, and being in ill-health makes me feel more. If you can oblige me with two quarters—one due and one in advance—you will render me a very great service. As I may be compelled to move hastily from the lodging I am now in, I beg you will have the kindness to direct to Mr. Cooper, Surgeon, Great Peter Street, for me, to the care of Mr. Cooper.

I saw Harry[7] yesterday. His looks are mended since I last saw him. I thank God that you have taken him and his poor chickens under your wing, and I hope you will hold it over them during the winter. I think they have merit, which, cheered by your kindness, will show itself. Mrs. Darnley is clever in Scotch and Irish characters.

Your affectionate mother,
M. A. Carey

P. S.—I am in a strange state of health. Two days before I saw Harry every one thought I could not live the night through. I am sorry that I live to trouble my dear child, and yet I cannot wish to die. *Let me see you.*

The appeal had its effect; loneliness and the shadow of death moved Edmund with compassion for the woman who had done nothing for him except bring him into the world, but who was also lonely and under the shadow of death. So she was brought to the Richmond cottage, where she lay very ill in bed and where Dr. James Smith saw her, a woman astonishingly like her son and looking scarcely older, so old did he seem. "She subsequently proved to be," wrote the doctor, "a low, dissipated, illiterate woman." But her dissipations, like Edmund's, were over; she was dying too. As soon as she entered the house, Aunt Tidswell, the grim irreconcilable, bounced out of it and back to her lodgings in Chelsea.

Three months after his reunion with his mother, moved by the same impulses of a dying man to forget old grievances and to draw to him once more all those who belonged to him, he wrote to Mary Kean the first friendly message that had passed between them since their separation.

[7] Henry Darnley, her son by father unknown.

Dear Mary,

Let us be no longer fools. Come home; forget and forgive. If I have erred, it was my head, not my heart, and most severely have I suffered for it. My future life shall be employed in contributing to your happiness; and you, I trust, will return that feeling by a total obliteration of the past.

Your wild but really affectionate husband,

Edmund Kean.

This letter was addressed from the Theatre Royal, Richmond, and was dated merely "Thursday, December 6."

What reply Mary made to this impulsive and most characteristic appeal we know not. Edmund had enjoined "a total obliteration of the past," easy enough for him indeed, but not so easy for her. She might forgive the Cox business, she might even obliterate Ophelia Benjamin and others like her, but could she wipe out of her memory the long aching years of loneliness, the ruin of her life, the heartless behavior toward her darling Charles? She may have gone to him and been reconciled—we hope so, and we know, at least, that she visited him as he lay at the point of death—but she did not "come home" nor did she accept of him more than that pension which was her due. She lived now wholly for Charles.[8]

Monday, September 24, Kean returned to the Haymarket for the third time that summer, opening, with Richard, an engagement of five nights which closed on October 8. He seems to have kept at home for the rest of the month; on October 26 he was playing *The Stranger* at Richmond, advertised as the last performance but two, and on the twenty-ninth, *Othello*.

[8] From Procter on this letter has been placed, by a careless suppression of its proper date, among Kean's last hours, where it gains certainly in poignancy. Its treatment by the three biographers is an illuminating commentary on the arts of biographical decoration. Procter simply says: "In one of these intervals [of lucidity] he wrote the following letter to his wife." Molloy makes Charles responsible for the overture: "He therefore suggested to the dying man that he should make peace with his wife." But Hawkins rises to the moment on wings: "The dying actor . . . only remembered that during that sorrowful period which elapsed between their marriage and his brilliant start into fame they had loved and slaved and starved and hoped against hope; and with all his old boundless affection revived, he called for his son to place his writing desk before him upon the bed, and with tears coursing down his pale and wasted face, he penned the following affectionate and repentant letter to his wife."

As a matter of fact the letter was written during a particularly busy run at Drury Lane. On the same night (December 6) Kean played Othello.

With Monday, November 5, he began his last season at Drury Lane, playing Shylock to the Bassanio of Cooper, the Antonio of Mathews, and the Portia of Miss Phillips. His appearances were on Mondays and Fridays as follows:[9]

November 9	*Richard III* (Richmond, Cooper; Ann, Miss Faucit; Queen Elizabeth, Mrs. Faucit)
November 12	*Hamlet* (Polonius, Farren; Laertes, Brindal; Claudius, Younge; Queen, Mrs. Faucit; Ophelia, Miss Faucit)
November 16	*A New Way to Pay Old Debts*
November 19	*Richard III*
November 22	*Brutus*
November 26	*Othello* (Iago, Macready; Desdemona, Miss Phillips)

That last bill brings us to a pause, and to a glance back over the last sixteen months, which had seen the passing of two notable figures from the world of the theatre. On July 8, 1831, Robert William Elliston, the eccentric, the unpredictable, the exasperating and lovable, had died. On May 30, 1831, Charles Mayne Young, in full possession of his powers, retired majestically from the stage at Covent Garden, explaining to the clamoring throng that he was "loath to remain before his patrons until he had nothing better to present to them than tarnished metal"—which sounds very much like a parting shot at his great rival. From Covent Garden the Kembles had departed, in summer, for the American El Dorado. So London was for the moment poorer in tragic actors of magnitude than, perhaps, it had ever been since the beginnings of Shakespeare. Only two persons rose above the mediocre level, Macready and Kean, and one of these was half dead. Yet his fame still lived, so that the conjunction of these two, recalling the conjunction of Kean and Young and that distant, but still memorable, night when Kean and Booth joined momentarily, stirred an immense interest, so great and so lasting that *Othello* was played twice a week through December, with the free list suspended and no orders issued.

[9] He also played at Richmond—for example, *The Wheel of Fortune* and *Paul and Virginia* (of all things) on Wednesday, November 14.

I remember [writes George Henry Lewes] the last time I saw him [Kean] play *Othello*, how puny he appeared beside Macready, until in the third act, when roused by Iago's taunts and insinuations, he moved towards him with a gouty hobble, seized him by the throat, and, in a well-known explosion, "Villain! be sure you prove," &c., seemed to swell into a stature which made Macready appear small. On that very evening, when gout made it difficult for him to display his accustomed grace, when a drunken hoarseness had ruined the once matchless voice, such was the irresistible pathos—manly, not tearful—which vibrated in his tones and expressed itself in look and gestures, that old men leaned their heads upon their arms and fairly sobbed. It was, one must confess, a patchy performance considered as a whole; some parts were miserably tricky, others misconceived, others gabbled over in haste to reach the "points;" but it was irradiated with such flashes that I would again risk broken ribs for the chance of a good place in the pit to see anything like it.[10]

Othello played November 29 and December 3, 6, 10, 13, 17, 20, and 28. Kean then went off for three weeks on a provincial tour. On January 21 he reappeared at Drury Lane as Richard, and was billed on the twenty-fifth with Macready in *Othello*, but was seized with an attack of gout as he was leaving for the theatre, and Cooper took his place. From then on, although he still fought valiantly against his multiple infirmities, he lost more battles than he won. Death was closing relentlessly upon him. On February 8 he was able to play *Othello* once more, and for the last time, with Macready. Then he collapsed again. But his demon still drove him on. He went down to Brighton to play on Tuesday, February 19, and was taken alarmingly ill in the midst of a performance; as he was borne off the stage he

[10] Alfred Bunn, at this time manager at Drury Lane, tells an anecdote of these performances (*The Stage: Both Before and Behind the Curtain.* London, 1840. I, 99): "Kean had a thorough contempt for Macready's acting; and the latter affecting to be indignant at the mode in which Mr. Kean had conducted himself (in always keeping a step or two behind him, whereby the spectator had a full view of the one performer's countenance and only a side view of the other), bounced into my room, and at first vowed he would play with him no more. He finally wound up by saying, 'And pray what is the—next p—lay you ex—pect me to appear in—with that low—man?' I replied that I would send him word. I went up into Kean's dressing-room, where I found him scraping the colour off his face, and sustaining the operation by copious draughts of brandy and water. On my asking him what play he would next appear in with Macready, he ejaculated, 'How the ——— should I know what the ——— plays in!' "

MACREADY AS IAGO

whispered, "I fear this is my last dying speech." On Thursday, the twenty-first, he could not play Macbeth at Drury Lane; had he done so he would have been pitted against his son Charles, who after many provincial wanderings and a visit of two years to the United States, had just returned to London, and played Sir Edward Mortimer in *The Iron Chest* at Covent Garden that night. On Saturday, March 9, Edmund gave his last performance at Drury Lane, as Shylock. He was billed for Richard on March 12, but gout prevented; at Richmond, on the fifteenth, he was obliged to give up Richard in the middle of the second act.

Living as he was on his current income, and not having played, as far as we can tell from the records, more than three times in London since January, he was badly in need of money. Bunn tells us that he now approached Captain Polhill, the lessee of Drury Lane, for a loan of £500, offering his future performances as security, but in view of his precarious state of health this request was refused. So deeply was he offended that, although his contract with Polhill had not yet expired, he betook himself immediately to Covent Garden, where, all gentlemen's agreements between the two theatres having long since become a dead letter, he was immediately received. The bills of Thursday, March 21, announcing him as Shylock, added that he was "engaged at this Theatre for three nights previous to his departure for Ireland." Drury Lane on the same day issued the following notice:

In consequence of the announcement, at another theatre, of

MR. KEAN,

The public is respectfully informed, that the engagement of that gentleman at this Theatre, does not expire until the 30th inst., which engagement has only been suspended by the receipt of the following certificate from Mr. Kean's Medical adviser:—

"Mr. James Smith presents his Compliments to Mr. Bunn, he is very sorry to inform him that Mr. Kean is confined by so very severe an attack of Gout in his right hand and arm, and some threatening also of the same sort in his legs, as to render it quite impossible for him to perform at present.

"Mr. J. Smith will be happy to inform Mr. Bunn from day to day, how Mr. Kean goes on, as it is impossible at present to fix the day for his reappearance. Richmond Green, March 12th, 1833."

It was all that Drury Lane was able to do by way of protest, for an injunction in the opinion of counsel could not be secured.

Kean therefore played Shylock unmolested, to the Portia of Ellen Tree, who was later to marry his son. On Monday, March 25, the Covent Garden bills announced that "Mr. Kean was last Thursday received in the character of *Shylock* with acclamations:—and in order to meet the generally expressed desire that he should appear with his Son, *The Tragedy of Othello* will be acted this evening, when they will perform together, for the first time." Charles of course took the part of Iago, Abbot of Cassio, and Miss Tree of Desdemona.

The theatre was crowded that evening. When Charles arrived he found his father in his dressing room, weak and shivering. "I am very ill," he said; "I am afraid I shall be unable to act." He was fortified with brandy and water, and encouraged by cheerful words, but a costume was laid out for Warde in case he should have to take up the part. Father and son were received with hearty applause. The play began. Edmund found that his son had improved: "Charles is getting on to-night," he said after the first scene, "he's acting very well. I suppose that is because he is acting with me." His own weakness was so apparent that it seemed impossible he should be able to finish, but he managed to keep going through the second act. As the third began he said to Charles: "Mind that you keep before me. Don't get behind me in this act. I don't know that I shall be able to kneel; but if I do, be sure that you lift me up." He got through the first half of the great scene well enough, to the point where Othello leaves the scene with Desdemona. But on his reëntry he could scarcely walk across the stage. The dialogue which immediately follows is thick with points which he had made heartrending or terrible. He struggled through,

I found not Cassio's kisses on her lips.

Immediately thereafter comes the famous "Farewell," which he had made one of the loveliest pieces of music in Shakespeare. He struggled through that. The dialogue goes thereafter:

Othello. Othello's occupation's gone!
Iago. Is it possible, my lord?
Othello. Villain, be sure thou prove my love a whore;
Be sure of it; give me the ocular proof . . .

With this speech he was used to summon all his fury; Lewes has told us how, only the last December, he seemed at this point to tower over a shrunken Macready. And now he tried desperately to do it once again. But he was spent, darkness covered his eyes, he felt his senses going from him; throwing his arms around Charles and sinking his head on his shoulder he whispered, "I am dying—speak to them for me."

He was borne to his dressing room, where he lay as if already dead. Several medical men, brought in from the audience, tried vainly to call back some appearance of life, by administering ether, burnt brandy, and other stimulants, but there was no discoverable pulsation. After a time he was carried in an armchair by two stage carpenters to the Wrekin Tavern, in Broad Court, and put to bed, but so great was his prostration that no attempt was made until the next morning to wash the coloring matter from his face. Under the care of his London physician, Dr. Carpue, he remained at the Wrekin until Saturday afternoon, when he was driven to Richmond.

There he was tended by Mr. Smith, who nursed him into such condition that he was able to drive out now and then in his carriage, and on one occasion went as far as Chelsea to call on Miss Tidswell, a trip which proved to be too much for him, for he was taken with a hemorrhage, returned home at once, went to bed, and never again left the house. On May 1 the press announced that his case was hopeless. His wife and son visited him May 2 and found him somewhat better. The next day he was able to be dressed; but it was a delusive sign. Mr. Douchez, the surgeon then in attendance, perceived on May 14 that he was dying. He passed the rest of the day and all the night in a state of insensibility; at five in the morning he seemed to recognize those about him, but could not speak; a little past nine, on the morning of May 15, 1833, in the presence of Mr. Douchez and his devoted secretary, Lee, he closed his eyes forever.

The news of his death fell upon the public ear with melancholy emphasis, reviving memories of his sensational début, of his stormy, wretched life, of his fitful but astounding art, marking, furthermore, the close of a great era. Kemble was dead, Siddons was dead, Elliston was dead, Young and O'Neill had passed from the stage. Booth was lost in America; only Macready and the entrancing Fanny Kemble were left to guide the destinies of high tragedy. Other actors would come, some of them great ones, no doubt, but the stage was weltering in chaos, having lost, with the passing of the masters, its two great schools of acting, the classic and the natural, which had given such character to performance and such vitality to criticism. Had anyone been gifted with foreknowledge he could have looked toward the apotheosis of polite burlesque under Vestris, the sentimental melodrama of Boucicault, the genteel comedy of Tom Robertson and the Bancrofts, the meticulously-dressed Shakespeare of Charles Kean, but would he have seen anything for which he would have exchanged the Coriolanus of Kemble, the Belvidera of Siddons, or the Othello of Kean? Or would tragedy ever again speak with such imperative and moving accent as it had from the mouth of that ruined mansion of genius and unregulated passions which lay awaiting burial in Richmond?

On Saturday, the twenty-fifth, a stream of curious and regretful people flowed out to Richmond, so many that extra coaches and steamboats had to be put in use. Twenty townsmen had been sworn special constables; the shops on the main street were closed; since Friday morning visitors had moved past the coffin of the dead tragedian. At three o'clock the funeral procession started for the parish church of St. Mary Magdalene; among the pallbearers walked Macready, behind the coffin was Charles Kean, supported by Sheridan Knowles and Lee, then came the chief mourners, including the dead man's physicians and John Forster, the friend and biographer of Dickens, next followed the members of the Drury Lane Fund Committee, after them a long line of actors from every London theatre, and at the end, the inhabitants of Richmond. With so much pomp and circumstance the body was accompanied to the old church, where, after a burial service with music by Purcell and Handel, it was interred.

On the following Monday the churchyard of St. Mary Magdalene received the body of Ann Carey, who had died on Thursday, May 23, eight days after her son.

Of all the hundreds of thousands of pounds which had passed into the pockets of the great actor, less than nothing remained. In June of 1834 his possessions were sold at auction—the house and furniture at Bute, his swords, cups, plate, medals, and theatrical wardrobe—all went for his debts. Charles had to buy in the few things he kept as mementos of his father.

Among the actor's papers was found a sheet headed "Edmund Keans last will," which passed into the possession of John Forster, and is now among the papers left by him to the Victoria and Albert Museum. There is no date on it, nor was it legally executed; probably it was the pastime of some idle and depressed moment, for it can scarcely be taken as a serious instrument, although the feeling in it is serious enough.

the Villainy of the Irish strumpet Ophelia Benjamin, has undone me & though I despise her, I feel life totally valueless without her I leave her my curses

My property in Bute, with the furniture of this House—Richmond I leave my mother (with the proviso) that no portion of it, shall be either sold or let if so,—the whole goes to the possession of the Drury Lane Theatrical fund.

My Dramatic Wardrobe, with all other clothing I leave to my worthy friend John Lee (forgive me oh Lord & receive my Soul with mercy)

No mention, herein, of Mary Kean or Charles. Were these words written before that letter calling Mary back to him? Or had the rift become too wide to heal? It is perhaps too empty a speculation; at any rate, he died reconciled to wife and son.

Mary, fortunately, had the staunch support of Charles, who had been moving slowly toward success, and would before long be wealthy. It is pleasant to know that he took care of her as a good son should, that in 1844 he was able to settle her comfortably on a property at Keydell, near Horndean in Hampshire. There, in 1849, she died. She is buried at Catherington, a hamlet near Portsmouth.

Miss Tidswell—the mysterious and irreconcilable Tidswell—lived on for a time at Chelsea, but for how long I am unable to say. What secrets she knew she kept locked behind her tight lips, and carried into the grave with her.

CHAPTER XV

TIME AND THE ARTIST

How great was Kean? In tradition he stands with the greatest, in the company of Burbage, Betterton, and Garrick. Burbage is hardly more than an honored ghost; of Betterton we know too little for comparison; Garrick must be allowed precedence if only for the versatility of his genius. Does Kean then rank second among the masters of the tragic stage whom we know well? No doubt a popular vote would say yes, for he is more alive today than any of his contemporaries except Mrs. Siddons, who is forever matchless among her sex, or than any of his successors until we come to Irving, who is *sui generis*. But a popular vote in his own day would certainly be divided, and we must take into account the very strong claims of Kemble, nor should we overlook that most original genius George Frederick Cooke.

Kean told John Howard Payne that he had never seen Cooke, which may be true inasmuch as Cooke was away from England after the spring of 1810. But we cannot trust Kean's word for that, and he would have had opportunities during his visits "home" or in 1806, when both were in London. At all events, his admiration for Cooke was remarkably strong to have been based on mere hearsay, and many have commented on the striking resemblance between their styles. Payne, who had seen Cooke in the United States, said:

> If Kean never saw Cooke, and he tells me he never did, the similitude in certain parts of their acting, as well as the conception of the true character, seems to me to be still more wonderful. Their leading features of resemblance in *Shylock* and *Richard* exhibit so marked a correspondence in their genius that it almost proves that both modelled themselves upon similar views of nature.[1]

It is not, of course, beyond the bounds of possibility that they both achieved the same result as a consequence of the same impulses to expression. The "similitude in certain parts of their acting," on the other hand, is more likely to have resulted from adoption by Kean of

[1] Harrison, Gabriel, *John Howard Payne*. Philadelphia, 1885. Page 67. The extract is from a letter of June 19, 1817.

GEORGE FREDERICK COOKE

some matters of business developed by Cooke, which would be common theatrical knowledge. Certain it is that Cooke was the first exponent, in the nineteenth century, of "natural" tragic acting, which, especially to younger people brought up on Kemble-Siddons, must have come with the force of real discovery. To Payne, also, he was a "discoverer"—"Cooke reminds me of no one but himself, and I have never been able to recognize the real *Richard* in any other actor."

His priority in Kean's field is therefore unquestionable, but he made little of it. For years he played amicably on the same stage with Kemble, often in the same play, without heading an opposition or even raising a party. Perhaps the times were not ripe, perhaps he needed a Hazlitt, but more probably there were not in his readings those audacities which provoke dispute, so that his acting impressed upon his spectators no more than a feeling of natural vigor. He was certainly great, yet he wasted his genius even more fatally than did Kean and his compass was narrower. He was known best in three rôles—Richard, Shylock, and Sir Pertinax Macsycophant in Macklin's comedy *The Man of the World*. In the last of these Kean could not touch him, but that means little to us nowadays, the rôle has so faded into distance that the greatness in it of Cooke and Macklin has lost reality. As Richard and Shylock he may very possibly have topped Kean, as he certainly did in parts of them, but even if we grant him so much, the superiority of Kean rests on his wider range, the intellectuality of his interpretations, and the greater impress he made on his times.

In the never-ending arguments over Kean and Kemble, the supporters of Kemble were wont to praise what Payne called "the steady, burning light" of his impersonations, in contrast to the intermittent flashes sent forth by Kean. Kemble, to them, was a model of classic justness, noble in figure and pose, graceful in movement, dignified, restrained, intelligent, never careless, never tricky, never "popular," but drawing the best from the high protagonists of tragedy because his mind and his conception of tragic action were likewise high. They admitted but one defect in the perfect ensemble, his voice. Ludwig Tieck[2] has left the most searching criticism of his elocution.

[2] Tieck visited London in 1817. His comments on the English stage, based on letters written at that time, are to be found in his *Dramaturgische Blätter*, of which I have used the Breslau edition of 1826 (3 vols. in 2). The passage above occurs in II, 138.

His organ is weak and tremulous, though full of expression, and every word is sounded with knowledge and feeling, only with too much emphasis; between every second and third word a significant pause is made, and most lines end on a higher pitch . . . This musical declamation, as one might call it, was a real hindrance to genuine acting, in fact made it almost impossible; for where all the energies are directed so unconditionally to the small nuances of speech, and every monologue and every bit of painting must constitute an artistic whole, then there can be no talk of character delineation, of true climax, or of the heightening and lowering of this or that passage.

One of his best effects, Tieck goes on to say, was got by falling from his measured stride into a hurried, natural gait, as for example in a speech of Hotspur (*I Henry IV*, I, 3) at the words:

> In Richard's time,—what do you call the place?
> A plague upon it, it is in Gloucestershire;
> 'Twas where the madcap duke his uncle kept,
> His uncle York . . .

Kean's manner, especially in his earlier years, was directly opposite; he spoke rapidly, with strong accentuation and irregular pauses; he achieved telling effect by interrupting the rush of words to utter a phrase with pointed deliberation. Indeed his whole behavior was a constant challenge to Kemble's. Here again Tieck is our best commentator.

His fixed gaze, his starting up, his turning about, his letting fall a speech, then suddenly snatching it up again with the greatest energy, his way of going quickly off, then returning slowly but unexpectedly—in all these epigrammatic surprises his action is too abundant, he is inexhaustible in devices for thus decorating his rôle with a thousand piquant *bons mots*, tragic or comic, and it is this intellectual virtuosity in remodelling, as it were, all of the business pertaining to him, that has won the general public, and especially the women, to his favor.[3]

Between artists so different it is hard to render a decision. Kemble's appeal was to order, moderation, chastity, grandeur, the high dignity of tragic acting; his weakness was that in only a few rôles could these

[3] *Op. cit.*, II, 179.

qualities find a suitable lodging—Cato, Coriolanus, Brutus, in which he was admittedly very great; at his worst he seemed to many people a starched pedant—"an icicle on the bust of tragedy," Hazlitt called him. Kean's appeal was to intensity, variety, naturalism; "he's terribly in earnest," said Kemble of his Richard, a significant comment from one who was never, even to his admirers, "terribly" in earnest; at his worst he was tricky, slovenly, common. Kemble's record on the stage was altogether more creditable, for with a very few exceptions he gave always his best to his public and his authors, and he labored unstintingly to maintain what he believed to be the best traditions of the stage. In consequence he enjoyed a vast respect, even from the enemies of his method, for his integrity. He was the last great bulwark of classicism in the history of the English stage; Young and Macready carried on his work for a time, but the spirit of the times was against them; intensity, variety, and naturalism won an easy victory through the nineteenth century over moderation, order, and high dignity; in Irving they found in turn their last great proponent; after Irving the twentieth century lost intensity and a good measure of variety, keeping only a perfected naturalism in the face of which Kean would feel strange and Kemble would be wholly at a loss. We have moved farther from Kemble, and because we have inherited the nineteenth century's belief that to be greatly moved is the test of great acting, we feel that Kean would be more at home among us. A supreme actor might have been compounded of the two, for harmony and order are not incompatible with intensity—indeed, the model of that union existed in Mrs. Siddons, whose genius rose above all party prejudices, though inclining, certainly, more to the classic mode than to the romantic. But taking the two men as they were, with all their faults, one must decide accordingly as one prizes energy or restraint, with all their attendant virtues, in histrionic art. But this at least may be said in way of judgment, that Kean had the greater natural capacity, a greater fund of that creative vitality, or inspiration, which is a prime element of genius. Kemble climbed laboriously, by force of will and discipline, to his high place. Had Kean subjected himself to a like discipline he would have settled every doubt as to his superiority.

Hostile criticism charged against Kean an imposing list of faults, some of which were admitted even by his friends. As to his voice, that was a fault in nature for which he could not be blamed except in the misuse but which told, nevertheless, against his effects. Although sweet in the lower register it lacked power, especially in the upper register, and when he forced it, as he too often did, it became a hoarse croak or screech that turned sense into mere fury. In his latter years, even at times in his prime, he gabbled whole scenes so inarticulately that one who did not know the play must have got little notion of what all the noise was about.

More serious are the complaints against his methods of elocution. For the broad, steady movement of verse in extended passages, except in a few striking instances, he seems to have cared little. Thus he never made anything out of Othello's narrative to the senate, although he gave the farewell to arms enchantingly and was praised for the Hamlet soliloquies, from which it seems probable that he had no feeling for the objective in poetry, whereas he was capable of everything where the mood was subjective and emotional. His treatment of the "level" or "common" passages and scenes varied between two extremes: either he galloped through them with indifferent haste, or he tried to avoid failure by laying on too heavy an emphasis, by forcing an energy out of harmony with the context. The latter is a fault against which Hazlitt frequently complains. Kean's great power, in the treatment of dialogue, was in his projection of short phrases or single words. In particular he loved to make them stand out by contrast with the words which immediately preceded them. Hence came those pauses which broke lines apart, those sudden variations of pitch, those startling transitions from one temper to another. The vice of his method was that it tempted him to make antitheses where they did not exist, and to apply the same pointed manner to all kinds of dialogue. It grew on him, if we may trust Hazlitt, almost from the moment of his appearance in London. We find that troubled critic complaining early in October of 1814[4] that his hero has got into these bad habits.

[4] Review of *Richard III* in the *Champion*, Oct. 9, 1814.

His pauses are twice as long as they were, and the rapidity with which he hurries over other parts of the dialogue is twice as great as it was. In both these points, his style of acting always bordered on the very verge of extravagance; and we suspect it has at present passed the line . . . The manner in which, after his nephew said, "I fear no uncles dead," he suddenly turned round, and answered, "And I hope none living, sir," was, we thought, quite out of character. The motion was performed, and the sounds uttered, in the smallest possible time in which a puppet could be made to mimic or gabble a part.

Later in the same review Hazlitt complained of another defect, a tendency to rant. "He merely gesticulated, or at least vociferated the part [in the latter scenes] . . . We doubt if a single person in the house, not acquainted with the play, understood a single sentence that he uttered. It was 'inexplicable dumb show and noise.'" This, too, was a frequent source of annoyance. Tieck, in 1817, found that in *Macbeth* "after the fashion of the French tragedians, he tore whole scenes to pieces, by leaning with all his might on every word and straining his voice to the utmost." By the time he reached America all these bad habits had gained on him, and offered a mark at which his enemies were quick to shoot. In Boston, on his first visit, a correspondent to the *Daily Advertiser* complained of his "feeble, broken voice" and his "cockpit style of taunting;" complained also of "his guttural throttling, likewise, in his high-wrought paroxysms of passion, which we have sometimes witnessed in the brute creation, but never before from the human form divine." "Betterton" in the Philadelphia *National Gazette*[5] likewise bore heavily on these failings. He abhorred "the sudden, mechanical depression and quick, violent vicissitude of tones—the precipitate strain and extreme volubility immediately preceding or following long pauses, or slow, repressed enunciation" as the tricks of a bad, flashy style; and he protested against the consequent violation of poetic rhythm—"His auditors can have no perception of rhythm or even verse, where a sort of amalgam is made of whole phrases either by hurry or hoarseness of utterance; and where long pauses are arbitrarily introduced not only between words, but between the syllables of the same word." There can be no doubt that

[5] For "Betterton's" whole critique, see Appendix 3.

in his worse moments, and even at times in his better, Kean slurred and ranted.[6]

Along with these capital faults may be noted one or two lesser. He was now and then checked for mispronunciation, but this was of small consequence. More serious were his lapses from the language of Shakespeare, which were the subject of frequent reproof. For instance, "Why thy canonized bones, hearsed in earth" became "Why thy dead bones hearsed in canonized earth," and "The native hue of resolution" became "The healthful face." But although ever and again a brief cry of anguish was raised over these innovations, they were never counted seriously against him. It makes one smile, however, to find him gravely informing Dr. Francis in New York that whereas the modern plays, like *Bertram* and *De Montfort*, were difficult to retain, "the language of Shakespeare was so noble and so eloquent that, when once acquired, it dwelt immovably in the memory."

In what might be called the physical department he was constantly blamed for want of dignity. This was partly laid to his insignificant stature (he was only five feet six inches), for which he was of course not responsible, but the chief complaint was that he kept up an incessant bustling. He was never still—eyes, facial muscles, hands, arms, body, legs were always in commotion. "His limbs," said "Betterton," "have no repose or steadiness in scenes of agitated feeling; his hands are kept in unremitting and the most rapid, convulsive movement; seeking, as it were, a resting place in some part of his upper dress, and occasionally pressed together on the crown of his head. I have remarked the process to be the same in his personation of different characters." This was extremely annoying to many, who thought it smacked altogether too much of harlequin. The New York *American* cried out against "the most unnatural union between tragedy and farce" and made odious comparisons with St. Vitus' dance.[7] Even the

[6] An interesting comment dropped by the Philadelphia *Democratic Press* (although an admirer of Kean) suggests that he had some of that barnstormer's manner which has passed away with the good old melodrama. "Again we have to regret that Richard not only the-ret-en-ed but again he *a*hated Lady Ann." I have no doubt that "my" in his mouth was always "me."

[7] The most violent attack on Kean was made in Blackwood's *Edinburgh Magazine*, XVI (1824), 271 ff. The following is a specimen: "Novelty will always command notice

admirers were sometimes moved to deprecate this extreme activity, or to condone it, as Hazlitt did, by explaining it as an attempt to fill by other means the deficiencies of stature. But of course they would never admit, with the detractors, that the bustling was "meaningless."

Criticism on this score was almost always general, so that although the modern inquirer has a pretty good notion of Kean's habit he has too little information as to his behavior in particular instances. One exception is "Betterton's" valuable note as to the hands fluttering about the upper part of the dress. Another is supplied by Tieck, who gives a detailed and most interesting account of the business which came between the ghostly visitations in *Richard III* and the soliloquy: Richard starts up.

He had his drawn sword beside him; supporting himself by it he tried to move forward, sank on his knee, started back as if to rise, lifted high his other arm, which shook violently to the finger tips: thus trembling, with wide staring eyes, dumb with terror he shuffled forward on his knees, impetuously but slowly, up to the proscenium, still shaking and gazing with dilated eyes toward the audience. I cannot say how long this stupid dumb show lasted, which seemed to me more like the art of a rope-dancer; but when at length he was ready for the monologue he was obliged to wait almost as long again, because of the immense applause, before he could begin.

This is a rare piece of precise reporting. The human eye has often a sharper sight for the things which displease it than for those which it likes.

Charges were also laid against Kean's general conception of a character. The hostile American press denied that he had any sense of keeping, that is to say of the harmonious relation of parts to the idea of the whole, a censure which, in the light of many energetic statements to the contrary from Hazlitt and others, must be looked at askance. It is true that in the latter years, when his art was crumbling with his body, and at all times in his slovenly moods, he was patchy

---

in London, and Kean's acting, happily, was a novelty on the English stage. His croaking tones—his one-two-three-hop step to the right, and his equally brusque motions to the left—his retching at the back of the stage whenever he wanted to express passion—his dead stops in the middle of sentences—his hurre hurre hurre, hop hop hop! over all passages where sense was to be expressed, took amazingly."

and tricky. But the best testimony goes to show that normally his interpretations were clearly conceived and firmly articulated.

Of more weight are the occasional strictures levelled at the worth of his conceptions. Here the case for the opposition is well put by John Finlay, an Irishman whose commentaries[8] on Kean have much sound understanding mingled with a Kemble bias:

> Therefore, as he cannot soar with his author, he sinks him to his level; and as he cannot, with Shakespeare, occasionally mount the skies, he is determined that Shakespeare shall walk the earth with him, in a sort of familiar chit chat, arm in arm. The grand soliloquies are accordingly broken up into *colloquies* . . . All the flights and eccentricities of Shakespeare's genius are levelled into a *conversational* form, and pressed into what is called a semblance of real life.

Well, there are always two handles to everything, and what annoyed Finlay brought joy to other men. For all that he says here is that Kean did not have the grand style, which must be admitted, but if you happened to believe that Shakespeare had suffered too much under the grand style you were likely to find this familiar chit chat a most agreeable change. The real question is whether, in walking arm in arm with Shakespeare, the actor debased the poet or merely pointed his humanity. Finlay believed the first, but he was too hardened a Kembleite to be trusted on this matter.

Hazlitt now and then, as in his long discussion of Iago, objected to the actor's idea of a character. But then he was notoriously hard to please and admitted that no human being could embody Shakespeare's heroes as they had formed themselves in his own mind. And too he always argued with Kean as one expert with another, firmly entrenched in his own opinion to be sure but willing to grant the intelligence of his opponent, glad furthermore to have so good a stone to whet his scythe on. It may be that Kean's Richard was too malevolent and his Iago too jocose, but these shadings were drawn with authority, they were not the product of incompetence, or ignorance, or meanness of spirit. Therefore the critic's purpose was not so much to condemn the actor as to inquire into the proper understanding of the poet.

[8] In *Miscellanies*. Dublin, 1835.

So much for the opposition, which makes indeed a formidable noise. But was it much more than noise? How is it possible, one may ask, that a mountebank in tragic clothes could still throw shudders of delight into such men as Hazlitt, Talfourd, G. H. Lewes, and Grattan, to mention a few more prominent names among a host of admirers? Was it the simplicity of scholarship which moved Dr. Samuel Parr to exclaim: "Madam, there has been a *frightful chasm* in the theatre from Garrick's time till the present, but now we can once more boast that we have an actor?"[9] Or was it merely from provincial ignorance that Richard H. Dana wrote: "The simplicity, earnestness, sincerity of his acting made me forgetful of the fiction, and bore me away with the power of reality and truth. If this be acting, said I, as I returned home, I may as well make the theatre my school, and henceforward study nature at second hand."[10] Dana and "Betterton" were seeing their man at the same time; how was it then that one of them found the acting to be "highly artificial and technical . . . elaborate, systematic, and ambitious," when the other was moved by its "simplicity, earnestness, and sincerity?" It is the two handles with a vengeance. But one wants to know which is the right handle.

Fortunately for Kean's reputation the voices of his friends have pretty thoroughly drowned out his detractors. Or we may say the voice of Hazlitt, who did much to build his contemporary fame and now maintains it. The voices of detraction are for the most part deeply buried in newspapers and magazines, but so long as Hazlitt is read the world will know what to think of Kean, and will know in the main rightly. There is scarcely another instance of a critic who owed so much to an actor or who repaid the debt with such abundant measure. Certainly the actor did not live and work and suffer in vain if he accomplished no more than to inspire some pages in the *View of the English Stage*.

The paradoxes of opinion cease to bewilder as soon as one comprehends that there was no middle way in feeling about Kean—either you were for him or you were against him. If he carried you off your

[9] Told by Mrs. Anne Plumptre in her *Narrative of a Residence in Ireland*. London, 1817. Page 377.

[10] *Poems and Prose Writings*. Philadelphia and Boston, 1833. Page 420.

feet you gladly forgave him all his sins; if he failed to carry you off your feet you sat discomforted in spirit, picking out his flaws, finding everything wrong, sorry for Shakespeare, and glumly homesick for the sublime Kemble. "Could audiences have remained unmoved," wrote Lewes, "they might have lent a willing ear to remonstrances, and laughed at or hissed some grave offences against taste and sense. But no audience could be unmoved." In every audience, however, some gentlemen sat stiffly, their chins buried in their cravats, looking at the stage with cold eyes, contempt thinning their lips. These were the men with whom the new manner did not take. They went home and talked with their friends of "humbug" and "a pot-house actor," or they wrote withering paragraphs full of spleen and comparisons. The unbiased critic in this case is as rare almost as the phoenix. We at our distance have to strike some kind of average between the extremes of opinion. We may easily dismiss the abuse poured on the actor by *Blackwood's* in 1824 as mere venom, but also we may shy at the anonymous enthusiast in the same magazine in 1820 who could write in his frenzy: "The opinion may seem bold; but we really do think that Mr. Kean has shewn more genius in *mis*-representing Shakspear as he has done in these two characters [Richard II and Coriolanus], and in parts of others, than any one else but Mrs. Siddons has in representing Shakspear."

Of the peculiar greatness of Kean in moments, the appalling lightning flashes of his genius, enough has been said in the course of this story. It is indeed the aspect which most lingers in tradition, so that we are inclined to picture him as a series of volcanic upheavals. But he was capable in softer moods and could sustain a part written in a minor key. Of all the plays in which he satisfied the critics (for we cannot always count his artistic successes as popular) *Oroonoko* was farthest from his natural bent. Yet he drew golden praise from two very different sources. Hazlitt was both delighted and surprised. The performance was of a "mild and sustained character," yet highly impressive "and most so where it partook least of violence or effort." All the passages of tenderness and pathos were given exquisitely; the occasional bursts of passion were moving rather than electric; the expression of the whole was "glowing and impetuous" and at the same time "deep and full." The actor Macready also found the performance "masterly." He cited in particular as "never to be forgotten" the prayer for Imoinda.

After replying to Blandford, "No there is nothing to be done for me!" he remained for a few moments in apparent abstraction, then with a concentration of feeling that gave emphasis to every word, clasping his hands together, in tones most tender, distinct, and melodious, he poured out, as if from the very depths of his heart, his earnest supplication:

Thou God adored! thou ever-glorious sun!
If she be yet on earth, send me a beam
Of thy all-seeing power to light me to her! . . .[11]

Similar and even more emphatic is Macready's appreciation of Sir Edward Mortimer in *The Iron Chest*, which because it comes from an actor and furthermore from one chary of praise, and because of the numerous details which help one to visualize this rarer Kean, I shall quote at some length:[12]

He had grasped the complete conception of the character, the Falkland of Godwin's "Caleb Williams," and was consistently faithful to it through every varied shade of passion. There was an absence of all trick in the performances. Scarcely once through the whole part did he give way to that unpleasant mode of preluding a sentence (an occasional habit with him), by a hesitation, or a sound as of a half-laugh, like a cue for the applause of the *claqueurs*. He had subjected his style to the restraint of the severest taste. His elocution was flowing, discriminating, and most impressive. In his deportment there was the dignified ease of one accustomed to receive obedience; the mild and gentle manner of his address to his dependents spoke the benevolence of his nature, while his woe-worn aspect told of some settled grief that was preying on his heart. The very mournfulness of tone in which, before his entrance, he called for "Winterton," prepared the spectator for the picture of blight and sorrow that his appearance presented. When in Wilford's utterance of the word "murder" the chord was struck that seemed to vibrate through every fibre of his frame, the internal struggle to regain his self-possession quite thrilled the audience. His trembling hand turned over rapidly the leaves of the book he held, as if to search its pages, that were evidently a blank to his bewildered sight, till the agony of his feelings overbore all efforts at repres-

11 *Reminiscences*. I, 138.

12 *Reminiscences*. I, 136.

sion, and with tiger fury he sprang upon the terrified youth. But to instance particular points in a personation disfigured by so few blemishes almost seems an injustice to a most artistic whole. Throughout the play the actor held absolute sway over his hearers; alike when nearly maddened by the remembrance of his wrong and the crime it had provoked, in his touching reflections on the present and future recompense of a well-regulated life, in pronouncing the appalling curse on Wilford's head; or, when looking into his face, in the desolation of his spirit, with a smile more moving than tears, he faintly uttered—"None know my tortures!" His terrible avowal of the guilt that had embittered existence to him brought, as it were, the actual perpetration of the deed before us; the frenzy of his vengeance seemed rekindled in all its desperation, as he uttered the words—"I stabbed him to the heart." He paused as if in horror at the sight still present to him, and, following with his dilated eye the dreadful vision, he slowly continued—"And my oppressor rolled lifeless at my foot!" The last scene was a worthy climax to a performance replete with beauties, that in its wildest bursts of passion never "overstepped the modesty of nature."[13]

Here is evidence enough—and elsewhere too (as in the comments of Hazlitt and Macready on *Richard II*)—to show that Kean was well able to do those things which he is commonly credited with not doing—to speak temperately and melodiously, to keep within the bounds of restraint, to maintain pathos, and to enter authoritatively into characters which are not composed of sharp edges. It is true that they did not come so naturally to him but required a more careful preparation, which is to say a greater effort, and it is known that he prepared *Oroonoko* and *Richard II* with unusual care. But Hazlitt is right in saying that he had a wider range of powers than he usually chose to display. That he did not more often choose to display them was due to a number of circumstances in his life and character—to winning too easy a victory at the beginning, to establishing a reputation for a certain style, to pride, indulgence, and laziness, and finally

[13] Hazlitt writes: "The last scene of all—his coming to life again after his swooning at the fatal discovery of his guilt, and then falling back after a ghastly struggle, like a man waked from the tomb, into despair and death in the arms of his mistress, was one of those comsummations of the art, which those who have seen and have not felt them in this actor, may be assured that they have never seen or felt any thing in the course of their lives, and never will to the end of them."

to the decline of his powers, which really began from the moment of his first success. He preferred the easier way. The public did not care much for *Richard II* and *Oroonoko*, but it loved to be thrilled by him. And to thrill was as easy as breathing.

The feature of his art which struck every one, usually into admiration, was his virtuosity in pantomime. A large part of the energy which went into his training of himself during his apprenticeship must have gone there. "He is the best actor we ever saw," wrote Finlay, "in what may be called the *pantomime of tragedy*; his acting is *inimitable* where there is no speaking." And again, "He is the best listener on the stage; whilst his partner in the dialogue is addressing him, the rising emotions are admirably displayed." His face was capable of expressing every emotion which he wished to convey. Lewes remembered how, in *The Iron Chest*, he used to deliver the words, "Wilford, remember!" with a long pause between them, during which "his face underwent a rapid succession of expressions fluently melting into each other, and all tending to one climax of threat." He adds that spectators who were too far away to catch the play of features considered the pause a mere trick, a point which was forcibly impressed on Hazlitt when on one occasion he saw Overreach from a box instead of from his usual place in the pit. The expression of the actor's face was quite lost—"all you discover is an abstraction of his defects, both of person, voice, and manner . . . The accompaniment of expression is absolutely necessary to explain his tones and gestures: and the outline which he gives of the character, in proportion as it is bold and decided, requires to be filled up and modified by all the details of execution." Only the strong marks of feeling, deprived of their links and gradations, reached the occupants of the boxes, who consequently thought the performance rather odd than moving. Hence the critic decided that "those who have only seen Kean at a distance, have not seen him at all."

He acted with his whole body. His hands were in almost constant motion, gesturing, pointing, often fluttering in aimless movements which expressed distracted anguish but which annoyed many people. Much of his by-play was tellingly effective, as when in *Richard III* he took hold of his withered arm, held it a moment, then flung it back in distaste, or when in *Othello* he brought his clasped hands down on his head, palms outward, in a gesture of profound Oriental despair. But no doubt a greater economy of movement would have improved his art. I find no complaints on this score against his Shylock, which seems to have been, if not his greatest, at any rate his most perfect representation. And there we have Douglas Jerrold to thank for one of the most memorable phrases that have expressed the picturesque in acting. It was, he said, "like a chapter of Genesis."

Despite all the spurious gimcrackeries and applause traps with which he tinseled his great art, there were vices to which he never descended. He did not, as some pampered favorites have done, play for himself alone or at his audience. He was always within the character and within the picture. Finlay tells us that he never appeared conscious of applause, even when it interrupted him, also that he was the "best listener on the stage," which is very high praise. Lewes also applauds as proof of his understanding the truth of human feeling, that his towering passions never broke off abruptly but diminished through the following dialogue. "In watching Kean's quivering muscles and altered tones you felt the subsidence of passion. The voice might be calm, but there was a tremor in it; the face might be quiet, but there were vanishing traces of the recent agitation." These are qualities belonging to the highest and most conscientious artistry, quite beyond the scope of a mere "mob actor." In only one point have I found that he regularly sacrificed coöperation on the stage to consideration for the spectators, namely, in keeping his face always to the front and himself always a little behind his companion, a manoeuvre which made Young and Macready boil. It must be admitted that he had none of the modern notion of ensemble in which the leading part is merged into the picture; he was always the "star" and felt, with his audiences, that he was in fact the whole show. But since the feeling and the practice were common in his day he can scarcely be blamed for them.

A word should be said as to his powers in comedy. The concensus of his contemporaries denied him any great success there. He had not, said they, the *vis comica*. Yet important testimony has been given to the contrary. The writer of an obituary in the Waterford *Mail* (May

25, 1833), whom I suspect to be Thomas Colley Grattan, thought that he had it in him to be the best comedian in England, and that his ill success was due entirely to a popular prejudice against seeing a great tragedian in an undignified rôle.

> His entrance in *Abel Drugger* [says this writer] was one of the most irresistible pieces of humour we ever saw on the stage. The face, that a few minutes before was the tablet of the tragic muse in *Richard the Second*, became transformed into an expression of such utter simplicity and credulity, that it was almost impossible to identify the tragedian in the disguise of so complete an antithesis to his other self.

The *London Magazine* (July, 1822), was charmed with his Tom Tug in *The Waterman*, which it called a "still, beautiful piece of acting . . . Like his tragedy, it has nothing in common with any existing school of acting; there was no grimace about it, no effort to produce a barren laugh by any trick of voice or manner; it was a true and perfect character." Hazlitt also spoke well of his comic powers. In the *Examiner* of July 2, 1815, he found his Leon, in *Rule a Wife*, ludicrous in the highest degree.

> The house was in a roar. His alarm on being first introduced to his mistress, his profession of being "very loving," his shame after first saluting the lady, and his chuckling half-triumph on the repetition of the ceremony, were complete acting. Above all, we admired the careless self-complacent idiocy with which he marched in, carrying his wife's fan, and holding up her hand. It was the triumph of folly. Even Mr. Liston, with all his inimitable graces in that way, could not have bettered it.

Against these encomiums may be posed the anonymous critic of the *Quarterly Review* (July, 1835) who settled the matter with one crisp damnation: "In comedy he was detestable." To find where lies the truth in this question is harder than in respect to his tragic powers, for the qualities of good comic action are open to easy appreciation, partly because the appeal of comedy is instantaneous and partly because there is less doctrinal prejudice to be reckoned with, so that it is really puzzling to know why one man finds detestable what is delicious to another. But since the weight of testimony is for the negative we can do no more than accept the general verdict, at the same time recording, with all due respect, the minority opinion.

And what would a modern audience think of Edmund Kean? The speculation is, I think, not altogether idle. For the answer depends not so much on Kean's own powers as on the justness of our current suspicion that the histrionic style of the early nineteenth century was keyed to a pitch which we would think too strident. Opinion is always relative to the standards in vogue, and what appeared to be the soul of nature in 1814 might in 1930 sound like artifice. Speaking for myself only, I have grave doubts as to this supposed evolution. For one thing, we have too much proof that our ancestors knew what constituted simplicity on the stage as clearly as we. The art of acting has not progressed along any constant line but has moved back and forth like a pendulum; periods of artificiality have succeeded periods of naturalism and been succeeded in their turn; in the two hundred and more years during which we have reasonably complete records of stage presentation we find that nearly every possibility in acting has been explored many times. The great changes have come about in the arts of production, where indeed we have moved an impassable distance from our ancestors, but acting has been, in the sum of its variations, a constant. Rant is no modern term invented to express contempt for a bygone fashion. Our great-great-grandfathers knew perfectly well what was not rant. They had heard the softest notes of Siddons' magnificent voice float to the farthest corner of the theatre; they had loved the melting sweetness of Miss O'Neill and Fanny Kemble; they knew everything that could be done with the human voice and body in expressing the widest range of tragic emotion—they knew indeed far more than we, who hear only the lower tones. Take for example the description by the actor, George Vandenhoff, of the way in which Kean delivered a passage from *The Merchant of Venice*:

> He hath disgraced me, and hindered me of half a million; laughed at my losses, mocked at my gains, scorned my nation, thwarted my bargains, cooled my friends, heated mine enemies; and what's his reason? I am a Jew.

This [says Vandenhoff] was always the cue for the most intense applause: it was the natural simplicity with which he gave it, the sort of patient appeal his tone seemed to make to your sympathy against undeserved oppression, that touched the heart and the intellect at once. He hurried you

JOHN PHILIP KEMBLE

on through the catalogue of Antonio's atrocities and unprovoked injuries to him, enforcing them with a strong accentuation, and a high pitch of voice; and when he had reached the *climax*, he came down by a sudden transition to a gentle, suffering tone of simple representation of his oppressor's manifest un-reason and injustice, on the words

"I am a *Jew*!"

and the effect was instantaneous.

And so would it be today. Neither the modern actor nor the modern director (however he may dress the play, or dispose his crowds, or manipulate his great batteries of lights) can add a grain to that handling of that passage.

The stage follows its literature, and the strong movement of naturalism in the drama has carried the actor with it. Yet our gains have been made at the cost of some expensive losses. No doubt we are well rid of everything that Tom Taylor and Dion Boucicault stood for, but as our stage has won a new solidity of prose and common sense it has been losing more and more its poetry and high passion. We are even a little embarrassed in their presence. We accept, with indifference or regret, according to our feeling about it, the fact that the art of writing poetic plays is dead and buried. Shakespeare still lives, but mainly through the momentum of past achievement, and the life which a century ago was a full torrent has fallen to an intermittent trickling. Not all the arts of production have been able to reinstate him in the regal authority which he then held by virtue of the actor alone, by virtue often of a single actor who could, in spite of crude scenery, incapable support, and slovenly rehearsals, stir two thousand people to excitements which most of us have never known. The picture is, I know, repugnant to the modern theory of production, in which actors are to the director much as the players in an orchestra are to the conductor. But the fact is that with the passing of the great tragic soloists a good deal of the magic has gone out of Shakespeare. And I believe that if a modern audience could see Booth or Salvini or Kean it would learn, with a sense of revelation, what high passion means to high poetic tragedy. There is not a Shakespearean actor living who would not give his eyes to be able to do what those men did. And if they could, the interpretation of Shakespeare, the conception of this or that rôle, the delivery of this or that point, and more broadly the technique of great acting, might again become the subject of argument in clubs and drawing rooms and in the press.

To consider Kean in relation to his times is to see that he fills a place which might almost seem to have been prepared for him by destiny. He is the fullest expression in his own field of the great post-revolutionary surge of revolt, the shaking loose from Augustan conformity and the assertion of the individual will which we call the Romantic Movement. No one can say, because no one can know, how much he was consciously responsive to the currents of thought and feeling. What were the influences which formed him? Did he himself know that he was giving voice to words which must be spoken? Or was he the unconscious instrument which the Time-Spirit chose for its communication? One feels drawn to the latter view. There is no reason to believe that, although he had considerable powers of intellect in the field of his own activity, he was what is generally called an intellectual man; that, except for his desultory attempts at self-education, he ever read anything, or thought much about anything, or had any ideas beyond the casually formed opinions which a man cannot help picking up as he goes through life. Even in respect to his own profession he shows a mixture of acute understanding and child-like simplicity; everything was grist that came to his mill, so long as it offered him a fat part; he had all the vanities common to the children of the stage, and their myopic vision, for he did not know a good play from a bad one, or else did not care; he could waste his talents on Malvesi, the Dwarf of Naples, and then play Othello like a god. He had nothing of importance to say about his own art, at least nothing has come down to us. His conversation, when he was in his flowing vein, was made up of reminiscence and anecdote; he could talk on but one subject, and hence avoided the companionship of cultivated men except for those, like Grattan and Dr. Francis, who could meet him on his own ground; but he took pleasure in the society of toadies and riff-raff. He was full of whims and fancies, of unreasonable generosities and unreasonable hatreds, of eccentricities and sudden uncontrollable explosions. Some have thought that he was touched with madness, the fatal legacy of his father, which may be true and may account for everything one regrets in him. His life he abused in a way to make one cry with rage. He was shameful, obnoxious, lovable, and pathetic.

One simply cannot see a man like that as the clear-eyed guider of his destiny. Beside Byron, Shelley, Coleridge, Wordsworth, and Hazlitt he is a baby. Yet fate, or the Time-Spirit, or environment, or whatever you may choose to call the impulsive drift of the age in which he lived put him up beside them, so that he gave preëminent expression in his own art to ideas harmonious with theirs, and filled his niche. In a nature like his are depths which cannot be fathomed. What gave him his demonic energy, his powers of application, his knowledge of the road he had to walk, and his confidence in his own rightness? He flashed upon the world, on the twenty-sixth of January, 1814, completely formed and astonishingly new, like a bomb thrown out of the mortar of destiny. Even the most matter-of-fact of historians must be struck by the fitness, the *Zweckmässigkeit*, of his eruption. And it almost seems as though destiny, having done what needed to be done with this lump of clay into which a divine spark had been infused, forthwith tossed her implement into the scrap heap, brushed her hands, and turned to other matters.

APPENDICES

1

THE STORY OF MRS. CLARKE AND KEAN[1]

It was at the house of the Father of Mr. Young the actor, that my friend first saw the mother of the late Edmund Kean. A circumstance that soon obtained for him a friend of unexampled benevolence and kindness. Mr. Young (the father) was an eminent surgeon in the City—highly esteemed for his professional skill, but of an irregular, not to say profligate life—passionately fond of the drama & what (he called) dramatic *genius* and *talent* and not very choice in his selection of intimates & associates even amongst such. His wife, Mrs Young—was a Dane by birth, of good family & beautiful, intelligent and amiable of most correct conduct—and universally respected, pitied & admired. My friend was one day descending the stairs after paying her a morning visit, when Mr Young rushed out of the Parlor and arrested her progress, exclaiming "Pray come in my dear Lady, I have a charming woman to introduce to you. I know your heart will warm towards her, she is the daughter of your admired favorite George Savile Carey (at whose recent "Lectures on Heads" my friend had been a constant and delighted attendant). Upon which, having drawn her into the room, he led up to her by the hand a rather graceful figure of a young woman, in exceedingly shabby attire, set off with faded finery—& cheeks highly rouged, though it was mid-day. In short such an appearance as she (my friend) would have rather shrank from, had not her demeanour been respectful & even modest and, moreover, her eyes of that dark and beautiful color form and brilliancy that could she felt, belong to none but the daughter of G: S: C. who had a similar pair in his own head. My friend recovering from the slight embarrassment occasioned by this abrupt introduction was about to speak when He interrupted "She is poor thing in very reduced circum[stances.] I know you will help her & be her friend—"What can I do?"—Oh the easiest thing in the world. She has been obliged poor dear Creature, to condescend to sell French perfumes. Here my dear, where is your basket—bring yr basket—Marechalle Powder, Jessamine Pomatum, Mille Fleurs, Hungary Water, Genuine Eau de Luce, all genuine. My Friend took some powder and lavender water repaying double for each. *Miss* Carey as Mr. Young called her then re-

[1] Victoria and Albert Museum, London, Forster MSS, Vol. VI. Anonymous. See above, page 18.

quested to know, if she might call at my friends house sometimes with her wares. To this she assented and gave her address—in the course of the next twelvemonth Miss Carey called eight or ten times, always well behaved, and always disposing of some articles out of her basket. My friend however was not induced to mention her to other Ladies—some communications—respecting Miss Carey's position in life, having come out in the course of her visits—that implied some little caution in giving her an introduction to other houses would be expedient. Very early she had spoken of a *son,* a wonderful little boy with an astonishing genius for acting. "Where is he"—"A Lady has taken him and brings him up quite genteely" —"I hope you will leave him under such good protection"—She had a brother who played on the guitarre and sang she said. They gave musical and dramatic sort of olios called Soirees now by the way—at Hampstead—Highbury Barn and other villages in the neighbourhood of Town. Her little boy's Protectress was a Roman Catholic. She had got him into her Chapel, where he sang and threw the censer about"—My friend's answer to all information concerning *him* was—"I hope you will leave him there, where he is safe"—From Mrs Young (who obtained the information at her request) she learnt that Miss Carey had lived with Mr Kean—a celebrated mimic, a man of talents—She thought now dead—& that she had given a true representation of her way of living & her brother who was talented too. So my friend at her request often gave her articles of Left off finery, such as artificial flowers, feathers beads, and dress hats. Once she made her a present of a tiffany painted skirt spangled too—for which she was very much obliged indeed. She had been sometimes silent respecting her son, & my friend thought her rather improved both in spirits and appearance. About the beginning of June, she was sitting one morning in her back drawing room when an irregular tremulous but rather loud knock at the street door struck her ear. It was opened she heard it shut again, and in a few seconds her old man servant came in with a sort of smile on his face, he said "Master Carey Ma-am is below and wishes to speak to you"—Master Carey? Yes Ma-am, he belongs to Miss Carey—that brings perfumes"—Tell him to send up his message. Ma-am I did, but he says he must speak to you.—Well show him up. Charles shut the door, presently threw it again wide open and in the centre of the threshold stood Master Carey—A slender pale diminutive boy really eleven years of age but not taller than nine—in a jacket and trowsers shabby almost to raggedness—one leg supported by an iron—his whole appearance that of half starved poverty but redeemed by a most superb head of hair full of rich though tangled curls and a pair of eyes larger more beautiful more brilliant even than those of either his mother or his Grandfather holding a fragment of a hat in his little thin hand he presented himself with the bow and the air of a Prince. My friend was so struck, and so moved, that she stood upright she told me, before him, and could not speak or rather could not tell what to say. He spoke in the most graceful and courteous tone & air—with a somewhat theatrical manner—& said—"My mother Madam desires her humble duty, and requests you will be so good as to advance her the loan of a shilling to take the spangled petticoat out of pawn you were so good as to give her. She would not have troubled you but *we* are going to play at Islington to-night. She has all, but one shilling"—What do you act too—"Oh yes"—I can act a good many things—What?—Chiefly Shakespere Madam—What parts do you act?—"Scenes from Richard the third—Hamlet and Macbeth—I can also play Harlequin and the Clown too—"Here is the shilling—but I should like to see you act"—"I should be so very happy"—Will you come to-morrow evening—"Oh yes—what shall I do—Madam"—"What you like best"—Oh that will be Richard the Third—Very well—I must have a tent—I begin with the Tent scene & he cast his eyes round the room. The Lady immediately opened the folding doors and led the way to a larger apartment handsomely furnished & with a bow window—You shall act here—His eyes actually blazed with delight—he threw off at once his theatrical air and became the natural animated child. This bow window is the very thing I can pin the curtains together to make a tent & this little sofa is the very thing. Have you a little bell Ma-am to ring when I am to begin? I ring it myself but may I have a little music before—"Yes"—"I know a young lady who will play the Battle of Prague"—Oh that is the best music. It was settled he was to come exactly at half past six the next afternoon, and he departed all life & joy—My Friend went immediately to a few of her intimates and neighbours to relate the interview & to engage them to play audience. The late, learned John Mason Good by the way was one of the number. The afternoon came, the guests assembled all seated in front of what was to present the Royal Tent on Bosworth Field. Half past six had struck, the lady's heart began to have some misgivings, when they were put an end to by the same irregular tremulous loud knock at the door. It was opened—he entered—she flew down to meet him and to take a survey before she introduced him to his audience. His general array was not mended, the same threadbare jacket & trowsers—but his face was quite clean and the delicate tint of his complection set off by the dark auburn curls now disentangled & shown in all their natural beauty—A white muslin frilled handkerchief of his mother's, was spread over as a collar the ends tucked into his jacket—and his hands were quite clean. His friend hurried him up stairs to her dressing room & with her own hands, not choosing to call a servant took the pack thread out his shoes and tied them with black ribbon—whilst performing this his eye caught sight of a black riding hat with feather—"Oh that is exactly what would suit Richard"—Oh and a real sword oh dear Madam may I have a real sword? I intended you should. With the hat & feather, the real sword fastened on with a real belt (It had belonged to her brother made for and given to him by his Godmother when a boy) Thus equipt and radiant with joy she introduced her protegé. He threw himself on the sofa—the little bell was in his hand—Richard was asleep. The Battle of Prague began but in less than ten minutes the bell was rung, and Richard started up from his uneasy slumbers—He had not got half through the scene when the Ladies were all melted into tears. They were prepared for his size his general appearance and the shabbiness of his dress—but when these were combined and contrasted with the grace, the energy and power that animated the delicate flexible little frame and the astonishing expression he threw both into his speech and countenance they were quite overcome—Loud applause crowned his exertions—and his kind entertainer then proposed the tea should be brought and that the young actor take a piece of cake—but no—he begged first to act the fight with Richmond—"What by yourself"—Oh yes—you'll see I can do it very well by myself—it was for this I wanted the sword" and in effect he did, to the astonishment of all who looked at him and died as skilfully as he ever did in after times—A gentleman with more good nature than tact had thrown half a crown upon the stage. Neither Richard nor Edmund Carey noticed or appeared to notice it, however the example was followed by a handsome collection of silver presented to him. He said he could not take it, he did not wish it. The Lady was his mother's best friend. The Lady however reckoned up the amount to him, and giving him a crown to take home, desired him to come to-morrow for the rest and after an ample refreshment of tea & plum cake she thought it best he should go home by day light—To pass over unnecessary particulars—A few weeks after this event my friend took the boy Edmund into her house, none of the comforts of which seemed to give him so much delight as his little bed probably the first clean one he had ever slept in. The curtains were of a cotton with roses printed all over it. He called it his "bed of roses." When my

Friend left Town on a summer excursion she placed him under the care of a motherly good woman she had long known and who lived near the school he went to—No boy could behave better in a house that [*sic*] Edmund Carey. He was always gentle civil and obedient honest and true. The servants all liked & one might almost say respected him. Even the milkman the Baker & the Butcher that came to the door. The husband of my friend a very benevolent gentleman but strict and impatient with children never found fault with Edmund. Nevertheless when he was out of the house he was full of quiet fun & daring & with all the flexibility & agility of a tumbler—his flexibility a very striking character in his after acting—My friend used to let him go to Sr John P—— (her relation) & the Honble G. F—— & two or three other Gentlemans houses in the neighbourhood of Town, to exhibit his talents. On these occasions she always required he should be fetched & brought back in good care & he was always presented with some little collection of money a portion of which was put by & given to his mother, the rest for his present use & future benefit. He made friends wherever he went & became known a circumstance he found very advantageous at the commencement of his theatrical career in London. After my friend's return from the Country she thought it advisable in every respect that he should continue where he was though he generally came to her house to take his dinner at the Luncheon. She often sent him to the Play when the Kembles performed, in the pit with her servant. He who was a person of some little taste & intelligence used to tell his mistress it was better than the play to look at Master Carey's face. All the play was to be seen in his face & he clapped louder than anybody & was ready to hiss when there was the least disturbance to interrupt the play. She went with him herself one evening. He placed his hand in hers I think, I must use Miss Mitford's beautiful words in her play of Chas the First, for they exactly describe what I have heard described on this occasion "The thrilling pressure of thy hand almost a language so, the ardent spirit burned and vibrated within thee." Chas speaking of Henrietta's hand. A short time after my Friend's return to Town, she received for a few days some visitors old friends out of her native country. A Gentleman of landed estate with his Lady and two daughters—fair gentle little girls of ten & eleven years of age. Edmund had a half holiday on purpose to come and amuse them, which he did in the most agreeable manner so as to delight the children and even the parents though high Tory country gentry, after the fashion of those days despising at all points such a one as Edmund Carey could not but own he was a very pretty behaved boy not less to their surprise than approval. Edmund was desired to come the next day to dinner. A party for the Theatre was formed of the visitors and two other friends & the Box taken. Edmund was seated at dinner between the two young ladies. The Play was to be Macbeth & he was able to answer their little questions in so intelligent & animated a manner that though in an under voice the persons nearest involuntarily listened there was a pause The boy blushed stopt—and in so doing excited an interest in all present save one. After the cloth was removed the division of the party in two carriages was talked of—Master Carey included when the Tory Gentleman who was seated next the mistress of the house said looking at the boy—"What—does *he* go with *us*—In the Boxes"—My friend was stricken somehow & before she could frame an answer she threw her eyes involuntarily upon Carey. His face was scarlet and his eyes flashing with indignant fire—He rose immediately from the table and slowly walked towards the door. In doing so he must necessarily pass along the back of the chair of the Lady of the House. She caught his hand which trembled in hers and grasped as it had done of old time. She whispered Go to Drew & ask her for three and sixpence and go to the pit. The answer was only a half shake of the head & he was gone. The next moment the street door slammed. She caught sight of him with head erect and without his hat passing along in a hurried pace—There was a pause—happily there was tact and feeling enough in the company to forbid a single word of comment. To the theatre they went my friend's pleasure damped though & her eyes continually turned towards that part of the pit in which he usually placed himself—No Edmund—The guests departed next day & when they were fairly off she sent her own maid to his lodging to desire him to come immediately She thought it quite right to give him a scolding & to take down his proud spirit, which by the way was called out for the first time in her presence, luckily her good husband was so much engaged in doing the honors of the table and talking with his next neighbour that Master Carey's flourish of trumpets had been quite unheard and unperceived by him. He did not go to the Theatre but to a meeting of the Society for the Suppression of Vice of wch he was an active member—The servant returned with the information that he had rushed into his lodging changed his best clothes for his old ones & rushed out again not saying one word, or giving any heed to her questions—My friend conjectured he had gone to his mother, & determined not to trouble herself about him till she brought him back a penitent which she fully expected. Two days past—no tidings—She began to be a little anxious, &

sent her servant Charles in whose discretion she could confide to make out without direct inquiry whether he was with his mother—Charles came back with the account that Master Carey had neither been seen nor heard of—my friend could think of nothing, but that he had thrown himself into the water or been crushed amongst the carriages at the door of the Theatre. The seventh day after his evasion early in the morning a good natured ostler from the adjoining mews who knew the boy brought him to the door in his arms—apparently insensible—He had found him fast asleep (as he thought) on the dunghill. He tried to wake him but when he got him to open his eyes he did not seem to know where he was, and when he set him up upon his legs he did not seem able to stand for he fell down again so he thought he'd "but take him and carry him to Madam at once" and joyfully was he received and travel worn mudstained, dirty, miserable, starved & wan as he looked, laid down on his little bed and attended with kind & watchful care till after some restorative refreshment he looked round him, restored to consciousness and said "Am I in heaven in my bed of roses again?—Strange to say my friend forgot to be angry or even to scold, but she did not forget her own suffering or what was both justice to herself and justice to the boy—*His* story was high anger at "that unfeeling man" His resolution, to go away forever—his Benefactress should never be vexed again for him. He had begged his way, I believe, really to Portsmouth & offered himself for a sailor but nobody would take him. He had been repulsed—rudely treated, beat half starved at last thought he would try to beg his way back & die at her feet—his beloved mistresses feet.

She comforted and forgave him, but was too sensible not to feel that himself and his passions must be placed under manly controul. She determined to call upon Miss De Camp, late Mrs. C. Kemble: whom she had known & esteemed from her (Miss D C—s) childhood & who knew the boy and his parentage & to consult her as to the disposal of him. She said he would never, she was assured, be anything but an actor, & that she was sure the moment he was let out of her my F^ds^ hands his mother and uncle would seize upon him. He had all his father's talent who was a wonderful mimic. They were on both sides, Careys & Keans too full of talent but the Carey family formed an objection to his being engaged at Drury Lane otherwise he was the cleverest child they had ever seen. He had also done himself an ill office in provoking the anger of Mr Kemble who had caught him at one of the rehearsals behind the scenes mimicking his tones & actions to the great amusement of the underlings gathered round. M^r^

Kemble had shoved him aside so roughly that he fell through a trap door & lamed himself for some time. A few days after this not very encouraging conversation my Fd received a visit from Capt Miller of the Staffordshire Militia then always in attendance at Windsor Castle. To him she confided her perplexities and asked his counsel. This very worthy and kind hearted gentleman immediately entered into the subject with the kindest consideration. It was presently arranged that Carey should go to Windsor with him, previously giving an evening entertainment with tickets of admission at half a crown both to leave an impression of his powers that might be hereafter useful, & to raise a little fund to set him off in the world with—A large room in Chancery Lane (then an Exhibition room) was engaged for the purpose. Edmund arranged all the entertainments himself—was indefatigable in his rehearsals at which he begged my friend always to be present for her criticism & applause. Everything succeeded. He was covered with glory as they say and carried away between forty and fifty pounds. I had in my possession one of the printed play bills which I gave away a few years ago to his son Charles Kean when he was in Bath. Capt Miller fulfilled all he proposed—Receiving & entertaining the boy at the Barracks where he performed to the officers—was introduced to some of the elder Eton boys who contrived to smuggle him into their rooms—Finally performed twice before the King & Queen and Princesses at the Castle—From Windsor he went to Oxford with a letter of warm eulogium & recommendation from one of the Etonians to his elder brother at Oxford—There a similar success attracted him. He was surreptitiously conveyed into the apartments of some of the most distinguished of the students amongst the rest to those of the late Revd. Worthy & accomplished Mr Conybeare, who had, he told me himself the honor & pleasure to present to the future Kean the first Copy of Shakespere's plays he had ever possessed.

2

KEAN'S LETTER TO DR. DRURY CONCERNING HIS DIFFICULTIES WITH ELLISTON AND DRURY LANE, UNDATED BUT LATE IN DECEMBER OR EARLY IN JANUARY, 1813-14[1]

"Vae Misero mihi. quanta de spe decidi."
Never, Dear Sir, has man suffered so many mortifications in the short space of three weeks, as he whom you have honor'd with your protection, if I have, through inadvertency been really in the wrong, most severely

[1] From the original letter at Harvard. See above, page 100.

am I punished for it, but till I am convinced by your Opinion of my fault, I will pronounce, with those to whom I have already Committed the Circumstances, I have been treated most unjustly, the whole Story Sir is such a chain of evil Consequences that I cannot unlink the Appurtenances without destroying the whole body of my Subject, I shall, therefore, intrude upon your patience, by stating Circumstantially the facts, that have caused my present Uneasiness, & trust to your wise decision in my favor—to get (in spite of powerful Opposition) Re instated in my Rights. however grateful I might feel, when you acquainted me, at Teignmouth, that you had employed your Interest to the promotion of my Appearance at Drury Lane Theatre, Yet I have been so much acquainted with disappointment (& particularly on the same subject) that I did not rely on the effort as a Certainty, & if I remember right, your own words were "do not let it impede any present engagement, for it is but uncertain though I have hopes of its success." while at Barnstable, I rec[d] a letter from Miss Tidswell my relation, dated Sep[r] 27th offering me a Situation, on the part of M[r] Elliston, for his new Theatre *in Wich Street* I was to be engaged as *Acting Manager* to have the choice of Characters, it was positively to open in the beginning of November, & my Salary 3£ per week. the Situation I was in not answering my expectations made me comply with these terms, which I expressed by letter to M[r] Elliston, in reply to which he answers me in the most vague, & opposite manner, totally Contrary to his first proposals, made thro' the medium of my relation, his letter, dated Oct[r] 8th tells me it is not in his power to fix the opening of Little Drury, that I am engaged *generally* in the business, (which is totally opposite to *principally*) is not certain of our meeting. but *if*! we shou'd, he does not fear of finding that meeting mutually Advantageous, & concludes by requesting me, to let him know my *residence*, in a month from that period—this cannot be termed an engagement on the contrary, it canceled my first acceptation of his terms, & I very justly concluded, that M[r] Elliston thought no more of the Correspondence,

Yours Sir of the 30th of October, was still Undecisive, with regard to Drury Lane, but intimated that in case of failure there, you wou'd exert your influence for the Haymarket, the Unfortunate delay of the Letter dated the 7th of Nov[r] has caused me all the troubles, I am involved in, which did not reach me till the 13th while at Dorchester, the increasing illness of my poor Child, which continued drawing near the fatal period, made me think it Adviseable, to procure a Situation, where I cou'd for some Months be settled & procure the best medical advice for the Occasion with these Sentiments I addressed Mr Elliston told him my engagement at Dorchester concluded at the termination of Six nights, & shou'd be happy to know whether he intended to open the Wich Street Theatre, as from the period I closed my engagement I cou'd be at his disposal (I was evidently engaged at Drury Lane Theatre, from yours of the 7th had it not been from the neglect of the Postmaster) which letter I had not received many hours when I was agreeably surprised, by the Unexpected appearance of Mr Arnold, whose great kindness then, makes more unaccountable the total loss of his friendship now—he extolled my talent, in the most flattering terms said he had not a doubt of my success in London, & stated in the language almost of a Parent, how Unadviseable it was to enter the Theatre on a *great Salary*, that such performers, seldom came up to the expectations formed of them &c & finally engaged me, for three Years, on eight, nine & ten pounds, handling at the same time so severely the Wich Street Theatre, that made me feel quite rejoiced I had escaped it—for to this hour, I do not allow it an engagement, Mr Arnold & myself parted on the most friendly terms, he assuring me, I shou'd in half a dozen parts, have a fair struggle, for public Approbation, with the great men of the day Shylock, I had chosen for my opening Character. this was all Confirmed by a Letter from Mr Whitbread—*Congratulating me, on my engagement at Drury Lane Theatre*! Novr 20th—to return to Mr Elliston, a letter from him dated the 15th of the same Month, informs me, he opened his Theatre in Christmas week, & shou'd *be glad to see me* —no Statement of terms,—no time specified for engagement,—nor what Services were required from me—I am not so ignorant of my profession, as to have entered upon an engagement, without the necessary preliminaries, had I not been the Servant of *D L*, I cou'd not have been so mad, as to bring my family to London, on a simple negotiation, with Mr Elliston—nor could I at all events, have afforded to lose so much time, as the Space from that period, to Xmas week. I therefore replied to him by the information, that I was a member of the Drury Lane Company, his answer of the 23d is filled with *Hauteur* & *Upbraidings* calls me a *deserter*, & says, he will claim his Man,

I believe Sir on this same day—or near it, it was my fate to endure the domestic Affliction, which has made an impression, never to be erased,— I replied to him in the most Submissive terms, Stated by great *Affliction* the Advantages I must forego, by Complying with his demand—in short, produced such Arguments, as I conceived wou'd have entered the heart of any liberal & feeling Man, & Concluded (so he tells me, but on my honor I do not remember it) that I wou'd wait on him personally when I arrived in London. Seven or eight days, passed in Dorchester subsequent to this, & I received no intelligence from Mr Elliston on my arrival in Town, the first thing I learned [was], that Mr Russell, late of Drury Lane Theatre was—& had been some months, engaged as the *Acting Manager*, for the Wich Street Theatre this put all my fears at an end, & on Consulting with Managers—& Veterans of the profession they advised me, to take no further notice of the transaction, for Mr Elliston must know very well, he had no claim upon me,

With no further apprehensions, I took my way to Drury Lane Theatre, & was received by Mr Arnold with more than Common appearance of pleasure. he informed me my engagement commenced from that time, & Conferred on me an Obligation, which in spite of his Unkindness since, I must ever acknowledge with Gratitude,—on the Saturday following—*I received my Salary from the Treasury* which Stamps me indubitably the Servant of the Drury Lane Managers. My hopes now I thought were realised, & I looked forward to my *debut* with an anxious pride & pleasure, what was my astonishment when on the Saturday following, I was informed by the treasurers, they had no account for me I flew to (my friend —I vainly fancied) Mr Arnold, whose cold repelling looks will never escape my memory, to enquire the Cause, he gravely told me, Mr Elliston had appeal'd to him, that I was engaged to M^r E—— & I must settle the matter with that Gentleman before I conceived myself a member of T D L [?]—the day passed in fruitless search after Mr Elliston for his various speculations, render him almost inaccessible, & I returned to my family late in the evening, with broken spirit, & empty purse. the features of Mr Arnold were now entirely changed he seemed to shun me as something noxious. & if by accident [I] caught the gleam of his Countenance, I was encountered by a frown, that seemed to crush every hope, I had so late enjoyed—after some Correspondence of little or no Consequence with Mr Elliston, we had a personal interview in the presence of Mr Arnold, in the beginning of the disputation M^r A—— dispirited me, by acknowledging I stood most Unfavourably in his Opinion & Mr Ellistons extreme volubility beat down by force every argument with which I cou'd oppose him even M^r A—— with all his authority cou'd but occasionally get in a simple no, or Yes, & the object of their resentment, was compelled to remain silent, & place his Cause unpleaded, solely to the judgment of these *Law makers*! the affair ended as undecisive as it began, Mr Arnold did at last condescend to say, that he thought the most *profound Submission*, was to be expected from me—& on my questioning the subject, told me I was undoubtedly a member of Drury Lane Theatre, & he cou'd enter an action against me for playing any where else, this was not my intention, for I decidedly told Mr Elliston I wou'd *never enter* the walls of Little Drury—(the name for his Theatre) here we parted, the end of the week approaching, made me dread the Consequences of returning a second time without money home, the embarassments I had already endured, are Indescribable, in short Sir had it not been for the generosity of Strangers, in whose house I had by accident taken apartments I know not what might have been the evils attending on it. Friday Sir, was appointed for payment at the treasury, I on Thursday waited on Mr Elliston again, who met me with an Unexpected degree of Complacency, told me, he had resolved on *relinquishing his claim to my Services, & all he wou'd exact from me, was to play a few Nights at Birmingham, in the Drury Lane Vacation,* this was rather a Compliment than otherwise, & I with pleasure agreed to it. Again Sir my hopes were at their summit my feelings were once more tranquil—how transient is the happiness allotted me—on the same evening after some previous Conversation in the Theatre, having passed between Mr Elliston & Mr Arnold I was called in to the apartment & told that a Gentleman, was sent from Drury Lane, to officiate for me in Wich Street, in Consequence of which, *I must pay his Salary* of 2£ per week I thought this *hard,* for it levelled my Salary to six pounds, which is very trifling in a London Theatre & for the necessary appearance that keeps up the respectability of the profession; but involved as I was—I found it useless to resist, & even complied to this, Mr Arnold then told me that he cou'd not again mention my name at the treasury, on the following day—without a written document from Mr Elliston which that Gentleman promised he wou'd give me—I conceived now the affair was settled, however repugnant to my feelings, & flattered myself that the next day I shou'd by receiving my Salary get rid of part of my difficulties, the day Sir has arrived *"Friday the 24th* from ten till three, I was employed in running East West North & South of this great City, after Mr Elliston, at three, I fortunately encounter'd him at the Surry Theatre & recd from his own hands the required document & hastened immediately overcome by fatigue & anxiety to Mr Arnold. I cou'd not then see him, therefore sent in my name & Lex Scripta, for nearly one hour I waited in the passage with *the rest, of the Menials* of the Theatre, had the mortification of seeing them all conducted to his presence before myself & when summon'd at last to appear, was with the continued brow of Severity informed, that I had no claim upon

the treasury, my engagement had all to begin again, *"I shall not forget the day of the month."* a second week Sir I returned to my family penny-less. at a period when every one appeared happy at the Celebration of the times, our fates appeared clouded & miserable. Your letter of the 23^{d}, reached me on Monday, & I forgot my cares in the hopes of seeing you, & perhaps, overcoming my disagreeables[2] by the public favor, *the balmy cordial, that heals all Actors sorrows,* judge, if possible, my disappointed hopes, on seeing another person, advertised for the very Character on which I built my fame,
Was this fair dealing? I cannot define justice if it was—Necessity again draws me to the treasury to day. & doubt not but I shall return with some additional mortification—
if I cou'd form any opinion from the conduct of Mr Arnold, I shou'd con-ceive all this, was a Subterfuge to get rid of his bargain, but his seeing & approving my humble talent before he engaged me contradicts this, & I must say, that in the present deplorable dearth of Genius in that Theatre, any man of ability must be an acquisition, my floating Ideas sometimes incline me to Imagine, that he may consider I have in this affair acted with duplicity in not mentioning the Circumstance of my negociation with Mr Elliston admitting even an engagement—wou'd it not have been madness to have closed my Casements, against the only ray of Sunshine, fortune had bestowed upon me, the whole life of an Actor (Ay—and of many who boast equal talent, with those of the metropolis) is sometimes spent, in the fruitless endeavour to obtain a London Situation, I knew those opportunities once lost are never to be retrieved, was I to resign my hopes of eminence, for an engagement, not certain, with Mr Elliston which even accepted, must have been the total destruction of every future exaltation, had I known the nature of the entertainments there I shou'd at the first have given a decided negative to all the proposals from Wich Street.
I fear—much fear, I have some secret Enemies Undermining me in the opinion of Mr Arnold, I cannot think that this plea alone is sufficient for his determined enmity—admitting the error on my side—the loss, both of time & money, is mine not Mr Arnolds, wherefore then, when the business is settled shou'd he still assume the Countenance of anger?

to all your questions Sir, the single monosyllable answers—No—I was not bound in any legal way to Mr Elliston—& I must ask, cou'd he have a legal claim on the service of any Man whose right of performing is by

2 Procter's reading, but uncertain.

all thought Illegal. I have now Sir given a Candid, & strictly true account of the transaction, trusting the whole matter to your Consideration, & friendly Interference, & believe me Sir, however the sudden reverses of fortune may perplex me, not for one moment do I forget the Obligations you have conferr'd on,

Yours Dr Sir

with profound Respect

Saturday Morning

E Kean

the Circumstances in this letter I shou'd not care (nay even wish) but were made public if you concur in that opinion—I shall have the honor Sir of paying my respects precisely at the time you appoint

3

"BETTERTON" ON KEAN IN PHILADELPHIA IN 1821[1]

February 6, 1821:

I know but few persons, and I am not of the number, who hesitate to acknowledge that Mr. Kean may be styled an extraordinary actor. As the hero of Drury Lane, proclaimed by a considerable party in England to be the rightful successor of Garrick, he ought to be seen by the Americans who are amateurs or would be connoisseurs in the affairs of the stage. Serious dramatic representation is of importance in its connexion with letters and with public taste and sentiment; we do well to avail ourselves of an opportunity of knowing what phasis it wears, what direction it takes, in the capital from which its character among ourselves is likely to be derived.

Nature has endowed Mr. Kean with a vigorous genius, and important physical qualifications, for his pursuit. He possesses a fine physiognomy, a most expressive eye, a muscular frame, well and even elegantly shaped, except in the shoulders, which, being round and heavy in appearance, detract much from the just effect of his other proportions. He has studied the mechanism or *art* of the profession, with great assiduity and success; he is fully trained in the trick of the stage. He can penetrate himself thoroughly with his part, and seem engrossed by it, so as to counterfeit a perfect abstraction from the audience. In every character which I have seen him personate, he furnishes at least *some* specimens of what is called brilliant execution; some felicities of conception and expression; some manifestations of superior power and consummate skill, that have an electrical effect, and give universal satisfaction.

[1] From the Philadelphia *National Gazette*. See above, pages 210, 335 ff.

He is eminently successful in situations which admit of intense fire and vivacity of action; inarticulate passion, or rapid alternations of countenance and tone. Sudden and strong vicissitudes of feeling are admirably pourtrayed in the movement of his features. His eye conveys the most opposite meaning and sensation with singular quickness of transition and versatility of eloquence. There was a fine development of this faculty in his dialogue as Shylock, with Tubal, in the third act of the Merchant of Venice; and, occasionally, in his performance of Othello, the character in which he appeared to most advantage in my eyes and left the most vivid remembrance, particularly on the second representation. The rage, despair, fell revenge; the wild tumult of the soul and fierce struggle of the affections, of which so much is to be pourtrayed in the Moor, gave scope for all the energies and significancies of look, the mastery and communicativeness of face and the impetuosity of movement, to which I have adverted above. In the last act particularly, there was signal excellence as regarded the execution of the murder; the air and aspect to be worn before and after the deed and in its commission, and all the evolutions of the general catastrophe. The previous scene, with Desdemona, in which the lost handkerchief is demanded, might also be indicated as of surpassing force in the manner.

I have so far spoken only of the pantomime or dumb-shew and might have included a special tribute to his general firmness of tread and occasional gracefulness of posture: a confident, elastic gait, attitudes bespeaking athletic vigor, with flexibility of limb, and presenting an easy and regular outline, are not to be overlooked in chronicling the deserts of a tragedian. I would emblazon the *dying scenes*, which are described by both his English and American panegyrists, as wonders of ingenuity and stupendous achievements of mind and body, but I must confess that I cannot distinguish their justness as imitations; being, as I am, under the conviction that no mortal, wounded and moribund, ever fell with the precision of pitch, and nicety of contour and straightness of prostration, which mark Mr. Kean's exits from the world.

Unless the copy be faithful, it resolves itself, in my humble opinion, into a mere feat of agility and posture; what the French call *tour de force*, which they exhibit daily, of the same kind, in equal perfection, at some of the minor theatres of Paris. Scaramouch does as much in Italy. Whether it becomes a modern Roscius to play the symmetrist in like manner, and seek distinction by fanciful, and elaborate pictures of that really *inimitable* extremity—giving up the ghost—I leave to your better judgment.

For my part, though there may be transcendant intelligence, beauty, and fitness in the operation, I cannot discover in it a particle of these qualities.

With respect to Mr. Kean's recitation, the combined use of the *understanding* and the voice, it is susceptible of praise in the enunciation of passages of a solemn, emphatic tenor, which he does not conceive to require vehemence of tone and velocity of utterance. His cadences are distinct and agreeable in measured and deliberate speech; if his voice is rarely musical, it is not always grating; and as there are feelings and language to which guttural notes, sepulchral sounds, even broken, harsh accents, are appropriate, he at times excels in the *oratorical* department of his profession.

February 7:

I have conceded as much to Mr. Kean, as liberality would grant within the limits of truth and judgment. Having noted his accomplishments and traits of superority, I have now to remark the objections to which he is liable. As a general stricture, it may be said that his excellencies are perpetually passing into extremes, or degenerating into defects. He is always in his happiest exhibitions of art, and most brilliant flashes of genius, on the verge of extravagance.

> When he appears most perfect, still we find
> Something that jars upon and hurts the mind.

His studied play of physiognomy borders on grimace; his animation of manner becomes incoherent bustle; what is spirited savours of turbulence; what is passionate, of phrensy. He obviously relies more on mechanical resources, than on his general mental preparation and powers, or his fervour of feeling and thorough possession of his part. He is called a natural player, but his style of acting is highly artificial and technical; it is uniformly elaborate, systematic, and ambitious. Nothing is left to the inspiration of the moment. I was particularly struck with this circumstance in witnessing his second representation of Othello. During the first two acts of the piece, it was, if I may be allowed the phrase, a *fac simile* of the first representation. The identity in every particular of look, movement, tone, pace, posture was a phenomenon in respect to stedfastness of method and force of habit. In the remaining acts, his gesticulation was less violent, and his manner in general more subdued; but this was plainly the result of calculation or physical accident, not of diversity in the momentary impulses of sentiment and judgment.

The stature of Mr. Kean is low, and his shoulders, as I have said, are not happily constructed. Garrick laboured under the first disadvantage, and Le Kain, the Roscius of the French stage, had to contend with both obstacles, and an ungainly visage in addition. These celebrated players counteracted their mishap by professional discipline and the more effectual correctives of an incessant display of genius, and nobleness of elocution. Garrick could be thought tall and majestic—Le Kain was believed by those who only saw him in his vocation, to be of lofty size and commanding aspect.

From whatever cause, Mr. Kean is not so fortunate as either. His most enthusiastic partisans and ecomiasts in England have been obliged to confess that there is an almost "habitual want of dignity and elegance about him"—a deficiency which, however, they pretend he redeems by master-strokes of art and nature, and the energies of passion and action. I have not been sensible of this amends but in a very few instances. The general impression produced by his carriage and mien is the reverse of awe or respect. There is, to say no more, not the least elevation in them, nor any gracefulness in his person and movement at large. As Shylock, he needs none, and nothing is missed. But even in Sir Giles Overreach you require more stateliness and a more magisterial feeling than appear; and in Richard and Othello, you find unremittingly an utter want of physical adaptation and patrician demeanour.

You do not see or hear in Mr. Kean, the magnanimous, high spirited Othello; the port of the general and veteran warrior is lost; his colour is not sunk in the swell of his generous nature; you cannot imagine how Desdemona could have been won by his narrations—all that is imposing and ingratiating in his character, according to the design of the poet, vanishes; and his credulity, rage, savage vindictiveness, and desperate atrocity only remain—so that you are ready to say, with the quaint old critic Rymer, when he is contriving a better catastrophe for the piece—"The fairy handkerchief might start up to disarm the blackamoor's fury and stop his *ungracious* mouth. Then might she, Desdemona, (in a trance for fear) have lain dead. Then might he (believing her dead) honestly cut his own throat, *by the good leave and with the applause of all the spectators.*" Hazlitt, the pit-trumpet of Mr. Kean at Drury Lane, says of him in one of his newspaper-reports, that he appears, in Lear, like the king of the Gypsies, instead of the truly royal, though credulous and choleric personage whom Shakespeare pourtrays. I found this remark verified on our stage. I could not have declared to Mr. Kean's Lear, with Kent,—"You have that in your countenance which I would fain call master." The character received a stamp of vulgarity and imbecility. I may go further and candidly confess, that the image of ebriety was in general presented to my mind. The tottering gait, the look alternately wildering and fatuous, the angry paroxysms and crazed humours of the old monarch, all mainly conveyed that image, in the cast which they wore in Mr. Kean's performance. This apprehension of the scene,—which thus became, to use a vulgar phrase, *quizzical*,—I would not venture to relate, had it not been, without intimation, that of others remarkable for sagacity of observation and sobriety of judgment.

Mr. Kean would seem to apply literally to his art, the lesson of Demosthenes with regard to oratory—action, action, action. His limbs have no repose or steadiness in scenes of agitated feeling; his hands are kept in unremitting and the most rapid, convulsive movement; seeking, as it were, a resting place in some part of his upper dress, and occasionally pressed together on the crown of his head. I have remarked the process to be the same in his personation of different characters, and I think I may assert that there is no eye which a habit of this kind would not strike as untoward and incongruous. The wild groping of the fingers about the neck and breast reminded me of Dryden's conceit in one of his tragedies, of the fumbling of the tenants of the cemeteries, at the day of resurrection, for their dispersed limbs.

Quick and irregular motion, vehement and perturbed gesture, are occasionally apposite; but there is a discipline and temperament even for disorder, whether as to action or to utterance, on the stage. Hamlet's lecture to the players has passed into proverb, but like much other *axiomatic* doctrine is oftener repeated than observed. Situations occur for the tragedian, calling for the highest powers of his genius, and the most curious refinements of his art, in which gesticulation is misplaced and detrimental. It has been emphatically said that dignity has no arms, especially where there is great force of expression in the eyes and other features. Dejection, lowly grief, profound reflection, tender sentiment, contempt, solemn or malicious menace, hauteur, rising passion of whatever nature, require but a look, a motion of the head. The energetic use of the limbs spoils the true and effectual expression. But I have occupied enough of your space for this occasion. The material part of my criticism is reserved for another day.

February 8:

The greatest physical blemish to be signalized in this tragedian, is the imperfection of his voice. This is universally admitted to be in general harsh and broken; while sweetness is, by some, ascribed to its lower tones.

Although I have found it in these tones, and in his few intervals of calm and regular declamation, sufficiently distinct and impressive, I can yet scarcely concede that it admits of "a touch of harmony." On these occasions even, you could say of it,

> From hollow chest the low sepulchral note
> Unwilling heaves and struggles in the throat.

It is artificial when not strained, and in the tempest of passion so frequent with the actor, is painfully hoarse and almost altogether inarticulate. I know of no more irksome noises than those which issue from his breast, when he labours to express rage or horror in their utmost intensity. The exhaustion of his lungs has a two-fold inconvenience; for there is always something contemptible in infuriate passion where the physical powers fail. His consciousness of the natural insufficiency of his voice, seems to stimulate him to more violent efforts in action and aspect, and thus carries him further beyond the bounds which he is otherwise prone to transgress.

The same insufficiency has, indeed, as may be at once perceived, a train of the worst consequences. It subjects him to the reproach which Churchill casts upon Macklin, of dealing largely in half-formed sounds; it causes him to play inordinately *to the eye*, and attach himself much more to the general, than particular sense and expression of his part; it robs his audience of a good portion of the literary beauties and ethical lessons of the poet. He has fallen into peculiarities in the management of his voice, which form an aggravation of the case. The sudden, mechanical depression and quick, violent vicissitude of tones—the precipitate strain and extreme volubility immediately preceding or following long pauses, or slow, repressed enunciation, which he so frequently affects, may be difficult achievements, but they are very foreign to the interests whether of the actor or auditor. The author is more and more suppressed, and a wider departure committed from the rules of reason and taste. I have amused myself with imagining what impression, Mr. Kean, with his system of declamation, and his dissonant, confused accents in his ebullitions of rage, would make upon a blind person critically conversant with the dramatist whose composition he might be reciting. Certainly it would not be one of much admiration. Nor would the result, I think, be very different, as to any auditory at large, if the tragedian wore a mask. We know that the face was entirely concealed on the ancient stage, and that, notwithstanding, even greater effects were produced than any which are recorded of the best representation of any player of modern times.

Hazlitt remarks of Mr. Kean's Richard on one occasion, that "every sentence was an alternation of dead pauses and rapid utterance," and properly adds that "the most common-place, drawling monotony is not more mechanical or offensive." The length of his pauses, with the studied play of the visage as the substitute of the tongue, while they are maintained, has something of the air and more of the effect of the memorable dispute in Rabelais, between Panurge and the English philosopher, "which was performed without a word of speaking," so that one portion of the audience made one inference and another, another; every one interpreted as he liked best. Garrick's contemporary and rival, Quin, was addicted to long pauses; and you may recollect the story which is told on the subject. When, in the Fair Penitent, Lothario gave Horatio the challenge, Quin, who acted Horatio, instead of accepting it instantaneously, made a long pause, and dragged out the words,

I'll meet thee here.

He paused so long before he spoke, that some impatient person honestly called out from the gallery, "Why don't you tell the gentleman whether you will meet him or not."

But Quin, notwithstanding his pauses, was distinguished for giving full sway to the language and sentiment of his principal the poet. Churchill says of him,

> His words bore sterling weight: nervous and strong
> In manly tides of sense they rolled along;
> Happy in art, he chiefly had pretense
> *To keep up numbers, yet not forfeit sense.*

Mr Kean has no pretense and indeed, no ability, to keep up *numbers*. His auditor can have no perception of rhythm or even verse, where a sort of amalgam is made of whole phrases either by hurry or hoarseness of utterance; and where long pauses are arbitrarily introduced not only between words, but between the syllables of the same word. I cannot conceive a more fanciful reading of the dramatic poets, or wilder havoc of their lines, than may be alleged against Mr. Kean, as a general charge. There cannot be the least affinity between the style of his recitation and that of Garrick's, whom he is said to follow in the imitation of nature. That master of the histrionic art was, it is true, energetic but without bombast; simple but without vulgarity; lofty and vehement, but not turgid or vociferous. He declaimed with the utmost truth, elegance and precision, and plumed himself upon setting in the strongest relief the merits of his poet in thought and diction; upon marking all the shades of excellence in a dramatic composition.—He avoided the stiff and stately, monotonous manner—as well as incoherent rant, but he loved high and weighty elocution. Heroic verse was, in his theory, to be metrically and majestically pronounced.—It may be seen by the verses I have quoted from Churchill, that, when his practice gave the tone to opinion, the preservation of rhythm was considered as a title to distinction and compatible with the full expression and efficiency of sense, passion and *nature*. I have now arrived at the topic which I think of real importance in the question of the Drama, and will therefore reserve it for separate consideration.

[In his fourth and last article "Betterton" leaves Kean to make some general remarks on acting.]

4

REPORT OF POST-MORTEM EXAMINATION OF KEAN'S BODY[1]

May 17, 1833.

The examination of the body of Edmund Kean, Esq., was commenced fifty-six hours after death by George Douchez, Esq., in the presence of J. C. Carpue, Esq., and James Smith, Esq., surgeons, Mr. Lee (Mr. Kean's secretary), and two of Mr. Kean's old and valued friends.

External appearance.—Face, neck, and the superior and the inferior extremities considerably emaciated. Decomposition rapidly taking place about the mouth, neck, and also about the face and extremities, but much more so about the former named parts of the body. Body well formed, and the external form of the thorax and the abdomen so beautifully developed as to serve as one of the finest models that could possibly be presented to the eye of the sculptor or painter. Body well proportioned, five feet six inches and three-quarters in length.

Head.—On dissecting the scalp from the cranium we found the occipito frontalis muscles more developed than they are usually found; likewise the corrugatores supercilii uncommonly strong. The vessels of the dura mater very much distended. On examining the dura mater and exposing the hemispheres of the brain we found that there were adhesions of the tunica arachnoidea to the dura mater, more especially on the left side. The tunica arachnoidea was likewise found to adhere to the pia mater. There was also a considerable quantity of serum and coagulable lymph effused between many portions of those two membranes. The vessels covering both the cerebrum and cerebellum were in a highly vascular state.

[1] From F. W. Hawkins' *Life of Edmund Kean.*

The convolutions of the brain unusually strongly developed. Substance of the brain softer than natural. Lateral ventricules distended with fluid. The plexus choroides much more vascular than natural. There were likewise about two ounces of fluid found at the base of the skull, which appeared to extend down the theca vertebralis and the thorax.

Lungs.—Perfectly healthy, with the exception of two or three old standing adhesions of the pleura pulmonalis to the plura costalis of the anterior lobe of the left lung. Heart excessively loaded with fat, flabby, empty of blood, and its muscular structure much less developed than when in a healthy state. The trachea and bronchiæ were filled with frothy mucus.

Abdomen.—On cutting through the parietes of the abdomen we found the muscles covered by nearly two inches of fat. The omentum as well as the mesentery were also much loaded with that substance. The liver was of a green colour, but natural in size. The gall bladder contained numerous biliary calculi. On examining the stomach we found the mucous coat much thickened, and that had evidently suffered from chronic inflammation. The duodenum was of a deep orange tint, the internal coat presenting a somewhat similar appearance. The other small intestines were healthy in their structure but much contracted. The spleen, kidneys, and remaining viscera were perfectly healthy.

J. C. Carpue.
James Smith.
Geo. Douchez.

INDEX